In a FOOL'S PARADISE

In a FOOL'S PARADISE

Memoirs of a Hawaiian Outlaw

Ellen Chalmers
Amanuensis

BY L. STAUNTON JR.

iUniverse LLC
Bloomington

In a Fool's Paradise
Memoirs of a Hawaiian Outlaw

iUniverse books may be ordered through booksellers or by contacting:

iUniverse LLC
1663 Liberty Drive
Bloomington, IN 47403
www.iuniverse.com
1-800-Authors (1-800-288-4677)

ISBN: 978-1-4759-6129-4 (sc)
ISBN: 978-1-4759-6130-0 (ebk)

Library of Congress Control Number: 2012921149

Printed in the United States of America

iUniverse rev. date: 08/13/2013

This book is dedicated to Mom, Dad and Lorna.

Contents

Introduction

When asked to describe Hawaii, the 50th State in our union, images of grass shacks and lovely hula dancers, swaying to the rhythms of melodious ukulele music, often come to mind. "Paradise" sums it up in a single word. Heaven on earth with infinite sunshine, blue skies, cool balmy breezes and, yes, white sandy beaches. Yours for the having 365 days a year. Even when it rains, the sun continues to shine. Hawaii is one of the few places on earth (if not the only) where it can be pouring rain on one side of the street and warm and dry on the other. The exact term for this particular phenomenon remains a mystery to me, but one has to experience it up close and personal to truly appreciate its magnificence.

Fortunate to be raised in such a picturesque environment, the "island lifestyle" was everything you could possibly imagine and more. However, like most places in this world, even fabulous paradise has a downside—cramped and overpopulated, you can easily feel a bit claustrophobic. Not to mention the high cost of living, limited availability of affordable housing space and ever-soaring unemployment.

Picture living on a gigantic inner tube, floating in the middle of the Pacific Ocean, surrounded by water in all directions, as far as the eye can see. Add to the mix, an overwhelming sea of humanity, busting at the seams, overflowing with ethnic and cultural idiosyncratic diversity. Like placing the entire human race into a blender and switching on the juice cycle. The final cocktail? A primordial ooze of microcosmic sludge! The melting pot of the Pacific. A far cry from the Hawaii most people envision.

Perhaps a little too harsh and critical of a description on my part. Well, sorry to burst your bubble! About this time, you may be confused as to the type of story you've chosen to devote your undivided attention to? Let me clear things up. First of all, you might find it comforting to know that no matter how disturbing the writing seems, everything you are about to read is true and actually took place at one time or another—the exact details extracted from what is left of this writer's lucid mind. Due to the nature of the subjects, I chose to use few, or no, names. The people who have the honor and privilege of reading this masterful piece of art know who they are.

All that aside, this book is an autobiography containing equal parts of realistic drama and ambiguity. Plus a dash or two of empty rhetoric, uttered from the lips of a disgruntled native Hawaiian son, teetering on the brink of insanity. A troubled soul searching for forgiveness, wrapped in absolute resolve. Hope you're satisfied? You be the judge! Whatever path your mind chooses to take on your journey to interpret the following pages, at the very least, you will be entertained, maybe even taken aback. Perhaps a bit moved. I'd love to spare you all the boring details, but there's really no fun in that. Besides, all great stories require this essential element in order to set the mood. To capture the audience's interest, stimulate the reader's curiosity. So please, continue at your own risk and enjoy the reading.

Chapter 1

Smiles, cries and lullabies

The year was 1957 when I made my debut on this big blue marble. Rock and Roll was here to stay and America was experiencing peace and tranquility. The average household still gathered around the television at night after sharing a home cooked meal at the dinner table. The nuclear family unit was the sign of the times. Born in this era (before the computer revolution catapulted us into communication oblivion) made one appreciate the simpler things in life. To be thankful for the little you had. A sense of moral obligation existed. You actually knew your neighbors. Life held so much promise for a family struggling to build a better way of life.

You could say the essential building blocks of my childhood rearing seemed to be in the proper order. My parents provided nothing short of unconditional love and support from the start. I never remember being hungry or worrying about staying warm and dry. I was not neglected or cast aside. However, I do recall my mother telling how she nearly died from shock the first time she laid eyes on me. Here was this strange looking creature, with flaming red hair peering out at her. Her exact words, and I quote, "that's not my baby! Where's my baby? You must have mixed my baby up with this one?" Then I started to scream my head off. There was no mistaking it now. At that precise minute she knew that I was, in fact, all hers. So began the life of yours truly. Happy Birthday!

Being the youngest in the family, I was dead set on claiming my rightful place in this world. Having lost an older brother at childbirth, I was left to the mercy of my older sisters. Too young to remember my eldest sister, Donna May, except from photos, she was the most beautiful child I've ever seen. Her face was like that of an angel, no doubt placed on this earth by the Lord above to warm the world with her smile. They say I was her favorite playmate. She'd spend hours cradling and cooing lullabies to me. She loved me more than her favorite hamburger joint, Wiggyburgers. Hence the sobriquet "Wiggieboy" was born; I carry it to this day.

Somewhere around this period, my father had been awarded the coveted "shield" from the Honolulu Police Department. His father, who was also once a member of the "Boys in Blue", had higher expectations for his younger son. Having a doctor or lawyer in the family would have been nice. As my Dad presented his badge of honor to his father, who lay dying in a hospital bed from a massive heart attack, he smiled. Proud to see his son, not the doctor or the lawyer, but the police officer who had followed in his footsteps, my grandpa passed away the very next day. He was only 45 years of age.

Raising a family on a single income, even in the 1950's, was a daily struggle for my parents. Although they lived in my mother's parents' house in an affluent neighborhood, times were tough. The house was located deep in the lush Manoa Valley, miles from my father's station house. With no vehicle to shuttle to and from work, he was left with the only mode of transportation available to him, walking. Each morning, come rain or shine, he'd wake before the dawn and commence his four mile trek to work. After roll call, he'd begin his day walking the beat down on the infamous Hotel Street. It wasn't uncommon for him to take a double shift to earn extra cash. After a hard day's work, drop-dead tired, he made his way home into the valley. Sometimes he was lucky enough to catch a ride from a fellow officer heading in that direction, but those times were few and far between. My father was a humble man who seldom asked people for favors. I wonder if I would have had the courage and strength to endure such hardship. The essence of a man is often defined by his ability to suffer in silence knowing he'll persevere.

Between my father's predicament and my mother's never-ending struggle to make ends meet on a shoestring budget, a better way of life was definitely their number one priority. One day, a proposition presented itself. My parents were afforded the opportunity to invest in a tomato farm. Though the business was located on a different island, and accepting the offer would mean moving us lock, stock and barrel, they jumped at the chance. At last, they'd have a place of their own. Free from living under foot of in-laws and family.

Dad took a leave of absence from the department, drew out whatever savings they had, packed us up and moved our family to the island of Maui. The farm was nestled high upon the slope of a dormant volcano. The weather was crisp and cool year long, with beautiful views of the ocean coastline. The scenery was breathtaking! The future looked promising. Prosperity and peace of mind. A whole new life! Then one day my sister, Donna May became violently ill. She had a high fever, began vomiting uncontrollably and complained that her head hurt badly. She soon became delirious. They rushed her to the nearest hospital, no more than a few miles away, where she slipped into a coma and later died. Only 5 years old, our precious angel with the beautiful smile was gone. Such little time in this world.

My parents were devastated! They couldn't understand how something so tragic could occur. They asked the question why Lord, why our little girl? They blamed themselves. What had happened? Perhaps she had ingested some kind of foreign substance, maybe a poison. There were lots of insecticides and fertilizers on the farm. Any one of them could have been the culprit. The autopsy later revealed that she had contracted spinal meningitis. The perfect family with the perfect life, shattered to pieces. We flew our beloved sister's remains, along with the rest of our lives, back to Oahu. Returning to the farm was not an option. She was laid to rest in a peaceful cemetery on the outskirts of the famous Diamond Head Crater. Here, she could be close to her brother Thomas and grandfather William.

Dad went back to the department and Mom went back to being a housewife and caregiver to my sister and me. With the death of Tommy and Donna May, my parents sought solace in the only thing that numbed their pain—the bottle. Alcohol became their way of dealing with the overwhelming guilt they felt. Too young to understand their grief, my sister and I were just going along for the ride. Soon the grieving was replaced by an extreme sense of dread and paranoia. Fearful that we would suffer the same fate and contract the disease, we were admitted to the Queens Hospital and placed into quarantine. Scared and confused, we were entrusted into the hands of total strangers. Our family had never been separated. I often wondered if this separation had been the reason of my fear of the dark. Following the quarantine, I was constantly haunted by nightmares.

In the hospital, we were bombarded by every antibiotic known to man. They kept us isolated in a special area, away from the other patients. Stuck in a room with no playmates but ourselves, we found new and inventive ways of entertaining each other. Along with singing and dancing, I exercised my artistic talents by painting murals on the pristine white walls, utilizing food items made readily available at mealtime—green peas being my personal preference. I guess I loved the way they felt all mushy between my fingers. The color green matched perfectly! The nurses didn't agree and stopped serving them altogether. Denied my favored source of creating pretty pictures, I devised a new plan of amusement. I discovered that I could escape the confines of my portable enclosure simply by lifting the mattress and crawling between the bars. When the nurses would finish making their rounds, I'd make my escape, scurry across the room to go play near my sister. She sure got a hoot out of that. I got it down to a science. I usually made it back before the nurses would return. Unfortunately, all good things must come to an end. Eventually I was caught roaming around the room free as a bird. Busted! The nurses, perplexed as to how I came to be loose from a crib that stood off the floor, did their best to extract the information from the two of us. We refused to divulge the secret to the enemy, even under the threat of torture. If you call taking away our dessert torture. My sister Lorna and I have a good laugh whenever we reminisce about those times.

Needless to say, we never contracted meningitis. We did, however, manage to receive identical sets of permanently stained yellow teeth. The dentist related to us that it was the result of all the antibiotics administered to us. All the whitening agents or treatments in the world won't get the yellow out. It was deep into the structure of the pulp and enamel. Talk about feeling self-conscious! Wasn't a whole lot of fun growing up with the other kids making jokes and teasing us about our "grills." You never realize how much of an effect something of that nature can have on a child's psyche. It's a pity how society judges a person by something so petty as their smile. Beauty is embraced and ugliness is shunned. And never the twain shall meet.

Released from quarantine, (comparable to a completed prison sentence) we were excited to return to our parents and the comforts of home. Our homecoming was a mixture of emotions. My parents welcomed us with the usual love and affection, but a sense of uneasiness filled the air. They seemed sullen and melancholy. Seeing them drink on a regular basis was disturbing. The liquor never seemed to interfere with their ability to perform the parental duties. Our lives were as normal as possible, under the circumstances. The good parents that they were, they covered up their flaws and misfortune behind a veil of false bravado.

My father was now a part of the police department's K-9 dog training corps. The program utilized specially trained attack dogs to serve as partners to motor patrol officers. The animals chosen lived side by side with the handlers and their families. These were not your average household pets. They were highly intelligent, highly trained animals. Countless man-hours were dedicated to teaching them to be absolutely obedient to their handlers and to carry out commands without the slightest hesitation. Failure to perform accordingly resulted in personal injury or even death to their handlers, fellow officers or members of the public being victimized by a predator.

Living in our home, these animals became a big part of our family. On the weekends, the dogs were taken to a training facility to evaluate their performance. At "Dog School" they ran an obstacle course and faced scenarios of confrontations from attackers. Training day was a family gathering with the other K-9 Corps families. The mothers packed picnic lunches and socialized while the kids ran wild. Watching the dogs perform their task was an amazing sight—beautiful specimens with different shades and colors. Each a precision-trained menacing instrument of death and destruction, capable of tearing flesh to pieces on command.

Rex was our first dog and the smartest on the force. Dad trained him to respond to both verbal and hand signals. A different hand gesture for each command, sit, stay, lay down, come and attack, could be given silently. When given the command to sit and stay, Rex would remain in that position for hours. My father often watched him from a distance, making sure he obeyed. People passed by him and he never budged. Not even a muscle when another dog or cat walked by. When Rex appeared to be losing his focus, my dad screamed "fooey" and he'd get right back on track.

Getting an animal to obey and perform in such a manner requires hours of repetitive training. The most important contributing factor is love and affection. You must gain the animal's trust and in return, the dog is willing to do anything to please his master. The animal is rewarded for his obedience and good behavior with treats, toys and lots of love. Raising and caring for such a special animal takes a lot of dedication and is a huge responsibility. The objective is to produce a lethal, totally controlled, weapon. When an animal is rebellious and refuses to obey his handler's commands, he is disciplined. All trainers know that their animals will, somewhere along the way, become stubborn. Breaking a dog's bad habits is all part of the training process. Every trainer has his own methods of dealing with resistant behavior. The universal rule is to refrain from any form of abusive measures, physical or otherwise. Beating an animal into submission is not an option and should, under no circumstances, be done. No animal deserves to be subjected to such cruelties, regardless of its behavior.

Sorry to say that I was unfortunate enough to witness an incident of such abuse on my father's part. I've seen my dad use a choke chain on Rex before to control him when he got out of hand, but up until this moment, I'd never seen my father strike him. For some reason, during the course of this training session, Rex had refused to obey my dad's orders. Frustrated and in a rage, my father lost his temper and snapped! He picked Rex up by the scruff of his neck and slammed his head against the side of the house. Shocked, I burst into tears. Hearing that poor animal yelp in pain broke my heart. The memory of that violent event was forever etched in my mind. In a culture where going out drinking with your buddies and then coming home and beating on your wife was acceptable behavior, seeing a dog get abused was a minor thing. Disquieting as the whole event appeared at the time, the resonating effect that it had on my subconscious somehow made it okay to discipline bad behavior with physical abuse.

Observing the training of these K-9 animals is one thing, seeing them actually perform in a real life situation is another. One day my father and Rex picked me up from school. On the way home, we met a friend and we stopped on the side of the road. Whenever Rex was in the back seat, the windows were kept rolled down so he could stick his head out. While saying their goodbyes, the man talking with my dad patted him on the shoulder. Rex, seeing this as an act of aggression, leaped out of the car and charged the man. If it weren't for my dad's quick reaction, the man would have gotten seriously injured. Rex had done exactly what he'd been trained to do. Flawless! The look of pride was evident on my dad's face.

Rex was eventually retired after a notable career and replaced by the next shepherd, Malama. Originally a house pet, Malama had no previous training and was more a companion to his original owner than guard dog. Like Rex, Malama became a beloved member of our family. Old enough now, I became more involved in the training program. I was taught to give commands and guide Malama through the obstacle course. It became my responsibility to feed, groom and exercise him. It gave me a better insight into how much work and devotion went into achieving the desired results from these animals. Soon, I became an accomplished handler and was able to perform with other members of the K-9 unit on training day. Gave me sense of pride being among the other officers, putting Malama through the paces. Glancing to the sidelines and seeing my parents smile made the moment even more meaningful. Malama was to be the last member of our K-9 corps. Although leaving the program, my father continued to assist in the training of other dogs. Malama spent the remaining years of his life as our family pet and personal protector.

Since then, there has always been a presence of German Shepherd dogs in my life. The one animal that had the greatest effect on our lives was Junior. Junior was a ferocious, untrained dog owned by a family friend. The owner, fearful of the dog's temperament, had thought of putting him down. The animal lover that she was, she refused to give up hope. Knowing of my dad's ability, she made arrangements to have the dog delivered to our ranch. The animal was so vicious, it took three of us with ropes tied around his legs and neck, to wrangle him into position. His new home was a chain secured to a wooden post under the house. There was no getting close to the animal without getting eaten! Every ounce of his energy was spent trying to take a chunk out of anyone who tried to get close. His food and water was pushed towards him with a long pole. He would work himself into a frenzy snapping and snarling until he collapsed from exhaustion.

After two weeks of the same behavior, it was clear that this animal could never be tamed. Then, somehow, in his over zealous efforts to take a bite out of us, he got his roped tangled around one of his paws. Each effort to free him resulted in the same vicious attacks. Eventually, the rope tightened to the point where he could no longer stand or move. His pain was obvious, yelping whenever he tried moving. The paw became raw and swollen. He refused to eat. We had no choice but to try and remove the tangled rope. We got another rope around his neck and shortened it so he couldn't move. My dad approached him and to our surprise, he just sat there, licking at his paw. He looked sad and vulnerable. He knew that we were there to help him. The minute my Dad unwrapped his paw, Jr. licked his hand and for the first time wagged his tail. From that moment on, he was a different animal. Gone was his violent behavior. It was an amazing change. The owner was astonished at the turn-around of the animal's behavior. Seeing how we interacted with Jr., hugging and petting him, she decided that the dog was happy right where he was and gave him to us. Though he was never trained to be a guard dog, he became the most loving dog we ever had.

For a dog with no formal training, Jr. had a special knack for opening doors. He'd stand on his hind legs and work a handle or doorknob with both front paws until it opened. Where he obtained this ability was an unknown to us. I never would have believed it if I hadn't seen it with my own eyes. He somehow made his way into the house one day and was busy running throughout the place when he got bored. The next thing you know, he jumped up, worked the doorknob of the back door, and click! He was gone! I stood there dumbfounded. That wasn't the half of it. Our family went out shopping one day, and returning home we were greeted by a bewildering sight of paper and tinfoil strewn about the yard. My father had inadvertently forgotten to lock the stand-up freezer in the garage before we left. Jr. had opened the door and practically emptied its contents. He got the meat and the cats feasted on the fish. They were still in the process of devouring the goods when we arrived. We couldn't help but laugh about it. After all, you can't blame Jr. for the unlocked door. He was just taking care business and looking after his family. That was some dog!

I watched him get sick and die from the disease that animals of his breed get stricken with, heartworm. We buried him in the yard, close to us, his family. I'd like to think that he'd gone to a better place in the company of other dearly departed family members. All of whom were currently looking down upon us from heaven.

Religion has always been an important part of my life. My parents, though from different religious backgrounds (my mother Catholic and father Mormon), taught me at an early age the need for having God in my life. I never knew how they decided on what particular religion we'd follow, but apparently my mother's devout Catholic practice won out over my father's lukewarm "jack" Mormon status. Attending mass on Sundays was a family affair. In the old days, the services were held in Latin and the priest stood facing the altar with his back to the congregation. Too young to care or appreciate the intricacy of the event, other than the fact that we were in some person named God's house, whispering words lost to me, I was content to be a part of the crowd.

I remember a time in church at five years of age when I began to shout out loud, "this is God's house. Mom, Mom, whose house is this. This God's house?" My mother smiling down at me, reassuring me of that fact as she attempted to quiet me. For some reason, I continued shouting the mantra over and over among the sea of smiling faces. Hopeful that my affirmation of that higher power witnessing my acknowledgment of his existence, approved of me. As if the Holy Spirit had entered into me at that very moment. An innocent child, touched by the hand of God, in his house. Years later my mother reminded me of that day in church. I remembered it clearly as if it were yesterday. I wondered how we had both come to recall that exact event.

Attributing our creation to a greater power other than man and science gave me a sense of peace. Trusting in something that surpassed the bounds of human frailty offered up a sign that man was greater, but not greater than he really was. The hope of life after death, where pain and suffering ceases to exist, can be a strong motivator for a person to live a clean lifestyle, free of sin. Insuring in ones own mind a place in Heaven. Protection from the devil and the evil that lurks around us. Salvation from our own evil deeds. These are some of the rewards of worshipping and serving a living and merciful God. Good enough reason for a child to want to kneel and beg forgiveness to an entity with omnipotent ability.

The thing with religious faith, its beliefs, and having it in abundance, is that in order for its bountiful gifts to make an appearance, one has to be absolute. You must believe with every fiber of your being. Anything less is worthless! When young, the actual concept of such dedication never crossed my mind. Although I felt that God was watching over me, my belief was uncertain. Lacking fervor, I was just going through the motions. Indifferent to the gifts and grace one could obtain by believing whole-heartedly. The real power of Jesus Christ and accepting him in all his magnificence would only become apparent to me later in life.

The reality of giving yourself over to God and all that he represents, can only be achieved by stripping oneself of all pride and attachment to earthly pleasures. The wisdom needed to be at peace with your acceptance is the gift presented to you through years of suffering and devotion. The key attribute in this process a person has to possess is "HUMILITY." On many occasions my father emphasized this word and the importance of it being a part of one's character. "Be humble in your life," he'd say. I found this a far contrast from a man whose temper controlled his emotions for a good part of his life. I never understood his meaning or his efforts to instill the concept of humility into me until later in my life. Only then would the true significance of its meaning become embedded in me. My father and I would later be confirmed into the Catholic faith together. The ceremony was held at the Lady of Peace Cathedral on the Fourth Street Mall in Honolulu. He was in his forties and I in my late teens. Although completing another phase of my journey to accepting God in my life, the true meaning would continue to elude me.

When a person becomes dependent on someone or something stronger than oneself in life, there is a tendency to reach out for help in troubled times and knowing it's there can be a comforting feeling. A promise that no matter how adverse the situation might be, things will be all right. The same safe feeling of reassurance you had as a child when you skinned your knee and your mother was there to place a band-aid on the wound. Her loving arms shielding you from harm. We, as mere mortals are weak and often need the help of others to overcome adversities in life. In times of dire circumstances, we look to friends and family for support. A shoulder to lean on in those difficult and unbearable moments. Only when these avenues of support are eliminated, can a person truly come closer to God. When you're alone in the world with no one to turn to, God is there for you. His constant love and strength never waiver. Call on Him in your hour of need and He will be there. Talking to God on a personal, intimate level can be the most rewarding experience any individual could have. Even more wondrous, receiving his answer. Recognizing the blessings that the Almighty Father bestows upon us is the greatest sight a person could behold. The gifts from God are limitless! His forgiveness and mercy endless! One only has to believe with all your heart and soul to bear witness to His glorious presence.

There have been countless moments in my life when God has spoken to me. However, only after many troubling events and bouts of endless suffering have I become attuned to His word. We often hear His calling, but His words fall upon deaf ears. The minute we give our lives up to Him wholeheartedly is when we begin to hear His voice. When you surrender yourself and trust totally into His care, you will receive His glorious gifts. Your eyes become open and you begin to see clearly for the first time in your life. He can take you to places and show you things that you've never seen before. More than in a geographical sense, but in the spiritual depths of your own soul. Prayer and devotion are the conduit to His reply. In times of crisis, I am never alone. His hand rests upon my shoulder, guiding me and giving me the strength to carry on.

In this crazy, mixed-up world we all experience many events of heartache and pain, from brushes with death to the loss of close family members. Each time I call upon my Lord and Savior to see me through and He is my comforter. Can you say the same about anyone or anything currently in your life? Can any one person or any one thing make you feel more secure, safer?

To those of you who remain skeptical and adhere to other principles and beliefs, it was not my intention to offend you in any way. I'm merely expressing my personal views and beliefs. For those of you who share the same beliefs of Jesus Christ and the Father Almighty, my prayers and thoughts are with you all. You are not alone in this world of grief, sorrow and evil. We are many! Warriors who strive to overcome the devil's handiwork by doing benevolent deeds—exchanging good for evil. We must start by forgiving our enemies for their trespasses against us as we pray for their forgiveness in return. For only with love for our fellow man and charity for those of us who are less fortunate, can we hope for a better life on earth, as well as our Holy Father's Kingdom of Heaven.

I've never attributed my illicit behavior to my religious beliefs. My running around this world like some madman, causing death and destruction, was never motivated by the belief that, no matter what despicable acts or heinous crimes I committed against my fellow man, God would forgive me. The prospect of having autonomy and exemption from eternal damnation for sins done in this world might give the individual with a demented mind and sadistic character reason to indulge in such behavior. I, for one, am not such a person. However, I do attribute my turnaround from participating in previous bad behavior and spiritual awakening to the Almighty Father and his Son, our Lord and Savior, Jesus Christ. Praise Jesus!

As children, we are expected to do things in ways that grown-ups, who were once children themselves, had at some stage in their lives also done. Call it the innocent behavior associated with youth. Being ignorant of most things in life gives us the excuse to act accordingly. Protected from the consequences and retaliatory measures that resulted from unacceptable behavior. That is, except in the case of corporal punishment doled out by our parents, who are the exception to this rule.

Sometimes, what we perceive as proper or natural behavior is, in fact, far from that. Not being the wiser to such impropriety causes us to indulge or act out according to our childlike perspectives. Then, when punished for said bad behavior, we become confused, perplexed as to the results of acting in a manner thought of as proper behavior.

Perfect examples of such behavior are when children play house or doctor with other friends. Sometime in our youth we've all played these silly games. We imitate the adults around us without the slightest notion of the impropriety. In reality, we just want to be like our parents. Grown ups! It was during an episode of playing one of these games with the neighbor's daughter that the meaning of right and wrong behavior confronted me.

I must have been five or six years old at the time and my next-door neighbor and I were under our house playing house. Like all actors in a play, we chose our roles according to the scene. In this case, she was the Mommy and I the Daddy. We began the whole coming home from a hard days work scenario and dinner together over polite conversation. The came the adult intimate bedroom moment that was basically, you show me yours and I'll show you mine. She went first, of course, and exposed herself to me. I then proceeded to drop my shorts and expose myself to her. We both stood there, like two deer stuck in the headlights, wondering what this whole thing was really about or what to do next. Staring at each other's private parts, I suddenly had the notion to reach out and touch it. With her permission, of course. The minute I touched her, she let out a scream and began to cry. Scared the shit out of me! She pulled her pants up and ran screaming for her Mom. Left me there with my drawers down around my ankles, shocked, with my little peepee exposed!

Don't ask me how I knew, but I knew I had done something terribly wrong and was about to get a good spanking for it. I felt frightened and for some strange reason, very ashamed. I hid beneath the stairs frozen! If a beating was coming, they were going to have to find me first. From my hiding place, I saw people gathering and milling around in the back yard. There were my parents and my neighbors with my playmate next to them. The look of worry and concern was evident on their faces. My Mom looked panicked and was crying. That scared me even more and I hunkered down lower to the ground to make myself smaller. The crowd grew larger. They appeared to be peering into a large hole that was dug in our yard. I saw a man that I had never seen before strip off all of his clothes. He stood there stark naked in front of all those people. Who would do such a thing? My Dad tied a rope around this guy and he just jumped into the huge hole! My Dad held fast to the rope the entire time. Soon, he was pulled up covered in sludge. He was filthy! My Mom looked hysterical, excitedly gesturing with her arms. By then the Fire Department had arrived and the crowd was even larger.

With all the excitement going on I couldn't resist getting a closer look. I crawled out from my sanctuary beneath the stairs and walked brazenly into the throng. My curiosity had gotten the best of me. You know the old saying about curiosity and the cat? Making my way towards that great big hole in the ground, I looked into its gaping maw. It was filled with swirling, smelly black water. The stench was overpowering! Someone in the crowd saw me and screamed, "There he is!" My blood ran cold and I knew I'd had it. Now the whole world knew what I did to my neighbor's kid. I was scared to death, but most of all embarrassed. My Mom bolted towards me and I braced for the spanking of a lifetime. She was crying and sobbing as she scooped me up and squeezed the breath out of me. Through her tears I managed to catch a few broken sentences. Evidently, when my playmate ran home to her house, crying and screaming incoherently, everyone thought that I'd fallen into the cesspool while playing with her. She never said a word about what went on under the house. The whole crowd cheered for my safe return and I acted as though nothing had happened. Mr. Innocence! At the time, I never realized the severity of my action. How could I have? I was just a kid. The privilege of youth—ignorance is bliss. Until this day, I remember that brave stranger who had risked his life by diving into that hole to search for me. That's all I could think about when my father introduced him and I shook his hand.

Chapter 2

Green Acres is the place to be

The most impressionable years of my childhood were spent growing up in the small country town of Waianae. This rural community on the island of Oahu was a replica of the many towns spread across the continental United States, with its lone stoplight, barbershop and Rexall Drugs Store. Down the road sat the open-air theater, where you could enjoy a movie beneath the starry skies or take in a matinee for 25 cents at the closed theater. Across the street, the grocery store and popular Dairy Queen, serving up their frosty cones with the famously distinctive curl at the top. The Texaco, Shell and Chevron gas stations with brightly colored logos advertising their cheap fuel prices, like prehistoric dinosaurs, part of a bygone era. The mouthwatering aroma of freshly baked bread and pastries from the family bakery filling the air. A peaceful setting that would one day be disrupted by a rash of criminal activity.

My parents, by now, had settled into a relatively acceptable existence. Their drinking continued, accompanied by sporadic bouts of arguing. No matter how heated the back and forth exchanges of verbal abuse got, there was never anything physical involved. As the drama unfolded, the results were always the same. My mother's tearful withdrawal, followed by my father's relenting and eventual concession. This topped off by the mutual silent treatment. Their issues of hurt and pain ran deeply. Regardless of all the drinking and fighting, they really loved and cared for each other. They were partners for life on this long road of disappointments. The everyday stresses of life had eaten away at them both, like some vicious animal devouring their souls.

I recall my father plagued by severe migraine headaches. His prescribed medication had little or no effect. The attacks began with a sharp pain in his left eye and spread to the whole left side of the head. Some headaches lasted for hours, others were shorter in length. The pain left him immobilized and at times, brought him to his knees. Some days he experienced multiple attacks or clusters. You could tell by the strange glazed over look in his eyes when one was about to occur. We kept damp towels in the freezer that he strapped to his head to help ease the pain. They'd happen at any time or anyplace. We'd be having dinner in a restaurant and a migraine would make an unwelcome appearance. Watching him endure such pain was agonizing. Leaving us, he withdrew to the car and suffered alone. It was impossible to sit there and eat a meal knowing how miserable he was. At family functions, when other kids were playing and having fun, I'd be at his side fetching cold towels, willing the pain away. I loved him too much to abandon him. His attacks left me mentally exhausted and drained. Just the thought of one made me sick to my stomach. I was a nervous wreck. Each episode broke a piece of my heart away. My very own private torture waiting to happen. Looming. We were slaves to his condition.

After the loss of two children in their lives, my parents doted on my sister and me. They did their very best to provide for us with what little they could afford. And often times could not. Many times they were stretched far beyond their means. I'd hear my parents arguing about money and my Mom's spending habits. When we went clothes shopping, I'd run for the toy department and grab an expensive toy from the shelf and refuse to let go. She struggled to drag me, kicking and screaming, but to no avail. Fed up and embarrassed, she resorted to the only solution. Selecting a cheaper toy, she'd convince that that her choice was much better than mine. In the end, we both won. Reaching the car, my mother was rebuked for giving in to me.

My sister attended the most prestigious private schools available. First, the native Hawaiian Kamehameha Schools and later the St. Francis Convent School for girls. Though every effort was made to enroll me in private school, I never got past the social interaction tests required for entry. My demeanor and obstreperous behavior was always a problem and I was prone to fits of violent rages. It wasn't uncommon for me to take a hammer to my toy collection reducing it to a useless pile of junk. On one particular interview, they placed me in a room with children my own age, filled with different toys. Standing behind a one-way mirror, my parents were shocked and appalled at what they saw. Here was their son, this monster, snatching toys from the grasp of other kids while pummeling them. The public school system was the only alternative.

Children at the elementary school level have a tendency to behave irrationally and impulsively. I was no exception. Regarded as an instigator and trouble maker, not a week passed without me seeing the inside of the principal's office, accompanied by frequent appearances at the blackboard writing endless, "I will not play in class" sentences. Finishing up with the after school clapping of dirty erasers. With all that punishment it's a wonder I learned anything.

Pushing the limits and discovering new and inventive ways of getting a rise out of my teachers was my goal in life. Being labeled a troublemaker had its perks. The other boys looked up to you and gave you their dessert at lunch period. You had your pick, and could trade, for the best sandwiches from anyone you wanted. Oh yeah, and the girls, they were all smitten with you. The cutest ones would lay their sleeping bags next to you at naptime. The Good Life! Just when I thought my tedious life of lackluster antics would never progress, I surprised myself. One bright sunny day, while horsing around on the lunch line with my friend Wayne, under the watchful and disapproving glare of my third grade teacher, my boring world was blasted into the outer reaches of space. Chided for our behavior, we were told, in no uncertain terms, "No playing in line. If you want to play, go play some place else." She seemed so sincere, we were more than happy to oblige her. Feeling liberated from the fate of my fellow classmates, Wayne and I walked away from the lunch line and headed out of the school grounds. We hadn't the faintest idea where we were going. Laughing and running, we hit the open road. Our journey to freedom had begun. In the background, receding cries of protest and pleas for our return scattered to the wind.

Clearing the school property, I formulated a plan of action. My friend Arthur was out sick that day, so I thought it a good gesture to pay him a visit. The problem with that idea—he lived about four miles away. The only way to get there was to walk along the highway. We'd be spotted for sure in the open. Making our way quickly, we kept a sharp eye out and tried to stay off the main road. Ducking for cover whenever a suspicious vehicle approached. The sun's scorching heat made our throats parched and dry. Thirsty, tired of walking and dying from starvation, we stopped at the nearest store. In our possession, only the meager 25 cents needed to purchase a school lunch. That isn't much by today's standards, but in 1964 you could get your money's worth. That wasn't going to be near enough in this case. The storeowner was a nice Chinese man and a family friend. He recognized me in an instant. "You the policeman's son. What you do here by yourself? How come you not in school?" When you've been in as much trouble as I have, telling lies is a breeze. "No worry Mr. Awong, my father dropped us off to buy candy and soda, he be right back to pick us up. He forgot to give me money, you think I can charge the stuff and he pay you when he gets here?" Worked like a charm. Grown-ups can be so gullible. A stunt like that would never work today, with all the Amber alert warnings. We loaded up our goodies, with a little extra for Arthur, and made our way to his house. We had come a long way, and with just a few streets left to go, Wayne had started to whine and complain. "I like go home. Take me back." Too late to turn back now. After some cajoling on my part, the whining stopped. We couldn't scrub a mission to bring aid to a sick friend.

Reaching our objective became nothing short of precision military exercise. Standing at the front door, knocking, we both breathed a sigh of relief—we made it! Safe and undetected. The surprised look on Arthur's Mom's face when she opened the door was priceless. "What are you two boys doing here? Why aren't you in school?" Time to turn on the charm. "Hi Mrs. Arthur, were here to visit and cheer up Arthur!" Reiterating my former statement, grown-ups can be so gullible. She swallowed the story hook, line and sinker. Ushered into the living room, there sat Arthur lounging on the couch in front of the TV. "Howzit guys, what you doing here?" His face lit up like a Christmas tree. Careful to keep our distance from the contaminated patient, we presented him with his goodies. We were, of course, invited to stay for lunch. The menu, hot soup and tuna sandwiches. Just the thing to soothe the weary travelers. Talking and laughing, I related the series of events that had led to our arrival—we were having too much fun. Arthur looked better already! His mom started to give us questioning looks when our ride failed to arrive. She began the old interrogation routine. That was our cue to split the scene. We had outstayed our welcome. She offered to call my parents to come get us. Casually declining, we made it for the door. She tried cutting us off in a last ditch effort to block our exit. Too quick for her, we scooted out the front door and on to glorious freedom!

Running down the road, it finally dawned on me that I was in a mess of trouble. I had finally out-done myself. The highlight of my career! I never thought for a single moment that our innocent excursion was, in reality, two kids who had run away from school. And it was at that very instant I envisioned my parents faces leering down at me. All the while, Wayne is ranting and raving, doing his utmost to remind me about how much trouble we were in. In all likelihood, more trouble than either one of us had ever been in. Reaching the highway, I had the strangest feeling that someone was watching us. I saw police cars passing back and forth at a slow pace. Drivers scanning the roadway and brush. Yup, the cops were on the lookout for us. My goose was cooked! Not spotted yet, we hurried across the road and hid beneath some Algarroba trees. The road was higher than our line of sight, so I climbed up one of the trees to get a better look. My parents drove right past us. I panicked and ducked as close to the tree as I could. Hugging it with all my might, I nearly lost my grip and fell. My heart was pounding in my chest like a jackhammer. I knew for sure that they had been searching for us. What the hell was I going to do? Our only hope was to sneak back to school as quickly as possible. Whatever story or excuse I gave when we got there, if we did make it, wouldn't matter. Wayne was wailing and crying uncontrollably. He had me on the brink of tears. Can't fall to pieces now; we came this far. I calmed him down and told him the plan. Leaving out the part about how, no matter what, we'd probably get the spanking of our life.

When the coast was clear, we made our way up the embankment and headed for the school. We must have walked about a hundred yards or so when I heard the distinct sound of gravel crunching behind us. Afraid to turn around, knowing what I'd see, I continued walking. Meanwhile, Wayne stood frozen in his tracks, screaming something to affect that, "your parents, dad, your parents" and so on. The horn sounded, causing chills down my spine. I turned to face my doom. There was my Dad's car staring me in the face. Two angry faces peering over the dash. Daggers of death shooting from their eyes. "Get in this car!" Our journey was over. Amid the din of Wayne's crying, I tried to explain why we ran away. They were flabbergasted! They had been searching for the last four hours. The school had called and reported us missing. Our teacher was beside herself and nearly had a nervous breakdown. Arthur's Mom had called and ratted us out. The store owner also. The whole town was looking for us. As mad as they were at me, I could see the relief on their faces. Knowing that I was safe in their care, their anger shifted to my teacher and the school. Looked like I'd escaped a beating. From them anyway. Never count your chickens . . .

Driving towards the school, my stomach was doing flip-flops. Somehow, I had the feeling that things weren't going to turn out right. Pulling into the parking lot, I almost lost my lunch. Soon, like a bad dream, I was seated in that familiar setting where many lectures had been given. The principal, Mr. Moore, sat behind his desk glaring, the look of disapproval evident on his face. My teacher in tears, fumbled along making her excuses, denying responsibility. When all was said and done, the blame was equally distributed, with Wayne and me on the short end of the stick. I couldn't help but notice that thick, heavy wooden plank with the holes in it hanging ominously behind the principal's desk. I've seen it there on many occasions, but never warranted its use before. It was agreed upon that though there had been a lack of communication between teacher and student, we needed to be taught a lesson. As my parents and teacher filed out of the room, my greatest fear had become a reality. The principal muttered some words of reproach as he reached for that paddle. My heart went straight to my throat. Wayne wailed like a bitch and blamed everything on yours truly in a futile effort to escape the inevitable. He was rewarded by facing the paddle first. Standing in terror, waiting for the fatal blow to be delivered on Wayne's backside, a thought flashed into my mind. People previously subjected to this form of punishment on numerous occasions said you should cry out in pain when receiving the first hit. "The first hit!" Failure to do so and trying to be the tough little soldier would result in more than one. Then whack! The crushing blow snapped me out of my reverie. The howling cry rang out, filling the room. My blood ran cold and chicken skin kine. Only one strike. Next . . . stepping to the plate, my body braced for the blow. And whack! It was over in a blink. I'd survived! Hardly felt it at all. Stuck in the moment, counting my lucky stars, I nearly forgot to react. I let out a shriek that could stand your hair on end. I even shed a few tears for dramatic effect. I should have been an actor. An award winning performance, if I may say so myself. No more hits were forthcoming. Relieved that the ordeal was over, I couldn't wait to get out of there.

My parents were content with the punishment already received so I escaped further cracks by their hands. That brought to a close to my introduction to Mr. Moore's dreaded paddle. We became the talk of the schoolyard. I wore my paddling like a badge of honor. My troublemaker status was launched to even greater heights.

Waianae town had a unique feature to it—there was only one way in and one way out. The single, two-lane blacktop highway ran the length of the town and community. It ended in a secluded area blocked by the mountains on one side and the ocean on the other. Only four wheel drive vehicles and drivers brave enough to travel the dangerous road ventured further—often times only to find the roadway washed away by storms or waves. Some large waves have been observed during the winter season at the end of Kaena Point road. Many of the less desirable residents used the town's geographical location to their advantage and to other's disadvantage. The green mountain scenery and sandy strips of beaches were magnets for tourists. Strangers who found themselves off the beaten path, enthralled by the landscape's beauty, could face the less than hospitable welcome from the locals. Many were robbed, carjacked or beaten. On a bad day, you could get the three-for-one special. The nightmare equivalent of a hat trick. These poor unsuspecting travelers left that part of the island broke, scared out of their wits and traumatized for life. Happy to be alive, many never return to Hawaii. Just the shot in the arm to help boost the state's economy.

Living in a rough community with your father as the police can be hard on a ten-year-old. The neighborhood bullies accosted me when I was alone in public and fights ensued with me often on the losing end. Not a particularly attractive kid with my squat build and chubby features, I was constantly teased and badgered. I was the butt of every practical joke imaginable. With the lack of confidence and low self-esteem, I withdrew inside myself. I compensated for the hurt by engaging in overeating. Food became my comfort. My parents none the wiser, indulged me. I was so obese, that my clothes had to be tailor made. Physical education classes were horrible. Awkward and ashamed of my appearance I shrank into the background.

Whenever the shirts and skins basketball games were played, I prayed not to be picked. The thought of running up down the court with my fat exposed belly, bouncing grotesquely for all the world to see, mortified me. Then there was the shower period. Kids at that age can be so mean and nasty. Made to endure a steady flow of derision, I lived in a state of high anxiety. When things reached a boiling point, I'd snap and lash out. Usually with physical violence. I was a social outcast, relegated to the shadows. My school performance waned and I became more introverted. I was in desperate need of a positive change in my life. A rescue from the pit of despondency.

My salvation came in the form of the ancient Japanese style of Martial Arts known as Judo. It was a standard of training for all police officers. Mr. Iona, the instructor who taught the program, was an officer himself and a close family friend. When not teaching at the station house, he ran a dojo for the public in his backyard patio. There was nothing fancy about the dojo—just a half-inch of house carpet over the concrete floor. Tumbling, rolling and being thrown around on that hard surface toughened me up real quick! I regained my self-confidence and became disciplined. I showed an aptitude for the art and later joined the Police Athletic League. My new instructor was Mr. Souza, whose dojo was outfitted with the best equipment available, which we borrowed when the police classes weren't in session. My new instructor was such an asshole! For some reason, he chose me as his personal practice dummy, demonstrating the different throws and holds on me without mercy. After the constant beat downs, something miraculous happened—I started to excel at Judo. I became so adept, that I easily defeated students of an equal rank. That earned me the privilege of sparing with higher ranking students, two of whom were my instructor's sons. The oldest held the rank of black belt—the highest ranking in the martial arts world. The other held the second highest,

27

a brown belt. They were both very good at what they did and had won many trophies in tournament competition. We were often matched against each other with me, in some cases, on the winning end. That certainly didn't sit well with the brothers and it totally infuriated their dad! Every time one of them lost a match to me, they were punished. Suffering defeat by a lower ranking student can be demoralizing, especially when you have dedicated your life to practicing a martial arts form.

And the reward for my audacious behavior? I was never promoted to a higher rank. This only deepened my resolve. I got more aggressive and lacked compunction when sparing with the other students. Heartbroken over my predicament, I found satisfaction in beating up on the other high-ranking students. Mr. Souza was beside himself! I was eventually kicked out of the school. His excuse was that my incorrigible and hard-headed behavior showed a lack of discipline and I would never amount to much in the Martial Arts world. Whatever. I was never picked on by the bullies again. My new found satisfaction? Beating the crap out of them!

A police officer's family had an unfair advantage. You were treated differently, with respect. People around you were law abiding, wholesome and hard working. You lived in this invisible protective bubble, shielded from the evil that the everyday public saw. The children wore halos above their heads that flashed a hands-off sign. My father, a server of justice and pillar of integrity, was considered a hero in the police community. We were special people in an exclusive club. No one had to mention it, you could feel it. An unwritten law wherever you went. More so in a small country town.

In the sixties, officers made a pretty decent living. My father worked lots of overtime to earn extra money. He was primarily a motor patrolman and used our family car as his official police vehicle. It was outfitted with the customary siren, red flashing lights and two-way radio. His beat was right in Waianae. I would watch the roadways for his passing car. At the end of his shift, he'd work another directing traffic at some busy intersection. Sometimes my mother drove us to his assigned post to see him in action. It was a treat to see him decked out in his uniform performing his duty. We'd drive by and he'd crack a big smile and wave us through.

He once worked a security detail guarding a movie set in Waianae. The set, at the outskirts of town, was for the movie *Hawaii* which depicted the missionaries' first arrival to the islands. At sundown, we drove over to visit and have dinner together. My sister and I looked forward to visiting. We'd run crazy around the set, playing and acting out our own scenes. The ritual lasted for the duration of the filming. Not only did we get the autographs of feature stars of the movie, Julie Andrews and Max Van Sydow, but my mother was hired as an extra on the film—that was the coolest! When the movie premiered, we all tried picking her out from the crowd of faces. An impossible feat with the amount of people in the shot, but it sure was fun guessing where she was. "A star is born!"

Back then, most of the families in our town were either living on state subsistence (welfare) or struggling with meager employment, living in a two-income family. We were considered to be in the middle to upper middle class bracket. My parents decided to purchase a color TV with money they made from the movie gig. Color television was still a new invention then. There were only two local stations broadcasting in color, channel 2, KHON that aired the Walt Disney specials on Sunday evenings and channel 4 KHVH, which had awesome cartoons on Saturday mornings. It cost an arm and a leg to buy a color set back then. Our Zenith was a huge brown monster made of metal on a metal stand with plastic casters to roll it around. The picture tube was one of those rounded on the sides deal. It was beautiful! Set my parents back about $500.

Before getting our own set, we'd often go to dinner on Sunday's to a close family friend's house to watch their set. The Portlocks had the only color set in the whole town. No one could afford that kind of money—you could buy a fairly new car for $500. All the kids at school would ask me about it and hope that I'd invite them over on Saturdays to watch cartoons. There was always a steady stream of folks coming over to check it out. My sister and I fought over which station to watch. You couldn't pry us away from that thing with a crowbar. When we got punished, that was the first thing that got taken away. It was torture watching the TV sit there, all silent and blank. No problem, because every evening, punished or not, the set came on so my parents could watch the six o'clock news. Even something as boring as the newscast was better than no TV at all.

Those were fond childhood memories of feeling, and being in a sense, special. Happier moments frozen in the time where the world around us remained oblivious to reality. The wonders of being young, innocent and carefree.

After years of attending private school, my parents placed my sister in a public school. The rising cost of tuition became too heavy a burden. From the start, you could see the disappointment in her. She had left all her friends behind. The upside to the change was her being enrolled into my elementary school. I was thrilled to have my older sister around. I became very protective of her and at times fought to defend her honor. In the beginning, she had difficulty adjusting. It's never easy being the new kid in school. But my sister Lorna was a smart, pretty and good natured person. Standing next to her you'd never think that we were related. We looked totally different, me with my pudgy frame and brown hair and eyes—she with a slim build, long brown hair and beautiful hazel eyes.

The drastic change in my sister's life had a far more reaching effect than we realized. She started to exhibit bizarre behavior. One morning, when my parents went to wake her for school, she was unresponsive. She just lay there, motionless. The only sign of life was the rise and fall of her chest as she breathed. Soon, tears ran down her face. Not a sound, only tears. My parents were stymied. After a few hours, she'd awake out of her trance and be back to normal. Usually long after school had started. Uncertain as to the cause of her strange behavior, my parents consulted a physician, and if I'm not mistaken, a shrink. They concluded that she had undergone some kind of emotional shutdown. Relieved that there was nothing physically wrong with her, they let her come out of this phase on her own, feeling only time will tell.

My mother decided that maybe Lorna needed something to help her get past her depression. One day, when she had finished work, she brought home a big surprise. Laying on the backseat of her car was the ugliest dog I've ever seen! The thing was so ugly, with its pushed in face and bulging eyes, that it was adorable. Her name was FiFi and she was a Chinese Pekinese. My sister was overjoyed. That's the happiest I'd seen her. FiFi became her constant companion. They were inseparable—the dog changed her life. Gone was all the weird behavior. More than a pet, FiFi was one of the family. We all spoiled her in our own ways. She was loving and a pleasure to be with.

Without tuitions to pay for, my parents were able to save enough money to purchase a new home. It was the first new home we ever had. Three bedrooms and two baths with a two-car garage and a patio in the back yard. The smell of fresh paint was a reminder of its newness—we loved it! FiFi had the run of the place. Located close to the beach, we'd take her for runs on the sand. She absolutely loved the beach. That was her favorite thing to do. Everyone who saw her with her short legs running up and down the beach fell in love with her. She really stole the show. FiFi was an extension of my sister. You naturally associated one with the other. Where one went, the other followed. The only time they were apart is when Lorna went to school. At those times, you would find FiFi curled up somewhere in Lorna's room, waiting for her return.

The Fourth of July holiday was near and we planned to spend the day at a family friend's house. They lived next to the beach, no more than a mile away. Walking distance, but because of all the stuff for the party, we drove. We spent the day running and playing with FiFi on the beach with the other kids. There was lots of food and fireworks. Towards the evening, we were exhausted from all the activities and anxious to get home. We said our goodbyes and packed up to leave. My Dad stayed behind to party with friends and my Mom drove Lorna and I home. For some reason, Fifi stayed behind too. Wasn't out of the ordinary for her to stay back with my Dad and she was having the time of her life. Such a beautiful summer day, who would ever think that it could end in tragedy?

While walking home that evening, FiFi got away from my Dad. She darted across the two-lane highway fronting our subdivision and was struck by a passing motorist. The driver, realizing what had happened, pulled immediately to the side. He was in the middle of apologizing profusely when my uncle grabbed him by the throat. They could have killed him! He wasn't at fault—it was an accident. They buried her on the beach where she loved to play.

Arriving home late, without FiFi in tow, there was no mistaking the look on both faces. Through his tears, my Dad struggled to explain to my sister that her beloved dog was gone. It was the first time that I ever saw my Father cry. My uncle, a cold-blooded killer by trade, stood there in tears. My sister was heartbroken and cried uncontrollably. Watching her broke my heart. We cried as a family for our loss and tried to remember happier times with FiFi.

Over the years, Lorna and I experienced numerous dying pets, my first turtle, a few fish here and there, each time we'd wrap the pet in something and bury it in the yard after praying over it. It had become a tradition between us. We never expressed the slightest emotion for any of those pets. With FiFi's death, that all changed. Her loss had a grave impact on us. The reality of death became apparent, unavoidable, and final. My parents exposed us to death on some level from an early age. We were taken to funerals and wakes of family members and friends. No doubt to help us understand the meaning of death and to prepare us for the inevitable. To accept it as a way of life, part of the struggle of living. We never once cried for any of those people who had passed on, but we cried like babies for FiFi. It would be years before my sister had another pet.

The atmosphere in our new home was peaceful and toned down. My parents continued to drink on a regular basis, but the arguing was less frequent. It seemed as if the new home had given them a fresh outlook on life. Regardless, I sensed deep, unsettled feelings in my Dad. My father had always possessed a violent temper. He never focused it on any of us, although I have seen it a few times. People who knew and worked around him called him "the man without a fuse." My uncle once explained the title to me. He said, "Some men when they get mad, you can see their fuse start to burn before they explode. With your dad, when he gets mad, he just explodes. He has no fuse." I never forgot his words. My father wasn't a big man by stature. Maybe 5'10", 200 pounds, solidly built with no fat. When he got mad, he became incredibly strong. He changed into a super human, easily mistaken for 6'5" and 300 pounds. There were instances where he'd explode and smash things to pieces in the house. One time, he snapped and threw a six foot stand up freezer, filled to capacity, right through the back door. I stood there in shock. There was no stopping him in those fits of rage. All we could do was huddle close to my mom until he calmed down. I wondered what could possibly cause a person to become so angry. I later found out that the thing that he cared about and worked so hard for, was the reason for all his hostility—the Police Department.

Somewhere along his career, my father had become disenchanted with the system of the "new" department. Back in the day, an officer could climb the ranks simply on his merit and hard work. There were no politics involved. Loyal to the previous chief, Dan Liu, he was promised a promotion for his dedication—placed on the fast track to gaining that gold shield. Before he got his chance, Dan Liu had gotten sick, or sick and tired, and retired. My father was left swinging in the wind. Under the new chief, Francis Keala, and his system, an officer was expected to have more than the necessary character attributes. The officers needed to have the "sheepskin"—a college degree. Going back to school at this point in his life would be a challenging venture for my Father, but there was no other choice.

One night, while our family gathered around the living room floor, my parents produced a stack of what appeared to be receipts from a cardboard box. Here before me lay all the hospital bills from when my sister and I were quarantined, some ten years ago. They were in excess of $25,000. That blew my mind! My parents had struggled for years to pay them off. They had finally made their last payment and wanted to share the joyous occasion with us. All these years they'd crawled out of the depths of debt. We celebrated as a family, thankful for our blessings. Life for our family looked brighter with the promise of even better things to come.

The funny thing about life is that it can change in a heartbeat. That's the way of the world. Nothing good lasts forever. Late in the evening, while on a routine patrol, my Dad and his partner answered a domestic violence call. Upon arrival, they confronted a couple in the process of beating the crap out of each other. Both were huge individuals by any standards. The male stood over six feet and tipped the scales at 300 pounds plus. His wife, though a bit shorter, weighed in at about the same. A heated exchange ensued between both sides. In a flash, the female attacked my father's partner, grabbing and pinning him against a parked car. The male then brandished a knife and lunged at the helpless officer. My father pulled his service revolver, shined his flashlight in the suspect's face in an effort to blind and distract him, and ordered him to drop the weapon. The man, outraged, turned and charged. A single shot from a .38 special brought the man down. An officer can work his entire career without ever pulling his gun, let alone discharging it. Due to my father's quick reaction to the event, his partner received only minor injuries. The suspect survived his gunshot wound, sued the Department and my dad for damages. The nerve! He almost won, but for one big mistake on his part. During the course of the trial, he opted to remove his shirt to give the jury a close-up look of his wound. No doubt a horrible railroad trace of a scar from the surgery. However, here was this mountain of a man towering over them playing the victim role. Seeing how my father was dwarfed in comparison to this monster, the jury found that the use of lethal force was warranted. The female members of the jury were later heard to comment on how frightening the big man was.

For some reason, my parents placed our new home up for sale following the trial. They may have done so before, to protect themselves from financial liability in the event the trial went the other way. Losing the house wasn't bad enough though and the least of our worries. It just so happened that the shooting victim's brother was one of the most powerful men in the underworld crime syndicate. A ruthless killer feared by everyone. Death threats were forthcoming and our family was forced to play hide and seek among different safe houses. Those were some scary times. Forced to live in fear for our lives, scurrying from one place to another like insignificant animals avoiding a predator. The pressure was enormous. It began to take its toll on all of us. Just when we were reaching the breaking point, things changed for the better. The threats ended and we returned home. By some unmentioned diplomatic means, an agreement was made between the forces of good and evil and our lives were taken off the chopping block. Seems like when you threaten the life of a cop, you feel the full wrath of the "brotherhood." Mess with one, mess with all. I guess the "Force" really was with us.

Chapter 3

Rancho deluxe

Now and then, even the downtrodden of the world get a lucky break. Ours could be referred to as a diamond in the rough. The gem was acquired in the form of a ten acre parcel of land that my father procured for the bargain price of $75 a month. Can you believe that!? You can't fill your gas tank for that price these days, let alone pay for your rent. We signed a 99 year lease with a renewal option clause. Insuring that future generations would have a home. The property, zoned for agriculture, was located on a private homestead in a remote area more commonly referred to as "the sticks." It came complete with a great big six bedroom dilapidated old house in desperate need of repair. The most beautiful sight I ever saw! A scene right out of a Norman Rockwell early fifties "Life in America" painting. The kind of place that people only dream about. Freedom with wide open spaces. Our closest neighbor was a quarter-mile away in any direction. There was, however, a slight drawback to the place. Sometimes the septic tank backed up and flowed into a stagnant pond near the back of the property, creating an awful smell. Whatever direction the wind blew, the odor was carried. At times, you barely noticed it; we got so used to it and thought it a small price to pay. Besides, aren't farms supposed to smell like that?

We called the place "the dumbshit ranch" with the name printed in red letters on a sign that hung from a white archway, with white double gates, which stood at the entrance to the property. The white fencing was eye-catching and added a certain appealing nature to the place. Your know, a touch of class. Though a far contrast to the overall picture of the place. The farm's name derived from a derogatory term one of my uncles used to describe someone outside of his good graces. Which he often screamed to his kids when they made him mad. You couldn't help but laugh when you drove up the driveway and were greeted by that sign. Just thinking about it brings a smile to my face, even after all these years.

There was an endless amount of work and we all chipped in to get it done. My dad and his step-father, Grandpa Joe, did the majority of the heavy jobs on the weekends. It gave my grandparents an excuse to escape the city life and their cramped condominium existence. A chance for them to kick back and relax at our very own private retreat. The therapy was great for everyone. The challenge of fixing up the place became more a labor of love than anything else. One of the first things on the agenda was repairing the roof. I'll never forget when the rains came pouring down—there wasn't a dry room in the house. Pots and pans lay everywhere. It leaked so badly in some areas, you could actually see the water level rise in the pots. We found ourselves shuttling from room to room emptying water akin to a fun game rather than an inconvenience. With the roof fixed and all of us cozy and dry, the next undertaking was the building of the many living spaces for the animals we intended to raise. We built coops for the chickens and turkeys, pens for the ducks and pigs, and hutches for the rabbits. Even a place for the Japanese quails to live in. The entire property was barbed-wire and a paddock was built to house the cows and horses. An uncle donated a boar and a sow, and I named them Bosco and Eleanor. I bred the pair and Eleanor gave birth to 15 piglets her first litter. Never worried about pork chops again! The farm was starting to come together.

My aunt Violet gave us a pair of humongous geese she called Hershey and Gertrude. They became the official guardians of the farm. Fearless and bold creatures, those rascal birds attacked anything or anyone that crossed their path. Not even the dogs messed with them. They were our version of a burglar alarm. Whenever strangers entered the property, they would sound the alarm, honking and trumpeting with displeasure. Not a living soul got passed those two. Hershey, the male, liked sneaking up on people from the rear and biting them. His bite was like a pit bull. Once he got a grip on you, he wouldn't let go. He hung on so tightly that you could lift him off the ground while he continued to grasp you with his beak. That bird must have weighed at least twenty pounds—hurt like hell if he got you in the right spot. One time I had by back turned and he snuck up and attacked. He caught me good in the wrong place. Startled and pissed me off more than anything else. Unfortunately for him, I'd been digging holes at the time and had a shovel in my hand. Without thinking, I spun around and smacked him with it. I guess the blow was harder than I had anticipated 'cause he went flying! He rolled across the ground, in a heap, and not only got his wing tangled over his neck, but was knocked unconscious. My sister Lorna witnessed the incident and totally freaked out. She came running to the rescue, unfolding his tangled wing and administering mouth to beak respiration—tears streaming down her face. Before you knew it, Hershey was revived and honking his disapproval as he waddled off in the opposite direction. I felt so bad watching my sister cry over that stupid gander. After that brief encounter with the shovel, Hershey gave me the strangest looks—more like the evil eye! He never sneaked up on me again and never let me get too close either. No big deal, he had lots of other targets to choose from.

My sister, who aspired to become a veterinarian, accumulated some fifty cats and fifty dogs as her pet project. She named every last one of them and they followed her around like the Pied Piper, each jockeying for her attention. The collection started with a few strays here and there. Next thing you know, she had her very own Humane Society. Lorna was a natural when it came to animals. They sensed that her generous heart and loving soul were their salvation. She had a big gray tabby tom called Purrboy. That cat was such a ham. His favorite thing was being draped around my sister's neck, like some dead fur stole, while they waltzed throughout the house. He would lay there lifeless and content reveling in being the star of the show. That big tom was the greatest contributing factor to my sister's ever-growing cat population. Then there was my pet Siamese named Maddal, who I lovingly called Deese, Deese. She was a gift from an aunt who raised pedigreed show cats but because of her broken tail, she'd never be considered show quality. She was adorable and her crooked tail only added to her charm. Each morning, like clock work, she'd jump on my chest and begin licking my face to wake me for school. Although the other cats were allowed to come and go in the house, they lived outside. Only Deese, Deese lived indoors. She was the queen of the house and she knew it. The cutest and most memorable talent was her singing. Somehow my sister taught that cat to sing the musical scales, Do, Ra, Me, Fa, So, La, Ti and Do. Lorna would sit her down in the middle of the living room and recite each note of the scale in a different modulating tone. After each note, she would wait for Deese, Deese to answer before she said the next one. Each note gradually increased in tone. If the cat hit the wrong note, Lorna made her repeat it until she got it right. It was hilarious watching that cat sing scales. Not exactly Carnegie Hall quality, but it would have given the Guinness Book a shot. That was a class act.

The biggest attraction and most entertaining spectacle of all happened twice daily at the ranch. That's when my sister fed her menagerie of pets. Especially her cats. Her bedroom overlooked the garage roof and every day before and after school, she'd climb through the window onto the roof and call out to those cats, "Here kitty, kitty, kitty." In a flash, a frenzy of activity began. Cats, the expert climbers that they are, would come dashing up the sides of the 4x4 post that held up the garage roof. The clamor of claws digging their way into the wood created a distinctive noise announcing the arrival of hungry felines. Pans held high in both hands, her feet disappeared in a sea of undulating fur and protesting cries, signaling that all were present and accounted for. Once she placed those pans down on the roof, a flurry of maneuvering, furry bodies was set into motion. Tails taut and twitching with excitement, each animal vied for the ultimate position. A crescendo of meowing was brought to an abrupt halt, replaced by the barely audible lapping of tongues. With the cats secured and out of the way, she headed downstairs where her entourage of starving canines barked in anticipation. Her pack ranged in size from puppies to full-grown. Everyone spread out on the front lawn, circling and prancing under her feet, every step of the way, in a vain attempt to reach the food. With hungry faces buried in pans, wagging tails set to the beat of satisfying bliss, and the consumption of huge amounts of food underway, all was indeed, quiet on the western front! Seeing the occasional duck, chicken or furious pair of man-eating geese strolling by for a casual peck, never seemed to upset the party. Perfect harmony! All God's creatures sharing—one big happy family. Lucky to be standing there at that point in time, watching the greatest show on earth take place, in retrospect, reminds me of how truly blessed our lives were then.

Farm life came with its share of responsibilities and obligations. All those animals depended on you to see to their every need. It was my job to make sure that all the animals got fed and watered properly. Each morning, bright and early, I made my way to the pens for the first feeding. The animals, hungry and anxious, greeted me in their unique style. The pigs stood up on their hind legs and squealed with delight as I filled the troughs and hosed them down. The chickens and ducks chimed in quacking and crowing as they ran about their pens with excitement. From the paddock, the cows loudly mooed and stood at the fence, poised and ready. Horses, frolicking to and fro, neighing with pleasure. An orchestra that only Mother Nature could produce. I could hardly wait to get home from school and repeat the ritual and be among them. Animals are more predictable than people and sometimes make better friends. They will never let you down and long as you keep them fed and safe, you are rewarded with undying devotion.

If caring for the animals weren't enough responsibility, my sister and I decided to expand our horizons and take over the local paper route. With fewer than fifty customers, we thought it would be easy. Not to mention the extra cash we could make to spend on junk. This was the first honest-to-goodness job that either of us ever had and we were both proud as peacocks. The reality of the endeavor soon showed its ugly head when the end of the month came around and dues had to be collected. It's one thing to place rubber bands around papers and throw them at houses, a whole other thing getting people to pay for those neatly folded periodicals. People made excuses in all shapes and sizes. Being the innocent little kids that we were, trusting people to make the choices was never an issue we thought much about.

The sobering truth became apparent to us all too soon when the amount of papers being delivered didn't jibe with the amount of dues being collected. Customer relations and service can be a bitch! There was one positive side to the whole situation; the route was on private property with dirt roads, so we'd use my dad's car to deliver the papers. My sister and I would take turns at the wheel while one of our parents taught us how to drive. We had a blast! Both of us became pretty good drivers from that experience. The best part of all was on Sundays when my parents would sleep in and Lorna and I took the car out alone. Needless to say, it was a longer route than usual on those days. The hassle of dealing with rude and obnoxious people was worth the effort. We milked that job for as long as humanly possible before calling it quits.

The ranch was a great place to grow-up. It was a peaceful setting away from the hustle and bustle of the everyday rat race and competitive lifestyle. Family members and friends would often pack their bags to get away from their mundane and crazy lives. It was all ours for the amazing price of $75 a month and we shared it with whoever wanted it. You can never put a price on the simple things in life. Those things that for the most part are right in front of your face, but you're too busy doing whatever it is that you do to stop and appreciate the glory of nature. The price for that ticket, by the way, is free!

Not only were the surroundings great, but so was life in general for our family. Dad made detective and mom attended the University of Hawaii to obtain her degree in urban development. She and a few of her colleagues were instrumental in opening the first community action program, known as the Manpower Center. At a time when "affirmative action" was in effect, this program was essential for the local people. The various projects they produced contributed not only to the beautification of the community but the advancement of the many underprivileged residents. Though travel was murder on both my parents, I never saw them happier. Life couldn't be better! Then one day, while driving home from school, a semi-trailer slammed into the rear of my mother's car. Though she survived the accident, she spent the rest of her life plagued with chronic back and neck pain. The doctors recommended surgery, but she opted for chiropractic treatment for alignment and medication for pain relief. None of the treatments worked very well. If anything, it only became the beginning of an even bigger problem. The doctors prescribed the drug Valium to deal with her pain, which grew worse as time passed. Combined with her alcohol use, she soon developed a neurosis that led to more medication and higher doses. Along with having to deal with menopause and taking hormone therapy for that, she was wound up tighter than a $2 watch! On edge most of the time, she became prone to fits of rage.

Like the average kid, being the teasing, joking aggravating brats that we are, I became the object of all her pent up rage. Because of my physical stature, slapping me when she lashed out only hurt her hands. Tired of that, she resorted to using cooking implements. Her weapon of choice, the wooden spoon. After breaking a few of those on different parts of my body, she changed to a metal one—the one with holes in it so liquid can flow through. Hitting me square enough in the right place vibrated the spoon and hurt her hand even more. Soon, she stopped using anything hand-held altogether. She simply picked up the nearest object, preferably a heavy glass ashtray, coffee mug, or even, now and then, a knife, and threw it with all her might. Young and agile as I was, she often missed. Sometimes she got lucky and at those times, I never saw her outburst as anything other than well-deserved dishing out of discipline. Only a jackass would run around the house teasing a person in that frail a condition just to get a response out of them.

Which I did as much as possible. Typical childish behavior. I love my Mom and never, for once, thought any less of her. It was a terrible thing to use her madness as a form of my own selfish amusement. Hey, I was just a stupid kid! Everything is fun and games when you are a kid. The emotional setbacks and constant bouts with pain took every ounce of energy out of my Mom. Just getting through the day exhausted her, both physically and mentally. Her delicate state caused her to put her college career on hold for the time being. But being the resilient person that she was, she'd win out in the end and face even more difficulties.

I don't claim to be an expert, but I often wondered if my deep seated emotional problems, such as hostility and hyperactivity, could somehow be attributed to those moments when I was exposed to fits of anger and violence in my household. Duh! I could easily be considered a live wire. My parents had the hardest time getting me to keep still. Whenever my mother took me out into the public, she had to use a leash. That was the only way for her to control me and hinder my movement—like walking a dog. People would stop and stare as I dragged her around the stores and shopping malls. They thought it was a cruel way to treat a child. Little did they know it was as much for their own safety as it was mine. My father once left me unattended in the shopping cart, parked next to a tower of glass jars of mayonnaise—the crash could be heard throughout the store. I'd reached out and grabbed hold of one of the bottles, from the middle of the stack. I was still holding on to it when he came around the corner. Lucky no one had seen the catastrophe—we ducked around the corner to the nearest aisle. He then guided our cart past the scene of the crime, trying to look innocent as the clerks cleaned up the mess. Whenever he told that story, we had a good laugh. There was never a dull moment when it came to me getting into mischief.

I have a female cousin who is named after my dad's mom—Marjorie. When it came to getting into trouble, we were two peas in a pod. Though we fought a lot as children, whenever our curiosity got the best of us, we'd partner up. There's this time when our family had a picnic down at the beach. Everyone was having so much fun, they forgot to keep a close eye on Marj and me. We wandered off into the parking lot area and thought it would be fun to amuse ourselves by letting all the air out of the tires of just about every car there. That's when they found us having our own little picnic with the tires. The family, to this day, tells the story and we all get a chuckle out of that one. I don't think it was very funny to them back then!

My poor cousin, she always seemed to get the ass end of the stick when we played. I really couldn't say who influenced who. I guess we both shared in that department. I know she got me upset about something once because I hit her in the head with a claw hammer. She still sports the lump from that. We don't remember what it was about, but she always brings the incident up when I see her. By the way cuz, I'm sorry for all the crap I put you through.

Around this time, I learned the proper usage of firearms. "For protection purposes only." Dad, being a former member of the Army's elite 1st Special Forces Tropic Lightning Division, was the best instructor available. The farm's isolated location was perfect for training. It was common to hear the echoing reports of gunfire so no one paid much attention to it. Who would be brave enough to venture into nowhere land to check it out anyway? A person could easily get ambushed out there.

Target practice at tin cans became an avid past-time and I soon became an accomplished marksman. I usually hit what I was aiming at. Every now and then, the unfortunate mongoose would cross my sights. They loved to chew holes in the feed bags to get at the feed. One had the nerve to chew the ears off

46

my favorite pet rabbit. Payback for that stunt was a bitch. I sent many of his family to the Promised Land. Not only was I a good shot, but I learned to clean and care for weapons properly. I could break down almost any weapon and put it back together again. I was taught the importance of the different types of ammunition and the effects they had on the target—objects or flesh. I learned volume of fire—to count shots and preserve ammo and make every shot count. Also fields of fire, suppressive and superior fire power and their advantages. How to attack and ambush an objective effectively. To survive a situation at any cost. I could live in the wild, track animals and human prey alike. Not exactly the kind of schooling the average kid received. The most important thing my Dad instilled in me, which saved my life a few times, was, "shoot first and ask questions later."

A mean streak started to emerge in me. I began abusing the animals. I'd hit the pigs over the head with the feed buckets and throw rocks at the cattle. I terrorized my sister's cats and dogs. I'd throw the cats into an empty chest freezer and run a water hose into it. You could hear them cry out in panic as the water level rose. When the water began to overflow, I would pop the lid and that cat would bolt out of there, soaking wet. Another good one was known as the cat siren. You take a cat by the tail and whirl it around like a crank. The sound they made resembled that of a siren going off. Cruel as it was, I never seriously hurt or killed any of them. Just for kicks.

My father never intended for me to put into practice the knowledge that I possessed. He too, wanted a better way of life for me. To become a doctor or lawyer. Anything but a police officer. It was clear from an early age that though aggressive, I was intelligent enough to achieve the desired heights of success in life. As to my aspiring to those things myself . . . well, that was altogether another matter. Unbeknownst to him, it was always my intention to follow in my dad's footsteps. To become a part of the brotherhood of boys in blue and wear the coveted badge of honor—the third generation of lawmen to do so. Perhaps, even surpass the ranks of my ancestors and rise to the level of chief. A proud heritage, no doubt.

The farm flourished. There was always an abundance of food to furnish those traditional Hawaiian luau that our family often held. The glorious summers were spent camping on the many beautiful white sandy beaches with my cousins. It was in these blue waters, during those summer months, that I learned to fish from Uncle Johnny. He was a master of the sport and he knew all of the secret spots where the fish would gather. You'd see him, perched on the rocks, still as a statue with his throw net draped along his back, sighting through his dark glasses. Just waiting for the opportunity to pounce on those unsuspecting fish. All at once, bam! The net was thrown and the bountiful catch retrieved. Fresh fish for dinner! What a life! To this day, I can still picture Uncle Johnny poised on those rocks. And in spite of his gallant efforts, I never amounted to much of a fisherman.

There was a special rite of passage that every male member of the family had to go through—the slaughtering of the animal for the traditional Hawaiian feast. The task of teaching us this art was given to my Uncle Johnny. He was an expert at butchering and preparing any animal. I remember the day that the honor was mine. The family held down the 300 pound boar while Uncle passed me the knife. This wasn't just your average run of the mill knife. This pig sticker had been in the family for years. Many a pig and cow had been laid down by the tip of that blade. It was a perfectly balanced, razor sharp boning knife, nine inches long. When the sun reflected off of it, it sparkled and shone. Looking at it gave me the chills. For the mere fact that, when the knife came out, something was going to die. I can recall my uncle saying, "alright boy. Just one quick stab here in the throat, straight to the heart, with one quick stroke." I struck. The shrieking made your skin crawl. My hand never waivered. It was the first time in my life that I ever killed in that manner.

From the backyard barbecues to the many police department gala events, the usual clique of friends consisted mainly of fellow officers families. The "old boy" network stuck together professionally as well as socially. There is nothing rowdier than a room full of drunken cops. You'd be surprised to see what went on. No matter what happened, when the shit hit the fan, they would circle the wagons. They took good care of their own, to the extreme. Being part of this great big family, you had a special "cloak of protection." If a family member was caught speeding, no problem, just a few words of advice, "slow it down." Your kid gets busted with some dope or stolen goods, no problem. A simple phone call to your parents and that was it. Like being invincible. We learned to use this protection to our advantage. Nothing too radical, innocent stuff at first. That all changed with time.

During this period, Hawaii was experiencing an escalation in organized crime activity. There was a series of unsolved murders on the leeward side of the island where we lived. And it was here that many crime syndicate figures resided and did their business. This town was considered a no-man's land. A person could easily disappear from the face of the earth and no one would be the wiser. Some of those crime figures were close family friends. I'd often spend weekends playing at their homes, with their children, while my parents drank and passed the time. It was so surreal. My dad the police, partying with known gamblers, loan sharks and even contract killers. Laughing and joking, without a care in the world. Looked innocent enough, just a bunch of friends having a good time. There was more than met the eye. Many deals and policies were arranged at these get-togethers. Lives, both guilty and otherwise, hung in the balance. You could always tell when the talk turned serious—the women would disappear and the men would yell at us kids to go play someplace else. You really knew something was up when all the men stood up and walked into the house. That pretty much went on throughout my childhood. I remember a time when I was staying at one of these homes and my aunty was busy helping her girlfriend pack her stuff up. We later drove her friend to an apartment in Waikiki. I couldn't help but notice how scared and paranoid they were as they hurried to get to that apartment. Like something or someone was after them. The next day, my dad asked me if I had seen this lady at my aunty's house. My aunty swore me to secrecy, not to tell anyone where she had taken her friend. It surprised me how this inconspicuous event was a concern to my Dad. I wouldn't reveal her whereabouts, though he said that her life depended on it. That night, we went to his office in the main Police station in downtown Honolulu. He said someone very important wanted to meet and speak to me. He sounded so serious; I could tell by the tone of his voice that the situation was nothing to joke about. Soon, in walked Francis Keala, the Chief of Police. I was awestruck! It was like coming face to face with your favorite sports hero or movie star. He introduced himself and related to me that it was of the utmost importance that they find this woman. I'm no rat, but when you are ten years old and the most powerful man in law enforcement is standing there asking for your help, well . . . there's really nothing you can do. They drove me to the apartment and I pointed to the room. I had a strange feeling. I felt that I had let aunty down. I knew that what I did was the right thing. That lady sure looked surprised when she answered the door, wearing that deer caught in the headlights expression on her face. She was so relieved to see my Dad, she just started to cry. The chief made a phone call and the next thing you know, the place was crawling with cops. They packed her up and whisked her away in an unmarked car. The Chief thanked me for my help and disappeared into the night. My Dad was so proud of me. I later found out that the woman was the girlfriend of an underworld crime figure and had witnessed a murder. Her boyfriend had been hunting her down to kill her—I saved her life.

Life got even more interesting later, when the son of a close family friend became involved in a murder plot. He didn't actually commit the act himself, but did help in disposing of the body. It all started when his best friend's girlfriend witnessed a murder. Apparently the killing had shaken her to the core and she couldn't live with the guilt. Her boyfriend, fearing that she would go to the police, killed her to keep his secret. This particular group had known each other since grade school, murder victim included. What the Hawaiian culture referred to as "hanabutta days." The slang describing those younger years when kids played together while snot ran out of their noses. Seeing how cold-blooded his friend was frightened him so much that he confided in his father the events that had taken place. He wasn't about to become another murder victim. His father convinced him to confess to my dad. That night, under the cover of darkness, he led my dad to the woman's grave site. I can still remember the stench of death emanating from the trunk of our car—an officer on the scene had mistakenly placed the shovels used to extract the body into our trunk. Our car reeked for days, no matter how much we cleaned it. The rest, as they say, is history.

The guy turned state's witness, giving evidence against his boyhood friend and was placed in the witness protection program. Thanks to his efforts, they were able to retrieve that other murder victim's body as well. Not to mention the solving of a few more crimes, including murder. Dad became the most celebrated detective that year. He was awarded the "Medal of Valor" and was voted Policeman of the Year—the most prestigious honor an officer could obtain. He was on top of the world and we were so proud of him. Promotion in the ranks looked imminent. We were sorely mistaken. Like those empty promises in the past, this time was no different. He'd gladly trade every award and medal for a promotion that paid more money. All the hard work attending the university to further his career was nothing but a waste of time. The promotion never came. He had reached his height in the department. A lifetime of devotion with nothing to show for it but a few framed pieces of paper and a wooden plaque.

My father's disappointment and bitterness towards the department was palpable. He drank more than ever, but the violent fits of rage all but vanished. He basically just drank, and mom drank along with him. They argued now and then, with less exuberance, mostly about her spending, but it was apparent that things had changed. Acceptance can be a bitter pill to swallow. Life never gives the suffering an even break. No matter how much shit you get, there's always a bigger pile to wade through. One night, while driving home from work, a single gunshot rang out into the darkness. The bullet shattered the rear window, passed directly through the driver's side headrest and exited through the windshield. Luckily, dad's head wasn't leaning against the headrest or he'd have been killed. He did survive the assassination attempt, but not unscathed. Fragments from the bullet peppered his face. The wounds weren't serious enough to cause permanent damage—the ambush had failed. Thanks to the grace of God.

All hell broke loose after the incident. Our farm was besieged by unmarked police vehicles. Being the middle of the night, we were awoken by their dramatic entrance. We knew something really bad had happened. One of the officers standing in our living room kept telling my mom not to worry, that everything was going to be alright and that my dad had been shot. No, "he's fine," or "he's dead" no nothing as to his condition. They didn't even have the facts. Then as quickly as they arrived, they all vanished. Gone. Leaving us alone and confused with no protection or the slightest inkling of the situation. So much for the efficiency of the department. Although my sister and I knew there was something terribly wrong, my mother refused to tell us what had happened. My father appeared later, shaken, but alive and surrounded by the group of officers who had abandoned us earlier. We all breathed a sigh of relief, followed by an emotional outburst, from my mom to all the officers who had left us hanging in midair.

Following these events, our world was turned completely upside down. They assigned a seven man security detail to our family, 24 hours a day, seven days a week. An RV, filled with radio equipment and weapons was rolled in to serve as a command post. All movements were strictly monitored. Attending school was out of the question, so we had to be tutored. Just performing the grocery shopping became a complex security task. A convoy of cars caravanned us to and from the market and while selecting our items, we were followed everywhere by men carrying automatic weapons. They literally blocked off the aisles when we were in them. No one else was allowed to be in those aisles while we shopped. That sure turned a lot of heads. The notoriety was pretty cool when you think about it, but the seriousness of the reason why was scary. That was the only outing that we really had, so my sister and I took turns accompanying my mom to shop because we both couldn't be in the same place at the same time. We even rode in separate vehicles whenever we went to the doctor or other appointments. I could empathize with the President and First Family concerning the hassle of security. The atmosphere was stifling!

To deter any further attempts on my Dad, he was flown to work via police helicopter. Each morning the helicopter would touch down on our front lawn and jockey him to his office. A scene right out of the movies! Didn't take long before the pressure took its toll on us. We needed a serious break soon or we would go crazy. After three months of this crap, we were allowed a family outing. We piled into cars and headed to the drive-in movie to see "The Rumble in the Jungle," the heavyweight championship boxing match between the then champ Mohammed Ali and challenger Joe Frazer. The circus event, orchestrating all that manpower around to just see a movie was as entertaining as the fight itself. Felt good to be out and about, even under those circumstances. A brief moment of normalcy.

Chapter 4

Get the hell out of Dodge

The state's budget for our security was staggering! Protecting our family became more of a liability than a necessity. They could no longer provide adequate security coverage. We were given a choice, or more like an ultimatum. We could remain living on the ranch, minus the security detail, or relocate uptown, closer to the police station. There, our family could be guarded by local patrol cars. Yeah, right! Which ever we chose, we had five hours to decide. After that, we were on our own. Exploring our options, there really wasn't much for us to decide. My parents weren't too keen about living out there in the boonies without the security. All those animals . . . what would become of them? Although leaving our peaceful existence was the furthest thing from our minds, we had no choice.

Once the decision was made, the fun really began. We contacted everyone we knew and they called everyone they knew. What could be sold, was sold, what couldn't was given away. The rest was packed up or left behind. The truck arrived and whatever was crammed in was carted away to our new home. Home, now that's an understatement, if there ever was one. Transported into the "Twilight Zone" was more like it. We went from a six bedroom house to a two bedroom apartment, smack dab in the middle of the city. Presto! Like magic. Needless to say, there was hardly any floor space in that tiny apartment. Boxes were piled three and four deep everywhere and I mean everywhere. You couldn't even get to the bathroom without running the obstacle course. It was so depressing. Welcome home.

Being uprooted, to a new location and way of life sure took getting used to. I kept playing over in my mind the last images of our previous life. That of my beloved Siamese cat, wandering the brush, lost and confused, we hadn't enough time to find her a proper home. Even more heartbreaking was watching my sister deal with the loss of all her animals. They say that in time, you can recover from anything. I agree to disagree on that one. Obviously, whoever believes that is a fool.

My sister and I were placed in different public schools. No friends or familiar faces, just stranded in a crazy world. To top it off, the department strongly suggested that we use aliases to throw the evil doers off the trail. How drastic is that!? So under new identities, we began our lives. I remember feeling totally alone and vulnerable. Cast aside. There wasn't much security coverage from that point on. Well, none that I was aware of. We were more or less forgotten. Left out in the cold. Victims of the very system that vowed to "serve and protect." From that time on, I felt nothing but hate and animosity for the law and all that it represented.

You could see how disturbed my parents were about our current situation, especially my dad. He wore the department betrayal on his sleeve. I could sense the disappointment. It was a living, breathing entity. The drinking got heavier and there was no more arguing. The hurt had turned inside itself. It was like watching a beaten man wallowing in his sorrow, resigned to his fate. Many a night, I'd sit and listen to him complain and vent his anger. How the department this or the department that. At times, he'd sit with the loaded gun on the table while he drank. It was like he was drinking to somehow muster up the courage to end his suffering. He'd drink and I'd listen, often we'd talk and we'd cry until he passed out. I'd put him to bed and think about the next time. Those moments left me physically exhausted and mentally depressed.

I started having problems in school. Fighting with other students and lashing out at the teachers. Eventually, I was sent away to boarding school on another island. Turns out that it was a school for troubled youth. Only the most hardheaded students were accepted to board there. No high SAT scores, no 4.0 GPA required. Just a bad attitude! The regimen there was nothing short of boot camp. I was already homesick, but that was the least of my concerns.

The days began at 6 am when a whistle sounded. We then rushed to one of the various job assignments, worked for an hour until the whistle sounded. We then had 15 minutes to get back to the dorm, shower, and dress and be standing, lined up, in front of the dorm. There, we were subjected to an inspection by the dorm matron and upperclassmen. If you failed, due to an unshaven face or winkled clothes, punishment ensued. This was in the form of overtime. Believe me, these overtime hours added on to your work period ain't no fun. Besides not getting paid, they usually consisted of the hardest, dirtiest, most backbreaking jobs. For those who wanted to step out of line, the overtime hours sure could add up. Then off to breakfast in the cafeteria and classes after that. After school the routine of working was repeated for two more hours, unless you had overtime to pay. That could cost you an additional two hours of work. You then had dinner around 6pm and finish the night with two hours of study hall. Lights out by 11 unless you had permission to cram.

The campus was located on the side of a mountain slope, overlooking the beautiful Pacific Ocean. The balancing act with work and school and sports, not to mention choir practice on Sundays, was the institute's way of building an individual's character. To instill discipline and responsibility. But being housed with 122 other boys soon led me on a totally different path to higher education. Every conceivable manner in which a person could get into mischief was explored and exploited. This included sneaking out at night to steal eggs from the chicken farm to snatching up watermelons from the garden. Perfect for that midnight snack.

I recall one incident in particular. During the holiday seasons we could either return home to our families or remain on the campus. One holiday, I chose to stay at school. I was walking along the hallway, in front of the home economics building, trying doorknobs, when one of them opened. That night, a few us snuck out and made our way to that classroom. Bingo! We hit the mother lode. We discovered a treasure trove of food items and proceeded to indulge ourselves. The party was on for sure! After stuffing our faces, we cleaned up the mess and vanished into the night. No one was the wiser. "Happy Thanksgiving."

I have to give thanks and praise to my dear old Mom, God bless her soul for teaching me the finer points of domestic life. She's the reason I became adept at not only cooking and cleaning, but ironing and sewing as well. Those talents came in handy when you were on your own. The other guys wondered why I was always so impeccably dressed. Needless to say, my popularity soon increased. Especially among the upperclassmen. Being a freshman sure did suck!

Regardless of the regimental programming that went on, the weekends belonged to us. For those of us who weren't busy working off those extra overtime hours, that was our time to cut loose. From Friday to Sunday we were allowed to wander the streets of the near-by town.

Lahaina was once a whaling village and port of call for sailors making their way across the Pacific in the 1800's. If you were lucky enough to catch a ride down the winding 1½ mile road that led into town, you could maximize your stay until the ten o'clock curfew. Like most small towns, there was a limited variety of social activities to choose from. There was the drive-in, the movie house and the corner pool hall; the latter being off limits to us, but that never deterred us the least bit. Most of us just hung out with our girlfriends or the day students and got into trouble. Some of the boys managed to get a hold of beer now and then, and spent the night drinking themselves into a drunken stupor.

It was during this period in my life that I began drinking—just beer at first and only on the weekends with the boys. But soon, my drinking increased along with my alcoholic beverage of choice. I'd get friends to purchase bottles of vodka which I stashed under a pile of rocks behind the dorm. A few of us would meet at the rock pile a couple times a week for a quick snort before morning classes. The process repeated after school before work line. We always drank vodka because it never smelled on the breath as bad. Nothing a tic-tac couldn't fix. Those tic-tacs were the rage of the time. Boy, did I love to drink, or should I say the effects of drinking. I took to it like a duck to water! All those years of watching my parents indulge in the spirits made it okay. I was an alcoholic by the age of 14. It was the crutch that I was looking for to cope with whatever issues or pain I was dealing with.

Then one day, while sitting around campus, a friend introduced me to marijuana. I had heard of the drug, but up until this time I had never tried it. "Have a hit" he said. "Just puff on it like smoking a cigarette, but hold the smoke in." After a bit of coaxing, I tried it. It really is true what they say about your first time. I felt great! The high was amazing! After a few bouts of uncontrollable laughter, we managed to contain ourselves enough to go exploring. We found ourselves at the pig pens, where we proceeded to throw copious amounts of fresh fruits and vegetables at this huge boar's genitals. I never laughed that hard in my entire life. My side ached so much I could barely stand. All at once, our laughter was broken by the booming voice of the work supervisor. "What the hell you guys think you're doing!" Our blood ran cold. This guy was a very large individual, not to mention the most feared person on campus. Many a student has faced the wrath of this gorilla. We took off running like scared jackrabbits in opposite directions. Every man for himself! Talk about bumming your trip, this was the ultimate nightmare! I found myself squeezing between a stack of plywood and boxes on a veranda of an old building. Sober now from the shock, I prayed I wouldn't be spotted. Suddenly, he came into view. Until this day, I don't know what made him stop and look in my direction. I was cornered. My only option was to bail out over the side. Luckily, I held on for dear life. There I was dangling off the side of this two story building. Nowhere to go but down. Beneath lay an unfinished portion of a new structure—nothing but tile blocks and rubble. This was going to hurt. Death before capture! I released my hold and bam! Perfect landing. I was outta there in a flash. Accompanied by a stream of screaming expletives. I can still see his eyes bulging out of the sockets, his face as red as a tomato. My friend and I met up at the dorm, safe and sound. Bursting into fits of laughter, relieved to be alive, we celebrated our victory with another joint. That, in a nutshell, was the birth of my drug habit.

Somewhere along the way, I became acquainted with one of the local girls. We were the same age, but that was the only thing we had in common. She was a tall, shy girl with alabaster skin and the most beautiful green eyes. They would change shade depending on her mood or outfit. I was mesmerized by them. Little did I know, at the time, that someday she'd be my wife. Life's strange that way. She fell madly in love with me. Although she was a beauty, my feelings weren't the same. We dated and hung out at school and on the weekends. I even flew her home with me on a vacation break. We were both virgins at the time, but she was more than willing to let me take full advantage of her, but I always stopped short. I thought that it wouldn't be fair because of the way I felt about her. Can you believe that! Yes I, the king of perve, had a conscience back then. To be young and innocent again.

It was during this trip that I met the love of my life. Talk about love at first sight! The minute I laid eyes on that girl I knew she would one day be my wife. She was, literally, the girl next door. She had become a close friend of my sister, who talked about me a lot. She was a dark-skinned beauty from Texas. Her father was a marine stationed here and as an only child, her parents watched her like hawks. I fell madly in love. I couldn't help myself. Just the sight of her made my heart melt like butter. I felt bad for the green-eyed girl that I had flown down with. She could sense that my mind was preoccupied—women have this radar that even the government envies. I found it difficult to leave for school. Reluctantly, I flew back after the holiday was over. Before I left, I made myself a promise; one day that Mexican beauty would be mine.

Things weren't the same when I returned to school. I became distant and aloof. I couldn't stop thinking about that girl. I'd call home on the weekends and my sister would put her on the phone and we'd talk for hours. I became homesick and fed-up with the whole boarding school trip. Eventually, my tenure at Lahainaluna High School came to an abrupt end, when home sickness got the best of me. It was a tearful event when I told the green-eyed girl that I was leaving school for good. I held her tight as we danced the final dance at the annual Boarders Dance. I packed up my stuff, along with my two newly acquired habits, and moved back to Oahu.

I was enrolled in McKinley High School, better known as Tokyo High—due to the predominately Japanese student body. The remaining part of my sophomore year flew by. I spent most of my time studying and getting closer to that beautiful neighbor. She was a few years younger than me, so our courtship was slow and rocky. Our parents became fast friends and they would often hang out. Her dad was a real piece of work—a short, solidly built guy, who drank like a fish and loved to hoot and holler. Add the USMC grunt factor and what you got was a force to be reckoned with. My dad had found a drinking buddy. This was my first experience with the Mexican culture, other than the language classes at school. At least her mom was a nice person. She was almost twice her husband's size and clearly wore the pants in the family. They didn't take too kindly, at first, to my intentions toward their underage daughter. But soon they softened. Besides, nothing short of death would have deterred me.

By this time I was allowed to drink in the confines of my home. I'd often have a few beers at the end of the day with my parents. At times, my girl's father would join us. See, the way my parents saw things was—we'd rather you stayed home and did it than run around behind our backs. I guess they thought they could supervise my intake. That was a mistake—it only gave me the green light to indulge. I was soon drinking with my Dad and my girl's father on a regular basis. We even went to bars and the O club together. And those times that I did go with the boys . . . the bar was open!

When junior year came along, I got involved with sports again. Although I had played football at boarding school, here was a whole new ball game. Football was a serious sport at McKinley and the kids that played had been doing it since grade school. Thanks to dad's idea of signing me up at the private gym, Mits Health Studio, I was transformed into a physically daunting specimen. Mits Kashiwabara and his wife, Dot, were two of the best health specialists on the island. They taught me a vast array of health and nutritional tips. If it weren't for their help, I never would have survived.

I excelled at football, but was shunned by my teammates. These guys had been playing together since Pop Warner days and didn't like the idea that an outsider had infiltrated their territory. I was treated like an interloper but I produced results on the playing field. Clearly, I had impressed the coach from the start and it didn't take me long to earn a starting position. The excitement, attention and physically violent nature of the game was a new high for me. To a certain degree I became one of the boys because of my ability. Well, you can't please everyone, especially the jealous ones. No matter what the beefs were, we all had one thing in common, we loved to party! And after every game, we did just that. I managed to corrupt my fellow teammates every chance I could. Besides I was the only one who had a license and the car to go with it. That qualified me for instant best friend status. Mr. Popular! The party train had a whole new element—mobility. My first ride was the same '69, four door Chevy Chevelle that my dad was driving the night they tried to kill him. I always felt invincible behind the wheel of that car. Me and that girl sure had some good times together.

I remember a time when me and the boys were out late one night joy riding on a mountain top called Tantalus, or Round Top Drive. A stretch of road about four miles that meandered through hills right in the middle of town. There was a lookout where tourists visited during the day and the lovers would use at night. Well, we would often make a run at the hill after a late night of partying before calling it a night. On this particular night, while in the process of speeding down hill, a blue and white patrol car showed up behind us. First, I outran him at breakneck speed—no one could catch me on that hill. I was the King! Finally, I decided to slow down and let him catch up before he killed himself. He flashed his lights and we pulled over like good, obedient kids out for an innocent drive. The next thing I know, I'm looking down the barrel of a 12 gauge shotgun held by some white-as-a sheet guy who looked younger than we were. As he screamed, at the top of his lungs, for me to place my hands on the hood of his patrol car, I couldn't help but notice how that shotgun was shaking in his hands. I casually commented to him to please stop pointing that shotgun at me before it went off by mistake. Through his ranting and raving, his fear was evident. As the rest of my crew was ordered out of the car, you could see the gun shake even more. A couple of the guys suggested that he lower the gun, "Why you pointing that gun at us? We're just high school kids out riding around." Then he made the biggest mistake of his life. As he climbed back into his car to call for back-up, he just laid that shotgun right there on the hood of his vehicle. Oh no he didn't? Hell yeah! Why, that that jackass, mother-so-and-so. As he peered over the dash of his car, speaking on the microphone, I told everyone to stay perfectly still. Don't even breathe hard. This guy wanted to kill somebody. Little did he know who he had stopped. Not some stupid kid dumb enough to make a grab for that shotgun, which was probably on safety, while he held his service revolver in his hand. When he got off the radio, all smug and arrogant, I told him how he had screwed the pooch on this one. "Officer so-and-so, you just detained the juvenile son of a detective and while in the process of a routine traffic stop, you did, in fact, brandish a shotgun in a menacing fashion. Then, while calling for back up, you did in fact, place your assigned weapon, loaded, on the hood of your vehicle, unattended, all the while holding your service revolver in hand, hoping that one of us would be stupid enough to reach for it. Now, since back-up is already on the way and the license number that called in came back registered in the name of Louis L. Staunton Sr., whose insurance card and other pertinent information has been confirmed by this time by the Department, and who no doubt has already been notified that his son has been detained by a rookie in a blue and white . . . well you can paint the rest of the picture. When I get through with you, you'll be lucky to be turning keys." This reference made to officers, mostly rookies and screw-ups, who spend their days locking and unlocking cell doors in the cell block. These cops don't even carry a gun. Just those keys. This is considered the lowest of the low assignment for an officer to have. Would be the best this guy could hope for. Soon, the place was littered with cops.

I recognized the Sergeant as one of my dad's close friends. Even the Lieutenant on scene worked with my dad. He said the reason he was there was because he had heard my dad's name come over the radio. I told him what the rookie cop had done and that I was sorry for all the trouble I caused. I was given some kind of lecture, a scolding and ordered to get my ass home. No ticket, no nothing. Invincible. Oh yeah, and the sergeant said that the guy was scared shitless chasing me at those speeds. And by the way, how fast were you going? "Oh, not that fast, you know, it's impossible to reach those speeds on this road. He probably got mixed up or his speedometer is wrong." We just smiled at each other and I walked away. As for that eager beaver cop . . . never saw him again.

Somewhere around this time I lost my virginity. She was two years older than I and was a former classmate of my sister. You know what they say about those Catholic school girls? I really didn't know squat about sex, but this girl was a pro. It was clear from the start that her obsession with sex was abnormal. No complaints from the audience on that account, but when she started saying she wanted my baby, well . . . see you later! I do thank her from the bottom of my heart for introducing me to one of life's simpler pleasures. I later found out that what she suffered from had a name, nymphomania. Bless her soul.

That year, our school football team was invited to play a pre-season game against O.J. Simpson's former high school, Galileo High School, located in San Francisco. For kids used to 75° weather all year round, this was a wake up call! The temperature was a cool 43° and prior to the game we were led to this freezing locker room where we changed into our uniforms. They must have shut the heater off to play some kind of pre-game mind trip on us. Let me tell you, it sure had the desired effect. We were shaking so bad from the cold, we could barely suit up. No matter how hard we played, there was no warming up. Not to mention we were at the mercy of two of the nation's leading running backs who would no doubt be on the All-American High School team. These guys were monsters! Took half of the defensive line to stop one of them. First set of plays, our linebacker broke his nose on the smaller one, trying the one-on-one action. He cried like a bitch when he saw his own blood. Six foot three, 245 pounds of solid freight train and that's the smaller one! Eventually, me and the big one met up as I tried to plug a hole on the line. Bam! I thought I'd hit a concrete wall. I felt every bone in my body dislocate! In sports, there's a certain experience players call "seeing stars." This phenomenon happens when two opposing forces collide at full speed. It was the first time I had experienced it on a personal level. The running backs always talked about it—it was a regular thing with them. My eyes were wide open, but all I could see were tiny dots flashing like stars. It would have been a cool, unusual display if I weren't being taken for a ride by this huge wave as I desperately clung to his massive six foot four, 255 pound frame. One of our corner backs tried to tackle this dude one-on-one. The biggest mistake of his life as he was literally tossed aside like a rag doll, head first into the bleachers. It took him three days to remember who or where he was. Sure was fun answering all his bewildered questions in the bus on the way to Disneyland, "Who are you guys? Where are we going? What's my name?" It was so comical; we thought he was faking it. I'd never seen a case of amnesia before. Needless to say, we lost the game. Sure was a great experience. Before then, I had never been to the mainland and I was happy just to be seeing the sights.

We made our way to Anaheim where we stayed across from Disneyland. I couldn't believe I was really here! That night I was dumb enough to lose all my allowance in a crap game to a teammate. My best friend, who also played on the team, was there to bail me out. I met him when I first moved from the country and since then we were inseparable. He was a product of a broken home, but a moral, clean cut guy. To ease my pain of defeat, he convinced me to accompany him to the nearest liquor store. There was no problem getting a six pack of Coors. We easily passed for legal age. Drunk and feeling better, off we went to Disneyland. The fireworks display at the park's closing was an awesome sight. The next day, slightly hung over, we made our way to the nearest diner for breakfast, then off again to Disneyland. One final day of sightseeing. It wasn't long before we were loaded up on buses on our way to the Farmers Market and Knox Berry Farm and the Japanese Deer Park. Once there, our attention was focused on that fabulous log ride. There's a point where this hollowed-out log exits a tunnel and takes a drop down this 60 foot flume. Whoosh! After a few sessions, we decided that it would be fun to try and stand up on the way down. Like a giant surfboard barreling down a sixty foot wave!

Picture ten people standing as this log made its way down. The look on the face of the ride operator was classic. More frightened to death than shocked, we were not only kicked off the ride, but banned from it. So much for that idea. We ended our journey at the Deer Park. A petting zoo of sorts, with an oriental theme. The tranquil surroundings were brought to an end with the arrival of the wild bunch. The boys went crazy there. The quiet, quaint little shops never knew what hit them. The boys stormed a shop, 30 strong, and proceeded to shoplift on a grand scale. The owners made a futile effort to keep track of all the activity. They soon kicked everyone out, in a last ditch attempt to save their stores, but not before losing a substantial amount of their inventory. This brought my mainland experience to an end, but not before borrowing a few bucks from my pal and securing a case of that Rocky Mountain goodness (Coors) for my Dad. Don't ask! Sure was nice to see that smile on his face when I presented it to him at the airport.

The rest of the school year was spent pretty much on auto-pilot; boring and uneventful. I did manage to hook up with that fine Mexican neighbor of mine. Between sports, getting stoned and her, I kept busy. If it weren't for being intellectually inclined, I would have never made it through school. My lack of enthusiasm and indifference toward attending classes caused me to seek other forms of activity. So, I spent most days cutting class to be with my girl or hanging out at the beach with the boys. I loved to bodysurf; it was the one thing I really enjoyed. The freedom of riding the waves, finding peace and being one with Mother Nature melted my cares away. I found that it consumed all my time. Not only would I cut school on the weekdays, I would also spend my weekends at the beach, sun up to sun down. It became an obsession. Another addiction to add to my collection. I never once considered the damage I was doing to my future. If I could take it back, I'd change every last part of my careless behavior. When you're young and immature, you act as though there isn't a care in the world. You have time on your side. Why take life seriously at this moment? Live a little. Before long, with all the Saturday night partying after football games and beach boy antics, my drug and alcohol abuse reached a point where my weekly allowance could no long stretch to cover all my bad habits. I was forced to seek alternative measures to supplement my income.

Chapter 5

Crime with passion

Comes a time, in everyone's life, when a critical decision has to be made. A decision, for all accounts that could make or break their lives. The imaginary picture that "Beware! Fork in the road up ahead" sign still reminds me of my failure to heed. Having the knowledge to choose the right path is not some magical mystical gift you receive in a moment of enlightenment—spiritual awakening. On the contrary, the ability to render such a decision is based on nothing more than pure and simple common sense. There's the right way and the wrong. Duh! Even a moron can get that one right. Unless, of course, that moron is hopped up on drugs and alcohol. Why should I be the exception? The smarter you think you are, the dumber your reality becomes. The problem with me taking the wrong path is that in my heart and in my mind, I knew the difference. Somehow, the wrong choice seemed more appealing at the time. It always is! Throwing caution to the wind, and in the process relinquishing a piece of my sanity, would later prove to have dire consequences. You might say, beyond my wildest imagination.

Regardless of my situation, or rather condition, I had every intention of joining the police force. I rationalized my current use of drugs and alcohol as a transitional period in my life. The typical adolescent behavior that all kids my age displayed. Once I graduated from high school I would get over it. That couldn't have been further from the truth. My nightmarish behavior would soon take a turn for the worse. It all began when I got together with a former boarding school friend. He was currently attending a private school on Oahu. His father, a retired police officer, worked with my dad years ago. After his parents divorced, his mother remarried a millionaire contractor. She now had the means to provide a better lifestyle for her kids. Stepdad paid all the bills. When he wasn't staying in the dorms, he resided at a palatial hilltop mansion in an exclusive neighborhood overlooking the entire city of Honolulu. An above average student, his mother had high expectations for his future. The only problem with that idea was her prim and proper son loved to party hearty and engage in questionable activities of an illegal nature. Wasn't long before we formulated a plan to make a little extra cash on the side. There is only so much even a rich parent is willing to pay for. When you party excessively, spending more than you have, at the same time concealing a bad habit, someone has to pick up the tab.

Enter . . . Butch Cassidy and the Sundance Kid! Or a reasonable facsimile thereof. Now, thinking about robbery and actually committing one are two altogether different things. It all looks good on paper up until show time. What ever prompted us to resort to such extreme measures I'll never know. What were we thinking? Shows you the lengths an addict would stoop to. Both of us were trained to handle firearms and decent marksman so the thought of using a gun wasn't an issue. We weren't going to use it, use it like shoot anybody but you never know. When you undertake such a risky venture, with a loaded gun and all, you have to prepare for the worst. This was no longer a game. Someone could end up dead. Every precaution had to be taken into consideration. We decided that we'd need at least three people to carry out our plan. Each person responsible for a specific task. My friend would be the driver and provide the transportation. His friend, Dave, a rich kid from Micronesia would be the bag man, or the one who holds on the to the loot after stripping the victims of their wealth. And yours truly was the gunman. The person who brought the element of terror to the show. It was my responsibility to provide the weapon. No one else had the guts to play this part. The other two parties involved wished to separate themselves from the more culpable aspect of the crime. If, by chance, things went wrong, they could always claim that the guy with gun made me do it. Who'd you believe? Not saying that they would have, but they could have. Those details aside, we were ready for the next step of our plan. We agreed that this would be a one or two time thing. None of us were keen on the idea of this becoming a habit. Limited partnership, limited venture. Just a couple of guys out on the town getting paid for kicks.

Finding the right job to pull, especially when it's your first time, is very important. Could mean the difference between success and failure. Getting caught or making a clean get away. Increasing the odds in your favor is essential to avoid being captured. Minimizing the risk by taking into careful account the unexpected occurrences. Leaving as little as possible to chance, we decided on the perfect target. Literally a walk in the park. See, the private school my friend attended was comprised of some of the richest kids in the Pacific. The sons and daughters of corporate CEOs, land developers, oil ministers, bankers, even royalty. Millions upon millions! On the weekends, like clockwork, an armored car delivered a ton of money to the school, which had its own bank. Yes, bank! Because of the number of students and the amount of cash required to meet the needs of these spoiled rich kids lifestyles, the school had a special banking system set up to cater to them. Every weekend, the boarding students were allowed to withdraw thousands of dollars from their accounts. Money that was splurged on whatever their hearts desired and the majority of it was spent on partying. With unlimited funds at their disposal, they wouldn't mind sharing some with the poor.

Anyways, there was this bunch of kids who had a habit of gathering in the park adjacent to the school. I guess they felt safe partying close to home. I can relate to that. On this particular night, while partying and having a good time, they bogeyman showed up uninvited. Surprise! "This is a robbery! Everyone get up against the wall. Listen and no one will get hurt. We're just here to take your money, not your lives." At first, they thought that this was some kind of prank. Until they saw the gun. After lining them up on the bathroom wall, Dave and I proceeded to help ourselves to the goods. Rifling through purses and pockets, I was shocked at the amounts of cash some of these kids had on them. The money was just crumpled haphazardly into wads, tens and twenties, fifties, even hundreds. Dubious at first about this whole ordeal, feeling the fruits of my labor clenched in my fist changed my outlook. My heart was beating a mile a minute. I felt the surge of adrenaline course through my veins—the high is hard to describe. I never felt so powerful with a high that was mesmerizing. We walked away with over a thousand dollars of cash and jewelry and vanished into the night.

For a limited venture, things got out of control real fast. The money was such easy pickings, why stop now? Not once had we thought about the risk involved or the people we hurt. Nothing came close to the thrills and excitement. With just a three way split of the profits there was lots to go around. We became a well-oiled cash machine. The weekdays were spent in the classroom earning our diplomas but the weekends were spent putting in work. Equal opportunity bandits, we never discriminated against any race, culture or age group. Everyone was susceptible to our attack. One night while cruising for a victim we came upon an unsuspecting couple sitting in their car in a deserted parking lot. Both were busy smoking a joint, obviously preparing for the night's festivities. Their night was about to be ruined. I stuck my gun into the driver's face and told him to hand over his wallet. The smell of marijuana smoke hung in the air. Stoned and confused, ignoring my request, he continued smoking the joint, protesting the intrusion. Smacking him upside the head with the barrel of my pistol to persuade him of my serious intent, I relieved him of the still burning joint and took a hit. Now that I had their attention, the female passenger turned and said, "You're not going to rob a poor college student. I have bills to pay. What a bummer." Giddy from the effects of the joint I burst into laughter and replied, "Sorry lady, times are hard. Now give the man your purse!" The poor students weren't all that poor on this night. Between the two of them, they had about $600. Pretty decent night's work for the kids. I felt sorry for the gorgeous passenger, so I let her keep her jewelry. The driver didn't get away so easy. Besides the lump forming on the left temple, he lost his watch, rings, gold chains and wallet. And so went our continuing means of gainful employment.

Perhaps not the safest occupation in the world, but it sure was the most fun and interesting. Though scary, it did have its advantages. We kept our own hours, never punched a clock and didn't have to answer to management. The pension plan left a lot to be desired. Not that we were overly concerned about that aspect of the job. Chances were we'd never reach retirement anyway. The stress factor was enormous! To take the edge off and relieve the pressure, someone came up with a crackpot idea of stealing parking meters. Sounded amusing, barely any risk involved. With all the cars out there that needed parking, we might even make a few bucks. Piling into my friend's Mustang, we drove to the busiest, but by now emptiest, lot in downtown Honolulu. Would've been nice to have a pipe cutter in our tool inventory, but the unprepared amateurs that we were, we settled for a crescent wrench. Held by four lousy bolts, removing the meters was a snap. I was reminded of Paul Newman in his role as "Cool Hand Luke." At the beginning of the movie, he uses a cutter to lop the tops off the meters, easy as pie. Even back then, he knew that the extra lengths of pipe that held those suckers would present a problem.

It wasn't long before we managed to rid that lot of a sizable number of meters. Loading our stash into the backseat of the Mustang, pipes and all, we hopped onto the Pali and made our escape; heads banging against the car roof, but we were too drunk to notice.

Having the meters in hand is all good and fine, getting to the change inside . . . lets just say we had our work cut our for us. Never having the pleasure of cracking open a parking meter before, the actual degree of difficulty was way more than we bargained for. Exactly how hard could it be? Like cracking open an egg, I'd suspect, to get at the yolk. Yeah, right! After a few tries, it was obvious that it would take more than a hammer and chisel to get at this yoke. An hour passed with only two of those bitches opened. Needless to say, nearly losing a few precious digits from our hands in the process. There had to be an easier way. Those buggers were built like miniature bank vaults. We definitely needed some heavy equipment. A mutual friend had a refuse company in the industrial area close by, so we loaded up the goods and raced out. Arriving, we found the place pitch black and devoid of life. No one was expected until morning. Just past midnight, we had plenty of time to get in, cut these suckers open with a torch and be long gone. Easier said than done!

Staring at the locked gate and ten foot high fence, barbed wired at the top, we faced our first obstacle. Pulling up to the gate, we quickly off-loaded and ditched the Mustang. We concluded that two would work on the meters, while the other kept a lookout. My friend, the only qualified welder, did the cutting and Dave and I alternated watch. Seeing the torch light up and sparks start to fly as he set to work, brought relief to my skepticism. Things were going smoothly and the cash was starting to add up. Then we hit a snag. My partner noticed that the oxygen was burning off too quickly. Something was wrong with the equipment. We needed every bit of fuel to burn through those tough casings. I looked around for another tank, but the rest were empty. We were barely through half the pile! We hoped that we'd have enough to finish. The stress was agonizing. Never had this much pressure sticking my gun in people's faces. This was supposed to be fun!

The sounds of rain splashing off the pavement washed away some of the tension and disguised our criminal activity. The heavy downpour can give the people engaging in crime a curtain of safety to hide behind. That false sense of security is akin to having a warm, fuzzy blanket wrapped around you when a tiger is about to pounce and eat you for dinner. All crooks think that rainy nights are the most ideal for committing a crime. Oh, and like the cops don't think the same thing! It was my turn to act as lookout, so I jumped the fence, found a spot in the shadow, and tried to remain vigilant. Shouldn't be a problem, being soaked to the bone and all. Standing in the pouring rain, drenched, I suddenly realized how utterly ridiculous this whole plan was. We'll be lucky to get a hundred bucks, total, out of all this. The idea bordered on the comical. Feeling, quite frankly, miserable and self absorbed, I noticed a slow moving vehicle approaching. And like a page out of some dime store cops and robbers novel, there appeared a police car. Pulling to the curb, he rolled down his side window and shined his flashlight smack dab into my face! Finding it hard to swallow, I reluctantly stepped to the open window and faced my impending doom. Most trained officers, given the situation, would automatically suspect that I was up to no good. "Run, run run! No, No No!" Think. Then it hit me in a flash. Tell him the truth . . . well, not the whole truth. Not the stealing part . . . the working part. The thing about police is, they have this built-in bullshit detector. They can tell right off the bat when a person is lying. Staring me in the face he said, "What are you doing standing out here in the rain?" "Yeah, what a night, huh? Too bad we had to work late in this stuff. We were just finishing up some welding for Al when I ran out of smokes. Can't finish without them, you know how it is." My legs were shaking so badly I could hear my knees knocking. I don't even know where all of that came from. Sounded convincing enough to me, but I wasn't the one that needed convincing. Glancing toward the fence at the sparks flying from the torch he replied, "Yeah, I know how it is. You guys going to be here all night?" "Nah, another hour or so." "Be sure and lock up when you leave." "Alright officer. Thanks for looking out." And with that, he drove off. I almost toppled over right there on the sidewalk. No doubt the rain had deterred him from getting out of his warm and cozy car to take a closer look. If it weren't for my calm, cool and collected demeanor, we'd all be on our way to the hoosegow

Clearing the fence, it was time to check on the gang's progress. With only a few more left to go, looked like we were going to make it. The money was accumulating nicely. That was a shit load of change! After telling them of my close encounter with the fuzz, they thought it best to clear out. Be a shame to neglect the rest of those meters and since we haven't been raided yet, the coast must be clear. Finally we cracked the last one and hauled ass out of there. The night air was clear and refreshed by the rain. Driving to our hilltop cruising grounds, we parked on the side of the road and proceeded to rid ourselves of what was left of those damn meters. While climbing down the side of the hill, I accidently stepped on a garbage bag that felt like a body. I let out a yell of disgust and made a beeline for the car. I told the guys I stepped on a body and we burned rubber out of there. The sun rose over the mountain top, painting the sky with iridescent hues. We went back to my place to divvy up the profits. When the final tally was in, we'd relieved the State of Hawaii of over $350 in dimes, nickels and quarters. Not a bad haul considering the headaches. Won't be doing this again anytime soon. My end came to about $120 and some change. We all laughed about our latest escapade as I paid for our breakfast. The puzzled look on the waitress's face was priceless.

The average criminal would never resort to cracking open parking meters for income, let alone kicks. When you're young, dumb and full of shit, well, you know what I mean. You'll try anything once. I look back on this adventure and wonder, "What the hell were you thinking?" Nothing lasts forever and it was only a matter of time before my brothers in crime started to get cold feet. I could read the writing on the wall when they came up with excuses every time I suggested that we put some work in. Can't say that I blame them. When you have rich parents who pay tons of cash for your private school education, I'd expect a return on my investment too. Can't turn a blind eye to your meal ticket. Be like tossing the golden ring into the trash. It was fun while it lasted.

The smart thing to do would've been to call it quits right then and there. Who said smart had anything to do with it? Selfish greed is a better description of my state of mind. I had gotten accustomed to the easy money and cheap thrills. Just another addiction added to the list. Going it alone seemed to be my only option. The thought of having nobody there to back your play can be a little unnerving. Feeding your need for a drug induced lifestyle changes all that in an instant. I rationalized that I'd give up this way of life before graduation. "Here we go with the excuses." "Hear me out." That way, if I never get caught I could still join the police force. My prior experience as a criminal could help to enhance my performance as an officer. How do you like that one? Goes to show you how seriously screwed up I was.

I tried limiting the amount of crimes I committed. Quick in, quick out jobs with minimum risk factor. I had no problem obtaining a weapon. Often times I just lifted my dad's old service revolver from his uniform days. It was a Smith and Wesson .38 special with a 4 inch barrel that held six rounds in the cylinder. The gun was handed down from my grandfather, who also used it in his uniform days. It was the standard issue sidearm for all officers for years. A family heirloom that was to be handed down to me when I became a patrolman, a longstanding tradition among law enforcement families. I was to be the third generation to live the legacy. Pretty tough act to follow. After a while, I felt really bad about using it. It was as if my grandfather's ghost was calling out to me. I always felt safe whenever I carried it on a heist, but it was the purpose that I was using it for that bothered me. All those years of being used for good things. Protecting the innocent and fighting crime . . . now here I was using it to do evil deeds and hurt people. Tainting its illustrious history. My conscience soon got the best of me and I couldn't bring myself to use it any longer. Left high and dry without a weapon, I was forced to acquire guns by other means. Mostly borrowing from friends and promising them one-third of the profits, one-half if I had to use the weapon. I had to take whatever was available. I found myself pulling jobs that required a handgun for concealment using a bolt action rifle—I stuck the long barrel down my pant leg to hide it. Covering the clumsy butt with a trench coat or leather jacket, I wore my pants loose so I could draw the gun. There'd be no way to run for cover with that thing down my leg. It was such a hassle, but nothing could stop me from getting paid. I once used a .44 magnum pistol with a ten inch barrel to rob someone. A huge cannon of a gun. At the time, it was considered the most powerful handgun in the world. Hunters took that beast on safari to hunt big game. When I produced the weapon and pointed it at the victim, he nearly pissed his pants! I'm glad I didn't have to shoot anyone with that monster; there'd be nothing left of the person. It was too much gun, but beggars can't be choosers. Eat your heart out Dirty Harry.

My friend and previous partner in crime somehow got his hands on a colt .45, 1911 army issue in mint condition. It was beautiful. Came with the serial numbers filed off so the gun couldn't be traced or linked to prior felonies. Holding it for the first time brought a surge of power throughout my body. Fit like a glove! The shine from its blue steel finish glistening under the streetlights' glare was mesmerizing. Chambering a round, I stuck it out the car window and squeezed off a few shots. Kicked like a mule! I was in love! Couldn't wait to use it. For those of you who are unfamiliar with handguns, the .45 caliber is a magazine-fed, gas operated, semi-automatic handheld weapon that packs a hell of a punch. It contains seven rounds in the clip and one in the "pipe" for a total of eight rounds. Pull back on the slide to chamber a bullet into the breach and just squeeze the trigger. Because of the weapon's heavy recoil, mastering the .45 is quite a challenge.

The American Army discovered the weapon's advantages during WWII while campaigning in the Philippines. Though allies, some local tribes' men would go crazy, run amok. Tying tightly wrapped vines or ropes around their body parts, they would run through villages hacking and killing innocent people with machetes. The tightened ligatures served as a tourniquet, suppressing bleeding when soldiers shot at the charging men. Smaller caliber weapons were useless against the armored attackers. Shot numerous times, they kept coming, chopping the shooter to death before falling dead. The stopping power of the Colt .45 would bring a man down with a single round.

This awesome firearm was perfect for stick-ups but convincing my buddy to let me hang on to it would be a problem. Reluctant at first to part with it, the thought of doing time in a federal prison for possessing an illegal weapon won out in my favor. The risk to me never even crossed my mind. Idiot! He really had no use for it anyway now that he was retired from the biz. No use letting the thing just sit around gathering dust. He could go back to worrying about college and pleasing his petite, "fine ass," oriental sweetheart for all I cared. Promising not to use it on jobs, he finally handed it over. You know what they say, "out of sight, out of mind." The gun came complete with its vintage WWII shoulder rig that fit perfectly under the armpit. I carried it everywhere. Even to school, sitting in the classroom, listening to my teachers' dull lectures. I wanted to pull it out and shoot them in the face. They hadn't a clue. For some reason, I needed to keep it close and handy. You never knew when opportunity would come knocking. The weapon wasn't for showing off. It was strictly for business and the only people who ever got a good look at it were my victims.

I've always known the kind of close personal relationship an individual could establish with a gun. Its alluring attraction and physical attachment can be hypnotic, no different than the feeling you get when you hug a beautiful woman, an anthropomorphic sense of reality attributed to an inanimate object capable of creating dangerous intent. This impending expectation of danger, matched with man's curious nature, the catalyst that propels us towards it like a moth to the flame. The love and affection shown to a bare piece of metal, is as good an explanation as any as to why many men give their weapons female names.

Unlike a woman, your gun will never cheat on you or let you down. Never turn its back on you or talk back. You can't always trust a woman, but you can bet your life on your gun. In the days of the wild, wild west, a man's life depended on his gun. Those pistol packing men of old lived by a strict code of justice. The nostalgia of the era captured me and I adopted the mentality of the classic renegade cowboy. An outlaw in the modern urban jungle. I remember my dad's words, "live by the gun, die by the gun." Reminding me of the destructive path I was following. My coyness was way beyond reason. Coming home in the wee hours of the morning, sneaking in as quietly as possible, I was greeted by a dark shadow sitting in the total darkness. The familiar voice inquiring in the night, "Where have you been and where is the gun? You been out pulling jobs again?" More of an accusation than question. He'd been on to me for sometime now. I kept the .45 hidden under my mattress and my trench coat hung in the back of the closet. He put two and two together and concluded that when both were missing, I was up to no good. I think my friend, who cared about my welfare, mentioned my nefarious activities to him. Nothing left to do but deny and lie through my teeth. I was just lying to myself. Surrendering my car keys to him, I was hoofing it for now. Never gave up my weapon though. In my twisted mind, my anger at him for trying to dictate my way of life was in fact his love and concern for an out of control teenager. Too stupid to see it then or even give a damn. Just another piece of hell I put my parents through.

By the way, I apologize to all the women of the world who may have taken offense over my seemingly demeaning references and comparisons. However, you know as well as I do what you are capable of. We'll leave it at that. The power you hold is greater than gold.

Mad at my buddy for squealing on me, it was only a matter of time before we banged heads. I knew he cared about me but somehow I had the feeling that his anger was manifested by a hidden desire to be right along side me. His current situation and inability to do just that further infuriating him. That's the trouble with denial. The difference between truth and fantasy is how big your balls are. After a tirade of lecturing, I reassured him that I'd quit the life. I would have promised him anything to hang on to that gun. The thought of giving it up affected me on a deep emotional level. I'd compare it to breaking up with a girlfriend, one that you really loved. I know it sounds weird, but like I said, the attachment is strange. I had to find a way to possess that .45 free and clear.

The chance to transfer ownership came on a hair-raising Saturday night. While drinking and cruising for a bruising we decided to go check on the outlaw drag races. The spot for this weekly event was a popular beach park called Sandy Beach. In the daylight hours, the place was bustling with the activity of body surfers and bikini-clad honeys. When night fell on the weekends, the roadway fronting the park was transformed into a quarter-mile race track.

Cars of all makes and models appeared from every part of the island to challenge and race for whatever a driver was willing to lose. Anything from cash to parts to drugs and, in some cases, pink slips exchanged hands. This was the happening place to be and to be seen. On this night, we were standing at the starting line watching the races with hundreds of people milling throughout the park. Seemed like an ordinary night with all the action and excitement, standing there with a beer in one hand, cigarette in the other, trusty Colt .45 casually tucked in the back pocket of my blue jeans. I glanced towards the entrance in time to see a motorcycle solo bike pull into the parking lot. That was odd. In all the times I'd been coming here, I never saw that before. I had this funny feeling and yelled at my friends that we better get the hell out of here quick.

By the time we reached the car, the place was over-run with undercover police. Four of them approached my car just as I started the motor. From the backseat my buddy's shaken voice whispered, "Don't let them catch us with that gun or we're dead!" I didn't see no "us" in this trip, just me. They had nothing to worry about, I'd be the one dragged out and arrested. Sensing the desperation and panic in him an idea popped into my head. No kidding, just like in the cartoons with the light bulb. I had him over a barrel, only he didn't know it yet. I made him a deal he couldn't refuse. "If we get through this, the gun is mine—free and clear." At that point, he would have agreed to anything. All this transpiring while the cops surrounding us were screaming at the top of their lungs, "Turn the fucking motor off and step out of the vehicle!" We all saw our futures melting away as this slow motion drama played out, and my friend said, "Yes, yes, whatever, it's yours. Just don't get us busted!" And that was the easy part. The next part would prove to be somewhat more difficult. I'd be damned if I was going to lose that gun now. Letting the cops find it anywhere near me wasn't an option. Things were about to get ugly.

The weapon was currently tucked under my left thigh. Shutting the motor off, I slowing opened the door and as I stepped out, I dropped the gun on the sand and nudged it under the car. Sounds easy as I read over that last bit on paper, but I was so frightened that I couldn't catch my breath and my heart was beating out of my chest. The officer, standing no more than five feet away, was too busy watching everyone else exit the car to notice. If this had been broad daylight, I'd be a goner. Presenting my license to the nice officer, I collapsed on the sand next to my friends. Staring at the spot where the gun sat, relieved that I wasn't at this very moment already handcuffed and heading for the station. Demure and motionless, we watched the cops tear my car to pieces. Whatever they were looking for, with the vigor and efficiency in which they performed their duty, I had no doubt they would find it.

The search failed to produce anything of value to them and by then, my ID and registration had informed them that the legal owner of the car was a detective and his son, Jr., the driver. One of the officers knew my dad and after a stern lecture, I was told to pick my shit up and get lost. Apologizing profusely, I bent over, retrieved the gun along with the rest of my junk. Jumping into the car I let out a deep breath. Now that wasn't too hard. The officer signaled us to exit the parking lot via the entrance. The police had set up roadblocks on both ends of the park and were routing traffic towards search stations. Every vehicle there was methodically searched for contraband. Glad all that was over and done with, I drove towards the block. The feel of my gun, yes mine, beneath my thigh, safe and sound made the whole ordeal worth it. Home free! My friend, baffled that we'd gotten away, asked about the weapon. Might as well have some fun at his expense, you know, twist the knife a little. "Sorry bro, couldn't take the chance, so I threw it in the bushes." Crestfallen, he said, "better than getting caught with it." Laughing inside, the joke was about to be on me. Pulling to the exit, the uniform officer stationed there, the look of disgust on his face, screamed at me to go back the way I came. No way! I couldn't believe it. All the protest in the world wouldn't, couldn't get us past the block. Here we go again.

I joined the procession of cars headed for the nearest search station. I looked around frantically for any of the officers who had searched us earlier. There were so many cops around, but

L. Staunton Jr.

not the ones I needed. Stopped and searched for the second time, I used the same maneuver. This time on the hard black top. Hearing the metal meet the pavement was like a gunshot. My legs turned to rubber and my heart skipped a beat. Maybe it only sounded that loud to me because of the guilt factor? With all the commotion and excitement going on, no one heard it but me and we were waived through to the next exit. Making it this far was nothing short of a miracle. My nerves were shot. How much can a person take? Luck only holds out for so long. The line of cars was moving at a steady pace and I could see the exit up ahead. Keep moving, less than 100 feet now. Moving, moving . . . almost there.

Suddenly, the line came to an abrupt halt and the cops starting searching the vehicle in front of us. An officer looking into my window and said, "Alright, turn the motor off and everybody get out." Can you believe this shit! Even in baseball, three strikes and you are out. Gripping the gun, thoughts of prison on my mind. I'd never get away with this again. The officer stepped back, turned on his flashlight, and pointed it directly at me. My life was over. Better to leave it in the car and let them find it. Too late, I couldn't let go without him seeing the movement. Staring intently at me as my leg hit the pavement, I watched in my minds eye as what was left of my freedom pass before me. Then, like some kind of divine intervention, the officers searching the car ahead, called back, "Jackpot!" Evidentially, the guy in the black Cutlass Supreme had been caught with fake police credentials, handcuffs, scanner and blue lights in his grill. He'd picked the wrong night to play make believe. Wrong for him, but oh so right for us. One leg frozen to the tarmac and the other still in the car, we were ordered back into the car and waved through. As we passed that poor schmuck, out eyes met for an instant and I saw myself as the one in handcuffs, on my way to jail. Leaving the area, my bad dream had ended but I now noticed my friend's disappointment over the loss of his beloved baby. With all the excitement, I had forgotten the funny joke, ha-ha. Made to suffer the agony and the ecstasy alone throughout the entire ordeal, I could no longer contain myself. When he uttered those heartfelt words, "Bum trip man. I lost my gun!" Mixed in with more than a few colorful words. Correcting his mistaken property rights, "oh, you mean my gun?" I produced it from the hiding place like the conclusion to a magicians fabulous act, "ta-da!" His jaw hit the floorboard. He was dumbfounded. "Thanks for saving my gun bro, how did you do it?" How quickly they forget. Reaching to snatch it from my hand, he was reminded of our deal. More angry at himself than anything else, he agreed. Letting go of something you love is never easy so I let him hold on to it on the drive back home. For old times sake. The man that he was, he handed it back to me when I dropped him off. So the ownership of that Colt .45 exchanged hands that night. His dismay would later come back to get me.

Armed and dangerous again, I set off on a spree of robberies. There was no stopping me. Throughout my senior year in high school, I continued to participate in many crimes, all the while with the intention of quitting and going straight after graduation, which I didn't. In all the years that I was actively involved in the commission of crimes, I was never captured. The exact number, though numerous, can't be determined. Upon graduating I made myself a promise to never return to that lifestyle. However, by now my drug dependency and alcohol abuse had reached alarming levels. In order to support my habits, I resorted to lesser, but by no means legal, methods of obtaining the money needed to feed my hungers. These hungers would one day consume me and ultimately ruin my chances of a happy and normal life.

Chapter 6

Trumpets in my head

There is no disputing that any form of drug or alcohol abuse over a prolonged period of time can alter a person's state of mind. It's not uncommon for an individual who poisons his body this way to have an adverse reaction, in both the physical and mental sense. Whether temporary or permanent, eventually your mind begins to play tricks on you. In some cases, hallucinations materialize—shadows and voices appear out of thin air, speaking to us on our subconscious and conscious levels. Who's to say which is real and which is make believe? Experts throughout the world agree and disagree on the subject. Can these trance-like visions be attributed to an insane person's rotting mind losing its grip on reality? Or could there be strange, dark forces that defy explanation at work? The answer to these questions is yes and yes.

When you take into careful consideration that person who has abused drugs and other substances for years to the point of going crazy, yes, that could cause a person to see and hear things. Now take the young innocent child never exposed to such abuses. Can early stages of his nurturing be a contributing factor in his experiencing ghastly apparitions and eerie

88

melodies? Nothing more than figments of the imagination? Perhaps it's the consummate example of these dark forces at work on the mind of a child lost in truth or fantasy. Maybe even something far more sinister than the latter? Whatever the reason, there have been moments in my life where I've experienced inexplicable paranormal events. These encounters usually took place while I was in a semi-dream state of sleep. The first time was when I lived on our ranch in the country. I must have been 10 or 12 years old. I'd gone to bed the same time as usual, around 10pm. While dozing, I began to hear an eerie cacophony, like horns blowing in the distance. The tune was unrecognizable, just an unfamiliar melody that increased in volume as I strained to listen. The louder it got, the closer the music came. I actually felt the music enter my head and encompass me. It was like wearing headphones. I tried to move, but my body was pinned to the bed. This couldn't have been a dream because my eyes were wide open. I gazed across the room, searching for answers, scared, confused and alone. I tried screaming but no sound came out. Only silence. Mouth agape, frozen pleas for help lost in the darkness.

There was a feeling of some force or entity there in the room with me hiding among the shadows. The pressure against my chest, holding me down to the mattress was incredibly strong. No matter how hard I resisted, I couldn't break its hold. As the blaring of the horns increased to its peak, so did the force pressing down on me. It felt as though someone was straddling me, holding me down with both hands. I could feel the palms pushing on me. I closed my eyes and began to pray, willing the evil to leave. I blinked several times in quick succession, convincing myself that this was no dream. The horns continued. I prayed harder! Then the horns began to soften. I could speak again, hear myself pray and swear. I was able to move. The horns were no longer in my head. Outside in the distance, I heard the faint tune playing. I peered through the darkness, hoping that the nightmare had ended but there remained a foreboding silence. Fully awake now and sitting upright on my bed, I wondered if the series of events were real. I lay back down and started to fall asleep. Within minutes I could hear the trumpets reappearing. They were coming from far away. I quickly stood up before they came any closer. I thought about waking my mom and telling her about it, but she'd never believe me. I hardly believed it myself. I stayed awake for hours, praying, afraid to close my eyes. Eventually, I slept. The rest of that night was uneventful. When I awoke in the morning, I remembered every single moment. Could it have been a dream? Possibly. Did I believe that it was? Hell no! Little did I know that the familiar blare would haunt me another day.

The next encounter happened when I was a junior in high school. I was living next door to that fabulous Mexican beauty in an apartment complex on the top floor. My partner and I were out drinking all night and had passed out on the living room floor. Next to me lay that classmate of my sister's who educated me in the finer art of sex. It had been years since my last experience with that evil presence and I never told anyone about it. This time, I began to hear a loud, escalating siren, like ringing. I felt cold. Like before, I was pinned to the floor, eyes wide open. I tried to speak but again, nothing but silence. The pressure on my chest was steady and unyielding. Pressed to the floor, my eyes raced around the room desperately searching for help. All the while, my friend lay motionless next to me, unaware of my plight. I suffered alone. Strangely, I felt more annoyed than frightened, like having a visit from a former adversary.

I was soon to experience an even more bizarre twist to this nightmare. Closing my eyes tightly, I swore to myself I could feel a presence somewhere close. An intense lingering heaviness hung in the air. I opened my eyes nervously, wondering what I'd see. I noticed that the door to our apartment was wide open. How unusual—no one else in the place was awake and next to me both figures lay motionless. Glancing toward the doorway, I saw a large, dark figure standing there. He wore a dark trench coat that reached to the floor and in his left hand he held a suitcase. His head was covered by a black Fedora, the rim blocking his eyes. Even now, describing the event all these years later, a chill runs down my spine. This scared me to death! I couldn't believe what I was seeing. I tried to look away, but I remained frozen, eyes wide open, unable to blink or turn away. He just stood there. His facial features were only a blurry image, unrecognizable. Somewhere in that dark blur, a smile spread across the cold black mask. It was an evil, menacing, smirk of a grin. Taunting me to focus on it, as if calling to me. Waiting for something, waiting for me. The sirens, ringing and blaring continued.

I closed my eyes and prayed to God to dispel the evil figure. At once, the ringing began to subside. I dared not open my eyes to steal a glance. The temptation to do so was irresistible though. I steadied myself and opened them. The dark man was gone, but oddly enough the door was still open. I quickly closed my eyes and feverishly began to pray. Soon, the noise softened and I risked another look. The door was closed and the room was quiet. The strange presence had vanished and I was able to move about. I looked at the two sleeping silhouettes calmly breathing, oblivious to my ordeal. A personal encounter, in my own private world, within my mind. Or was it? I lay back and tried to fall back asleep. Suddenly, the faint ringing tones began again and with them the forceful pressure to my body. My eyes flew open and I saw the open doorway. Missing was the figure. I started to pray again and swear obscenities, in an effort to rid myself of this evil once and for all. I sat upright and continued with my vigil until the episode was over. There would be no sleep for me that night. Somehow, I knew that I hadn't seen the last of these visits.

Chapter 7

Changes in latitude

Heartbroken, disgusted and plain fed up, my dad finally called it quits with the Honolulu Police Department. After years of empty promises and repeated disappointment, he accepted the fact that he'd never be promoted past the rank of Detective. The problem with being a cop for twenty plus years, it's impossible to walk away gracefully and hang it up for good. The job stays in your blood until the day you die. There are tales of retired cops unable to cope with their newly found status as ordinary civilians going nuts and blowing their brains out. The policeman's version of post traumatic stress syndrome. To prevent themselves from going stir crazy, and satisfy their hunger for law enforcement, many take jobs as security heads for the big hotel chains or department stores. Wandering throughout the house and moping wasn't doing my father any good. His drinking increased and he became prone to fits of melancholy. Frustration mounted and a change was desperately needed. Then opportunity presented itself.

When a position for an investigator with the city prosecutor's office became available, dad interviewed for the job and was hired. The timing was perfect. Chief investigator Dewey Allen was a former police officer and friend who worked with dad in the early years. Along with his oldest son, the investigative team was complete. Nepotism ran rampant back then in the city and state workforce. Officials who weren't guilty of the practice themselves, turned a blind eye. With city elections over, Prosecutor Maurice Sapienza was at the helm and a fresh new regime was in place. Facing public scrutiny, the office was under extreme pressure to produce results. I was happy to see my father back to working in his element again and this job was tailor made for him. From the start, I noticed the change in his attitude. He was resurrected, but the drinking continued, even escalated.

The prosecutor, a heavy drinker himself, of Italian descent, often met with his investigators after a day's work at their favorite watering hole to relax and unwind. More occupational pleasure than hazard of the office, I sometimes went along to have a few with the gang. Drinking and engaging in casual conversation with one of the most powerful men in the state judicial system and his staff was no different than kicking back and having beers with my high school buddies. The only difference was the topic of discussion. Shop talk. Though treated somewhat as an equal, I did my best to blend into the background. No one gave much thought about contributing to the delinquency of a minor. I wasn't there to argue the fact; I was just there to get drunk. Who cared about government hypocrisy!

O'Tooles was an establishment frequented by law enforcement personnel from all branches of the city, state and federal levels. Judges, public defenders and powerhouse attorneys all met there after their courtroom battles with their "opposition" and they would formulate strategies to sell the next poor unsuspecting schmuck down the river. With their custom suits, handmade shoes and air of arrogance, the atmosphere buzzed with the high voltage energy of the influential. A virtual who's who in the justice community. I was supercharged with the feeling of power, the alcohol a mere anticlimax to the already natural high I was experiencing. In light of my younger years, watching my parents' abuse alcohol, it seems odd that some of the happiest moments that I ever had with my father were while we were drinking. A disturbing statement and totally improper at best. Some may even find appalling. And though the alcoholic inside of me loved every second of it, the closeness I felt to my father at those particular moments was the real prize.

Alcohol used as a common denominator in a father-son relationship is not very healthy. Were the love and affection experienced obtained by crossing the moral boundaries of responsible parenthood? Clinical mumbo jumbo! I agree whole heartedly and don't dispute the fact that parents are, and should be, held accountable for their actions in setting examples of wholesome behavior for their children—hoping that their children will mimic said behavior. But who can fault, or blame, a father who expresses his love for his only son by treating him as an equal? For treating him like a man? Irresponsibility on the parent's part? I beg to differ. In primitive cultures throughout the world and in past civilizations, a man is defined by his ability to hunt and kill to provide for his family. To endure extreme pain and to suffer through feats of endurance, not by his age. It's our present day society that dictates the standards and rules by which a child becomes a man. In the process, the male child loses a part of his manhood due to the babying that he's subjected to, in essence, making him a weaker human being. There's no lesser degree of love or affection in their process. The rites of passage into manhood are decided on by an individual's personal attributes, his strengths and weaknesses. Does it make their methods immoral because our society is different? Our society is so advanced, yet so prejudiced and cynical that everything and everyone is judged by labels and rules adopted conveniently to fit the needs of the privileged. One thing is for certain; a parent's love for their child is absolute and extends far beyond any and all boundaries. And with all my love and respect to my father, God rest his soul. And that's my opinion on the matter.

Spending quality time with my father under any circumstances, moral or otherwise, made no difference to me. It was all I cared about. If drinking was the platform for our relationship, so be it. We spent countless hours in bars or drinking beers and watching football games on Sunday. I looked forward to those moments of one-on-one. I wish every son could experience the same closeness I felt at those times. It really never mattered what we were doing or who was with us, at those times it was the close feeling of friendship that made it right. Though we never talked about it, I know the feeling was mutual.

There was this one time that sticks in my mind above the rest. I had an uncle who was on the state liquor commission. His job was to visit the local bars and restaurants that sold liquor in the Honolulu district. One night he invited my dad to go along. Naturally I followed, not being able to resist the temptation to get plastered for free. It was like a gambler winning an all expense paid trip to Las Vegas. From the moment we set foot in an establishment, we were given the royal treatment. The owners would greet us at the door and seat us at the best table in the house. The liquor would flow non-stop and the finest selection of mouth-watering steaks and seafood, served to perfection, delivered in excess, to our table. Compliments of the house. The cost could amount to hundreds of dollars. After a couple of hours of being waited on hand and foot, we headed for the next place. Then the next. And so it went until the early morning hours. Each time, each place, the treatment was the same, some outdoing the others. Reaching our final destination, drunk beyond words, I watched my uncle, a seasoned drinker, slumped down in the booth next to me, barely conscious, while my dad and I finished our drinks. The word bribery is a dirty one in any language. Right up there with blackmail and treason. For some reason, I couldn't get it out of my mind. It had been a long night and I had found immense pleasure drinking my uncle under the table. I looked over to my father and his eyes, now blurred from the alcohol, held a dim sparkle of pride and satisfaction. Feeling no pain, but still functional, we carried my uncle to the nearest cab, thanked him for a wonderful evening and bid him goodnight. With my arm draped around my father, we walked the distance home, laughing and weaving all the way. I never forgot that night and smile whenever I think about it.

It never ceases to amaze me how, as children, we look up to our fathers as idols. Super human beings who can conquer all and overcome anything in their efforts to protect us. Regardless of their flaws, we desire to become the mirror image of them. And though the trials and tribulations of our adolescence keep us occupied and caught in the business of survival, somehow, somewhere, in the process we lose track of that childhood vision. We evolve and develop into our own individuality, our own self. In the long run, whoever we perceive ourselves to be, we all become our fathers. To me, that's a good thing.

While transitioning to their new office space, the city Prosecutor's Office was temporarily located at the Neal Blaisdell Center. The center, besides offices, also housed a concert hall and huge arena where rock and roll concerts were held. This arrangement worked perfectly to my advantage. The Prosecutor's Office received complimentary tickets to all the featured events—operas, symphonies, Broadway plays, and my favorite, rock concerts. Staff members didn't care much for the loud and screaming rock music, so they passed the tickets on to dad who gave them to me. That was a very good year for me and the boys. The tickets were often the best in the house, sometimes no more than a few rows from the stage. We were treated to the likes of Elton John, Rod Stewart, Peter Frampton and the Average White Band. In those days, you could fire up a doobie anywhere in the arena without the fear of being arrested and the whole place reeked with the smell of marijuana smoke. High times for sure.

One of the most vital responsibilities of the Prosecutor's Office at the time was the state's witness protection program. Essentially, to provide protection to those brave citizens who came forward to give testimony against the criminal element. A potentially dangerous undertaking, even under ideal circumstances. The level of danger was further increased due to the prevalence of underworld crime activity. Local syndicate factions were locked in violent disputes over who would control the lion's share of the lucrative drug, prostitution and gambling trades. Many of the accused facing stiff sentences for murder and other crimes, had ties to these syndicates, famous for their fierce reputation for silencing witnesses. In some cases, these people also had family members on the police force and sheriff's departments, making protecting these witnesses even more difficult. Keeping them safe here in the islands was impossibility. In order to ensure their safety, many were held in safe houses on the mainland, guarded by state and federal marshals. To prevent a breakdown in security when witnesses flew in to give testimony, few local law enforcement agencies were utilized. Many of these witnesses had prices on their heads or contracts put on them by syndicate leaders. Trust being the issue, or lack of, my father opted for a more unorthodox method of dealing with the threat. Though controversial by official views and standards, it proved to be highly effective. He chose to hire individuals from the private sector. The chief investigator, familiar with dad's expertise in these matters, gave him total autonomy. Only people my father knew on a personal basis for years were selected to serve on the security details. Though legally a minor at the time, I was chosen to participate. Regardless of the legal ramifications, he was confident that I could handle the job. Trained by the best to perform just such a task, my involvement in operations was kept on the down-low. As long as no one got killed in the process, we had nothing to worry about.

Another member of the team with a colorful history I'll simply refer to as uncle Freddy. Not a blood relation, but as close as you could get. He had once been a hired killer for one of the local organized crime families. He was the last of a few surviving members whose boss had been murdered by a rival gang. Because of his past, he possessed an intimate knowledge of the present day syndicates and their members. Enhanced by his coldblooded nature and ability to handle weaponry, no doubt when push came to shove, there was no better person to have in your corner. I felt a hell of a lot safer with him covering my back. He had a fondness for that Colt .45 of mine, so I often loaned it to him. When I think about it, our motley crew, under different circumstances, would have seemed amusingly outrageous. You had an under-aged kid carrying a loaded gun, backed up by a former underworld hitman packing an illegal firearm, protecting crucial witnesses in state murder trials. I wonder what the criminal justice system and current fearless leader of the state's prosecuting attorneys office, would have thought about that.

Brings to mind my first security detail protecting a witness who had informed on a crime family. Marked for death, an assassin walked up to him in public and shot him six times with a .38 caliber revolver. One bullet entering his brain, he somehow managed to survive and turned states evidence against the shooter. The high profile case had everyone on edge. For obvious reasons, the witness and his family were kept in a California safe house, guarded by the sheriff's department. Prior to the trial, my father and a few team members flew up to retrieve the witness. Deputized as Federal Sky Marshals, they were authorized to carry their weapons on board the plane during transport.

The upcoming trial was awash in a media frenzy, presenting us with a security nightmare. Any mishap in the scheduled arrival of the witness could be disastrous. Trusting their safety to no one else, my father had arranged to call me at a designated time and at an undisclosed phone number. I sat at the phone impatiently waiting on pins and needles for that call to come. Then, in the early morning darkness, ringing broke the silence. It was a relief to hear my father's voice. Things were set on his end and now it was up to me. I placed a call to Dewey Allen and the security team was placed on standby. I felt the weight of the responsibility that had been placed upon my shoulders. It was crucial that everything went according to plan. All I thought about was my father's safety. If it came down to gun battle, I could care less about the witness, I'd kill anyone who tried to harm my dad. As far as I was concerned, the rest of the people were collateral damage. Compared to that fear, everything else was a cakewalk. I felt up to the challenge and confident that the situation was under control.

Less than twenty-four hours before the trial, the witness was flown in and greeted on the tarmac by the security detail. Ushering him into the limo, I was relieved to see my father exit the plane. His face was haggard and tired from the journey. Our eyes locked and a smile spread across his face. The witness secured, we proceeded to the baggage claim area. And here is where things got a little hairy. Standing next to the limo, waiting for the luggage, 12 gauge shotgun at the ready on the front seat, scanning the terminal and the throngs of passengers lost in confusion, I became aware of the seriousness of my situation. The stranger in the back seat chatted on aimlessly in a vain attempt to solicit me in conversation, as though he hadn't a care in the world. Least of all, in fear for his life. The tension in the air hung, like a heavy steel curtain. My eyes darted in all directions searching for signs of possible threats. That indiscriminate person moving too slowly in the crowd, or paying too much attention. Anxious drivers speeding inches away, hurrying to get to nowhere and everywhere. Anyone of them a potential threat. Then, the realization hit me. I was all alone with the witness! Where the hell was the rest of the team? They'd all disappeared. The hair on the back of my neck stood straight up and goose bumps covered my arms. I had the strangest sensation that someone was watching me and something bad was about to happen. The child in me emerged and fear took hold. Meanwhile, the guy in the backseat kept rambling on and on, his nonsense lost in my peripheral train of thought. Unaware of our vulnerability; that at any moment a stranger could have easily walked up and killed us both. That quick and it would have been over. But not before I took a few of them with us. I tried to remain calm and in no way alarm the witness. I found comfort as I gripped the gun tucked in my front waistband. I stared for a second at the shotgun on the seat and thought about reaching for it. That's all I needed—a panicked crowd on my hands. Feeling naked and exposed like a painted target, palms clammy with sweat, I braced for the impending attack. The scene smelled like a set-up. It was as if a diabolical plan was put into effect, by a sinister organization to make good on a previously botched attempt.

Suddenly my father exited the terminal, accompanied by a detail of airport security. Relieved to be alive, the bewildered look on his face at seeing me there all alone soon turned to anger. He asked, "Where the hell is everyone?" As the airport security blocked off traffic, preparing for our departure, I replied, "I have no idea. I thought they were with you." He was livid. The team arrived then, loaded down with enough bags and boxes to fill an apartment, most of which were gifts paid for by the citizens of Hawaii for the witness's family and friends. Without missing a beat, my dad lashed out at them. At least the witness could find comfort knowing that his luggage was well protected. Uncle Fred stood there shaking with rage, hatred for the other team members oozing from his pores. He had a strange habit of blinking and stuttering when he got angry. This he did, as he inquired about my welfare. No mistaking that under different circumstances those who screwed up would be dead by now. Felt good to be appreciated. Apparently there had been a breakdown in communications regarding assignments. A plausible explanation to the unfortunate event, no harm, no foul. Nothing as ominous as I made it out to be, just a case of my imagination getting the better of me. Thank God. Nursing the wounds from their battered egos, they loaded into the vehicles and we sped off for the safe house.

The witness spent an uneventful evening and was delivered to the courthouse bright and early the next morning. Taking the stand, he presented the jury with his gruesome tale and a flawless testimony. In the end, the accused was convicted of his crime of attempted murder in the first degree under the murder for hire statute. The conviction carried a maximum sentence of life without the possibility of parole, which the judge later awarded him. The person responsible for ordering the killing was never brought to justice. He was, however, a victim in one form or another when gangland war erupted among crime factions in Hawaii. I never saw the witness again, but I would one day cross paths with the killer. Poetic justice on both our accounts. My path in becoming a third generation law enforcer looked promising. The only problem with that idea was my other presently chosen field of gainful employment. I somehow can relate to those comic strip super heroes and the villains that torment them. They dash and spring about in their fancy disguises, each playing their parts while the world looks on, shielded from their true identities. Only, in this story, I play them both.

Sometime during my junior year of high school, my sister Lorna believed she'd found the man of her dreams and decided to get married. He was a likeable enough guy that came from a good Catholic family. They met while our family was vacationing on the island of Maui. While I attended Lahainaluna High School, my sister and mother would fly up on the weekends to watch my football games. It was on one of these short trips that the courtship flourished. Born and raised on Maui, my mother had many family members residing there. In fact, my future brother-in-law was actually related to my mother's side of the family by marriage. Her brother's oldest daughter Terry, was married to his cousin, so that would amount to first cousins being married to first cousins. My cousin Terry's house is where we stayed on those vacations. The families all lived across from each other in a cul de sac. How convenient! I remember the entire family playing matchmaker between the two of them. The ever protective brother that I was kept a watchful eye on things. It was apparent that my sister had strong feeling for this guy so I cut him some slack. She was the only sister that I had and I wanted nothing more than for her to be happy. I got along okay with the guy and we even became friends. No one expected the relationship to develop into anything serious, but when Ricky proposed, the families were delighted.

Everyone switched into high gear as they planned for the big event. It would be a lavish affair, with the bride and groom being married off in style. The families went all out, sparing no expense. The couple would exchange vows in a typical Hawaiian wedding ceremony with a touch of Catholicism. The priest performing the marriage, Father Keahe, was a teacher at Ricky's former high school and a close family friend. The wedding would take place in the tiny town of Makawao. The groom and his family had been members of the church there since his childhood. The bridal party consisted of my sister's best friend Lurline as the matron of honor, with Ricky's two sisters, Honey and Cookie, as bridesmaids. I was elected as the best man with Rick's best friend, Everette and younger brother my attendants. I felt honored to have been a part of such a meaningful event.

It's amazing what can be accomplished when friends and family unite to benefit a common cause. Preparations were well under way with the Eddie Tam War Memorial gym selected as the reception site. With its ability to accommodate the more than 600 guests, it was the perfect choice. The liquor tab alone for an event of this magnitude could rupture a bank account. All of which was donated to the couple as a gift, compliments of the groom's cousin Teko, who owned a bar on Oahu. The menu for the evening would consist of the typical Hawaiian luau feast: poi, lomi salmon, Kalua pig, haupia and other exotic delicacies. The food and liquor were loaded onto a barge and transported by tugboat from Honolulu to Maui. Included on the shipping manifest, along with the honored guests, five, four hundred-pound pigs, alive and kicking (for now). The matron of honor's brother worked for the Dillingham Tug and Barge Company, so everything was shipped for free. Her gift to my sister.

Bride and groom entered the bonds of holy matrimony dressed in the informal, all white attire, with green Maile lei around their necks. These lei, made from the highly prized leaves of the Maile vine, are only found in the wild on the wet mountainous regions of the islands. They produce a delicate fragrance reminiscent of the sweet forest. Standing at the altar, slightly swaying, watching my sister, beautiful on this day made especially for her, reciting her vows to the man she loved, I found it impossible to choke back the tears. They were a perfect couple, made for each other and this was their perfect, fairytale wedding. The party started on my part from early morning and by ceremony time, I'd already consumed a case of Bud and smoked more than a few joints. Thus, the reason for my inability to remain upright at the altar. With barely any sleep, the previous night was spent in an old abandoned house, freezing my ass off. Drinking bottles of cheap champagne and smoking joint after joint with Rick and Everette, while the rock music from the boom box echoed throughout the empty house. Our rendition of the bachelor party.

The reception, all but a haze in the back of my inebriated mind, was the grandest affair seen in the small community for years. By the end of the evening, over 1000 guests attended the reception to celebrate the occasion. There was plenty of food and drink to go around with the entertainment provided by a local band. Every woman dreams of having a wedding like this and my sister Lorna deserved all of it. The entrance to the hall was piled high with enough gifts to fill the new condominium "love nest" they were moving to. The bridal purse contained thousands of dollars to help kick start the couple's life journey. For those trips to the grocery store, my sister was given a brand new Chevy Chevette. A gift from her father-in-law who worked at a car dealership. My parents later took my sister on a shopping spree to furnish the condo. Life for the newlyweds was off to a good start. We all wished them the best that life had to offer. My parents, happy beyond words, could now look forward to bouncing their grandchildren on their knees in the not to distant future. After all their years of hardship, Lord knows they were deserving of a little joy in their lives. With one of us on our way to fulfilling our purpose in life, that left me to contend with. It would prove to be more than any set of parents could deal with. But, however difficult, they'd never give up. Real love conquers all!

The trouble with drugs is that you begin to believe that the world you exist in is the true reality. You stumble about in a permanent haze, blinded from the truth. Your constant desire to satisfy the cravings with instant gratification becomes the first and foremost objective in your life. All responsibilities are trashed in the bottom of a can. Throw into the equation the mister-know-it-all attitude and the fact that you're a high school kid hanging precariously on the verge of flunking your senior year and what you have is a formula for destruction. When confronted with the truth, the mind shifts into overdrive and locks gears in the panic mode. And that's where I sat on this fine spring day in the Athletic Director's office with my father seated next to me. The shit was about to hit the fan big time! "Did you know that your son has over fifty unexcused absences and is currently short 1.25 credits for graduation?" he asked. The look, or should I say piercing glare, on my dad's face said it all. The party was over. Above the ringing in my ears, I deduced from their conversation that I had just three months to make up those credits and blah, blah, blah . . . his only recourse is to attend the Special Motivation Program. This program was designed to afford the student with problems an opportunity to obtain a decent education and, hopefully, a diploma. These classes were filled with all the rejects, the worst of the worst students the school had to offer. Most of them had trouble putting sentences together, let alone thinking.

Classes began each morning at precisely 7 am and showing up late could result in suffering the wrath of Mr. Ho, an enormous Hawaiian with hands the size of telephone books.

Tardy students were greeted with a smack upside the head with those huge paws. I've seen students buckle at the knees or even reach levels of semi-consciousness from a blow—even the females. Mr. Ho was an equal opportunity smacker. My first day was a scene out of a freakazoid comic relief show. Greeted by my peers in the form of cheers, laughter, heckling and more than a few degrading comments. How the mighty have fallen! I felt right at home. The majority of these degenerates were kids that I partied with. The only difference between them and me was that I possessed what could be construed as a brain. Where as all they had to show for on the top of their necks was a container for holding empty space between their ears.

The curriculum consisted of the basic see-spot-run, 1+1=2 stuff that might have peaked the interest of a pre-school student. Even if I fell asleep in class, I would be able to complete the course. What the hell did I get myself into? It was a small price to pay for all those months of partying. If it wasn't for my ass being stuck in a sling, the whole thing would be outrageously funny! As reluctant as I was to participate, I really had no other options. Hunkering down, I concentrated hard and focused my eyes on the prize. In a few months, I would be outta here. I just wanted to get it over with. If it weren't for those early morning smoke-out sessions before class in the parking lot, I would have had a hard time making it. When the dust cleared, the underdog prevailed, making up the credits and graduating with cap and gown with the class of 1975. Finally! Free!

Graduation day brought not only relief and satisfaction, but a sense of trepidation. Here I was on the brink of freedom when the reality hit me square in the face. You're no longer considered a kid. You're an adult. No more excuses or passing the buck. Its all about working, paying bills and, yes, responsibility. All the fun stuff that your parents have been taking care of since you were soiling your diapers. Just the thought of it all ran shivers down my spine. Let's put all of those nasty thoughts on the side for now because there was a lot of celebrating and partying to take care of. The party animal that I was got right down to business. Let the festivities begin! We were all gathered into the main auditorium for commencement exercise instruction. My band of notorious friends assembled in the back rows where packs of fireworks were distributed. I then lit up a bunch of joints and passed them around to the willing. Clouds of reefer smoke filled the upper sections of the auditorium. The strange aroma summoned an overwrought teacher to the scene. Beneath the sounds of her tirade of disapproval, we laughed and carried on. Nothing or no one was going to ruin this day. Feeling ignored, she left us to our vices.

Instruction complete, we were chased out to our assigned seating areas on the bleachers. Those of us who held the fireworks, sat at the very top of the stands. Wouldn't want to accidentally burn any innocent victims up on such a happy occasion. However stoned or overcome with excitement, when the speeches began and the actual presentation of diplomas was underway, a profound sense of pride and accomplishment swept over me. Here I was, I made it! Seeing my parents among the crowd of family members and well-wishers, their happy, smiling faces beaming with pride. Suddenly, the whole drama was revealed to me in an instant. The meaning of it all. It's a moment in time forever frozen in my memory. The proudest day of my life! Everything else good, bad or otherwise that previously happened in my life was meaningless. Tears welled up and I was overwhelmed with emotion when given the instructions to transfer our tassels. Staring down at the fancy paper held in my hand, I was reminded of all the years of struggle and sacrifice that went into obtaining it. Now the journey was over. Being part of such a special occasion only comes once in a lifetime.

The congrats over, it was time to make some noise and on cue we lit the fuses and tossed the fireworks towards the back of the bleachers. The sound was deafening, echoing through the cheering and applause.

We made our way to the tree-lined field facing the school's charmingly landscaped entrance. The large Banyan trees, strong and green the year long, held a designated letter displayed atop their leafy foliage representing the last names of the graduating class. Footsteps followed by previous graduates. Here, family and friends gathered after the ceremony to present their loved ones with the typical expression of affection in the form of the traditional Hawaiian fresh flower lei and to snap photos. Lei piled high above the heads of former students were a welcome sight. Each of them seeing who could collect the most, then passing them around to the less fortunate. The camaraderie and spirit of Aloha felt everywhere spread throughout the throng of happy people. Posing for pictures with my parents and friends, I took one last look at the campus, knowing that I would never set foot on it again. Hell yeah! Good riddance.

My parents arranged a little get-together to celebrate my freedom. Nothing elaborate, just a few close friends and family, some homestyle cooking and ice cold beers to wash it all down. The gang split up for now to go do the family thing, but everyone knew that my place was where the action was. No picky parents dictating proper behavior with a no booze, no drug policy in effect. The drinks were on the house. To make sure that things got off to a good start, my friend Richard and I rolled up a bunch of doobies from the bags of stash, yes bags, that we procured the night before. Though we've done this exact same routine many times before, somehow it seemed different now. Can't explain it in any other terms other than to liken it to when kids grow out of playing with their toys. Beer in hand, we caught the elevator to the rooftop for some fresh air and to contemplate. The panoramic view, always spectacular, was even more so today with the last glimpse of the fiery orange sun changing the colors of the ocean on one side and on the other, the rich green mountain valleys of the Tantalus hillside covered in dark shadows. We lit up a joint and sat there in silence sipping on our beers, basking in the glory of it all. Though few words were spoken, in our hearts we knew that the life we had come to know was ending. What our futures held was still a mystery, but for now, we could care less. The mood was set and it was time for some serious partying.

The party was rocking with guests coming and going all night long with many guests stopping by briefly for a drink before continuing on to the next one. During the course of the evening, I received two very precious gifts. The first one was a large blue star sapphire ring in a silver setting. This was given to me by my uncle Freddy. Yes, that uncle Freddy! The next was a bloodstone ring set in 14k gold band from my father. The flat green stone with tiny flecks of red was a family heirloom given to him by his father. I was speechless! Caught totally off guard. Holding it in my hand, I had no idea of its worth monetarily but I knew the sentiment was priceless. The remainder of the night was spent with my girlfriend Elvira, whom I snuck out to pick up. The celebration wouldn't have been complete without her. A fitting close to a memorable moment in my life.

Now that I was no longer in school and considered to be an adult, there were some serious issues that I needed to address. The most immediate was my college education. While all the other athletes were fulfilling their obligations to Big Ten colleges across the nation, I was busy vacillating between two distinctive choices. I could either accept one of the two offers from junior colleges in Walawala Washington and Lienfield Oregon, both intent on having me participate in their gridiron programs. Which was the proper choice? Or I could take a break and continue doing what I have been doing—partying, hitting the surf with the boys and cruising with my gorgeous Mexican beauty. Now that's a no brainer. If you were a kid fresh out of high school with an alcohol and drug habit, what would you do? Why spoil a good thing?

Messed up on sex, drugs and rock and roll, stupid me chose what was behind door number two. I still had delusions about joining the boys in blue, but it wasn't my number one priority. Just thinking about making money wasn't gonna pay the bills in the adult world. Since the armed robbery gig had ended, I replaced that career with hauling trash full time at the waste management company. To support that draining drug habit of mine, I started dealing dope on a small scale. Mainly pot, because it was safe to handle and cheap to obtain. I purchased it from the same dealers who sold it to me in high school. Things worked out pretty good for a while. Until the good turned bad—"the larger the need, the larger the greed!"

I'd like to pause for a second to send out a message to all those hard working, ambitious graduates with a single purpose in mind. To go on and attend the college of their choice, and if luck have it, obtain that all important status symbol that bankrupts many parents along the way. I dedicate this regrettable moment in my life to your quest for higher learning. Youth has its privileges—irresponsibility, indecision and ignorance, just to name a few. With your whole lives ahead of you, why even worry or stop to consider all those once in a lifetime opportunities that you'll have laid at your feet? I mean, surely they grow on trees? Of course, they do! I had one of those dangled in my face. I was offered the chance to attend the Merchant Marine College in Boston on a full ride scholarship. A close friend and fellow co-worker of my dad had a brother who was the Dean of Admissions there. He had no family of his own, so he offered the scholarship to me. At the time, I didn't have the sense enough to realize how great the opportunity was. The institute was considered the civilian version of the Navy's Annapolis Academy. Many captains and first mates who sail the seas and pilot the large oil tankers and luxury liners around the world today, have either been graduates or attended the institute at one time or another. Without giving it a second thought, I declined the offer. Among the many, perhaps the biggest, mistake and most regrettable moments in my life. Never take anything for granted.

Chapter 8

When love dies

Soon after graduation, my girlfriend's father (the grunt) was transferred to Okinawa. This meant that she and her Mom would be moving back to Texas. I dreaded the thought but always knew the day would come when they would have to leave the islands. Her parents had finally found a fool-proof way of splitting us up. Our parents said that what we had was nothing more than puppy love and that we would get over it. We were convinced that our love was real. We were living on borrowed time and spent every possible moment together. With her still in high school, that was difficult. We looked forward to the weekends, which seemed to take forever to come. The two days we had was never enough. She started cutting classes at first, then school altogether. She would catch the bus to my house in the morning and arrive just after my parents went to work. We had the place to ourselves the whole day. In the afternoon, I would drive her back to the base and drop her a block away from her house. Everything was going smoothly until two unfortunate incidents occurred. First, my mother came home early from class one day and caught us in a compromising position. Then, her mother received a call from the school counselor complaining about her absences. She was grounded and our weekends cancelled. Her mom watched her like a hawk and for added measure, drove her to and from school. Time for us was running out and the clock kept on ticking.

She rebelled and ran away from home on the spur of the moment. Calling before she snuck out of the house, we planned to meet at the nearby Safeway. She never even made it off the base. The MPs snatched her up from the side of the road. Better them than some nut case. I had no idea that she'd been discovered. Nowhere to be found when I reached the rendezvous point, I got worried and went looking for her on base. When I drove to the front gate I was detained and taken into custody. I was escorted to the Provost Marshal's office where I was confronted by her angry parents. After a good ass chewing, they forbade me to ever see their daughter again. If I refused, they would have me arrested. I apologized for all the trouble I caused and told them I'd never stop seeing her. Throughout the entire ordeal, she sat crying in the backseat of their station wagon. I wanted so much to hold and comfort her. I'd never get close to that car with that pair of formidable MPs standing at ease behind me. They were itching to haul me off in chains. I was cornered. Here I was trespassing on government property on the verge of being locked up for love. I'd be released if I promised to stay away from her. Might as well shoot me now because that wasn't going to happen. These people just didn't get it. Haven't they ever been in love? Right now, I had to get the hell out of there. So I lied, telling them what they wanted to hear. Deflated, but not deterred, I escaped to fight another day. I took one last look at her and left.

A week went by and I could no longer contain myself. I had to see her. Though the odds of that happening were against me, I'd do anything to get to her. She called whenever she had the chance and those few stolen minutes we shared only strengthened my resolve to be with her. Desperate times call for desperate measures and on this particular night I put my plan into action. I snuck onto the base and climbed through her bedroom window. Getting through the window was the easy part. Visions of prison bars and cell doors slamming shut flashed into my mind as I approached the front gate. If any one of those MPs on duty recognized me I'd be arrested on the spot. No ifs, ands, or buts. My heart thumped in my chest as they waved me past.

Safe in the confines of her darkened room, I tried to relax. That proved to be a bit of a problem with her little Chihuahua barking and nipping at my heels. I locked the mutt in the closet to shut him up. Problem solved. His muffled cries could still be heard, but were ignored for obvious reasons. Dawn nearly here, I quietly tiptoed out the front door. No sooner had I reached the sidewalk, I was caught by her mother. She asked me what I was doing there after being warned. She had no idea that I was on my way out and thought that we were just talking outside. With all the commotion, her dad appeared at the door. He had a menacing look about him and her mom all at once took on this sad, pouty face. The kind you see at funerals. Inquiring as to how I came to be standing outside their door step, he glared at me. I was speechless. Lost for words, I searched mindlessly for the right thing to say. Soon, I'd be on my way to jail. I begged their forgiveness and said that I intended to marry their daughter. They went silent and after the initial shock wore off, I was invited back to the house that afternoon to discuss the matter. Elvira looked even more shocked than her parents were and broke past them and wrapped her arms around me. I told her I loved her and that everything was going to be alright.

I showed up that afternoon with hat in hand and was greeted, surprisingly, in a welcoming manner. It reminded me of those traditional Spanish prearranged marriages where the couple met for the very first time. Her parents sat all serious and business-like on the sofa opposite us. She held my hand as they grilled me about my intentions and told me of their expectations. I proposed then, with her hand in mine, and she accepted. There were congratulations and hugs all around. Everyone was overjoyed. Especially the two of us, because now we could see each other again. Their only wish was that we wait until she finished school. Reasonable enough request. We had planned on waiting anyway.

My parents were happy for me but worried about how I would handle her leaving. Unlike her parents, mine were far more lenient and understanding. We left the topic open for discussion at a later time.

Before we knew it, the clock had run out for us. On the night prior to their departure, our parents met at their hotel room for our final dinner. We didn't have much of an appetite, so we spent the evening alone in the room. We clung to each other and cried over our helpless situation. They were scheduled to fly out the following night via the MAC flight. We thought of running away together and hiding out until her parents left. She didn't want me to get into trouble and since things were going so well, why spoil it? She would graduate in two years then we'd be together. Forever—a lifetime to wait. They say you find true love only once in your life. When you do, there's no mistaking it. The feeling is electric! It flows through your entire body like a warm wave. Warmth that reaches into your very soul. Seeing her off at the airport that night tore at my heart. Saying our tearful goodbyes and pledging our endless love to each other, the scent of her perfume lingered as I watched her plane climb into the darkness and out of sight. I missed her terribly. The drive home was filled with the memories of our life together.

When we first met, our late night visits on opposing lanais, trying to keep quite while everyone slept.

I had just finished delivering some paperwork for my dad at the Pearl City Police Station when a drunk driver sped across the median strip and smashed into me, head on. Obviously the dumb ass didn't kill me, but he sure gave me one hell of a headache. I didn't have my seatbelt on and had struck my head against the roof of the car and was knocked unconscious for a split-second. I awoke to the sound of the engine, still running and making the strangest clicking noise. Dazed and confused, I sat staring into a shattered windshield, wondering what happened. The last thing I remembered was a white blur at the corner of my eye. It was over in a blink. There was no time to react—I could have been killed. It was a scary thought. The driver of the other vehicle had exited the Pizza Hut parking lot on the opposite side of the highway and flooring the accelerator, he crossed two lanes, through the median and smack dab into me. The initial impact pushed the left front end of my car over the roof. Motor and all. From there, both cars continued on a spiral path of destruction, wiping out the whole driver's side from bumper to bumper. Both cars were totaled. I shut the motor off, silencing that annoying clicking sound. Squinting through the spider-webbed windshield, I noticed a dark, oddly protruding object against the night sky. Gingerly exiting the vehicle, the extent of the damage became clear. My father's fairly new Chevelle was history. I had some explaining to do. I couldn't believe that I had survived such a devastating accident. Wobbly and unsteady on my feet, I went to check on the other driver. Approaching his car, I was assaulted by the strong stench of alcohol. Except for a gash on his forehead and cut on his arm, he was fine. He wasn't wearing his belt either. I wanted to punch his lights out. He was drunk as a skunk.

By now, a crowd of curious onlookers had gathered by the roadside—the "lookey-loos," anxious to feed their thirst for blood. A few bystanders wandered up to me and one asked, "Did you see what happened?" I pointed to the tangled mass of metal and said, "I was driving that." They panicked and walked me to the curb, inquiring about my condition. Someone called for an ambulance and minutes later it arrived and whisked me away to the hospital. I was amazed at their quick response. My parents, having been notified, were waiting for me at the emergency room. I'll never forget the looks on their faces as the attendants unloaded the gurney. I reassured them that I was fine and the relief showed in their hesitant smiles. It was that moment I thought about what all parents with teenage drivers fear the most—that late night phone call. After a few x-rays and a couple of tests, I was released. My parents looked old and tired. I felt bad for wrecking the car and apologized. They cared less and were just happy that I was alive and uninjured. As we hugged, there in the emergency room, tears of relief and joy burst forth from all of us.

The accident shook me to the core and I became gun shy about driving. This was the second accident I'd had, the first being just a fender bender. I thought the car was jinxed, not once attributing the accidents to my inexperience as a driver. There was no way to prevent the recent crash, but the first definitely could have been. I guess having a close call with death brings to mind all previous infractions causing even more uncertainty. But like everything else in life when you take a fall, you pick yourself up, dust yourself off, and jump back into the fray. I think about how my sister Lorna felt the day I begged her to let me drive on an errand for my mom. The ink on my learner's permit was barely dry when I hit that attorney's expensive car. I blamed her for telling me to go when I should have stopped.

I tried to make her feel guiltier than I did and worse than she already felt. No one expects you to accept responsibility for your actions when you're a kid. Not even yourself.

Sick with grief over my girlfriend's departure, I had difficulty dealing with the separation and heartache; I drank excessively and did whatever drugs I could get my hands on. Anything to ease the pain. Sitting in my room one afternoon, morose and wholly in sorrow, I looked up to see my father standing in the doorway. Tears rolling down my cheeks, I told him that I just couldn't take it anymore. I've always considered myself to be an exceptionally strong, manly type individual—physically and mentally, but when it came to that girl, I was a weakling. Even Samson had his Delilah. He sat beside me and suggested that I take a break and go visit her. Texas seemed like a million miles away and easier said than done. I'd never be able to afford the trip on my own. That glimmer of hope vanished in an instant and I was crestfallen. He left the room briefly and reappeared holding a plain white envelope in his hand. Giving it to me, he said he had been saving it for a rainy day. The envelope contained an insurance policy that he had been paying on since I was an infant. One of the many back up plans they invested in to secure my future. My parents often joked about how reckless and hyperactive I'd been as a child. They resorted to taking out extra insurance policies to pay for all the damage I did. We figured out the cost and ironed out the details together. My spirits lifted and I was overcome with emotion. I never felt closer to or felt more love for my dad then at that moment. I raced to the phone to tell her the good news.

Taking a week of vacation from my illustrious job at the trash company, I cashed my paycheck and added it to the pot. Minus the plane fare and a few other items, I had over $1000 for expenses. I could hardly wait. I flew to Dallas Fort Worth and caught a connecting flight to Houston. With an hour layover,

I had some time to kill so I searched out the nearest watering hole. Perched at the bar, excited with the anticipation of seeing my girl again, I threw back double shots of Chivas and almost missed my flight. Hearing the departure call, I downed my drink and left for the gate. Missing the shuttle, I had to run the entire distance, over half a mile away, reaching my destination just as the doors were closing. I was out of breath and sober after running the fastest marathon of my life. Settling into my seat, all nice and comfy, I signaled the flight attendant and asked her for a cocktail. There was a no limit consumption rule in those days. So unless you went ape shit on the plane during the flight, you could pretty much indulge until you passed out. I drank my way across the entire trip and landed safe and sound in Brownville, Texas.

The welcoming committee consisted of my girlfriend, her mom and a few curious family members. It felt good to squeeze and hold her tight in my arms again. We could hardly wait to be alone and ravish each other. The Spanish people share a similar cultural belief system as the Hawaiians—family oriented and overly protective of the younger women in their households. I was given her bedroom and she would sleep with her mother. I prayed that her mom was a heavy sleeper. She introduced me to her grandmother, who'd be staying until I left and was to be our official chaperone. She was a frail, delicate, sweet little lady in her eighties. Speaking no English, when hugging me close, she whispered words of endearment in her native tongue. Her eyes were still full of life and sparkled when she smiled up at me. In her younger years, she must have been a beauty. Elvira volunteered to show me around the town and we made our escape. Ardent with lust, we hurried to the closest hotel room. In the heat of desire, like two impatient honeymooners, we stumbled and fumbled through our lovemaking.

The next day, I was taken before the panel of judges for passing review. Her whole family had gathered at her uncle's home for a fiesta in my honor. I got along great with her uncle and cousins from the start. They were gracious, down to earth and fun-loving. We drank and laughed and teased El about her life as a baby. Of course, the pictures came out and embarrassed she ran snatching them from everyone's hands. I felt right at home. Her uncle asked if I'd like to see Mexico before I left and we made plans to do so. From the looks of things, I met with their approval and passed the test with flying colors. Acceptance by her family, the first gigantic step towards our happy life together. The worst was over with just a little way to go. I wondered if I could do it all in a week.

Time sure flies when you're having fun. The week flew past much too quickly and I never even made it across the border. We'd decided to see Mexico the coming weekend. I was having a fabulous time and wasn't even close to leaving. What I really needed was an extension to my holiday. I called my boss and asked for an additional week. Having a family member as President and General Manager of the company has its advantages. Granted another week, I was off to the races. I was riding an emotional high that could have lasted forever. Then one evening, after a long day of visiting with friends and family, I happened to notice bits of ripped up paper in the trash can next to her vanity. Alarms sounded inside my head and my heart began to pound. Curious, I reached in and collected them. There are only a few reasons a person discards letters in that fashion. Obviously to protect a deep, dark secret from prying eyes. Whenever concealing the truth, one should always take better precautions. My heart raced faster and faster and I pieced the tiny scraps together. Something inside told me to stop; sometimes the truth needs to remain hidden. I was committed to knowing. In my heart, I think I knew what this all meant. I felt faint, dizzy and had trouble breathing. Reading the legible parts, I recognized the familiar handwriting from the many love letters I received over the years. Letters cherished and kept in a shoebox in the bottom of my closet. Denial is a strong defense mechanism we use to safeguard our sanity. I somehow found the strength to assemble the remaining parts of the letter and laid it on her bed. Then the tears started falling.

I was stung by a sense of guilt, knowing that I had invaded her privacy and crossed the line that bordered on trust. My discovery overrode all ethics in that department. Driven, I rifled through her drawers, searching for answers. I came upon a neat stack of letters from a person in Hawaii. It appeared as though they'd been having a relationship for sometime. The torn up letter no doubt in response to one of his. My arrival had caused her to recant. The pain was too much to bear. In an unsteady and shaky voice, I called out to her. Entering the room and seeing the scattered bits of paper, stunned, the smile left her face. The look in her eyes confirmed her betrayal. Handing her the stack of letters, I haphazardly began packing my bags. I wanted out of there in the worst way. She lamented, grabbing the clothes from my hands and flinging them to the floor. My shattered heart was deaf to her cries of forgiveness and excuses. I felt as numb as a rock. I needed a drink. Through her tantrum of tears, amid her protests and attempts to impede my exit, I stormed from the room. She chased me, franticly professing her love and spouting apologies. Her mom, lost in confusion, tried in vain to console her hysterical daughter as I brushed past and out the front door. It was going to take a lot more than a few sorry's or I love you's to fix this mess.

Rambling down the empty streets, my mind flooded with thoughts of her betrayal, anger rose and replaced the hurt. Engrossed, I broke from my trance and realized that I was lost. In my haste to create the greatest amount of distance between us, I failed to take into account my lack of knowledge of the surrounding area. I came close to making an about face and retracing my steps. There was no way I could deal with that shit now. The hole in my chest dictated my next move. Finding civilization, I called a cab and told him to find the nearest bar. Stepping from the taxi, the night was still and cold, with an air of loneliness. Entering the establishment, my eyes were assaulted by the gaudy interior of red. Red velvet curtains, red shag carpeting, red upholstered bench seats with gold buttons, and fake marble statues completing the classic roman palace motif. Who cared what the place looked like as long as they served booze? Finding a spot at the bar, I ordered a triple shot of Chivas with a cube of ice. Just enough to bruise it. Like my ego. Halfway through my second drink, preoccupied with self pity, I heard a loud commotion at the front door. Glancing over my shoulder, I saw a bunch of drunks enter. Great!

They sauntered up to the bar and boisterously demanded drinks. Annoyed, I tried my best to ignore them. The way my night was going, the last thing I needed was to get into a bar fight. Though the thought was appealing, good therapeutic benefits and all, I'd decided against it. Strangely, I recognized a familiar voice among the group. Who could forget such a distinct, aggravating tone? Turning, I stared directly into the face of my long lost friend Hector. He was a Marine private who was stationed at Kaneohe Marine Corps Air Base before rotating back to the mainland. We met while having drinks at the NCO club with my future father-in-law. Hitting it off from the get go, we became good friends. After that initial meeting, we spent weekends drinking and getting high on pot. Before leaving, we invited him over for dinner. Saying his goodbyes at the end of the evening, he removed his silver chain with a Marine Corps emblem pendant and gave it to my Mom. Now here he sat less than a few feet away. What were the chances of that? Hector let out one of those infamous Mexican war cries that ruptured eardrums and nearly knocked me down when he hugged me. I was glad to see a friendly face here in the middle of nowhere. We proceeded to drink ourselves into a stupor and talked about old times. I felt better already and after a couple of rounds, we withdrew to the parking lot to partake of the marijuana. Hector lit a joint and passed it on. Smelled like someone started a brush fire. I took one puff and threw it to the ground. It was awful. Like smoking wood. I reached into my pocket and produced a product of Hawaii's finest. The sweet fragrance drifted on the wind, filling the lot with its pleasant aroma. Dynamite in a small package. I laughed as they smoked and coughed their lungs out. A tribute to the strain's potency. I lit another. The men in the circle tapped out and I smoked on alone. As the drug seeped into my brain, my troubles forgotten for now, I said goodbye to Hector and his pals. I shook his hand, hugged him and handed him a few more of those kryptonite joints as a gift. He smiled and let out a final yell, with his friends joining in. Could have woken the dead. Feeling no pain and standing all alone, I looked around the vacant lot and had no idea where I was. The bar had closed by now, so getting another drink wasn't an option. It had been a long night—time to call it quits. I called a cab; thought about getting a hotel room. Instead, I asked directions to her house. Somehow I managed to remember the street name. After driving past house after house, I recognized the place and was promptly delivered to the front door. The porch light burned brightly, signaling that I was expected. Weaving up the sidewalk, I was met by none other than my cheating sweetheart. Her arms encircled me and we held each other briefly before she guided me to her room. I was passed out before I hit the mattress.

The early morning sunshine spread across the bedroom walls, its glare stinging my eyes. Through the fog of my much deserved hangover, head pounding like a jackhammer, my previous night's attempt to erase the heartache caused by Elvia's infidelity, I decided to catch the first available flight home. Glancing up, there seated on the bed next to me was the object of my desires. Looking sad and guilty, with those black puppy dog eyes, staring at me. Bursting into tears, she apologized and did her best to convince me of her devotion. She begged me to forgive her and stay. I saw the hurt in her eyes, and it touched a part of me. She looked and sounded so sincere, but how could I ever trust her again? Rationalizing in my mind her disloyalty, I searched for an answer. Any excuse to remain. Would have been easy to just reach for her. To hold and reassure her that everything was going to be fine. Tell her I loved her. The pain was agonizing. What she'd done was unforgivable. I stopped fooling myself at that point and came to a conclusion. Regardless of her dirty low down behavior, there was no disputing the fact that I was still and always would be, madly in love with her. She was my first love. My one and only. Put all the old cliché stuff aside, and get to the heart of the matter. From the moment I first laid eyes on her, something went boom. I'd spend the rest of my life with her. She was the food I hungered for and the water that quenched my thirst. There'll never be another. And like the weak, pathetic, pussy-whipped sorry individual that I was . . . I stayed.

We crossed the border into Mexico and made our way to the small, sleepy town of Metamores. The place was a picture from out of old western days. With its adobe brick buildings and dirt streets, I expected John Wayne to come riding in on his horse at anytime. Only the occasional automobile passing belied the peaceful setting. I suddenly heard a crashing noise and turned to see a bicycle rider pinned between a taxi cab and parked car. Apparently, the taxi driver had misjudged his angle while attempting to parallel park his cab and struck the rider. Without the sense of mind to move his cab the driver had exited the car and started yelling at the biker. Like some comedy skit, the two continued to argue until the police arrived. They ordered the driver to move his cab, freeing the innocent rider. He didn't appear to be injured and continued to rant and rave. Neither man was willing to accept guilt and it was obvious that someone was going to jail. In all probability the taxi driver. This being a foreign country and all, I couldn't have been further from the truth. The driver shook hands with one officer, jumped into his cab and drove away while the other officer handcuffed the cyclist, threw him in the patrol car, and tossed his bike to the side of the road. Unbelievable? Turned out that the cab driver was the officer's relative. Corruption . . . you find it everywhere.

I strolled the streets to the bazaar in the middle of town to shop for the family back home. Along the way, I was approached by three beautiful senoritas. Dressed in their traditional floral print finery, they couldn't have been older than fifteen or sixteen years of age. They began speaking Spanish to me and though I hadn't a clue as to what they were saying, it was simple to see that they wanted something and my host was happy to translate their intentions. He gave me a sly smile and told me that these three gorgeous women would love it if I bought them lunch. Of course, in return for a small favor. He then winked, and shocked, I replied, "you mean with all three of them at once!?" If you wish he answered. I gave each of them five dollars and went on my way. He laughed and told me that I'd probably get more than just a good time to remember them by. I counted my blessings.

The center square was crowded with little stalls, each peddling their wares. The colorful mix of architecture and style depicted the native culture and history of its people. Prices for items were ridiculously low and could be haggled even lower.

My shopping out of the way, the heat of the day had me parched, so we stopped for cervesa at the closest cantina. The place was nothing more than a small room just big enough to hold four tables. A counter ran the whole length of the room and doubled as the bar. Pleasant and quaint, the tables all had matching red and white gingham checkered tablecloths set on dirt flooring. We ordered beers all around and they were served ice cold in bottles. The bar was sweltering from the merciless heat of the sun and I gulped down the first three bottles. Amongst the laughter of my three companions, El's uncle for some reason, warned me to slow down. An accomplished drinker, I chose to ignore the advice and ordered round after round. The beers went down nice and smooth, satisfying whatever thirst I'd had. Six bottles later, I felt a bit woozy and thought it strange. It usually took an entire twelve-pack to get me drunk. Something wasn't right here. Realizing that I'd been had, my fellow comrades let me in on their little secret. Beer in Mexico isn't regulated like it is in the U.S. Therefore, the alcohol content can be as much as double what we are used to. Yeah, laugh at the dumb pineapple. That was just the start. To compliment our drinks, the waiter served us tortilla chips and salsa. They suggested that I try the local favorite, the freshly made green and red chili salsa. It looked inviting and from the way they were wolfing it down, must have been delicious. I selected a chip, dipped it into the sauce, scooped out a huge portion and tossed it into my mouth. It was so hot, it gagged me. I never tasted anything that hot in my life. The burning sensation was indescribable and my lips went numb. The cold beer did nothing to ease my pain. If anything, it made it worse. They all had a good laugh and I was happy they enjoyed themselves at my expense.

We ended my visit with dinner at a popular, out of the way, food stand. The house special was tiny burritos filled with turkey, ham and roast beef, carved from this long, stainless steel spit. The combination of meats and barbecue sauce was scrumptious and for a mere fifty cents a dozen you couldn't beat the price. I couldn't resist ordering several dozen to take back with me. Standing next to the pick-up, finishing the remaining dozen I'd started on, I suddenly became distracted by loud popping noises coming from up the street. There was no mistaking the reports of gunfire. I looked across the road and saw a person running down the sidewalk. As he entered the circle of light from the streetlamp he collapsed. Another figure soon appeared, stood over the motionless form and fired more shots into the body. Stunned, but intrigued by witnessing a real live murder, I ducked behind the safety of the truck. That was more excitement than I'd bargained for. We loaded into the pick-up and made our way back to the good ole US of A. I looked back at the stranger lying dead, alone under the street light. No one came to his rescue. Not even in death. I had enough of Mexico to last me a lifetime. Stopping for inspection at the border checkpoint, we were detained pending investigation of the contents of a suspicious brown paper bag. In my rush to hide and avoid becoming the next shooting victim I had left the bag of taquitos on the step side of the truck. And there they sat until a diligent border patrol agent recovered them. Handing the bag over to me, smiling, no doubt disappointed it contained no drugs, it was just another reason to laugh at the pineapple.

The days passed much too quickly and I had trouble leaving. I could've stayed forever. What was supposed to be a short trip had turned into an extended leave of absence. I phoned my boss and talked him into another week. He said if I wasn't back to work the next week, I was done. Fired! Even family can bend backwards only so far. I thought about just quitting. Find a job doing whatever and moving to Texas. The thought scared me. Leaving Hawaii for any reason, even for love, was too much for me to handle. The memory of her unfaithfulness popped into my mind. I wondered if I'd ever get over it. Not likely. I started to feel homesick. Make the best of what you got and get on with life.

The final week of my vacation was spent in bed sick with the flu. Bummer. It was a miserable way to top off my trip. The harsh cold weather finally caught up to me. It is weren't for those shots I had from their family physician, I might never have made it home. Most difficult part about being sick was not being able to get too close to Elvia. There was an urgency for us to spend every possible second as close as we could—time was running out. I may forgive, but I'll never forget. All the bullshit aside, I have to admit that I had a great time in the Lone Star State. She was a good hostess and taught me a lot about myself. The inevitable day arrived and it was adios amigos. Driving to the airport, the rain began to trickle, mirroring the dull, somber mood we were in. I held her tightly the entire drive as she cried softly. Because of the fever during my bout with flu, my lips had broken out with blisters so I couldn't even kiss her goodbye. An awful sadness stretched through the group of family gathered to bid me farewell. The rain hid our tears as I gazed into her dark eyes. There was a strange finality to our parting. Somehow I knew then that I'd never see her again. Casting that thought from my mind, I boarded the plane and prepared for the long flight home. I drank my way across the Pacific, feeling empty and alone. I couldn't forget that faraway look in her eyes, or that final thought I'd had. Seeing the Islands come into view in the fading sunlight, I was filled with wonder. I lived in the most beautiful place on earth. It was good to be home.

I've known my share of women and of them all, Elvia had the greatest influence on me. Both heart and mind. She would become the standard for which every relationship, casual or otherwise, would be judged. Her betrayal had caused me to mistrust all women, even to the point of becoming insecure.

It compelled me to control and dominate the women in my relationships; to possess them inside and out. Fearful of abandonment, I smothered them. When the relationship finally ended, I was so grief stricken that my heart turned cold. Heartless women were treated as things. Objects used and abused for my own selfish pleasures and desires. Compensating for my pain by projecting my hurt onto them. Essentially, victimizing all the poor, innocent and not so innocent, females who have had the misfortune of becoming involved with me. My lame excuse for such deplorable behavior is having first-hand knowledge of how young love blossoms, fades, and then withers and dies. In the process, killing those pure hopes and dreams associated with innocent youth. Burying deeper still, all the caring feelings that we save up like so many precious gems. Gems we plan to someday share with that special someone we meet and spend our lives with. Friend, lover, wife, mother, confident, foe . . . true love forever. For those victims, the women who by chance honor me by reading this book, you know who you are. Especially my ex-wife Kahili, I'd like to apologize for my selfishness, lack of compassion and immaturity; I pray that I may someday earn your forgiveness. To quote the Good Book, the greatest piece of literature ever written, "Charity suffereth long, and is kind; love envieth not; love vaunteth not itself, is not puffed up. Doth not behave itself unseemly, seeketh not her own, is not easily provoked, thinketh no evil; rejoiceth not in iniquity, but rejoiceth in truth; beareth all things, believeth all things, hopeth all things, endureth all things. Charity never faileth; but whether there be prophecies, they shall fail whether there be tongues they shall cease; whether there be knowledge, it shall vanish away." Maybe a slightly altered rendition, but the words themselves say it all. Praise God!

Arriving home, safe and sound, but dead on my feet, the welcome wagon consisted of Mom, Dad, my good friend James, and a magnum of champagne. Feeling the effects of jet lag, alcohol consumption and heartache, I popped the cork on that extra large bottle of bubbly and took a big swig. Champagne spurted from my nostrils like a ruptured fire hose. James twisted up a few numbers from his bag of tricks and we sat there drinking and smoking until the bottle was empty. He made his exit and I made it to my bed, lying there, drifting off into la la land, as my mind played back the events of the last three weeks. Even in my semi-conscious state, the emptiness and pain could still be felt. Home only a few hours and I already missed her something fierce. Her lack of fealty was my final thought as sleep took me. It all felt like someone else's dream, but the hurt was real and all mine.

Life continues for the living as we struggle with the everyday drudgery of our lives. If my own problems weren't enough for me to contend with, I went and volunteered for watch duty for my former partner in crime. His future on track, he eventually went away to college in New Mexico, leaving me behind to babysit his 1973 Chevelle SS396 and little Japanese girlfriend. She turned out to be more trouble than the car. I'd suspected that she had been creeping around on him, so I started trailing her. I hit pay dirt when I saw her with a guy I had never seen before and they were acting too friendly to be just friends. I felt terrible for my friend and could relate to how he would feel when all this shit came down. I walked up to them casually and said, "Hi." She nearly jumped out of her skin! The surprised look on her face was classic. They should package those "cat caught with the canary in its mouth" look or in this case, pardon the pun . . . pussy . . . and sell it in gag shops. She introduced him as a fellow classmate. Yea right. I shook his hand and squeezed as hard as I could, trying to break it off. I thought I heard him squeak, rat that he was. I said, "Nice meeting you" and told her that I hoped to see her again soon.

Needless to say, my phone rang off the hook and, knowing it was her on the other end, I let it ring. I finally answered and she asked me to come over. She sat crying and told me of my friend's controlling ways, drunken rages and fits of jealously. Since their relationship started, I had gotten to know her on a personal level and considered her a friend. Listening to her blab and make excuses about her behavior, her cheating . . . I wanted to beat the hell out of her! This bullshit had me insane, crazy mad. I said that if she didn't stop seeing the guy, I'd make him disappear. She told me she loved this guy and wanted out from under my friend. She pleaded with me to help her. There was no way in this world that I was going to explain this shit to him. She wasn't getting off the hook that easy. I gave her two choices. Either she could tell him the truth herself, now, today, or I could beat the crap out of this new boyfriend. Knowing what this bitch meant to my friend, the news would kill him.

He showed up unannounced, but expected at my house in the middle of the semester. The mad look on his face told the story. "Let's get wasted!" he said. Seeing a close friend go to pieces before your eyes ain't a pretty sight. He wanted to spend the rest of his life with this cheating bitch and before this fiasco he had made plans to marry her. The story had such a familiar ring to it. I tried reasoning with him to let it go. I even gave him the "plenty of fish in the sea" speech, but he wasn't buying any of it. He couldn't leave it alone. I felt his pain and after sitting around getting bombed out of our minds, we did what all close friends and brothers do in the same situation: we plotted that poor unsuspecting fool's murder. In the beginning, I went along with it to calm him down and make him feel better, hoping that overnight he would come to his senses and change his mind. Before the night ended, knowing how serious he was about it, I looked him dead in the eye and said, "If you still feel like killing that s.o.b. tomorrow, when your head is clear and sober,

I'll help you do it." Then we passed out cold. I woke the next day, hung over, with him waiting for me with a drink in his hand. He looked at me and said, "I want that punk motherfucker dead!"

The guy worked nights as a parking valet at an exclusive private club. Perfect! We trailed his every move, day and night for days. Throughout, I tried, without success, to dissuade him from committing murder. He, on the other hand, kept begging her not to leave him. Also without success. We decided to kill him on a week night when business was slow and he worked alone. Parked in the shadows, shotgun at the ready, we sat chugging on a bottle of Jack Daniels and waited. The killing would be an easy one. The parking lot was deserted and not a soul was in sight. All the guests were long gone and only a few employee cars, including the target's, remained. Suddenly, the guy exited the building and made his way across the lot toward his car parked less than fifty feet away. My partner took one last sip. I passed him the Remington 12 gauge, filled with 00 buckshot and said, "Don't let him start the car, blast 'um just as he enters. Two quick shots to the head. Almost there, nice and slow . . . now! Now!" He sat there frozen next to me. I should have known. He never had the guts to stick a gun in someone's face when we robbed them and didn't have them now to kill his girlfriend's lover. Instead of being relieved, I was furious! I grabbed the shotgun and heard him starting the car just as I was making my exit. I felt him reach out and take hold of my arm just as the guy drove past. Disgusted, I jumped in, closed the door and drove off. The guy never knew how close he came to death that night. No doubt in my mind that I could have smoked that chump. All the cajoling in the world couldn't get her to come back to him but he had one trick left up his sleeve that none of us saw coming.

Several weeks later, while relaxing at home, the phone rang. Answering, I was surprised to hear her voice on the line. She was panicked and crying uncontrollably. Through her excited sobs, I hear her say that my friend had been shot. My blood ran cold. He was in surgery and it looked like he was going to make it. I went nuts! I asked her who shot him . . . someone for sure was going to get killed before the sun went down. The phone went silent, just her sniffing wetly. Then she said that it was an accident, he shot himself while cleaning the gun. Bullshit! The guy knew more about gun safety than anyone. We were raised in the culture from small kids. Cold chills ran through me as the truth set in. I braced as I calmly asked her the details about the gun he used and the location of the wound. I could hear the guilt in her voice as she explained. "I guess he finally got your attention." I was beside myself with anger. Again the line went silent. "You stupid bitch. This is all your fault!" I slammed the phone down and raced to the hospital.

When I arrived, his surgery was over and he was out of recovery. He was in a private room that was already filled to capacity with family and friends. Awake and talking, our eyes met when I entered the room and the message was clear. All the casual banter, witty comments, false bravado, nothing would save him from the conversation to come. To make things worse, that bitch sat on the bed next to him, holding his hand and playing the loving friend role. The other hand was heavily bandaged and in traction. I wanted to reach over and smash her face in! Then, slap him upside that stupid head. I asked everyone to please step outside while we talked privately. No one objected and as the last person left the room, he broke down and cried. I walked up to the bed and something inside of me snapped. I screamed, "you stupid asshole! Over that bitch?" I wasn't about to show him the least bit of sympathy. I then said, "what, you never had the balls to suck on the barrel?!" He told me he tried sticking the barrel in his mouth and pulling the trigger, but lost his nerve. His hurt was bad, but not enough to end his life. It was all about the sympathy to get that bitch to notice him. Well, he certainly got that! That's about all he got because she still intended to leave his dumb ass.

What my brilliant friend failed to take into account was the gun he chose to shoot himself with. Of course, if you're going to kill yourself, might as well use your favorite weapon. In his case, a Colt AR-15 semi-automatic, gas operated, magazine-fed rifle chambered in caliber .223. The exact same weapon adopted by the military in the early days of the Vietnam war. The bullet fired from this weapon had a unique impact capability. Because the casing of the round was larger in proportion to that of the projectile, the bullet had the tendency to either tumble upon impact or fragment. Thus creating a buzz saw effect. Lucky for him, when he pulled the trigger, his hand was flush against the barrel. The resulting hole was the size of a quarter that went right through his hand. Cool. He said after the shot, he lifted his hand and could see clean through it. If his hand had been even a fraction of an inch away from the barrel, his hand would have blown clean off. Jackass! Not even this extreme act could persuade the cheating bitch to come back to him. Goes to show you . . . when a woman makes her mind up, ain't no changing it. I wanted to kill her and that punk she was seeing. If he didn't love her so much, they'd both be in a hole someplace.

I never really saw much of my friend following the incident. We sort of went our own ways. We kept in touch on and off and got drunk now and then. Took a bunch of surgeries to put his hand back together. With unlimited funds at her disposal, his mom made sure he had the finest medical treatment available. They managed to repair the damage and he eventually regained full use of the hand. Even back in those days, well over a million dollars. He went on to graduate from college and become a special agent with the ATF. How he passed the psychological evaluation test beats the hell out of me. I was happy that at least one of us had reached our goal. We met for one final bout of carousing after he emerged from an undercover assignment. His investigation of an infamous Oakland motorcycle gang suspected of illegal gunrunning led to multiple arrests and convictions—single-handedly closing the club's chapter down. Cruising down the highway, beers in hand and the top of the 4x4 rolled back, sun on our faces, wind blowing through our hair, felt like old times. Handing me a joint from his pack, he flashed that wry smile of his and said, "Relax bro, smoke up. The law can't touch us. I got a license!" He flipped his Federal credentials at me for dramatic effect. I lit the joint, took a big hit and passed it to him. He did the same and we broke out into laughter as we headed to the beach to watch the sunset,

Chapter 9

We all fall down

The sinister world of drug addition is a cold and lonely place. A cruel, deceptive world filled with an army of lost and misguided souls. Each one wandering the earth aimlessly in search of themselves. Emotional vampires that suck the very life out of everyone they touch. They leave in their wake a pathway of destruction. Tormented by the only thing that they embrace as their god, their constant need to feed becomes the most important purpose in life. The drugs that hold them hostage, their closest friend. Many sacrifice all they once held sacred as decent human beings—relationships dissolve into thin air; friends, family and loved ones all consumed, fuel for the fire. We are society's outcasts, shunned, hurt, confused and weak. That person standing next to you at the bus stop or checkout counter, your fellow workers and employees. The neighbor who tells you good morning each day. That person watching TV in your living room. Drug addiction knows no bounds, favors the rich and the poor alike and does not discriminate.

Like all habits, drug addition is acquired slowly. It sidles up to you unnoticed, as subtle as a thief in the night. Working into the very fabric of your being. That ever present voice whispering in your ear, demanding to be heard. From the moment I smoked that first joint, I knew my life would never be the same again. The intense high was liberating. A feeling of freedom, transporting me into a state of serenity. I never imagined that it was the beginning of what would become a long and troubling life of pain, struggle and addiction. Alcohol and marijuana became the stepping stones that eventually led me down the road to both the agony and the ecstasy of drug abuse. Bringing me at times to the brink of insanity.

Drug addicts basically share a common rule. Stick to your preferred drug of choice and never deviate unless absolutely necessary. In which case, that drug isn't handy, you take whatever is available. Use the one that gets you high, keeps you high and doesn't cost an arm and a leg. The majority of drug addicts are broke. I've never met an addict who could afford his habit. It may appear as though they can and do have things under control, but that's just an illusion. No amount of money is ever enough. Sooner or later, the cash runs out and that's when most turn to dealing or crime. Like items in a supermarket, the selection of highs out there for the enthusiast to indulge in is vast. Some are cheap to purchase and easy to obtain, for example, liquor, marijuana, inhalants and some prescription pills. And although you're hooked on them, to some degree, staying high on them doesn't take much effort, or time out of your daily life. Other drugs, like heroin, cocaine, meth and certain types of pharmaceuticals are expensive and require a mammoth amount of effort to stay high. These drugs take total control of your life and the lives of the people around you. Staying high on these substances takes an exhausting 24-7, day in, day out, effort. It becomes more of a job than just a habit. You become the drug and the drug becomes you. The addict will stop at nothing to obtain what he needs. The sad part about all of this is, while in the process, the ones who love and care for us the most fall victim to our abuse. They try to save us. Giving everything they have. They give until they no longer can. In the end, their love for us is just not enough to save us. So they become enablers to our curse. Their love fuels the fire.

Up, down, or sideways. Any which way I could go to get high, I went and I experimented with anything that I could get my hands on. Young and strong, my body and mind were up to the challenge. A little coke here, some LSD there, I got acquainted with barbiturates in my early stages by stealing my Mom's pain medication. She had a variety that ranged from Valium to Percodan. I discovered that they complemented the booze rather nicely. I rationalized that my drug use was merely an escape vehicle from life's everyday problems. A passing phase that I'd grow out of. I can't say I remember the exact moment when that notion was forgotten and my love for being high all the time emerged. Everyone who becomes dependent on a substance, be it animal, vegetable, or mineral reaches that point in their lives. We end up crossing the line that leads us along the path to self-destruction. The boundaries of right and wrong—good and evil—become blurred. Obliterated! Your addiction eventually manifests itself into a living, breathing entity with a life of its own. Apparent to everyone but you. So you keep fooling yourself, caught up in the vicious cycle to feed the need. Resorting to whatever means necessary.

A perfect example to describe the lengths to which an addict will stoop to get a fix is an event that occurred while my dad was a detective at Juvenile Crime Prevention Division. One of his assignments was to visit the local schools, lecturing about juvenile crime and the evils of substance abuse. For this purpose, an aid in his presentation was a drug display kit in the trunk of our car. I used to sneak out at night when my parents were asleep and raid the display for joints. There was so much to choose from, I never thought he'd miss them. Some of them came rolled in that sweet and tasty strawberry flavored paper. The rave at the time. Long after my father had retired, over beers, I mentioned it to him. He smiled and said he knew all about it. He'd discovered them missing and had a hunch I was stealing them. That's why he stopped storing the kit there. After all, he was a detective. And a good one. Besides that you can never pull the wool over your parents' eyes for long.

The more you use, the stronger your tolerance grows. Your body and mind undergo significant changes. Soon, you're convinced that you can't live without it. You start to expand the types of drugs, experimenting with new and different ones, like a mad scientist searching for the elixir of eternal life. Only your search is for the perfect high. Peer pressure and your curiosity take you deeper into the realm of addiction. Each experience brings you closer to finding the answers. When you find that perfect high, and every user does, we choose to exist there forever. No matter what it takes. We beg, borrow and steal. Reluctant to resort to drastic measures as I had in the past, I was forced to seek full-time employment to support my ever increasing habits. My job choice was more of a convenience than anything else. Not exactly glorious or spectacular by any means, it paid well at the time. Still sick with heartache over my girlfriend's departure, the long hours I worked kept me busy and my mind off of her. After I returned from my trip to Texas, I had trouble adjusting. My drinking increased and drug use skyrocketed. Though I maintained and managed pretty well, my life was on a downward spiral.

I viewed my job at the rubbish company as a temporary thing. My introduction into the average Joe's real life, 9-5 work drama. I had every intention, even at this point, of joining the Boys in Blue. The thought drifted further and further into the back of my mind. Becoming a cop seemed to be too serious of a choice now. I didn't think that I could turn back from what I had become. There was always a chance—I still carried the hope somewhere inside of me. Maybe I didn't want it bad enough like I once did? Here we go again, making up excuses.

There really wasn't much to my job at all. Any trained monkey with half the intelligence could do it. I drove around in one of those funny-looking pick-up trucks with the bed cut out and a fork lift attached to take its place. Starting at 4 am, I drove to the Honolulu International Airport, pulled the 3-yard rubbish bins out of their chutes and lined them up on the runway. The looked like neat little green blocks, waiting to be dumped by the front end loaders. That lull in the routine, waiting for them to arrive, was the most peaceful and calming moment of the day. Smoking a joint and watching the sunrise over the horizon while 747s, silhouetted in the distance, taxied for take off. All to the beat of the radio playing rock and roll tunes of the 70's. An awesome sight. It was something I looked forward to every morning. I found a sense of peace at those times. Made me think about how insignificant my problems were, compared to the magnificent creations of God.

After a hard days work, all the employees gathered outside the job site to raise a few beers and unwind. It's at this daily ritual gathering I was introduced to a fellow driver named Walter. Walter was a drug dealer who pedaled his drugs to all the guys. Naturally, we became good friends. It was an obvious fact that we shared a common interest—drugs! He wasn't a particularly attractive guy, so I flipped out when I first met his wife Dolly. She was an Asian beauty with dark, almond-shaped eyes and long, silky black hair. They were direct opposites. I guess they really do attract! She must have seen the generous and caring person hidden beneath his deceptive exterior. Walter would be the person responsible for introducing me to the drugs heroin and PCP. Invited to dinner one evening, dessert was served in the form of China White heroin. I can't get the image of him sitting at the coffee table preparing his syringe, while his gorgeous wife looked on, out of my mind. It was as natural as washing the dishes after we had eaten. So casually scary, I for one, being extremely terrified of needles since childhood, the sight sent chills through me. I remember a time when I ran out of the examination room, the second the nurse walked in carrying that syringe. My father chased me through the parking lot as I cried my heart out. Though appalled at his action, my curiosity got the best of me and the drug addict in me couldn't resist snorting a line. It made me sick to my stomach. I hated the feeling, but that would all change one day.

Walter and I started spending more and more time together. He was an avid hang glider who was determined to get me up into the air in one of his contraptions. I drew the line at that. My fear of heights would never allow me to take the leap. Watching him participate in the hobby was enough excitement for me. I felt his spirit connect with nature as he soared on the currents of the wind high above me. Late into an afternoon of motocross riding, for which he was also gifted, he asked me to accompany him to a drug deal of his. He said he had a friend with a pound of angel dust to sell, and he was going to broker the deal. Up until this time, I'd never been involved in such a big transaction. My deals had all been small nickel and dime stuff. Mostly grams of coke and bags of weed for personal use. This was to be my first big deal involvement. PCP, better known as angel dust, is a strong chemical substance often used as an animal tranquilizer. When ingested, the high causes a state of euphoria where the user feels as if he is floating. Your body vibrates from head to toe as though sitting in a massage chair. You loose all track of time. It's like you blackout, but you're still awake. Dealers and bathtub chemists who produce the stuff would spray it on marijuana leaves. When dried, the leaves were crushed and sold. It produced a strong and distinctive smell that was far more deceptive than the pleasant aroma. California drug dealers popularized the drug by spraying it on the custom cigarette brand Shermans and sold them for $10 a stick. Hence the name Sherms becoming associated with the drug angel dust, the drug of the angels. Sent down from heaven above. Until now, I'd vaguely heard of it, but had never tried it.

Sitting in the room with Walter and his hippy friend, waiting for the money to arrive, Walter lit up a joint of dust and passed it to me. The room filled with the sweet minty smell. I hesitated for a fraction of a second before he urged me on. Taking a small puff, the smoke seeped into my lungs. It tasted exactly as it smelled. The effects were immediate and intense. Unlike anything that I'd ever experienced before. It was pretty unnerving at first. Now I knew why the joints were rolled to tiny twists, called pinners. I couldn't believe how potent the drug was. After two hits, I was done! I sat back and got lost in the drug's effect. Around me people came and went. The deal got made and the sun went down. I knew that I was present and witnessed the entire day's events, but it was like I was asleep. The time had flown by in an instant. In reality, six hours had gone by. When I came to, because that's what it felt like, the same feeling as when anesthesia wears off, Walter laughed and threw me a three-finger-sized bag of the stuff. He said his take for making the deal happen was an ounce of the stuff and that this bag was mine for being there. I stared at the bag in my hand and thought about what just two hits of that shit had done to me. It scared the crap out of me. But not enough to make me give it back. All I could say was thanks. Thanks for the madness. I couldn't wait to try it on my friends.

The next morning, I came upon five of my friends playing basketball at the nearby park. I asked them to join me in a smoke and they all agreed and dropped what they were doing. I handed them three of these little, pin-sized joints and they all started to laugh and tease me about it. Same thing I did. They all greedily inhaled and the sweet aroma spread on the wind. After two hits, no one was laughing any longer. Everyone slumped to the ground and was lost in their own thoughts. Jaws gaped open in disbelief. They never even noticed me leave. That's how I found them four hours later. Exactly how I left them. I stuck around until they came to. It scared the living daylights out of them. I asked if they wanted another hit and they declined and called me crazy. I should have known then and there that the stuff was poison. Too strong to mess with. Should have thrown the shit away. Drug addicts never throw their shit away! Besides I had the best dope in town. Might as well enjoy it. If that's what you call going crazy, fun.

The word got around about this insane drug of mine and people came far and wide to try a taste. Each time, it had the same effect. By now, after smoking the stuff for a week, my tolerance was so high that I could smoke more of it and function in a more or less normal capacity. I even drove on it. That's a scary thought. I had no way of knowing that it was driving me crazy. I can say in all honesty, that my short, but constant use of PCP, which lasted no more than three or four weeks, contributed to a major part of my bizarre and often violent outbursts. Behavior that changed character. It was only a matter of time before the drug drove me totally insane. If I didn't stop taking it, it would soon drive me over the edge. That moment came late one night while partying with three of my friends. Bored out of our minds, we decided to roll up a couple of cigarette-sized numbers and see what happened. The effects were fast and intense to the point of sheer panic. I can remember my whole body vibrating so badly that I couldn't move without feeling as if I was being shaken apart. So I stayed perfectly still, my eyes were wide open, watching a blinding rainbow of brilliant colors that covered the entire light spectrum. My hearing became so acute that the slightest breeze sounded like a hurricane. I could hear my buddy's girlfriend somewhere within the myriad of sensory overload whimpering like a child. She kept repeating, "Why did you do this to us?" Her cries more of a desperate plea for keeping her sanity than anything else. Every time someone got excited, spoke too loud, or raised their voice, even a pitch, we all shared a rushing effect that washed right over and through us. It was as though we were all connected into one body. Thinking, seeing, hearing and feeling the same things in unison. It was an eerie, agonizing experience. I've been fried on LSD, to the point where I couldn't even move, stuck frozen within my own mind, fighting to achieve any motor function. But this nightmare took the cake. This is why medicine men and shaman priests claim they can see visions. Perhaps, but maybe they're just plain crazy. Reaching such heights of altered states, by means of hallucinogens or other toxic chemical substances, could easily convince someone that they had a direct connection with their god. Finally, after five hours of torture, the drug wore off. We had made it without losing our marbles. I saw the face of the devil that night. He'd touched a part of me that would never be the same. Nothing in the world, from that moment on, would ever frighten me to that level again. Not even committing murder. I left them that night feeling lucky to be alive and mentally intact. On the drive home, I tossed the remaining contents of the bag out the window. I promised myself that I'd never touch the stuff again. I drove two blocks, realized what I'd done, turned around and went back to retrieve it from the road. Pitiful, but true.

Dad soon had his fill of dealing with the state's bullshit and retired. It wasn't long before boredom got the best of him again and he returned to the work force. This time as a sales representative for the same waste management company that I worked for. It was a cushy position that came with a brand new company pick-up and expense account to woo clients. Thanks to Conrad, my cousin Noe's husband, the family was running the place. Life was good! With all the extra cash flow, dad thought we should all move into a bigger home. We packed up and moved to a three bedroom, two bath single level house in Pearl City. It wasn't new, but it was roomy and nice. My parents also decided to purchase an entire house full of furniture for my sister and her husband as a sort of belated wedding gift. I was happy for her but felt a little left out. Sensing my dejection, my parents had offered to buy me a car. They said I could buy anything within reason. Dad would put up to $5000 on the down payment and co-sign the loan with his bank for the rest. I was ecstatic! My first choice was a Porsche Turbo 912 Targa. I had always dreamt of owning one. I saw the exact make and model parked in a downtown car lot. She was all black, had a sport roof that detached, with chrome custom rims set on Pirelli R7 radial tires. She was beautiful and about to become all mine. The sticker priced was $10,000 and some change. My parents weren't too thrilled about my selection but if that's what I wanted, Dad said as long as I could handle the monthly payments, he'd agree. Perfect!

That month, a family member passed away and we'd all attended the wake at Williams Mortuary. During a smoke break, I happened to notice a custom van parked in the Dodge dealer showroom across the street. Drawn to the beautiful airbrushed painting on the side, I couldn't resist the urge to get a closer look. Standing in the showroom, I was awestruck. It was an industrial work of art. The brown metallic paint gleamed under the lights of the showroom. It's colorful airbrushed painting of a cantina and sunset enhanced the western theme of the modern day version of the stagecoach. The salesman gave me the guided tour. It was loaded with extras like four captain's chairs that swiveled to provide comfort and easy access; plush wall to wall carpeting and rich walnut paneling; custom tailored cabinets for storage next to a portable sink and miniature refrigerator. The rear seating area held two bench seats that could be folded down into a double bed. I could live in here. It was a sweet ride and I fell madly in love with it. I had to have it! The price for all of this luxury was just $10,000 and some change. I dragged my parents to the dealership and they loved it. We placed the van on hold pending approval of the loan.

The loan passed with flying colors and I became the proud owner of that one-of-a-kind custom van. The monthly payments were $250, a considerable amount of money in 1976. I made a decent living hauling trash so meeting payment deadlines was a breeze. For now. When I took possession of my van, the Hawaiian sun shone above in the usual cloudless azure sky. Driving off the lot, I was exhilarated and overcome with a sudden sense of pride and accomplishment. I had the world at my feet. A steady paying job, comfortable living accommodations and a brand new ride. Life couldn't be better. Forgotten for the moment was the empty space in my heart. With all the hours I worked, there was no shortage of cash on hand. Living at home with my new financial obligation, my parents never expected any rent. They were content, spending their weekends cruising in the van. With all the extra cash on hand, my drug and alcohol abuse went through the roof. The party scene suddenly had a whole new look. We were rolling down the highway in style and comfort and everyone lined up for a ride in my dream machine. Mainly the fairer sex. I had become a self-contained carnival on wheels. The party was never ending. The saying, "gas, stash, ass or cash, nobody rides for free" became my motto. Party on.

Financial independence can be one of the greatest illusions. Especially for a young, inexperienced newcomer to the world of high finance and the responsibilities that go along with it. Youth has a tendency to make a person with the world at their feet feel Herculean. Able to leap tall buildings with a single bound kind of complex. The problem with that attitude is that no one sits you down and tells you of the consequences involved in taking that leap. The fall is fine and harmless, but the sudden stop will kill you in the end. All of which I would soon become aware. Having a class A credit line with the bank afforded me the opportunity to borrow money from different financial institutions. I was confronted with the same tempting urges that people in my position face. The urge to spend, spend, and spend some more. "Thank you very much for your business, just sign on the dotted line and here's your cash." You become so caught up in spending that you forget that you have to pay it all back, with interest. Irresponsible behavior kicks in and the next thing you know, your credit cards are maxed out and you owe more money than you make. Reality slaps you in the face and panic occurs. Barely staying afloat, I worked feverishly from dusk to dawn to pay for my lifestyle. The only glue holding everything together was my job at the trash company.

Even under the immense pressure to meet payment deadlines, you become tricked into believing that you are beating the system. Surviving, winning even. In reality, the system has already gotten its deadly grip on you. Up to your eyeballs in debt at the tender age of twenty can be as fatal as a double-edged sword. Wielded in the hands of an expert, cutting through those challenges that you're presented with (in an attempt to reach heights of financial security) the results could be glorious and very rewarding. Attaining a lifetime of happiness, of course, is reserved for those diligent hardworking individuals free from all social or personal vices. That same sword wielded in the hands of an incompetent, inexperienced drug addicted, alcoholic fool . . . the results could be devastating. Life changing. Either you stab with the sword or the sword stabs you. Once the mistake is made, recovery from such a messed up situation, for an idiot that is, is hopeless. Thus, one of the reasons for our nation's current economic downfall. The average Joe, ignorant of the country's intricate financial structure or basic theory of economics, becomes blinded by the American dream. Falling victim to its never ending consumption of human greed and frailty. Totally spent, all used and abused, they're left tossed aside like discarded confetti on the empty roadways following a grand ole parade. Cannon fodder for a great nation's status and claim to fame as a dominant world power. "God bless America!" So great, that they can't even feed their poor or pay their bills.

For awhile, my fencing skills were adequate enough to fend off the powers that be, keeping them at arm's length, from snatching the shirt from my back. I was paying my bills on time and living in the style that I had become accustomed to and beginning to think that I could actually pull it off. Make this whole real life drama work out. In the far reaches of my slowly deteriorating mind I had convinced myself that victory was within my reach. In the outer limits of thought I still harbored the notion of joining the police force. It was also my intention to attend college and get some kind of degree. That prospect had become nothing more than a faded idea lost within the soft gray matter of my brain. For now, I was just too busy struggling to survive. Each day that passed, I dug myself deeper and deeper into debt. When you stop and take a serious look at my life at that point, the fake façade of control removed, all you'd find is a person hanging on by the skin of his teeth.

Some people would reason that all recently graduated students from high school, mostly those lazy students themselves, should be afforded the freedom to explore their options. Payback earned after twelve years of dedication of putting nose to grind stone. No small task by any means. The smart ones either go straight to college, enter the family business or start work at the career choice they'd dreamed about as a kid. The not so bright ones procrastinate and dawdle, using their previous educational encounter as an excuse to cruise. I have to admit there are a few confused individuals that are slow to start but achieve greatness in the long run. But after two years . . . who do you think you're kidding? Yourself for sure! Everyone else who you were smart enough to maneuver into buying your bill of goods, for the time being, sure. Your parents mainly. Parents are eager and hopeful creatures. They want nothing but the best for their children and would do anything to help. Anything!

For those of us who are aware of our parents' vulnerability, who have selfish motivations and devious intent on our minds, it's easy to take full advantage. Their only weakness is to provide your stupid ass with unconditional love. The very trap they use against themselves in their attempt to please a loved one. And though they're fooled into believing your sincerity and promises for a little while, you can't deceive them forever. That's why they're the parent and you're the child. They haven't lived this long and raised your dumb ass to be fooled by an amateur. And the sorry thing is, even though they know you're a worthless liar, strung-out on drugs, they stand beside you. They never, ever, give up or turn their backs on you.

Young adults who find the nest hard to abandon, often discover it's in their best interest to remain at home, living under the roof of such devoted parents. All they really want is to see their children prosper. To be successful and become self-sufficient and to live independent lives with financial stability. And if God would have it, someday raise a family of their own. Isn't that everyone's goal in life? At least it is for normal people. For the average kid with enough common sense to know this golden rule, that's how life plays out. But what about the poor, mentally impaired kid whose parents make excuses for because of their handicap? Parents facing this burden are compelled to shelter and guard their special needs child from the atrocities of this cruel and unforgiving world. They know, without a doubt, that it's their duty to protect that poor helpless child. The responsibilities of parenthood. Now consider the useless, lame, alcoholic drug addict kid who resides under your roof. Should he or she be entitled to the same loving care and affection? For some twisted reason, the answer is yes. When you become a parent, you'll know precisely why. As sick and deplorable as this may seem, parents are hardwired this way. It's their natural instinct to protect and provide for their weak, helpless offspring, no matter what the circumstance. I use the word offspring loosely and in a derogatory sense, appropriate for individuals such as myself. Those who can consider themselves selfish, bloodsucking bastards and predators who feed upon the love and good intentions of the very people who have sacrificed everything to bring them into this world. These people who, for no other reason than that selfless act, deserve better from their progeny. Those of you who can relate to this . . . "Get a life!" You're not fit to kiss the ground they walk on. You never know how much something is worth until you lose it. Once it's gone, it's gone forever. Too late for sorrys or regrets. So kids cherish your parents and treat them with respect. Honor them and make them proud of you.

I don't know if it's bad luck or just plain karma catching up to dumb people who think they know it all, but somehow it always seems to find us. Just when life is running smoothly and things are great you go and do something reckless. Take for example the beautiful sunshiny day I had decided to go skateboarding with a friend of mine. We had chosen a portion of the newly built H-3 freeway that wasn't yet open for public use. With no traffic to contend with and steep hills, the place was ideal for riding. After a few tries, I got braver and started taking the hills faster. Soon, on one of my thrilling attempts,

I lost control of my board and plunged headfirst into the pavement. Luckily, at the last moment, I tucked my head to the side. In all probability, this act saved me from living the rest of my life as a paraplegic. I settled for a broken collarbone and a back that resembled raw hamburger. Laying there, feeling rather ridiculous and staring at the blue sky, I knew that something was definitely wrong here. The injury took six weeks to heal and thanks to my family connection at work, my job was secured. Not only that, but I managed to claim the injury as work related and got paid while recuperating. That was just the beginning of my nightmare. Returning to work amidst the questioning stares, I broke my collarbone again the following week. This time I needed corrective surgery and it took nearly four months to mend. Because it was a recurring work related injury, Temporary Disability Insurance paid me $300 a week to stay home. That was my very first, but not last, insurance scam. Staying home for that long, a person can get lazy and I dreaded going back to work. I was having way too much fun, partying and getting paid for it. The bills needed to get paid though. Up until now, I managed to hold on to my wheels. Even that would eventually prove too much for me to handle.

I should have paid attention to the warning signs that read "slow down or crash!" It's hard to focus when your mind is blurred and besides, stupid people don't take time to read signs, they're too busy being stupid. Anyways, not one to sit still while a weaker person is getting taken advantage of, my knight in shinning armor character kicked in. I found out that my cousin's boyfriend was using her as a punching bag. She got tired of the abuse and their dirty little secret and mentioned it to her sister, who mentions it to her older brother, who then mentioned it to me. There's no way in hell we could let it slide—this punk had to be dealt with—with extreme prejudice. One evening, we lured him to a deserted park for some partying. He had no idea that we had planned to beat the shit out of him there. Earlier, I'd stolen my dad's .38 snub-nosed revolver for insurance purposes. As the night wore on, the subject of his beating on my cousin was casually introduced into the conversation. In his drunken stupor and amid his vehement denials, my cousin cold cocked him right in the face and he went down like a rock. The I started whaling on him. Somehow, in the middle of all this, he managed to get to his feet and broke into a flat out run. He was a big guy, over 6 feet and 250 pounds—big and slow. We gave chase and right as I reached out to grab him, I stepped into a shallow hole and broke my ankle. Damn that hurt. Just thinking about it makes my foot hurt today. Tackling him to the ground, the beating continued. I was so pissed off about breaking my foot that I stood up, pulled the gun from my pocket and pointed it to his head. Consumed with anger I was ready to shoot. My cousin, taken aback at seeing the weapon, stepped between us. I wanted him dead! Suddenly aware that his days on this earth were over, he began pleading for his life, sniveling and crying like the little bitch he was. If it weren't for my cousin intervening, he'd a been dead on the spot. My foot throbbed badly and I struggled to my van. I couldn't even stand on it. By the time I reached home, it was the size of a football. It was 3:30 in the morning and I had to be at work at 4. There was no way that it was going to happen. I saw my whole life go down the drain in that instant. I was faced, once again, with the task of lying to my bosses; this time with less than favorable results. Speaking to the shift supervisor, using every excuse in the book, I was gruffly told to "either show up for work in the next fifteen minutes or find another job." I hung up and went to bed. The party was definitely over. I'd have plenty of time later to worry about how royally screwed I was. I felt really bad for my parents. I had let them down again.

Why should all the bad stuff stop at me? The hits just seemed to keep on coming. Not long after, my sister Lorna's marriage ran aground. She caught her cheating punk ass husband with another woman. I went ballistic. I wanted to kill him and everybody like him. She begged me not to touch him. My heart broke for her badly. He was her first love and she was living the dream that any woman in the world would have died for. The only good thing that she had to show for a relationship on the rocks was her son, my nephew Rickyboy. He was an angel and reminded me so much of his mother. Her life shattered, she and Rick moved back home. My parents were overjoyed to have their first grandchild running about the house and spoiled him. We all did. Our family was once again united for the first time in years. Plus a new addition. By now there was peace and tranquility in our home. The drinking continued, but there were no more fights.

Having my sister home again, though under sad circumstances, reminded me of our younger childhood days, especially during the holiday season. Those days always held a special place in my heart. A time for happiness and joy, where friends and family gather and celebrate together, washing away the cares of the world and cleansing the soul. I can still smell the aroma of freshly brewed coffee, filling the house in the early morning dawn, signaling my mother's presence in the kitchen, hard at work preparing her much anticipated turkey feast. Her acclaimed stuffing recipe I have had the honor of memorizing. Grandpa Joe, her number one fan for the latter, and Grandma Marjory at the top of the guest list. Uncle Pat, a former navy man and bachelor, befriended by my dad over the years, always present. A tradition that, through the years, has seen their numbers lessen. The sounds of laughter and merriment forever captured in our hearts and minds.

The coming of Christmas and the spirit of giving puts everyone in a cheerful mood. The annual tree selection, a family affair in our household. My poor parents chasing my sister and me through the maze of trees, as we decided on the perfect choice. The closeness we shared while decorating. Each of us with an assignment; Dad stringing the lights as my sister and I placed the delicate bulbs, some handed down through generations, precious and irreplaceable. My mother, the most patient of us, took her time draping the thin silvery icicles, every strand in its proper place. Her relaxation she'd say. She spent hours getting it just right. Their glistening shine bringing the tree to life—a shimmering display of brilliance. Last, but not least, the shining star at the top. My dad always helped one of us aloft as we placed this final ornament. Plugging in the lights, the room became awash in the bright glow of multicolored hues. The shadows danced off the walls, creating images of imaginary reindeer flying through the night.

The stage was set for the happiest time of the year. With presents tucked safely (or so *they* thought) beneath the tree, my sister and I could hardly wait to tear into them. Like all the other children of the world, the excitement and suspense was killing us. Never the patient types, over the years Lorna and I adopted a ritual of sorts. Whenever our parents went out to Christmas parties, we'd put our covert plan into effect. Soon as they drove away and the coast was clear, we'd snatch up our gifts and carefully unwrap them. I know, I know, not very Christmas-like, but we sure had a lot of fun. Turns out we were only kidding ourselves. Like I said, parents had our number. Always smarter than the kids they bring into the world. They later told us of how they knew all about our escapades, but never let on. Apparently, faking genuine surprise wasn't our strong suit. As the years passed, our curiosity faded and those memories continued to bring smiles to my face. Even today. How I long for those days.

My little nephew Rick, too young to fully realize what was happening, stuck his head in the doorway and made the grim announcement, "Uncle, the tow truck is taking the van away!" I felt bad for biting his head off for intruding on my sullen mood of denial. I did, however, marvel at how his young innocence was the armor of protection from harsh reality. The repo man had come knocking, bringing to a close a chapter in my life that was more fantasy than truth. It was like watching a close family member die—much too hard for me to witness. Even the likes of a child had more strength in him than the empty shell of a man cowering in defeat. Not savvy in the ways of banking and the system that makes them rich, we failed to secure the loan by purchasing the special insurance. In the even that I became sick, injured or dead, the insurance would continue to pay the note. No doubt we weren't the first customers to fall victim to the fine print. The van itself was more than adequate to cover the cost of the outstanding balance of the loan. The custom rims, tires and stereo I added were enough. All of which was paid for by money borrowed from various loan companies. Money still owed to them as well. Stand in line people. I really didn't care that much about losing it because I knew it was coming and was prepared. It was watching my mother cry over losing the thing that hurt the most. She sure loved cruising in it. Another nail in the heart and in the coffin. Stripped of my status symbol and chick magnet, I fell into despair. And deeper into my addictions. Sometimes you stab with sword and sometimes the sword stabs you.

The house of cards can't stand very well when it begins to tumble. Because of my cousin's husband Conrad's improprieties at the trash company, he was eventually fired. Seems he was having an affair with one of the sales persons, who was also married. It wasn't much of a secret except to my cousin. At least my dad didn't have to play the game of helping him conceal the relationship any longer. With the captain of the ship thrown off the plank, it was only a matter of time before the whole crew got the ax and dad left to fend for himself in shark infested waters. Rather than get eaten alive, dad chose to save himself by quitting. Back to the life of leisure again.

If things weren't bad enough, one day while grocery shopping with her sister, my mom slipped and fell in the produce section of a prominent store. Too proud to lay there in front of all those strangers, she stood up and refused to be hauled away in an ambulance. Although hurt, she had no idea the extent of her injury at the time. By the time she reached home, she could barely stand up straight, let alone walk. We rushed her to the hospital, where the x-rays told the story. She'd bruised her tail bone and broke a few disks in her spine. She would need back surgery to correct the damage. They removed bone from her hip and fused it into her neck in two places. Watching her suffer during her recovery broke my heart. She was bedridden for weeks and needed to be practically carried to and from the bathroom.

I spent whatever time I could helping my dad take care of her. That was the only good thing about my lazy stint of unemployment. She eventually recovered and was able to walk normally again. However, from that day forward, she was plagued with chronic back and neck pain. She was looking at a big payday from the store whose popular chain of retail stores had recently been purchased by a Japanese conglomerate. Should have been in the millions of dollars due to the store employee who failed to remove the water from the floor after spraying the vegetables, but due to the lawyer's ineptitude, they got almost nothing. They did cover her medical bills, which we could have never paid. If she had just lain there and let the ambulance take her to the hospital, our family would have been set for life. I miss my mother terribly and hate myself for putting her through so much shit. God bless you mom, rest in peace.

With the lack of cash flow, things were about to get rough. Our family was faced with a transitional period of readjustment. My sister, heartbroken over her marriage, was busy working and mustering her priorities, living her life for two. She concealed her hurt bravely, but I sensed the change in her. She was determined to become totally independent. My feelings of failure overwhelmed me and caught up in my guilt I spent all my time stuck on the pity pot. I was lost and even more useless to anyone. I saw myself as a liability and not an asset. I fell deeper and deeper into despair. Like a drowning victim struggling for every precious breath, I was desperate. When backed into a corner, it's difficult to recognize the solution to your problems. Add to that a habit that hinders any possibility of lucid thought, you wouldn't notice the answer to your problem if it reached up and slapped you in the face. Your choice is relatively simple, "get off your ass, stop feeling sorry for yourself and get a job!" Any job. It was as if I was too devastated to function. I was too far gone smothering myself in drugs and alcohol to even see the obvious solution to my situation. The weak get weaker. So in a rash fit of desperation, I did the one thing that I'd live to regret for the rest of my life . . . I went back to robbery.

Chapter 10

Point of no return

There's really nothing to committing a crime. You just have to be desperate enough. And this may seem funny . . . cowardly enough to resort to such extreme measures. The money is out there to be had. By the bundles! They hang like so many tempting apples from an orchard of trees and all you have to do is pluck them. Going back to robbing folks as a means of financial support was a no brainer for me. Just like riding a bike. Take a fish out of water then throw it back in again and watch it swim. Take it out one too many times and it dies. Ambivalent over the prospect of my decision to retrograde into previous encounters of crime caused me to become even more dependant on drugs and alcohol. My sister had moved on and was set to move out, but not before I dealt her another bitter pill to swallow. Jonesing to get high and no money to do it with, I called a friend who said if I could get to his house the party was on. My sister was out with her friends for the evening and had left her car home. I stole it and sped off to get my fix. On the way, I took an off ramp too fast, hit a curb, flipped the car over and smashed into a guardrail. The car was totaled. I should have been killed, but survived. Would have saved me from all the shit

I had to take for my actions. That car was sister's only means of transportation and independence. Stupid me had taken both away from her in a blink. My heart broke for her and watching her cry over it made things even worse.

With my sister gone, there was no need for such a big house. So we moved. Still a jobless bum, I had no choice but to tag along. I started to hang out more and more with drug dealers and people involved in the drug life. I soon began to formulate a plan to limit not only the risk factor associated with robbery, but the guilty conscience I was feeling. Somewhere along the way I'd grown a conscience and didn't feel good about victimizing innocent people for the sake of my habit. I rationalized that since the dealers had all the cash and the product I might as well just take both off their hands. Be killing two birds with one stone. I started off by setting up deals between the parties looking to score. First, you find the stash, then you find the cash. Doesn't matter which side you're on because the one always leads you to the other. Similar to a salesman or broker. The good thing is when you set up a deal, you take a percentage from both parties involved. Your commission depends on how much money is involved and the amount to be sold. No different than any other business transaction in the world of commerce. Only in this business, the people carry guns and kill you if you're not careful. I tried to keep things on the up and up most of the time. You could make tons of money if you know the right people and are lucky enough to get in on a big deal. If worse comes to worse, you found out who was making what deal with who. Very discretely of course. Then you take them down. You meet lots of people in the drug world and the circle of dealers, and many are connected in one way or another. So the last thing you need is for any of them to know that you're a pirate. Otherwise, the word gets out and you're ostracized. Even hunted down and killed. It was not a job for the weak at heart. And certainly not for the posers. People who talk the talk but don't walk the walk. At any given moment, you have to be willing to kill or be killed. You can't have one without the other and only the really cold-blooded survive in this business. I had no qualms about either issue. When you are young, you are foolhardy and not afraid of anything. Dying is always a frightening issue on any level and always in the front of your mind. But you can't think about that, can't get hung up on it or you will never be able to function. You'd most likely end up dead. Fearless yes, reckless no. If you are willing to give it your all, you can make a pretty good living. Competition is fierce and to stay on top of the ladder you have to prove your ruthlessness at one point or another. You know, set an example. Just so the people out there know that you are serious. This is usually accomplished by means of physical violence. Could range from torture and beatings to killings. Like I said, this job ain't for the weak. Being trained in weapons and hand-to-hand combat, I had the jump on many of my competition. There were, however, a select few individuals in this world that were a cut above the rest. The real deal hitmen and killers that specialized in the art of extermination. These cats were very serious fellows and were to be avoided at all costs. That is unless absolutely necessary. These guys would kill you just because you looked at them funny and they usually killed people in the most gruesome manner. There was a man who, with the very mention of his name, brought chills up and down my spine. I did have the pleasure of meeting and doing business with this one guy who was at the top of the list. I reminded myself that if things went wrong, I'd have to be faster to the kill than he was. No matter how big the person is in legend or size, he's only human and bleeds like the rest of us. It's the repercussions from your actions that are scary. The killing part's easy.

This whole crazy lifestyle sort of reminds you of the wild, wild west. You better believe it. The normal public who go about their business day to day could never imagine this life. They hear about the killings and the drugs on the news, but have no idea of the reality. They choose to disassociate themselves from the truth for fear that the badness will somehow find its way into their small, safe little world. They depend on law enforcement to be their savior in the event that the monster comes calling.

Society wrapped up nice and safe. Sanitized. As it should be. Everyone else outside of the bubble be advised, keep your dirty, hostile world to yourselves.

Cruising at light speed through the underbelly of society is no different than swimming through a cesspool. All the showers or clean changes of clothes can't wash the stench out and I loved it! No one to answer to except yourself. A shadow with venomous fangs ready to strike. The scum of the earth. The word on the street got around and my reputation preceded me. I was in demand—gun for hire. It was about this time in my life that my sister Lorna introduced me to her new boyfriend. More like a sugar daddy. His name was Ralph and he was almost twice her age. He was a white dude, or as we locals say, "haole." He was a taut, wiry, wild and crazy guy. At first, I couldn't understand what my sister saw in the guy. That would all change quick. Turns out, this guy was once a millionaire land developer who loved the finer things in life. Fast cars, fast women and good dope. She'd met him while running from her past, whatever it was. I could tell that the guy was hooked bad on her. The only way he stood a chance was to meet the family and be accepted by all. My parents were reluctant, at first, but the guy did all the right stuff to please them. He really went way out of his way. That was sort of a red flag and I was just a little concerned. I sat her down and we talked about it. I was worried for her safety. The guy made me nervous and I told her that if this clown ever hurt her, I'd kill him. She smiled and told me to sit back and enjoy the ride. She had it all under control. This she convinced me of as she broke out her stash of cocaine. We sat there, snorting lines and reminiscing over old times. I've never seen this side of my sister and I was somewhat surprised. She was a different person altogether. Her talk, body language and the drugs. She'd never indulged in dope before. That punk-ass brother-in-law of mine must have really messed her up. I wanted to kill the son of a bitch.

Cocaine had never been a real habit of mine. Occasional use and only if it was free. That would all change real soon. Leave it up to my older sister to introduce me into the world of the rich and famous. By now, her and Ralph were an established couple. They lived together now and his grandiose, flamboyant visits never failed to amaze and intrigue me. The guy was off the chain. Whenever he had small menial tasks to do, my sister made sure I was included. These tasks usually involved the heavy use of cocaine. For which I had, thanks to her, become not only accustomed to, but addicted. Ralph taught me everything there was to know about the drug. How it was made, where it came from and how to process it and bag it up for sale. I had become a cocaine connoisseur and entrepreneur overnight. I was now running, from time to time, among the rich and privileged. It was a strange world for me. No one said it at the time, but I must have been a bit of an oddity to those "turned-up nosers." One thing for sure, they knew not to offend or mess with me. They could feel the scary boogieman persona on me. Some even did their best to avoid contact with me at parties and events. I was the bull in the china shop. Deep down inside, these people were no different than me. They just dressed better. Oh yeah, and they were filthy rich. Must be good never having to worry about money. That's one experience I wouldn't mind having.

These people had no choice but to be nice to me, because I carried the briefcase that held all the coke. Yes, that was the one job Ralph assigned me that I loved the most. There was five ounces of dope in that bag at any given time. The majority of it he used to impress his clients. He just gave the stuff away. Literally! Why not? He got it all free anyway.

How is a person given such a coveted position you say? Well, let me explain the circumstance to which I was introduced into the inner sanctum. One bright and beautiful Hawaiian sunshiny day, I was home lounging on the patio at my parent's house, when the phone rang. I had just finished smoking a joint and had popped my first brewsky. My sister on the line asked if I was busy. If not, she said, would I mind coming over and helping with something. I asked her if she was in trouble and she just laughed and said to hurry up. She sounded so matter of fact, like she needed some curtains hung. Boy was I in for a surprise. She met me at the door, wine glass in her hand. She had become a wine imbiber recently—not the cheap stuff either. Nothing but the best. Entering the living room I was greeted by Ralph who immediately tossed a 100 tab Tylenol bottle at me and said, "Here, fix yourself up!" I unscrewed the cap and saw that it was filled to the top with cocaine. My sister smiled and her eyes twinkled. Go ahead brah, go for it. She poured me a huge glass of wine from her personal stash. It was cold and sweet. It was delicious! Ralph motioned me towards the bedroom and said when I was done getting high, he needed my help in here. Totally blown away and greedily filling my nostrils, I headed for the room. What I saw floored me. I never expected to see such a sight in my life. It was just like the movies! They had a king size bed in the middle of the room and on it was all these bundles of cash. All stacked in neat piles, according to their denomination. Ones, fives, tens, twenties, fifties and hundreds. Hundreds of thousands of dollars' worth. My jaw hit the carpet. I stood there shocked—never saw so much money in one place in my life. It scared me and I looked around, as if expecting a bunch of bad guys to start kicking down the front door.

Ralph sensed my apprehension and told me to relax. He said that he needed me to help him count all of this cash and get it ready for pick-up. Dumbfounded, I just stared, speechless. He said there was no rush as he turned his attention and mine to the dresser. There, atop the dresser, sat the biggest bag of cocaine I'd ever seen. Must have been two or three kilos. I shook my head in disbelief and they both just laughed. He said he needed me to start weighing out grams of coke first. "Just grams," I asked? "For now," he replied. I went crazy! I got busy right away.

When I first opened the bag, I gagged and almost passed out from the ether fumes. "Be careful when you open that," he said—a little late. The whole room now smelled like a hospital. It turned my stomach, but in a good way and I nearly shit myself. This was heaven. My mind raced in all directions. I got higher just off the fumes. I began the task of breaking down that mega-bag of cocaine. I began pilfering a few here and there when no one was looking. Soon every pocket was filled. My sister, observing, wandered over and said, "you don't have to do that brah, Ralph would give it to you." I felt bad that the drug addict in me had shown itself. All the while, I continued helping myself, snorting humongous lines on a mirror and drinking wine. I must have packaged about 100 grams before I took a break. I was insanely high on coke. Youth has its advantages. A lesser, or older man, would have been dead of a heart attack.

I moved on to my next task of counting all of that beautiful money. There was so much of it—every denomination was counted twice. Once by me and then my sister. We first made stacks of hundreds, and then placed them in bundles of $1000.00. Counting by hand isn't an easy task, no wonder drug dealers prefer using a money counter. After a few hours of counting, I was exhausted. I had even begun to perspire. I never thought handling cash in that fashion could be so tiring. My finger-tips turned black and my hands cramped. If it weren't for the cocaine, I would have passed out from all the wine I'd drunk hours ago. I was having the time of my life. So this is how the rich live. Welcome to the big time! As the hours passed, my mind began to play tricks on me. That voice inside my head started telling me to do unspeakable things. I walked to the kitchen to freshen my drink and the paranoia from all that coke suddenly hit me. I had the craziest idea. I opened the kitchen drawer and picked up a large French knife. I was all set to go back into the room, stab Ralph to death and rip off all that cash and stash. That's how my sister found me, in mid-thought, holding on to the knife. Sensing my intentions and seeing the crazed look in my eyes, she blocked my way and said, "Brahses! (the nickname she always calls me) What you doing?" The tears started running down her face. All of that money and dope had driven me nuts. I said to her, "let me do this. Think of Mom and Dad and how hard they worked all their lives. We'd be set for life. All of us!" She pleaded for me to put the knife down. I could hear Ralph in the bedroom, busy talking on the phone, clueless that his life hung in the balance. She had just split seconds to convince me to change my mind. She told me that the people whose money that was would stop at nothing to get it back. They'd hunt us down and kill all of us, our parents included. Even that wasn't enough to deter me. She looked into my eyes and said, "Please . . . he's so good to me and I love him!" I could see the sincerity in her eyes. I dropped the knife back into the drawer and she hugged me. Clinging, relieved and maybe both of us crying. Ralph walked in at that moment and was puzzled, "you guys okay?" We both smiled. I would later regret not killing that bastard.

With still thousands of dollars of cash to be counted, he enlisted the help of both my parents. When they arrived and set eyes on all that cash, they were nearly knocked off their feet. It became a family affair as we all got down to business. We counted and drank, then counted and snorted coke, then counted and drank, and on and on. Night came and my parents were beat and left. But not before being paid $500 each for their efforts. The three of us continued throughout the night and into the next day. By the afternoon, people started to show up to pick up the cash. There were many different types of people, mostly white. You'd never suspect them of anything criminal. There were teachers, businessmen, students, lawyers and architects. After the third day of running this marathon, I was totally out of my mind. Most of the money had been distributed or counted. There was still lots left to be counted, but I'd had enough. I had never been so high in my life. Ralph gave me about $700 and a sandwich bag of coke for the road. It was a profound experience that I would never forget. It took me an entire day to fall asleep. Glimpsing the fabulous lifestyle of the rich can be hard for the average person. Once spoiled, you hunger for the action. You wait around hoping that the phone would ring again. And ring it did, many times. Ralph had become a permanent fixture in our family life. He was a generous person who always went first class. Showering my family with gifts of cash, I saw that he cared deeply for my sister and did everything to please her. She was easy to love. She had that special way of practicality and honesty about her. Even her pets sensed it. Animals have a keen intelligence about them when it comes to humans. Many of her cats would catch birds and mice and present them as gifts to her. She'd find all these dead animals around her room. Whenever they gave birth to their young, they would lie on her lap before birthing. She means the world to me and I'd kill an army to keep her safe and happy—or just to see her smile.

Needless to say, I began to do odd jobs for my sister and Ralph. He taught me everything about his real estate practice. How to purchase land without a dime in your pocket and make a profit. Drugs were always intermingled in all of his deals. It was common for me to run errands or drive him to and from appointments. Everywhere we went, I carried a briefcase with ounces of cocaine to give as gifts to his many friends and clients. At first, it unnerved me to walk into a prominent law firm and break out a huge bag of coke and place it on a senior partner's desk. The list of businesses and clients was staggering. Seemed like, no matter how law abiding or attached to the system that ran our great country these people were, corruption was at the heart of it all. It was a sobering reality. It was also scary!

The way things were escalating, it was only a matter of time before somebody got seriously hurt. The last thing I expected was that person to be me. Ralph with his trusting, ignorant self-righteous character chose to do business with a bunch of crazy locals. These people were a gang of thieves that went about the drug world ripping people off. They would purchase product from you and even paid you on time just to gain your trust. Then you got stupid and fronted the dope to them on consignment to pay at a later time. Needless to say, they had no intention of paying you one cent. When you pushed the issue, they pulled a gun. In the drug business, you have to arm up at some point. Every dealer carries a gun for protection. It's law. Well, Ralph didn't believe in guns or doing things in any other way. He believed that gentlemen don't have to carry guns and that your word is your bond. Stupid ass! It's that exact way of thinking that almost got me killed. It always bothered me, the blasé way he took this whole drug business. This was a dirty, low down business—nothing casual about it. That day, when I showed up at their apartment and saw all that cash and dope, the first thing I asked him was if he had a gun. He laughed at me and said I should relax. Then he gave me this whole lecture about that being the trouble with us locals—we were too violent and needed to chill.

I guess I was a little too relaxed that Thanksgiving Day, when the guy who owed us money walked into his partner's house and tried to kill me. We were invited to have holiday dinner with this guy who sold drugs for us. I had no idea that his partner, who we'd been looking for, had argued with Ralph earlier that week about money owed. Apparently, Ralph had told the guy that I was looking for him. Now, you don't go around telling a gun-toting cocaine fiend that the guy you owe money to had somebody looking for him. He might get the wrong idea. In this case, he did. You certainly don't do that without letting the guy know that you blurted his name out to this person in a threatening manner. I wondered why, when I saw this guy exiting a hotel lobby a few days earlier, he took off running. Too high on coke at the time, I failed to put two and two together. So here I sat, on this festive occasion, drinking my beer, engaged in conversation, when I saw this guy enter the front door. He walked directly to me and I saw him scratch his ass. A term gunmen use for a person who is reaching for his weapon concealed at the small of his back. It looks just like a person scratching an itch. The movement is subtle and to the untrained eye, innocuous. Realizing his deadly intent, I dropped the bottle, stood up and tried to intercept his progress. He was too far across the living room. Too far for me to get to in time. Luckily, the partner saw the whole thing and stepped in front of him. It was all the time I needed to pounce on him. I grabbed the gun with two hands and wrestled him out the front door. We fell down the steps of the porch and onto the ground. By now I had taken the gun away and had thrown it to Ralph, who was nearby. I proceeded to punch the guy senseless. I shouted for Ralph to shoot the bastard and his partner. Ralph held the gun, frozen. I could see the shock registered on his face. I jumped up, reached for the gun, ready to kill the pair. Ralph panicked, pointed the gun at me and said, "Stay there!" It totally blew my mind. I pleaded for him to give me the gun. I was insanely angry. He refused. Instead, he gives the gun to the guy's partner, who goes back into the house with it. In the meantime, the guy I was beating on wakes up and runs into the house.

I stood there screaming at Ralph, telling him that now we're both dead. Any minute, I expected the guy to come out with that very same gun and shoot us dead. I was furious. I was lucky, in more ways than one that day, and lived to tell about it. After that incident, Ralph and I parted ways. But we'd meet again one day under different circumstances.

With my steady supply of drugs severed, it was back to nickel and diming with the boys. I could never afford the lavish cocaine lifestyle that I had gotten used to. I was still unemployed and too messed up to even consider doing the nine-to-five trip. I did whatever it took to get high. For some reason, my armed robber tendencies had been put on hold. I was getting by just from dealing. I was an adult now and if busted, could do some serious time. No more slap on the wrist shit. Been about three months since I last heard from my sister and Ralph. She was totally freaked out over the incident on Thanksgiving. They went to California after that and hadn't been back since. Out of the blue, the phone rang and she was on the other end. I was surprised to hear from her. She put Ralph on the phone who asked me to do him a favor. He said that he needed me to go pick up some luggage that was being held at the front desk of a Waikiki hotel. They drove by to give me the use of their rented Lincoln and gave me the lowdown. The whole thing sounded fishy from the start. He finally admitted that in one of the suitcases was about five pounds of weed. All he wanted were the other bags, I could keep the weed. The hair stood up on the back of my neck. The cops could be waiting for whoever came to pick up that bag. I had no choice. Well . . . I did, but I didn't. I sure could use that five pounds of marijuana. I hesitated for all of two minutes, grabbed the keys and walked out the door. The car was a beautiful Continental coupe, fully loaded, sunroof and all. Driving to the location, my heart raced and I could feel the adrenaline pump through my veins. If I was going to get arrested at least I'd go in style. Walking though the lobby, time slowed to a crawl. I couldn't believe what I was about to do! I glanced around, trying not to look conspicuous as I searched for the heat. Can I help you sir? The front desk clerk looked like a local who could have been a relative of mine. I told him that I was here to pay for Mr. Stewart's bill and pick up his luggage. Here it comes. He tapped on the keys to the computer and gave me the strangest look. Any minute now. That will be $240.00 sir. I asked him are the bags still here. He nodded and said they'd be right here. I couldn't help myself and asked, "All the bags?" He smiled and replied, "Yes sir all the bags are here." There were four of them and a porter helped me to the car. Making our way across the lobby, my heart beat a mile a minute. "Here it comes?" Closing the trunk, I tipped the porter twenty bucks and sped off. I zigzagged in and out of traffic, trying to avoid the imaginary police. I drove to a friend's house, removed the bag from the trunk and opened it to check the goods. Yes, it was all there, and it was all mine! I threw the bag to my friend and told him to hang on to it. I arrived home, slammed the bags down on the living room floor, handed the car keys to Ralph, kissed my sister goodbye, thanked them and was gone.

After a few weeks, the phone rang and again Ralph asked for my assistance. This time, when I went to their place, he had all of this hashish that looked like the bottoms of shoes. There were pounds of the stuff! Also, he had all of these Tai sticks, marijuana that was tied to bamboo sticks laced with opium. They were about six inches long and tied together in bundles of fifty. There was a whole Styrofoam cooler filled with them. Hundreds upon hundreds! And if that weren't enough, he had liters of honey oil. This is a very potent type of hash oil made from the buds of Afghanistan rock hash marijuana. The thick viscous liquid, amber in color, resembled honey, thus the name. Once again, I was amazed at the volume of drugs. He asked casually if I could use any of this stuff. (You think?) He gave me some ridiculously low price for whatever they cost and told me to help myself to however much I wanted. "Don't have to ask me twice." I loaded up and was off. And so it began again.

It was hard to dispute the fact that Ralph was anything else other than a big time drug dealer. Among his many talents, this one distinctive attribute of his seemed to encircle everything in his life. The extent to which he was involved in the drug business was even far greater than I could have imagined. Handling drugs on this scale is reserved for only the upper echelon in the drug world. Drug cartels and smugglers like Pablo Escobar, Carlos Leader and the Ochoa brothers to name a few. These people ran countries and their governments. The only thing missing in this equation was the bloodshed associated with these men. It was common practice for these people to eliminate the entire infrastructure of a drug ring just to escape justice. And though Ralph was against using violence, there was no doubt in my mind that the people he answered to and did business with had no such reservations. Behind every man in the suit is a guy in overalls, holding a pick and shovel. The thought made me uneasy. I just worried for my sister's sake. These people were vicious and did not discriminate between male or female when it came to setting examples. My suspicions were laid to rest, confirmed, when he showed me a torn hundred dollar bill that he carried around in his wallet. It was ripped in half, right down the middle. He said that the other half was in the possession of a Catholic monk at a monastery in Peru. He also told me that it was a credit card to purchase cocaine in any amount. Even tons. No money was needed to exchange hands over the deal, just the matching of bills. When the two halves were put together, they matched perfectly. He then described how they transported the drugs in a special 100-foot yacht. The entire interior of the boat, all the cabinets, sides of the hull and flooring, was hollowed out to accommodate the cargo of drugs. His tale was mind boggling, but I never doubted it for a second. The crew that sailed the boat to its destination were professional smugglers with nerves of steel. And there it was, the story behind the man. He later explained to me how he laundered the drug money through various bogus shell companies he had set up. Also, by the purchase and sale of land parcels. Over the years, he'd built and developed subdivisions and housing tracts throughout Hawaii and the mainland. The reason for his real estate license, and the architecture firms and the law firms and the multi-millionaire clientele. The picture, once cloudy, was now all too clear. Ralph was, for all intent and purposes, an international drug smuggler, money launderer and confidence man for an organized crime faction. That was the most frightening part.

Meanwhile, dad had accepted an offer to work as a night security head at a popular Japanese-owned hotel. The security chief was a retired cop and personal friend of his. Even after the Department, the boys in blue look after their own. It's a family that sticks together for life and I still longed to be a part of such a family. As each day passed, I moved farther and farther away from that reality. Dad's workplace was located directly across the street from our apartment building, so he walked to work. His nightly work schedule made it easy for me to conceal my movements from him. When he wasn't sleeping during the day, he was busy at work. Mom was the only one who saw the comings and goings. It wasn't like I was trying to fool them about my habits. They were hip to it all long ago. In my own way, I was trying to protect them from actually knowing how bad my involvement had become—the despicable things that I had done. And although they turned a blind eye to my addiction and alcohol abuse, they'd never condone the lengths I went to support both. I'd have been out on the streets. So, I kept it like the Army's don't ask don't tell. On the down-low. Their failure to take action, or lack of stern control, could be summed up as their way of coping with it. Regardless of me being an adult at the time and living under their roof, I did adhere to certain rules. I just spent the majority of my time out. It's when I began to cross the line and merged the two separate lives that the trouble started. It doesn't matter how careful you are or how courteous and considerate you are, sooner or later the drug-induced individual that governs your world takes over. Morality is cast aside and the monster within always has his way. The people around you, especially your loved ones because they have a weakness for you, their love, become the frontline casualties. The thing is, you know that you love them with all your heart and consciously would never do anything to hurt them. You'd probably kill anyone that tried. You're just too screwed up to know that you are the one hurting them the most. The instrument of destruction. Such a pitiful situation. Families everywhere suffer the very same dilemma. It's a love that kills. That same love that once comforted us and made us feel safe and secure at night we now use as a weapon against them to get our way. We become the masters of heartless, devious intent. Plagued with a fatal flaw.

Somehow, through all this madness, I had started an on and off relationship with my high school green-eyed girlfriend. She was a completely different person from the individual that I'd known way back when. Gone was the innocent virgin. The new version was, strangely enough, a lot like me. Her sweet character had blossomed into a candid, no nonsense, assertive, to the point of aggressive, woman. The transformation pulled me in and captured my undivided attention. And the most prominent change was her addiction to drugs and alcohol. This defect in our characters would become both the attraction and destruction in our relationship.

When you walk around day to day with a substance abuse habit as large as mine, it takes an awful lot of dedication to support. Like I mentioned, it's all consuming. I spent every waking moment chasing down my next high. Any form of criminal activity made readily available was taken full advantage of. Up until now, I'd been extremely lucky. Nobody stays lucky forever. The odds of that constant are mathematically impossible. Why would I be an exception? Not a person to learn his lesson any other way than the hard way, I chose to go up in smoke. The events that led to my collapse happened rather quickly. You never think about how life can change for the worse in a heartbeat. Particularly when you're in denial about the quality of the life you are living. Believe me, a life of crime ain't no life at all and certainly doesn't contain the word quality in it.

Well, here's how the whole thing started. Remember that cousin of mine who recruited me to help beat the crap out of his sister's boyfriend? Yes, the incident where Karma caught up to me and I broke my ankle? I should have known from the get go, when he asked me to help him bring down some dealers in his area that I was in for a bumpy ride. The whole thing just didn't feel right, but the promise of all the drugs and cash they had to offer was just too tempting to pass up. Be a simple home invasion. Break in, tie everyone up and threaten the dealers with bodily injury. We even had an inside man who'd been purchasing drugs from these guys for the past week. A white guy himself, they'd befriended him. Goes to show you,

you can't trust anybody. This was a two-man operation, so I got the help of my cousin's husband, another drug addict and dealer. He agreed to go along for a piece of the pie. That made it a three-way split, since my cousin would pay the inside man out of his share. Of course, I'd take most of whatever I wanted, who was going to argue the point with me? If they had the balls to do that, they didn't need me in the first place.

The house was located at the end of a dead-end street, fronting the beach. Perfect! I reconnoitered the area and formulated the plan. They did the majority of their sales at night and slept in the daytime. We'd use the cover of darkness to conceal our movements and approach the house from the beach. There'd probably be anywhere from five to ten people in the house when we entered. Taking control of the situation quickly was key. Rounding everyone up and placing them face down together in one area. According to the inside source, these dealers were young and trusting and didn't carry guns, but you never know. Someone in the house might have a weapon. I know that I would. And it would be important for me to let those people know that I have no problems using it. It was a cake walk. After three days of observation, it was on.

On the night of the hit, we met at my cousin's house before midnight and went over the game plan. The inside man would go to the place and make a purchase to insure that there was ample product on hand. If he went into the house that was the signal that they had drugs. If he didn't enter, there were none and we call it a night. Watching him enter from our observation point on the beach, we had a clear line of sight. We'd break in the minute he exited the front door. Kneeling on the sand my pulse raced. I could barely contain myself. I was unable to get a handgun for the job so my cousin provided me with his long-ass rifle. The thing was clumsy and hard to conceal. Not exactly the ideal weapon for this type of job, but it was real and loaded and could kill you. That's all that mattered. It's not the gun, but the man behind it. Any moment now our man would exit and we readied for the attack. We made our way closer to the house and hid behind a tree.

He appeared on the porch, said his goodbyes and walked down the lane. The person still held the front door open as we rushed it. I grabbed him by the hair and slammed him on the living room floor. The two men seated on the sofa froze as I pointed the gun at them, "on the floor!" I shouted. My partner, who held a huge 12-inch French knife, searched the house for others. There were just the three of them home. We proceeded to bind their hands and feet with duct tape. I taped their mouths shut and began to interrogate them. At first they dummied up and refused to give up the stash. I emptied their pockets and relieved them of their cash. They still denied being dope dealers. I pulled a switchblade from my pocket and caressed their cheeks and necks with it. In a low, menacing tone, I whispered, "I don't have to shoot you to get what I want . . . one way or another, you're going to give me what I want if it takes all night." They began to squeal beneath their taped lips. Releasing the tape on one of them, he began to give up the hiding places to all of the drugs. "Please, take all of it, but please don't kill us!" We gathered up the loot and escaped into the night.

Running down the sandy beach, we made our way to the getaway car. My heart pumped as the adrenaline surged through me like a fiery bolt of lightening. Driving down the deserted streets, I experienced the quiet. Not a siren or patrol car in sight. We'd done it! Gotten away clean! The familiar feeling of that natural high associated with committing the perfect crime took me back to that special place. Before the hit, my cousin and partner offered me some marijuana to get me in the mood. I refused and told them that no one was getting high until this was over. Work first, then play. Besides, I never got high before a job. It was a rule that I lived by. A rule that I would break just once and live to regret. In total, the heist had netted some four or five hundred in cash, an ounce of pot, a quarter ounce of cocaine and an eighth of an once of PCP in powder form. Not the big score that I was expecting, but not a bad night's haul for half an hour of work. Apparently they'd sold most of their goods earlier in the evening. We missed the boat by a few hours. Next time, I'd get it right.

The mentality of a criminal is as predictable and simple as a rat in a maze. However basic the level of intelligence, unlike the rat, we have (or should have) the ability to decide whether to run the maze or not. After all, that's what separates us from the other species that walk the earth. Given the gift of discernment on a higher plane of thinking, it should be easy even for the criminal to decide when enough is enough. In this case, I give points to the rat rather than the criminal. Which brings us to my decision to rob those poor dealers again. After finding out they were up and running, you would've thought that they had learned their lesson the first time. It was me who should have learned the lesson. And school was about to commence on that account. So it went as before—the exact same scenario. Why deviate from a perfectly executed plan? The only difference was I had stolen my grandfather's .38 special. We were unable to get a weapon for the hit and the plan was already in motion. I should have seen that as a bad sign from the start. The hairs on the back of my neck stood up when I took the gun. I had a funny feeling and didn't stop to read the signs. My greed and hunger for the drugs and action was more powerful than logical thinking. So what else is new?

We'd elected to pull the robbery earlier and on a weekend when the prospect of better pickings were right. These dealers were as dumb as rocks because they never figured out that their newly acquired friend was our inside man. He continued showing up at their house and partied with them as usual. Walking down the sandy beach, the anticipation of what was to come filled me with excitement. My heart pounded in my chest. Closer and closer its rhythm increased and that familiar feeling rushed through me. In the distance, I caught a glimpse of shadowy figures moving about. We came upon two party goers who had strayed from the house. The man and woman greeted us and even in the darkness, it was obvious they were stoned.

They asked if we'd come to join the party and we responded in kind. I questioned them about how many people were there and if there was enough drugs to go around. They said the crowd had dwindled to no more than ten and that there was lots of dope when they were there. I couldn't see their faces and no doubt they couldn't see ours. The house was about a hundred feet from where we stood and from the looks of these two, they'd be none the wiser of what we were doing, but I couldn't take that chance. I pulled out the gun, jabbed it in the male's chest and ordered them on the ground. The female started to protest and I shoved her to the sand. We duct taped the pair and left them next to a log. That's when something stupid happened. My partner looked at me and said, "Why we got to hold these people, they're not involved." His sudden bout of conscience enraged me. We were arguing the point when I saw our man approach the front porch. That's when my partner did a stupid thing. He cut our captives loose. I watched our man at the bottom of the step talking to one of the dealers. At first, they stayed outside and talked. That was the signal that they had no drugs. Then he went inside. The whole scene was wrong. I turned and saw that the hostages were gone. I freaked! Our man exited the house and I made a split second decision. I should have left, instead I charged the door. Entering the front door, pistol pointed at the surprised man's head, I saw four people seated on the couch. Three guys and a woman. The shock registered on their faces instantly as I told them to lay face down on the floor. The clock was ticking inside my head. There was no time to waste. We had to get the hell out of there fast. We duct taped everyone except the girl who said she had a sick kid in the bedroom. I left her with her son and told her that if she tried to escape, I'd kill the kid's father. Things were already too complicated. Then I did an even dumber thing—I looked down on the coffee table and saw a mirror with lines of a white powdery substance. It called out to me. I bent over without hesitation and snorted two huge lines. I had broken the cardinal rule. What I had thought to be cocaine turned out to be PCP. The effect was instantaneous. Realizing my mistake, I rushed through the house to tell my partner it was time to leave. Heading to the bedroom, I looked down and saw a few dollars lying on the floor. I snatched them up and put them in my pocket. By then, the drug had taken ahold of me. My partner was busy searching the place for loot. Time slowed and a comforting calm overcome me. I wandered through the house losing track of all time. I was spaced out. It was over without me knowing it. I felt so peaceful. I surrendered myself to the high.

For a brief moment, I remembered what I had come for and dragged the two dealers into the kitchen. I sat them in chairs and began to ask them for their drugs. They refused to cooperate. I proceeded to encourage them by the use of a Bic lighter. I turned the flame all the way up and placed it near one man's bare nipple. "Tell me where's the stash?" Seeing my intention, he began to sob. I removed the tape from his lips and he said that there was no stash. I taped his mouth shut and flicked the lighter. I showed it to him and held it directly to his naked nipple. He leaped straight into the air as the hot flame crackled against his burning flesh. The smell of cooking flesh filled the kitchen. Taped securely to the dining room chair, when landing, he fell over onto the floor and banged his head on the cabinet door. I righted him, removed the tape and asked him again. He begged me to stop, but answered the same. No more drugs. I re-taped his mouth and flicked my Bic again. This time, I stuck the flame right up his nostril. The flame popped as the soft flesh burned. I saw the flame shining through the side of his nostril, the way the light flickers from a candle inside a pumpkin on Halloween. Again, he leaped and fell over. The guy duct taped to the chair next to him, witnessing the torture of his friend, had tried to escape by hopping. He'd fallen over also, and hit his head on the floor. I sat them up, removed the tape from the jack-o-lantern man and asked him again. He responded the same. There was no way anyone, except for a CIA operative or Special Forces soldier, could take such torture without giving up the truth. The guy was telling the truth. Maybe he didn't know the "real" truth. Maybe the other guy knew? No use letting one guy have all the fun.

I approached the next victim, who was white as a sheet. Blood ran down his face from the gash on his head. I let him bleed. Something about seeing your own blood makes a man squeamish. Again, I flicked my Bic and held it to the man's bare body. The results were the same. Righting him and removing the tape, he pleaded and confirmed the truth. There were no drugs or cash to be had. They'd given all the money to their supplier and were waiting for him to bring the load. This whole damn caper was a bust. That was the least of it. Bored, I headed to check on the others. In my preoccupation with the two dealers, I had forgotten about everything and everyone else. I checked on the woman who was lying next to her son in the darkened bedroom. I reassured her that this whole thing would soon be over. I also told her that she should give up the drug life and think about her son. My partner was guarding the other two men in the living room when I heard a car drive up the drive way. The driver called for one of the occupants. I grabbed the guy on the floor and asked him if he knew who that was. He said the guy was supposed to show up earlier. I held the gun on him, opened the front door and told him to get rid of the guy. They were busy talking when the guy pushed me back and dove over the railing. Before I could recover, he'd took off running down the lane. But not before shouting to the driver that they were being robbed. The car sped in reverse out of the driveway. That's it! We're out of here!

I gathered up what little drugs they had on the table, stood the guy on the floor up and told him to get his car. "No funny stuff, I got your family!" I got the girl and the kid from the room and said that we were all going for a ride. I stood at the front door and looked at the girl's husband who had the car idling. At that moment, for some reason, I'd stuck the gun into the waistband of my pants, concealing it. It was the one action that would prove to save my life. I ushered the girl and her son into the front seat and jumped in behind her. I looked at my partner next to me and heard a voice shout, "Drop the gun now!" I turned and came face to face with three gun barrels pointed directly at me, inches from my face. They kept yelling, "Drop the gun, drop the gun." I replied, "what gun, I don't have no gun!" I then slowly reached into my pants, as slowly as possible hoping to hide my movements, slipped the gun out and dropped it on the floor. They'd convinced me to do so by slamming the barrels of their guns into my face. Boy did that hurt! The door flew open and before I was yanked off my feet and thrown to the pavement, I glanced over to the left at the empty seat and open door where my partner used to be. With all the excitement, I never even noticed that the couple was gone. Under arrest! Busted to the max!

Smashed face first on the ground, the police encircled me and proceeded to beat me mercilessly. They kicked, punched and took turns having at me. One officer held the barrel of his shotgun and used it like a baseball bat, swinging for the fences. I covered up as best I could, but there was no way to avoid the onslaught. There must have been ten or more taking their anger out on me. Lucky for me I wasn't cuffed at the time or I would have been dead. There was blood everywhere, but I managed to stay conscious. I looked over to see my partner 20 feet away getting the same treatment. There were fewer guys on him though. Maybe it was because I had the gun. You think! All the while, I kept seeing my father's face in my mind. The beating lasted for at least ten minutes and was so brutal that the crowd that had gathered started shouting at the cops to stop. That snapped them out of their frenzy and they handcuffed and left me on the ground in a pool of my blood. Some gigantic plain clothes cop, for whatever reason, yanked me to my feet, punched me in the ribs and threw me back down on the ground. He then came up behind me and applied a choke hold. I'd learned this exact same hold while a student of Judo. There was a right way to apply it, in which the neck is placed in between the crook of the forearm and bicep, chin and elbow facing in the same direction, cutting off the blood flow and rendering the victim unconscious. Then there's the wrong way, when the person applying the hold fails to place the neck in proper position, crushing the windpipe and causing the victim to drown on his own blood. Many police officers mistakenly apply this hold improperly and cause the death of the suspect. That's why today, the choke hold has been barred from being used in most police forces. Just so happened that Supercop had me in that death hold. I was seated with my legs straight out in front of me with my hands cuffed behind my back. He was seated on the ground behind me with his legs tucked over mine, locking me in place. I started choking and he applied more pressure. I fought back, but knew that if I didn't get out of this now, I was dead. Thanks to the pcp I had ingested, I had the famous super-human strength attributed to those under the influence. In a fit of panic, my adrenaline spiked and I somehow stood up with this gorilla still attached to my neck and threw him to the ground. I was free! I yelled at the man looking up at me, "I couldn't breathe asshole!" The stunned look on his face almost made it all worth it. Almost. I was beaten back down to the ground by three other officers who had witnessed the whole thing. At least I was alive. Live to fight another day.

They carried me to a waiting ambulance after one of the officers recognized how badly I'd been beaten. The attendants were disgusted by the sight of me. They'd seen the beating incident and said they would be happy to appear as witnesses on my behalf in a brutality case. They also remarked that they'd never seen a person so badly beaten without being critically injured. I lost all respect for the police department that night. I resented, no hated, them and the law they stood for. Throughout the entire ordeal, all I could think about was how I was ever going to face my father. Up until this very moment, no matter what bullshit antics I was going through, no matter what crimes I had committed, the hope was still alive. The hope of me carrying on the family name in law enforcement. Well, the dynasty was dead. Killed off by an out-of-control drug addicted, self-centered, immature kid. Now I would forever be referred to in the circle of law abiding citizens as one of the bad guys.

We were driven away in separate unmarked vehicles to the Pearl City substation. An ominous sign to say the least. The last time I was here, I was nearly killed in a head on collision. I had a feeling that my visit here tonight would be no different. Three officers escorted me to the Sergeant's office for questioning. If that's what you call being slammed headfirst into the concrete wall next to his desk. Blood squirted from the gash in my head like a sprinkler. I was way beyond feeling pain to consider it by now. Rather amused by the way it shot forward, I began to point the flow in the direction of his neatly arranged desk. The blood splattered everywhere, covering his paperwork and cute little family photos. I guess he wasn't the least bit amused. He screamed for the other cops to take me away but not before landing a few well-placed blows to my body. They removed the blood-soaked shirt from me and threw me in a cell with nothing but the pants I wore. It was freezing cold in there. I'll never forget the finality of hearing that metal door slam shut. My hair was matted from the dried blood and was stiff and plastic against my skull. Body aching in every imaginable place and eyes swollen shut, I passed out. Sometime during the night I was awakened by the sound of the cell door opening. "Finally," I thought, "some humanitarian assistance." That couldn't have been further from the truth. Looking up through the thin slits that used to be my eyelids, I heard the sounds of shuffling feet enter the room. Their voices conveyed their disdain and disapproval for my action. The men began to beat me. Kicking and punching as they swore and made it known what they thought of me. They finally left and I found comfort again in the cold and lonely cell. This treatment went on and on for the first night I was there. Got to the point where no matter how dead asleep I was, when I heard the cell door open, I covered up. They never failed to disappoint me. I was refused all contact from the outside world, no food, clothing, mattress or blanket. Hawaii's finest Boys in Blue. The organization that all my life I had aspired to belong to was nothing more than a bunch of thugs. The only difference between them and me was that they carried a badge—a badge that they could hide behind. I hated them. Don't get me wrong—there are many honorable men on the force. There just weren't any of them there that night.

Chapter 11

The aftermath of shame

No longer able to keep my whereabouts a secret or the situation to himself, my cousin John was faced with the task of notifying my father. Sitting there in my cold, lonely cell, I could only imagine the effect the news would have on my parents. Of all the stupid things I had gotten myself into over the years, this took the cake. Lying motionless on the floor, doing my best to keep warm, I was interrupted by the sound of keys opening the cell door. I braced myself and prepared for the worst. Two officers entered and said I was being transported to the main police station in Honolulu. I had lost all track of time and as they loaded me into the waiting blue and white, I could see through my swollen eyes that night had descended again. I had refused to cooperate with any of their questions. Even reluctant to give them my name. The beatings no doubt attributed to my resistance.

Arriving, I was placed in a single cell, isolated from the rest of the convicts. Up until this time, I was still denied any type of contact. It was strange that I hadn't heard from anyone. Deep in my heart, I had hoped that my father would somehow rescue me from this nightmare. I fell into a deep restful sleep. I was awakened sometime in the early morning hours by the stern voices of authoritative figures entering my cell. I looked up and squinted to see nothing but shining brass, dazzling in the cell's gloom. There, before me in the small room stood a Sergeant, a Lieutenant and a Major. They were overwrought with concern over my condition. One of them called me by name and said, "Are you alright?" I almost laughed myself to death at that one! All I could reply was, "Do I look alright to you guys?" "Don't worry, we're going to get you fixed up," was all he said.

At the time I had no way of knowing that my father had something to do with the sudden interest in my welfare. Apparently, after hearing my cousin's story, my dad called the Chief and was granted a visit. They patched me and I was escorted to a visitation room with a clear Plexiglas partition. I sat there, apprehensive and ashamed. I knew that any moment, my father would walk through the door. We were not allowed to make any contact. Given the situation, even a phone call would have been a relief. Soon as he entered the opposite room, I started to cry like a baby. The look of hurt, concern and disappointment on his face would be forever burnt into my memory. Through the tears, I tried to apologize but all the sorrys in the world would never be enough. I wore the bruises and scars from the beating like a mark of shame. For a man who had witnessed firsthand many victims and corpses throughout his career, he was appalled at my appearance. The tears in his eyes mirrored his feelings. I told him not to worry and he assured me that he'd do everything in his power to get me out. I felt safe then. I would soon come to know the extent of his power. Before leaving, he said, "You are so hardheaded . . . you always have to learn the hard way!" We looked into each other's eyes and volumes were spoken. In that silence, I knew that he would move heaven and earth for his son. That's what he saw staring back at him through that Plexiglas. Not some notorious, hardass criminal that needed to be locked away forever—just a scared, lonely boy who'd lost his way.

I went before the judge the following day for arraignment and plea. As I gazed at the crowd of curious onlookers, my eyes came to rest on my mother's sad and tired face. She was seated in the gallery beside my dad and next to my sister Lorna and Ralph. When our eyes met, she started to cry. The tears rolled down her cheeks and the sight broke my heart. I smiled at her and did my best to put on a brave face. I refused to let her see me cry. I felt weak and vulnerable, my legs weary and nearly buckling. I wanted to rush into her arms. To be cradled safe and warm the way it was when I was a child, comforted in her embrace and protected from the suffering of the world. The pure love that only a mother can provide. Those days seemed so far away, like shattered glass from a broken mirror, distorted and irreparable. The charges against me included burglary in the first degree, robbery in the first degree and possession of a firearm, drugs, kidnapping and maiming. I was facing 20 years to life. All this for just a lousy $3 and half a gram of pcp. I entered a plea of not guilty and bail was set at $150,000. A ridiculous sum. There's no way in hell my family could afford that. Exiting the courtroom, I took one last look at my family's faces. The smile had vanished from my face, replaced by a tight lipped frown. Lorna and Ralph said not to worry, they were already working on my release. I went back to my cell with a dim glimmer of hope. It would take nothing short of a miracle to get me out.

Sometime in the night, I heard the footsteps of the turnkey approaching. He called my name and announced that my bail had been paid. I was out of there! I couldn't believe my luck. I guess miracles do happen. I was greeted at the receiving desk by the happy faces of my family. There were hugs and kisses all around as we headed up the ramp into the warm Hawaiian night. There was the sweet smell of freedom in the air and the clear starry sky was even more prominent that evening. I felt as if a heavy blanket had been lifted off of me. And although this was just the beginning of a long hard road to be travelled, I was content to revel and live in the moment. Ralph and Lorna had come through for me big time! Not only did Ralph put up the ten percent cash retainer for my bail, he managed to do it without producing any collateral. It was no surprise that a man as resourceful as he was had a friend who owned a bail bond company. That was only the first of many miracles that would liberate me.

It was a strange feeling arriving home, knowing that my life hung in the balance. I was free, but yet I wasn't. The happiness, though joyful, would be short lived. The underlying feelings of my shame and disappointment for my parents was buried beneath the surface for now. It was the 800 pound gorilla in the room as we all gathered. Ralph lit a joint and handed it to me. My dad passed me a beer and we toasted my freedom. It was good to be home and among family. You never realize just how much they mean to you until you think you've lost them. I'd put my parents through so much shit, but here they were, standing strong next to me. There's much to be said about a parent's love for their children. This, by far, is the greatest example of such. The epitome of the parent-child relationship. Unconditional love at its finest. I was not worthy, but felt truly blessed.

My battered body had begun to reveal the effects of the beatings. Ice packs had relieved the swelling around my eyes and the lumps about my head and face, but they couldn't take away the bruising. Removing my shirt, the extent of the damage was evident—I was covered from head to toe with purple to black marks. My mother cried as she put her delicate hand to them, as if to gently smooth them away. I hugged her close. I saw the revulsion in my father's eyes. Ralph had called a professional photographer to snap some shots of the injuries. Documented proof of the excessive force and brutality I suffered at the hands of the police department. These photos would later be a key bargaining chip in my sentencing agreement. When all the excitement was over, I retired to my bedroom. I was exhausted! Laying there in the dark, waiting for sleep to come, the feelings of guilt and shame overwhelmed me and I wept. Crying myself to sleep, I slipped into peaceful slumber.

The next day, my dad summoned my cousin and our "inside man" over for a meeting. His anger was apparent by his quiet demeanor. I knew that he'd blamed my elder cousin for my involvement in the crime. He had been a troublemaker since childhood and labeled as the black sheep of the family. My father may have suspected, but not known, that my criminal activities had far surpassed my cousin's by now. It was impossible to hide the obvious fact. It was time to set the record straight, before they arrived. I looked at him and said, "There's nobody to blame but me . . . nobody forced me to do it." The realization really hit home and the truth of the matter I could see registered, by the disappointed look in his eyes. Still, didn't prevent the good ass chewing they had for being involved. They got off easy that day. If it had been years earlier, they'd have received the beating of a lifetime. Seems like they were more afraid of my father's wrath than me ratting them out. They knew that no way in hell that would happen.

The criminal justice system in this glorious nation of ours leaves little to be desired. Its cold, no nonsense approach to dealing with the criminal element of society is swift and as for being just goes, as good as it gets. That is, if you have the unlimited funds at your disposal to acquire the best legal representation available. In which case, the relative facts in the case of the accused can be influenced greatly in his favor. There is, however, a totally different slant to this unwritten rule of mine. "It's not how much you have or what you know, but who you know." Being the only son of a retired detective who was one of Hawaii's most decorated police officers has its advantages. Our family name was well known within the state's law enforcement community. My father's brother once worked for the Department of Corrections and held the rank of captain at the Oahu State Prison. He later went on to form Governor George Ariyoshi's state capital security force known as the "green shirts." I can only imagine his dismay at my behavior. He'd married my aunt, who was of Japanese descent, back in the days then their kind were just barely recovering from the attack on Pearl Harbor. She always had a high opinion of herself. What we Hawaiian's call "Ho'okano" or conceited. My cousins were always picture perfect in every way. We used to visit their fabulous home in an exclusive part of the island on Sundays. And though I got along well with my cousins, I always felt out of place. The animosity ran deep between my Mom and her sister-in-law. She used to complain about my late sister Donna's exuberant behavior when they visited. Story goes that at my sister's funeral, my mom attacked her and had to be restrained by my father. Over the years, they had become cordial with each other, but my mom had never forgiven her. The tension was palpable whenever they were in the same room. Now, she had something good to gossip about. Sorry for embarrassing you Uncle Wally, may you rest in peace. No matter what went on in the family, my father always loved you. I'd like to think that you had a hand in some way of me receiving preferential treatment over the years. Thanks for that.

The legal issues that not only I, but my family, were facing were insurmountable. To put it mildly. Thanks to Ralph's connections, I'd obtained legal counsel from one of the top criminal attorneys in the state. The cost for his services was much too high for the average person. In exchange for representing me at my pre-trial hearings and at my kidnapping trial, my mom would sign over the deed to a parcel of land that she had inherited from her mother. It broke my heart when I heard of the deal. That land had been in her family since the days when Hawaii was a monarchy. It was to be passed on to my sister and me as her legacy. All that was forever gone now because of my selfish stupidity. I watched my mother cry the day she handed the deed over to the lawyer in the courtroom. A mother's love is immeasurable.

During the trial, my parents sat hopeful and expectant. The lawyer was worth every penny and to see him work his legal prowess was magical. For some reason the couple who had been victimized in the crime had testified on my behalf. They stated that even though we were committing a crime, at no time did they feel that their lives were in danger. The female's son, who was also present at the house that night, was sick. So I had allowed her to stay with him alone in the room, away from everyone else. My compassion had saved me. I was found not guilty of the kidnapping charge. The attorney had done his job and then asked the court to be excused as counsel for all future proceedings, due to my family's inability to pay for further services. The court agreed and I was back to square one. Another miracle had been granted, which made way for the next.

Being free on bail is like being pressed together in a vise. The pressure produced from the law on one side and your false sense of freedom on the other places an enormous strain on you. The conditions of bail are usually strict and the bail bondsman watches you like a hawk. His major concern is that you show up at court for your hearings and trial. If you skip out, or run, while on bail, he runs the risk of losing everything that he put up to release you. In this case, $150,000 worth of property that he didn't have. I can see how that would make the average bail bondsman nervous. Thanks to Ralph, I didn't have to worry too much about that. His friend owned the company and was a cool, rotund black fellow, who frequently walked on the wild side. Most of the people associated with Ralph did. The only thing that I had to worry about was getting busted again for any reason. Even the smallest infraction could get my bail revoked and land me back in the pokey. The thought of ending up back in jail was scary enough to deter me from committing any more crime. However, it wasn't scary enough to stop me from doing drugs and alcohol. In fact, the idea of spending a good portion of my life behind bars caused me to get high even more. The only difference is, I did it privately, behind the closed doors of my parent's condo. My parents, knowing my dire circumstances, as usual, enabled me. Other felons out on bail often had to submit to random drug testing by the bondsman. A failed urine analysis could result in a bail forfeiture. Go directly to jail, do not collect $200. Fortunately for me, that was one less hassle I had to contend with. Looking back, there is no way I would have made it through those troubled times without getting high. But that's just the warped opinion of a dope addict.

I lived a sheltered existence for the entire time of my relative freedom. The bottom line, when all of this was said and done, I would end up in prison. The only question was for how long. My parents had given everything they had, money-wise to staunch the flow of oncoming justice from taking its course. There was no way we could come up with the cash needed to do battle with the state. Just when we thought that our situation was at its bleakest, another miracle materialized. Somehow, the prestigious law firm of Have, Aoki and Chun had heard about my case and offered their services pro bono. It was a sign straight from heaven. The stuff movies are made of. Things were looking brighter, but there was still a long way to travel.

It would soon become apparent to me the extent of my father's influence. The weight of our family name, though tarnished, was still powerful enough to be the deciding factor in the outcome of my future. I would become witness to one of the prime examples of influence and power within the government ever seen. The stuff of legend. Very few people in the world ever have the opportunity to experience, yet alone became a part of, such a covert operation. Just being privy to the information necessary to pull off a complex coup of this magnitude, could get you killed. At the very least, destroy the careers of numerous government officials. Including judges and administrators within the Department of Corrections. We, the mere lowly populace of the world, are ignorant of the realities of how our government really works. Behind the truth and justice and all that Constitution bullshit, stands a veil of surreptitious truth that we know exists, but never can prove. The old adage of "it's not what you know, but who you know" would never be more true than in this case. And the truth will make you free!

The wheels of justice were about to turn in my favor. In the middle of all this excitement, my father had entertained the thought of accepting a job from his millionaire hotel mogul cousin on the Big Island. This all depended on the outcome of my legal problem. One afternoon, my parents and I were summoned by my attorneys to discuss our options. The firm had been busy preparing my defense for the trial. They were also putting together a police brutality case against the state. I felt confident, seated there next to my parents, across the huge oak desk of those powerhouse lawyers. Both names appeared on the law firm's signs and letterhead. Evidently, my case was substantial enough for these two heavy hitters to handle personally. From all outward appearances, their professional conduct did nothing to ease the tension. Pleasantries aside, one of them said, "We have good and bad news." I opted for the good news first. They said that in light of our brutality case against the state and the evidence showing that the victims were probably drug dealers and that no one was badly hurt, the state was willing to deal. A plea bargain of sorts. Of course, I'd have to plead guilty to all the remaining charges I faced. And drop the multimillion dollar civil suit against the police. In exchange for my guilty plea, and handing over all the pictures taken of my injuries from the beatings, the state would allow me to receive a Deferred Acceptance of a Guilty plea. The deal would clear my criminal record upon completion of my sentence. It was a fabulous, one of a kind deal that was rarely offered. My lawyers themselves were amazed at the state's leniency. In all their years of practicing law, they'd never heard of such a deal. They made it clear that even if I did decide to change my plea to guilty and take the deal, the sentencing judge had the final word as to the amount of time I could spend in prison. Yes, the bad news. No ifs, ands, or buts. I will be spending time in jail. The cold hard reality hit me square in the face like a bat. I've had enough of jail to last a lifetime. "No way. I'm not going back to jail!" I ask them the alternative if we went to trial. They were willing, but did I really want to take the chance of spending the next 20 years or so in prison?

That thought made my skin crawl. "What about the lawsuit?" I questioned. They said we had a good case and in all likelihood, the state would settle out of court for a substantial amount. There it was, the bottom line. Either I could be rich and go to jail forever, or I could take the deal and "roll the dice." Throwing myself at the mercy of the court. They also mentioned that the sentencing judge was not bound by the agreement. The whole thing was just too much for me to handle. I had a week to decide before the state took the deal off the table. I'd need every minute that week to decide. I left their office sick to my stomach. I needed to get wasted!

In the long run, I took the deal. It was the way my father had persuaded me to take it that convinced me. He sat me down one day during that week of indecision when I was sober and talked to me. He said that I still had a chance at a normal life if I took the deal. We both knew that all of his dreams and mine of ever becoming a part of the law enforcement community were over. That all died the night I got arrested. It was all about damage control and survival at this point. His main concern was keeping me from doing hard time. The rest we could live with. He said that I had to get used to the fact that I was going to prison. What he feared the most was me in that prison filled with hardened criminals, even killers, that he had personally put there. He knew that they'd seek retribution.

Prisoners spend their empty days locked behind concrete walls thinking about killing those responsible for putting them there. If you can't get to that individual, the next best thing is to get to his family. Killing one is like killing the others. Sometimes it's even better. Throughout our conversation, he assured me I had nothing to worry about. That he would take care of everything. It's the way he said it that comforted me. The same way a mafia don says not to worry about things. The confidence and conviction in his voice convinced me beyond a doubt.

We met the following week with my attorneys to finalize the deal. I signed the necessary paper work to get the ball rolling and handed them the photos. They said not to worry and that they would see me before my change of plea hearing. Funny how everyone kept telling me not worry. That's the same thing they tell stage four cancer patients. I was far passed worry. I was a nervous wreck. Sticking guns in people's faces and beating the crap of them is one thing, but switching out sides of the coin reduced me to a sniveling fool. It's not even the least bit amusing when your life rests in the hands of others. Strangers you have no control over. And in all this mess of legal issues and self pity, not once had I had the decency to empathize with any of my victims. Such is the case of the self-absorbed coward, hooked on drugs with no moral values.

In the middle of all the drama, Lorna and Ralph had moved to the Big Island to enter into a huge land venture. It was a coincidence that my parents had also chosen to move there when my father accepted the position as night manager of Uncle Billy's hotel in Kona. The only thing holding them back was the outcome of my court appearance and sentencing. To appear less of a threat and menace to society, while waiting for all of this trial stuff to happen, I did two strategic things to help place me in the good graces of the court. First I applied and had got into the Kapiolani Community College Food Service program full-time. Next, I obtained gainful employment at the Victoria Station restaurant washing dishes at night. It was a way of showing the court that I could be a responsible member of society. It was a strategy that would prove to be effective. My schedule was grueling. I attended classes at the college Monday to Friday from 8 am to 4 pm, then I caught the bus to my job and washed dishes until midnight. Thank God for the tips from the waiters and waitresses after work. Not to mention the free beers they bought. Nothing like an ice cold beer after a hard day's work.

On the day I was to sacrifice my life to the state, we arrived at the courtroom early. I met with my attorneys who did their best to calm me down. My entire future was on the line. When court was called to order and my case was announced, I stood there alone on rubbery legs. I glanced over to my parents seated behind me and sought comfort from their forced smiles. The look in my father's eyes told tales of unforeseen knowledge. Known only to him at the time. After entering my guilty plea, the prosecutor entered a motion for my bail to be revoked and for me to be remanded into the custody of the Department of Corrections until my sentencing. My lawyer objected and argued the fact that I was presently in the custody of parents, the father a retired police officer. He also stated that I was presently attending college and working a full-time job. The judge agreed to let me remain free on bail until sentencing. The strategy had worked brilliantly! I was free once more. For now. My parents were overjoyed and we embraced right there in the courtroom. My lawyers were flawless in their duties and I thanked them profusely before leaving. They said to keep up the good work and not to get into trouble. There was one final obstacle to overcome. And that one was a doozy! The miracles just kept coming.

My parents moved away before my sentencing date and I was left behind to continue with my hectic life; work and school and school and work. Before leaving, they'd paid the rent on the condo and I had the place to myself. It was empty except for the mattress I slept on, a portable radio and a 13" inch black and white TV. I was so busy I barely had time alone in the empty apartment. School was a welcome relief. The courses were easy and the people were nice. On Tuesdays and Thursdays, we had a lab class that lasted the whole day and into the night. The purpose was to give the students hands-on participation in the restaurant industry. We'd prepare a prearranged menu which included appetizers, soups, salads, entrees and deserts. The food was then served to the public at reduced prices. Just like in a restaurant and our performance was graded accordingly. The students often brought cases of beer and we'd have a party before calling it a night. Although totally illegal (consuming alcohol on a college campus) my baking instructor let us slide. He even joined us. Considering that he was an alcoholic, we all got along just fine. No one knew of my legal problems or all of the bullshit I was going through. There really was no need to complicate my life any further. Besides, it was none of anyone's business.

As my sentencing hearing got closer I began to panic. The anticipation of entering the penal system had me frantic. With my family living on another island, the loneliness started to weigh heavily on me. I knew my father was doing everything humanly possible to get me out of this jam, but I felt abandoned. I called them almost everyday just to hear the reassuring sound of their voices. It was the only thing keeping me glued together. Just when I thought I couldn't go another day, my dad called and said that he wanted me to fly over to meet someone that weekend. I caught a cab and headed for the airport. I looked forward to seeing my family again. The short respite from the grind would do me some good. All the stress had caused me to abuse drugs and booze at an alarming rate. It was like I was racing to do as much junk as I could before going to prison. Feeling that perhaps I might not make it out of there. My tolerance for both had become impossibly high and I spent all of my money sedating myself, trying to numb the pain. The more I did, the more it took. As usual, there was never enough.

Seeing my parents happy faces upon arrival made all the bad feelings disappear. They looked fit and healthy and hugging them close was all the tonic I needed to lift my spirits. The hotel they worked and resided at was a storybook rendition of a tourist vision of paradise. The beautifully manicured grounds, green and flourishing, accented by the surrounding palms. I was happy to see that my parents were living in such a beautiful place.

Dad ran the hotel at night as the manager and mom worked days at the switchboard fielding calls. It was a comfortable relaxed atmosphere that agreed with their tender age. I understood why they preferred to relocate from the craziness of Honolulu. The next day, at poolside, my dad introduced me to a friend of his. The man was about the same age as my father, late fifties, gray hair and wisdom in his eyes. They had known each other for years from the department. Back in the days before politics ruled. He was currently the head of corrections in the state. And now it was plain to see the motive for me being there. The gentleman was polite and straight to the point. He rebuked me for my bad behavior and said how much he respected my dad. He told me how lucky I was for having him. With that set aside, he said he was aware that soon I'd be entering the prison system. Even though it was my first time, with the crimes that I had committed, he said I'd be going to a hardcore facility. There was no avoiding that. Once there, he'd arrange to have me moved to a safer environment. That was the only way to do it without calling too much attention to his involvement. Until I actually entered the system, his hands were tied. Sitting there, discussing my imminent doom, brought to mind the severity of my situation. The talk had shaken me to the core. Before leaving, the man reminded me of how lucky I was and reassured me that everything would be taken care of. Alone again with my father, I broke down and cried. He hugged me and said, "don't worry son, everything's going to be alright." I believed him with all my heart, but that couldn't stop my fear. And the miracles kept coming.

I returned home to the madness of my temporary life and an empty apartment. Sentencing was a few weeks away and my fate would be sealed. It would occur two weeks before the semester at school ended. My attorneys said they would ask the sentencing judge to defer execution of my sentence until school was over. It was a long shot, but no harm in trying. And that's where my father's influence came into play the most. And the greatest miracle of all was about to happen. Right before I left to fly back to Oahu, my father had mentioned that I'd be facing Judge Walter Heen for sentencing. He said this was the judge's last year on the bench and that he would be retiring. He also said the judge was a very good friend and that he owed him a favor. I was stunned. He said it so matter of fact. It sounded so casual, as if he'd be asking the judge to fix a parking violation. Believe me, this was by no means even close to it. It was an incredible debt to collect on. Throughout the years, I've seen many things take place behind closed doors, some of which I had been a party to. But this was, by far, the greatest yet. It was all that kept me from falling to pieces as the days passed too quickly.

Came the day of sentencing, my family was all there to support me. My mom looked tired and the worry showed in her eyes. My father said to relax and that everything was set. I found this whole nightmare hard to believe. Being in a courtroom is frightening, especially if your ass is on the line. My stomach was doing somersaults and I wanted to throw up. I watched the judge sentence the man before me to 99 years for his crimes. I nearly collapsed. The bailiff read my name from the docket and I stood there trembling. The judge acknowledged my presence with a stern look and said, "I know your father. He was a fine police officer . . . what happened to you?" I choked up and was at a loss for words, but did my best to answer. And the rest was as my father had said. The judge accepted my guilty pleas under the DAG agreement. He then said due to the nature of the crime and the use of a firearm, he had no choice but to sentence me to a prison term. If it weren't for the gun charge, I would have walked. Then he boomed, "I hereby sentence you to ninety days in the custody of the State Department of Corrections and five years probation. Don't get into anymore trouble." He then hit the gavel and said, "Next." I was so caught up in my fear that I thought I heard him say ninety YEARS. My lawyer reached out to congratulate me and I was out of my trance. They had also gotten the judge to delay the execution of sentencing until school let out. I had thirty days of freedom before I had to surrender. The prosecutor was exasperated—he wanted me locked up immediately. I turned to see the smile stretched across my father's face. My mother cried, but her relief was evident. Her son would not be spending a good portion of his life behind bars. Standing there, embracing them, was like winning the lottery. I had gotten my life back. The scary thought of entering the prison system seemed trivial compared to the victory we'd just won. I put all of that in the back of my mind and celebrated our triumph.

My father looked at me and said, "that's it boy, I can't help you anymore. From now on you're on your own." The finality in which he'd spoken said it all. He'd cashed in every favor and then some, to save me. If I tried the rest of my life, I could never repay him. I hugged him tight and said, "Thanks dad. I love you . . . I'm so sorry." And at that moment, I really and truly was. I meant every word, but no matter how sincere, the evil demons that resided deep within me knew me better. Those demons would once again come to call and demand their due.

The school semester ended much too quickly. So did the lease on the condo. I had two weeks left before I had to surrender with no place to stay. I went out on the road for one last party train. I'd saved most of my money, so there was no need to keep working. I stayed with friends and pretty much moved from place to place. I drank and got high off whatever I could get my hands on. The days ran into one continuous stupor. I woke mornings in strange places, forgetting how I'd gotten there—next to women I never knew. I often thought about fleeing, but after everything my family had gone through, I couldn't bring myself to do it. I'd rather take my chances behind bars before disappointing them again. I concentrated on my future instead of the present. I had my whole life ahead of me, why compound the damage by doing something rash?

I decided to go back to college after doing my 90 days in lock-up. Things wouldn't be easy for me when I got out, but I had already done the school and work thing before. Why not again? I could finally fulfill my dream of getting a college education. Maybe not in the area I originally had chosen, but a degree none the less. I mentioned the idea to my parents over the phone. They were less enthused than I expected. They were too worried about my survival in the urban jungle environment to consider it. They wanted to have me relocate to them on the Big Island and work at the hotel. I already had a job waiting for me helping to renovate a wing of the hotel. The place would be undergoing a complete make-over around the time I was getting paroled. I didn't have the heart to protest. After what I had put them through, I didn't have the right. So I agreed.

My last day of freedom was spent cruising the streets, taking long looks at places that I knew I'd miss. My favorite haunts. Dives that I loved to eat at and out of the way hides where we congregated. The very last stop was the place I loved the most. A place I loved and admired from my childhood. The beach. I had to feel the cool ocean breeze on my face for what could be the last time. The sand between my toes brought back memories of my youth. When I ran barefoot along the white sandy beaches of the Waianae coast. The beautiful blue Pacific calling to me. The soothing rhythms of the waves breaking against the shore washed away my fears. Carrying them aloft within the calm peaceful reaches of my mind. I could exist here forever. Dreaming of better days, wondering what was to come. For now, I felt content, though the fear of uncertainty loomed close by. I smoked a final joint there among the tranquil surroundings and readied myself for the next step in my life. A step that would prove to be the hardest test of my manhood ever. All at once I was filled with elation over life. It was good to be alive and I wanted to live. And no matter what it took, I'd make sure that I survived this coming chapter.

I was dropped at the gateway to the Halawa Jail facility located in a lush green valley. The endless chain link fences, topped with barbed wire were a daunting sight. Intimidating. My heart began to race and I broke out into a fearful sweat. My palms were clammy and my breath came in short spurts. My legs went weak as I approached the guard shack at the entrance. I gave the occupant my name and he checked me off his list. Opening the gate, I made my way up the hill along the yellow painted line that he directed me to follow. I thought of the Wizard of Oz and how Dorothy danced along and sang as she followed her yellow brick road. Each step I took up the path, my footsteps became heavier and heavier. I thought that my legs would freeze up altogether at any moment. There was nowhere to hide. The nightmare had become a reality. Nothing could prepare me for the world that I was about to enter. I thought about my family. How much I missed them. I prayed to God for comfort. I was all alone. You never fully realize how much the idea of freedom means until it's taken away. It's the scariest feeling in the world, but it was time to put on my game face and look mean and menacing. That'll be a tough act at this point.

Chapter 12

When prison walls surround you

That long walk up the hill was the longest of my life. I know now how those condemned prisoners who faced execution felt when they walked to the gallows. Dead Man Walking! Maybe a trifle dramatic on my part, but none the less my feelings at the time. For all I knew, this could be the end of my life. The anticipation of the unknown was killing me. I could barely move. It took all of my strength to put one foot in front of the other. Reaching the top, I was greeted by the prying eyes of the inmate populace busy working at various jobs. They all stopped to stare me down. Oh great! Fresh meat! And that's exactly what their stares said. It chilled my blood and the hairs on the back of my neck stood on end. Among the curious pack I recognized a familiar face. I called out to him and he acknowledged me with a wave. Not even a shaka sign—the local universal greeting. It's commonly used to show another that he's welcome or cool. Although I'd only met this guy a time or two, I knew his older brother well. We played on the same championship football team in high school. His father was an infamous underworld figure who was accused of running a heroin ring. His son took the rap for his dad and ended up in here instead. Solid as a rock. I'd do the same if it was me. I hoped that he would remember how I used to go to his parents' house and get stoned with his brother. I could use an ally in this place. From the way he whispered with the other prisoners, the word on me was already out. Before I even set foot in the door the prison grapevine would be red hot. And I would have the pleasure of being the topic of conversation. Now the enemy had the advantage. So much for my down low entrance.

Entering the main building, I was directed to the admissions office, or intake. Hi, checking in, Presidential suite please. I was then escorted to the laundry to pick up my linens and blue denim wardrobe. Then, downstairs into the bowels of the prison. To the lower levels where my cell and home for the next, who knows how long, awaited me. I was escorted down the dingy hall amid the cat calls and jeers of my fellow brethren. It was the most humiliating and uncomfortable feeling I'd ever experienced. I was subjected to the worst verbal vulgarities on earth. Called every derogatory word and phrase imaginable. I put my head down and stared directly at the floor. The guard did nothing to deter the ruckus. He even laughed at some of the taunts. As luck would have it, my cell was located at the very end of the hallway. After running gauntlet, I was rattled and exhausted. Opening the cell door, the turnkey locked the door behind me and said, "Welcome to Halawa Jail!" The loud slam of the door jarred me out of my skin.

The cell consisted of three separate areas, two dormitory sections adjacent to a dayroom. I stared directly at the latrine situated at the far end of the room. It stood there in the open without partitions or doors to conceal it. Like some Greek statue to be admired. The showers, located in the open area beside it, were the next disturbing feature of my luxurious accommodations. Obviously, modesty and inhibitions were cast aside here. The thoughts of gang rape and homosexuality flashed instantly through my mind. If I ever got the chance again, I'd never gawk at a beautiful woman in public the same way. I was jerked back to the present by the stares of my cellmates. Five in all. I hoped they had their lunch. They approached in a group and I prepared for the worst. The beating they'd put on me could never match the one given by the cops. The only difference here, there'd be no one around to stop them. I'd take a few of them with me for sure before I went down. One by one, they began to introduce themselves, rather than sticking me with a shiv. I tried my best not to show the relief on my face for fear they'd see my weakness. Can't say that I felt very welcome, but it was better then a sharp stick in the eye.

One of them showed me to the bunk area. I chose a bed on the bottom rack. Closest to the floor in case I had to do some fancy footwork. The last thing I needed was to be thrown from the top bunk in the middle of the night. At least on the bottom, I could jump out quickly and hit the ground running. The drawback to that was the predators had easy access to me. Well, you can't have everything. I noticed a dark skinned individual seated alone at the table in the common area. He was the only one that didn't approach me to introduce himself. He appeared older than the rest of convicts. I got a strange vibe from him. I'm not sure what it was, but I knew it wasn't good. Finishing unpacking and making my bed, I made my way to the dayroom area to watch TV. The set was in the hallway fronting the cell next to a huge fan. No sooner had I sat down to watch the news, then the strange fellow approached and sat next to me. He stuck his hand out and said, "hi, I'm Gypsy Jack . . . you want to see something trippy?" We shook and I said, "why not." He then took a long sewing needle that he produced from thin air and stuck it through his forearm. "Whoa!" I was stunned. He held it up to me so I could get a better look and just when I thought the show was over, he pulled it out and said, "that's nothing, check this out." He then pulled his penis out of the side of his shorts and plunged the needle right through it. "How do you like that?" he asked. I jumped back in horror. I felt as if I'd just been kicked in the balls. The dude was certifiably nuts. Scared the living daylights out of me. I had landed in a cell with a bunch of crazy people. I'd sleep with on eye open tonight. I can't get Gypsy Jack's face out of my mind. The way he smiled with pleasure at his performance. This world is full of freaks. I was still in one piece and that was the main thing.

I learned the prison hierarchy and what being the low man on the totem pole was all about. As the old saying goes, shit always runs down hill and lands on the person at the bottom. No sooner had I began to kick back and relax on my bunk, a beefy white dude walked up to me, handed me a broom, and said, "Clean the cell area!" If this had been anywhere other than here, I would have jumped up and whooped his ass. Then I noticed the rest of the gang, hanging out close by, smoking cigarettes. Just waiting to attack. I've had my share of beatings, so I complied. I guess my willingness to go along got me accepted. The atmosphere lightened and the boys started to loosen up. No matter how compliant you seem to be, this is a place of predators. Where the strong take full advantage of the weak. You either become a wolf or a sheep for the slaughter. I had no intention of letting anybody punk me, however scared I was. I'd fight to the end before I let that happen. Comes a time in this prison environment when you have to do just that. To prove yourself a wolf. You don't have to look for trouble in this place, trouble comes looking for you.

That night, while shooting the shit with the guys, that buffed up white guy started throwing karate kicks to my head. He was getting a little too close for comfort so I told him to chill out. He didn't take to kindly to my protest and said, "What you going to do about it?" The rest of guys spread out to make room for the inevitable fight. I'd have to make quick business of this guy and be ready for the next one. I noticed that this Chuck Norris wannabe had one flaw in his technique. A weakness to his form when throwing his head kicks. He had a habit of turning his head. You never turn your head away from your opponent in a fight. Even an idiot knew that. He kept throwing those kicks and taunting me. I'd had enough. He threw a kick and turned his head again. I just blocked it, stepped in and swept his other leg. I slammed him to the floor and grabbed him by the throat with my free hand. He turned purple and I let him go. The guys stood there in shock, their eyes bugging out. My Judo skills had kicked in just when I needed them. I readied for the rest of the pack to attack, but nothing happened. None of them were prepared for what they had just witnessed. I helped the guy up and told him that I didn't want any trouble. He shook my hand and asked if I could teach him a few moves. We became instant friends. Nobody bothered me from that moment on. We even took turns cleaning up. Still, you can't trust anyone.

Now if the rest of my stay in this awful place could transition as smoothly as that, I'd stand a good chance of making it out of there alive. Only time would tell. One day, making my way to the chow hall, I happened to see a guy from my grade school days. He and I were fierce competitors in the fifth and sixth grades along with another bully. We'd fight almost on a daily basis to see who would hold the title of "bull" of the school. A tradition among the males in our country town of Waianae. We'd meet before school started between the portable classrooms and fight. Whoever beat the crap out of the other held the title for the day. Then, after school we'd meet again and try our luck once more. There were times when we'd fight each other back to back to find a winner. Or I'd fight one guy in the morning and the other in the afternoon. This went on throughout elementary school. We all eventually became good friends and made a pact to stick together when we reached the intermediate school level. Which we did. Now here he was locked up, standing in the chow line, passing opposite me in the hallway. Our eyes locked and he smiled that big toothy grin of his. Mike was a huge Hawaiian guy who stood about 6'3" and weighed in at around 240 pounds. All of it solid muscle. He was a tough no nonsense guy and good with his hands. Rumor had it that he had gained quite a reputation behind prison walls as a strong arm. We shook hands as we passed and he said, "I heard you were coming. Don't worry about anything, no one going mess with you." And he was gone. Those words echoed in my head and were all I needed to hear. And with that, my stay in the joint was set. How far his reach was remained to be seen. The guys who saw our exchange of friendship were convinced. One of them even commented to me after chow, "Hey, how do you know Mike? You better be careful of that guy, he's a scary dude!" I told him about how we'd met and he shook his head, bewildered.

Things were going pretty well and I settled into an amicable existence. The everyday routine of prison life is dull and repetitive. There's really nothing much to do but read, watch TV, work out and write letters home. So far, I'd gotten along okay with the rest of the cons. There were no more challenges of male dominance in the house. I even began training with the haole guy. Apparently Mike had been good to his word. There was, however, a day when my paranoia got the best of me.

I'd fallen asleep in the afternoon, before chow, and woke with a start. The cell was deserted and the front door was wide open. I jumped from my rack and chills ran through me as the hairs on my neck stood. I walked to the hall and noticed that there wasn't a single soul in sight. Not in the corridor or in the cells. The whole thing smelled fishy to me. I felt like I was being set up for a hit. I ran to the chow hall, fearing for my life.

That's where I found everyone else. Sitting down, eating their lunch. The last time I had that feeling was when I stood guard outside the limo at the airport protecting a witness. It was no less frightening now as then. I never fell asleep around chow time again.

The rumor mill began sending messages our way that a vicious killer was being released from the special holding unit, aka the hole, sometime this week. They said he was headed our way. Everyone was walking on eggshells in expectation of our new celly. We were all scared to death. This guy had a bad rep and was mean as hell. No one was safe from this type of shark. The rest were considered gold fish in a barrel next to this guy. Came the day of his arrival, the whole gang huddled together to welcome the gigantic specimen of a human being into our midst. No doubt to garner favor by kissing his ass. I stood back and continued with my workout routine, eyeing him through the bars. I tried not to look too obvious. The guy was super huge. About 6'6" and well over 300 pounds. His name was Kepa, but I called him Kema. He moved into the cell next to the common room by himself. No one argued. I looked up in time to see him staring at me. He sat there unpacking and watching me workout. His stare was like hot coals being heaped upon me. It made me self-conscious and distressed. I've seen wild animals eye their dinner in just that way. If this guy decided to target me, there would be no stopping him. If cornered, I'd have no choice but strike first and hit a vital area, hoping he'd go down right away. My mind was swimming with defensive scenarios to save my life. And possibly prevent me from becoming someone's girlfriend. Ain't no way that was going to happen. I averted my eyes trying not to appear as if I noticed his greedy stares. Maybe I was imagining the whole thing? Maybe I was being paranoid? Better safe than sorry, to be on guard than relax and get blindsided.

Just when I began to think that all of this was my mind playing tricks on me, he walked over in my direction. The closer he got the larger he looked. I mean, this was a monster of a man. He may have been fat but he was solid enough to break me in two with little effort. I continued my workout, praying that he detoured in another direction. He sat down on the bed across from me. I stopped doing pushups, got to my feet, and took a step back. Just in case I had to make a break for it. The rest of the guys scattered for cover. Here was this incredibly scary man less than six feet away from me, sizing me up. I remained silent. Afraid to even speak. Fearful that I'd irritate him. To my surprise, he said in a thick gravelly voice, "You workout often? I was watching your routine, looks pretty good. I got to lose some weight . . . maybe you can help me out?" I was blown away. We began talking and I showed him some exercises. Though a little skeptical as to his real motive, I was relieved. For now. While we were in the middle of our conversation, a guard called him over to the bars and handed him a sandwich-sized, brown paper bag. He walked to his bunk, sat down and dumped the contents onto the bed. He called me to come over. Hesitant but curious, I went. There, spread upon his blanket was an array of drugs. There was marijuana, heroin and all kinds of pills. I was amazed. That was a whole lot of dope to have in prison. Was I seeing things or did that corrections officer really give him drugs? Sure looked like it. Not only was this guy scary, he was well connected. That made him even more dangerous. If a guard was willing to do this for the guy, he'd have no problem looking the other way if something went down. He asked if I want any of this stuff. I wavered for a moment, wondering about the cost. Money I had, but it was other payment that worried me. He saw the look on my face and said, "Don't worry. I ain't no fag!" That's what they all say. Just then, I smelled the familiar sweet aroma coming from over in the corner. The guys were busy smoking joints off to the side. It sure smelled good. Kema handed me a few joints and said, "Here, help yourself to anything else." Then he asked the strangest thing. "You related to the captain that worked in the old block at Oahu Prison." My blood ran cold. Before I could answer, he said, "I knew a guy with the same name as you used to work there . . . he was a great guy, did me a few solids." I blurted out loud, "That was my Uncle Wallace." And with that, it was like a magic door had been unlocked. The guy opened his locker, which was filled to the hilt with everything imaginable. Cigarettes, candy, cookies, you name it, he had it. Each of us had a stand-up metal locker to store our clothes and commissary. The kind you find in high school. This guy had two, both filled to the top with stuff. He asked me what kind of cigarette I smoke, reaches in and grabs two cartons of Kool's and handed them to me. I protested at first, but he insisted. Didn't want to make the huge guy angry, so I accepted. He also gave me a shit load of junk food. I was flabbergasted.

I couldn't even begin to think about how he had known who I really was. After all, this was prison. 'Nuff said. He then reached down into his stash of goodies and gave me two number 10 valiums. As I shook his hand and thanked him exuberantly, he said, "If anyone messes with you, let me know . . ." And the miracles kept coming.

If no one screwed with me before this, they sure didn't now. I was, from that moment on, pretty much protected and having the time of my life. I'd climbed to nearly the top of the prison hierarchy, literally overnight. It was a relief to still be in one piece at this point—you can't do any better time than this. I was getting high on a regular basis and enjoying my prison experience. Kema and I worked out regularly and he even started to diet. I thought about how fortunate I was. Things could have easily gone the other way for me. If the situation stayed as is, I'd have no problem doing my ninety days. Easy street. I'd forgotten all about my meeting on the Big Island with that Department of Correction head. About the time I was beginning to think that I was stuck here (only half way into my second week), a guard appeared at the bars and said the Warden wanted to see me. I was ushered into his office and stood at attention while he spoke excitedly to someone on the phone. After hanging up, he looked at me, shook his head and said, "I don't know what the hell's going on or who you know, but I just got a call that your life is in danger. You got ten minutes to pack your shit, you're being moved!" Looked like the powers that be had spoken. The wheels had started to turn. "Where am I going?" "They're moving you to the main Police Station in Honolulu as a trustee." Off I went. The bewildered look on the Warden's face was more precious than gold. The guard escorted me back to my cell with orders not to let me out of his sight. Not moments before this went down, Kepa and I had smoked a joint. Now the adrenaline pumping through my veins had sobered me up a bit. I said my goodbyes to the gang, but saved my large, newly acquired friend for last. He grabbed me in a bear hug, lifting me off the floor, sad to see me go. I'd made a good friend in him. I knew that I'd never see him again because I didn't intend on coming back. He shook my hand and I felt the pills in his huge paw. His eyes danced with pleasure as he told me to have a good life. I swallowed them on my way down the hall.

I was driven away to the main city cell block at the Honolulu Police Department. It was the same one I was taken to for medical treatment for my beatings just after my arrest. As I made my way through the booking desk in the receiving area, I couldn't help but notice all the cops. They were coming and going, but none even gave me more than a glance. I was part of the furniture as far as they were concerned. They thumbed a button and an electric switch buzzed me into the cell block proper. There, I was met by Officer Chong, the turnkey who we lovingly referred to as "quick draw Mcgraw." He was an asshole who enjoyed making life hard for the prisoners on his watch. Rumor had it that when he was a patrolman, he had a bad habit of drawing his firearm too often. To insure the safety of the public they are sworn to protect, he was given a new assignment. I guess his attitude towards us convicts was due to losing his gun-toting privileges. He showed me to my new home through a steel door that was never locked, next to his desk. Upon entering, I was introduced to the other three trustees who lived there. Each had a specific job to help run the cell block. Howard, who'd been there the longest, about a year, worked in the kitchen. Russell and Mike were the floor boys who cleaned the puke and shit up after the overnighters. It was a rotten job, but someone had to do it. And yours truly was responsible for setting up the orange cones on the roadway to make room for the officers coming on duty for the 3-11 shift. The place was lacking adequate parking for all the personal cars so this was the solution. I also pumped the gas at the station's garage for the motor patrolmen. The civilian workers filled the blue and whites and motorbikes in the mornings and topped them off at night. It was a cruise job and I was the only one allowed out of the block. I looked forward to those afternoon bouts of fresh air and warm sunshine. There was a small park on the corner where I'd lay the cones out. I'd kick back and relax on the soft grass, watching the traffic pass, waiting for the last officer to hit the streets for duty. It was refreshing and the shade from the tall trees was heavenly. I was free and unattended for those brief moments each day. There was no easier way to do time anywhere in the state. Every inmate wanted the position. But only the best behaved prisoner in the system was rewarded with the job. Some waited years and worked their tails off to get it. Now, here I was, not two weeks into my sentence, living the good life. Miraculous!

The living area was a single large room about 20x50 feet with a separate space for showers and toilets. We each had a single bunk located in our own little space, away from the next guy. There was a color TV, a stereo and a ping pong table. All the comforts of home. It was sweet time. What were the chances of this happening? I owed it all to my dad. All of us here were short-timers, finishing off the remainder of a stretch. Out of the four, I was the only one without a criminal history. I fell into line quickly and tried not to make waves. They gave me the nickname "Geese" because I looked Portuguese. We all got along great. On the weekends we'd order takeout from the Chinese restaurant, pizza parlor or KFC down the street. Life was great! My parents would fly down on the weekends and we'd picnic in the park on the corner. Being away from my family was difficult and those weekend visits were uplifting. On Sundays, before they flew back, my dad would buy me six packs of beer and snacks. They'd drive through the pump, hand me the bag, say their goodbyes and drive away. The two civilian workers were cool as shit and we'd become good friends. They'd watch the pump while I went to the back of the garage and got smashed. I even kept the beers in the motorcycle cops' ice box. Since it was a Sunday, the place was slow and deserted. Every once in a while, me and the butchy chick that worked there too, would sit on the bench next to the pump and smoke a joint. We'd have a blast laughing and watching the cars pass. She was a good person and understood my plight. Yeah, I know your probably asking yourself by now, "Didn't that dummy learn his lesson?" What can I say? When you're an alcoholic and drug addict, placed in an environment where you have access to indulge in your vices, you go for it. And as for my parents catering to my habits, you should know better than to even go there.

Being that sorry individual that can't control his urges to partake of illegal substances, anytime, any place or anywhere, it's only natural that I'd be on the lookout for the opportunity to obtain those substances. Especially when they're laid out before you on a silver platter. All mine for the taking. Let me explain. On one beautiful, sunshiny day, while making my way home after a hard day's work at the pumps, I happened to notice the sweet smell of marijuana lingering in the air. The place had the distinctive aroma of a freshly cut patch. I looked down at the ramp that led to the entrance to the cell block and saw all these buds laying there. Must have been hundreds of them, just lying there! I looked around to see if anyone was watching me. I then proceeded to pick them up and stuff them into my shoes. They were green and sticky and of pretty decent quality. Standing at the booking desk entrance, I waited to be buzzed in. The place was crawling with cops! Change of watch just ended and everyone was busy preparing for their shift. The smell of green pot, wafting from my work boots was so pungent, I seriously thought about turning around and scratching the whole idea. My heart fluttered in my chest. Then, the loud click of the door opening. Last chance. I walked in, eyeing the room casually even as I felt guilty as sin. Probably looked it too. They hardly ever searched me thoroughly, most of the time they just patted me down quickly. I placed my hands on the holding cell bars and assumed the search position. I hoped that with all the busy confusion, someone would notice me and say beat it. The whole squad room smelled like pot, so even if someone did frisk me, they'd never smell the weed. Out of the crowd, someone called my name and said, "You're good." And just like that, I walked right past a room full of cops with two shoes full of pot. About half an ounce worth. The irony of it, what made the whole thing laughable, was the pot was courtesy of the boys in blue themselves. Thanks to the marijuana eradication program, special units with the use of helicopters would comb the targeted areas searching for the pot plants. Back then, growers would use the cover of the sugar cane fields to hide their crops. When discovered, the pot would be yanked or chopped out, loaded into dump trucks and brought to the main station. There, they were off-loaded and taken to the Narcotics division and weighed. The whole process of unloading and reloading resulted in the magic buds appearing for me to find. Perhaps if you guys hadn't beat the crap out of me I'd have a slight twinge of conscience about abusing my trustee status.

There was never a shortage of drugs. Whenever my stash got low, a friend would visit during the weekend and bring me some more. We had contact visits at the ramp parking lot area, unsupervised. So passing stuff was never a problem. The visitors were always nervous with all the cops moving about. With all the training they undergo, they never once gave us a second look. We usually smoked at night when Officer Chong went home and Officer Mitchell worked. He was a lot more mellow. When he found out that his dad and mine were on the force together, and friends, he never bothered me. He's even given us access to the kitchen at night to raid it for snacks. That's why it was a shame when we broke his trust over a stupid incident.

It all started when Russell begged me to ask the desk sergeant for permission to go outside and help me set up the cones during watch change. While sitting in the park waiting for the last car to hit the streets, we noticed this tall lanky white dude carrying a brown paper bag walking towards us. Without the slightest hesitation, the guy sat next to us on the grass and said "hey, you guys want to buy some pot?" Russ and I just looked at each other, dumfounded. Didn't this guy know who we were? Apparently not. We asked him to show us the goods and he proceeded to dig bags of weed out of his package. There was no shame in his game! We had already decided to rip the guy off from the moment he made his sales pitch. The problem was how to do it without drawing too much attention while doing so. After all, we were in the middle of a public park with people all around and just two hundred feet from the police station. If we scared the guy and he yelled out, our goose was cooked. Just when I was about to snatch the bag, he got spooked somehow. It was as if he had suddenly remembered a prior appointment. He stood up abruptly and said he had to split, but he'd be back in ten. I don't think so! What was the chance of that happening? It was already a miracle, that out of the entire island, with the thousands of places and thousands of people to choose from, he landed in this exact spot. Right in our laps! And before we could do anything about it, the guy turned and walked away. We looked at each other and swore up and down. Playing the blame game accusing ourselves for being too stupid to make a move. We sat there sick, thinking about the missed opportunity. Frustrated! Just when we were getting ready to leave, I saw the guy walking towards us. Talk about chance, what would be the odds of that? We made a quick plan. I told Russ that I'll grab an ounce of weed from the bag and walk away. He'll tell the guy that I was a hardcore criminal and that his best option was to take the loss and split. I thought about taking the whole bag but that for sure would make him chase after me. He'd think twice if I left him most of his stash. The guy sat down next to us, opened the bag and asked what we needed. I asked for an ounce and as casually as he handed it to me, I stood up, shoved it in my pocket, told him thanks and walked away. I could hear him protest and I turned to look. I saw him stand up and run out of the park. Russell sat there laughing and I knew we'd done it. Now came the hard part. Where to put all this weed? I couldn't risk taking the whole bag through the cell block. I started sweating and began to panic. I kept walking. I saw the garage to my left and without thinking, headed for the traffic cops bathroom and locker room area. I walked in and listened for signs of life. The place was empty. I entered a stall and started taking some of the weed out and stuffing it in my shoes. All the while, I listened for the door to swing open. My heart was beating a mile a minute. The last thing I needed was to get busted with all this shit. And in a police locker room. They'd have my ass on a stake for sure. I exited the stall and searched frantically for a hiding place for this monkey on my back. I looked down and saw a space between the bottoms of the lockers. I crouched down and pried my fingers into the small crack and I lifted with all my might. It was hard but I managed to fit the bag beneath it. The place smelled of pot. So did my shoes. If anyone walked in at that moment, I was dead! Just as I stood up to walk out, the door flung open. There in the doorway stood an officer. He was a menacing figure dressed in his motorcycle outfit, with the boots and helmet, wearing those mirrored shades. He stood there not two feet away from me, smoking on a cigarette. After being startled out of my wits, the sight of him puffing on that smoke was a sign from heaven. He said what's up as I walked past him. I nearly shit myself!

Now that was just the beginning of my troubles. It's when I started handing out joints to the others that the real problem happened. The trouble with convicts and being locked up in an atmosphere where the alpha male, big man persona, can't help but take over an individual's character; they're bound to do stupid things. I knew the moment Howard the kitchen trustee asks me if he could give a friend of his a few joints, it was a bad idea. The guy was a career criminal who was recently arrested and was being housed in the cell block awaiting arraignment. I advised him against it but left it up to him. He said if anything went wrong, he'd take the jerk. That night, while relaxing and watching the tube, Mitchell opened the door and told Howard and me to meet him in the kitchen. By the tone of his voice, we knew something was up. I looked at Howard and said, "I told you not to give Walter the shit." We entered the kitchen and the first thing I saw was the two joints on the table. The look on Mitchell's face said it all. He was totally bummed out. We sat down across from him looking guilty as shit and he said, "Which one of you gave Walter the joints?" The dumbass had got caught smoking and ratted us out. I don't know how my name got mentioned but that didn't matter at this point. Howard, the man he was, took the blame. He was a head trustee and had another year to do before his release. This infraction would get him sent back to Halawa to finish his sentence. I sat there stoic, relieved that I was off the hook. Besides, it was his fault in the first place. If he hadn't played the big man part we wouldn't be in this mess. Howard looked at me as Mitchell chewed his ass out. His eyes were sad, questioning and expectant. Guilt overwhelmed me at that point and I spoke up, "I gave Howard the weed." Dumbass! It was a stupid thing to do, but it was the right thing. The relief showed on Howard's face. We would both take the burn. My solidarity was forever sealed in that instant. The idea of going back to Halawa on a new charge and violating my plea agreement didn't appeal to me. It was too late now to reverse. Mitchell turned his attention to me disconcerted that I'd have anything to do with this. He went off! "You should know better . . . I trusted you . . . blah, blah, blah." When he was done ranting, we both told him we'd pack our stuff and be ready for our trip back to Halawa. He then asked it there was any more dope in the house. I said yes and he wanted to know how much. I lied and said a couple more joints. I thought about that bag under the lockers and snapped back to the present. He went off again. When it was over, he looked at the two of us and said, "that's bullshit . . . get out of my sight!" I stared at the two joints on the table and ask him what about those joints? He looked at me and said, "What joints?" Howard and I looked at each other, caught up in our indecision, wondering at his true intentions. I reached over, grabbed the joints off the table and walked out. Fearing he'd change his mind and come after, we went to our house and began smoking up whatever dope we had left in the house. We were stoned out of our minds. Howard was beyond words and grateful for saving his ass. He heard Mitchell say in the middle of his ravings, "If it weren't for your father's friendship, you'd be history." The expected goon squad never showed up. We'd dodged another bullet. I couldn't help but feel a twinge of guilt for breaking the trust between me and Mitchell. He was a great guy and deserved better from me. Things were never the same between us and soon after he was promoted to motor patrol driving blue and whites.

That left us to the mercy of Chong. The guy who took Mitchell's place at night was alright but could never be as cool as he was. Anyone was better than Officer Chong though. He was worse than a slave driver. Once, he made us scrub the entire cell block on hands and knees. He made us use bleach and Ajax together which we were too stupid to know could, and almost did, kill us. Yeah, he got a good laugh at that one. Every chance we had to get one over on him, we took. We'd pretend to be sweeping the hallways, then when we heard him snoring at his desk, we'd sneak into the women's side of the block and coax them into sexual favors. Most were prostitutes or drug addicts who got a kick out of it. Always made me nervous, looking back at that small one-way mirrored window. You never knew if there was a matron staring back at you. Made it hard to concentrate. Only the brave, manly Howard and I would chance it. Wasn't long until Chong overstepped his boundaries and tripped himself up. He thought that his power over us was absolute. All of that came to a screeching halt when he made us (as punishment for something) paint the whole cell block with just a small brush. We had the last laugh on that one. What he failed to consider was that the care and maintenance of any City and County building fell under the City's maintenance division. The desk sergeant showed up looking for a prisoner and saw us covered in blue paint. He went crazy on Chong! Wasn't long before he was transferred out and our life was bliss.

I counted down the days I had left. I spent the weekends at the park with my mom, picnicking. I'd given up getting drunk or high toward the end so as to not risk blowing my release. I got off giving away free gas to my father's friends instead. Officers who used their own vehicles for duty had a weekly gas allowance. Each was tallied according the distances they travelled to and from work and during their shifts. Some of them went over their quota for the week and couldn't fill their tanks. That's why some cops invented this ingenious device to help them change their odometers. Basically it was a motor that attached to the back of the car's odometer via a cable. The motor was plugged into the car's cigarette lighter as a power source and ran up the mileage. Even with an electric motor, it took hours to reach the desired numbers. Don't ask me how I knew all this. And I don't think you could do it with the cars today. That whole unit is inaccessible, welded shut to prevent cheating. Whenever someone I recognized drove up and had a limited amount to pump, I'd shut the pump off after a few gallons then start again, topping them off. Somebody's going to be in trouble when the pump readings don't match up, but by then I'll be long gone. See ya later!

I must admit that my time spent in lock-up wasn't as traumatizing as I envisioned it would be. You could say that it was more of a summer camp. It was, however, none the less frightening at first. Thankfully, I wasn't exposed to the more vicious aspects of prison society. I have a lot of people to thank on that account. Mainly my father. I never would have survived the ordeal without his intervention. I couldn't begin to imagine how doing years of my life in such an environment would be. I hoped I'd never find out. But the future holds true to no one. Besides the obvious regrets I have, there are but a few minor things that I look back on and sigh. The first was the passing of my great-grandmother, whom I never new existed. She was the pastor and founder of a Hawaiian church. She was pure Hawaiian, a rarity in this day and age. In her nineties, she went to rest with the Lord while I was incarcerated. I was granted permission to attend her burial and was a pallbearer along with the others of my generation. It struck a cord in me as to my ancestral heritage and what it was to be Hawaiian. I wish that I could have gotten to know her better. The next was that, though given the opportunity, I decided against returning to college. My need to be close to my parents following my release was much greater than my desire to pursue a food service career. It's a shame because I had a natural talent for cooking. Brought about, no doubt, by my younger years spent under my beloved mom's tutelage. Often, when people go through a traumatic experience in life that leads them down a path of cold reality, a change occurs. The result is a sobering slap in the face that leaves a person's sense of self lost and confused. You're filled with indecision and your need to be with family supersedes everything else. We seek the comfort and assurance from those we trust, and have always trusted, the most. We return to our roots . . . to our family.

And as the buzzer sounded for the final time in my life, I walked out the door and into the warm Hawaiian sunshine. I breathed the air of freedom and was embraced by the man who had made it all possible . . . my father. He had journeyed to bring his son home. Home to a place that was new. Change would be good for everyone. Where we could all cleanse our souls and start a new way of life. Hope for the future was bright. But, after all, life is a mystery that holds promises to no one.

Except maybe to those who control and build it. In that regard, we are all equal and are afforded the same chances to excel at greatness. Only the people smart enough to make the right decisions while the rest of us . . . we go on to repeat our careless, destructive lives. For us, the road ahead is rough and dismal.

Chapter 13

Change is relative to being the same

We spent the last night on Oahu celebrating my freedom. I couldn't help feeling paranoid in public. I felt as if people were watching me. Being in prison, even for a short time, had really messed with my head. I could hardly wait to reach the safety of the hotel room. My father brought a co-worker along, Jim, who was the maintenance man at the Kona Bay Hotel. He was medium build, in his forties, with sandy blonde hair and piercing blue eyes. A throw back from the sixties, he was a genuine party animal. I could tell from the moment we met that we'd get along fine. Our flight to the Big Island departed early the next morning, which left us the whole night to catch up. Soon as we reached the hotel room, my dad popped me an ice cold beer and Jim handed me a huge joint. Welcome home! Things were off to a good start. We drank the night away after a delicious steak and seafood dinner fit for a king. I don't even remember passing out.

Morning came before I knew it. Hangovers all around, we each had an eye opener for the road to clear the cobwebs. Jim insisted that we take a few hits to compliment the beers. I was high when we jumped into the taxi. I stared out the window and said goodbye to the place that I called home for the majority of my life. I reflected on how it felt when I last heard the door buzzer at the cell block. Exiting and seeing my father's happy face, beaming, as he greeted me with a welcoming hug. It was a feeling like no other. Sitting here now, beside him, I couldn't help but be overwhelmed for this man who had given so much of himself. Tears filled my eyes and I wiped them away. How can you ever repay such a debt? There's no amount of money, gold or treasures in the world that could cover the tab. But that's not what is expected. Not what is asked. The price is simple enough. It lies within and can't be purchased. All it cost is your willingness to change. And yet even that is a price that is much too high. I already flunked the first test on that account. The joy of freedom had managed to compromise all of us in that department. Leading me once again down that path to destruction.

The Big Island is both the largest and youngest island in the chain. Because of the Kilauea volcano's constant activity, the island continues to grow. Tourists from around the world gather at night to see the red hot lava flow, glowing in the darkness, as it makes its way to the sea. One of the most beautiful sights on the planet. An eruption can be seen for miles as the goddess Pele spouts her angry streams of bright magma high into the air. As the plane touched down, the vast, sparsely covered region depicted how my new life would be. There's been many times in my life when relocation from one area to the next occurred—country to city, city to country, then back again. But this was altogether different. Although we moved from island to island in my childhood, this was not the same. I felt empty, as if I'd lost my home. Uprooted in a sense. When you are a baby, the whole world around could change. Back then, all that mattered to you was a warm place to sleep and hugs from your parents. I didn't look forward to my new life in this strange place. All that paled in comparison to my being free. After that experience, nothing could faze me. It was good to be united with my family again. My mom was there at the hotel, waiting with open arms. She cried, wrapping her arms tightly around me. "Be a good boy now," she said. Her words rang in my ears. I'd put them both through so much pain. At that very moment, as we stood there locked in her embrace, I would never, ever, think to break her heart again. But the weak, though they feel, can never help themselves. We are destined to repeat our careless behaviors. When something tragic happens and we survive, we step back and fall into a period of hibernation. We refrain from our bad habits but we can never truly give them up. No more than a dog can resist licking up his own vomit.

They planned a welcome home party for me with friends and family that evening. Jim had already planned an outing at the beach with his wife and daughter for that afternoon. A sort of sight-seeing tour. We hopped into his beat-up station wagon and were off. But not before his wife handed me a few Quaaludes for the ride. The beers were cold and they just kept coming. Along with the joints. All of which totally kicked my ass. By the time we reached our destination, I was nearly passed out. The ocean was lovely and the breeze on my face was cool and refreshing. I slept the entire way home. What a lightweight I was! After the home cooked meal my mom had put together, I was beat. It was a beautiful homecoming . . . the final thought that went through my mind as I fell asleep.

I started my job a few days later, helping with the hotel renovation. I worked for my cousin's husband, who was a fat, greasy, asshole. He had the demeanor of a big, overgrown baby. I picture Nero, in all his splendor, watching Rome burn to ashes as he looked on and played his harp. We got into a small misunderstanding one day during lunch and I told him to go fuck himself, and quit. Not exactly the smartest thing for a parolee to do. Who cared at that point? If I had to sit there and watch that pig slop his food down in such a disgusting manner for one more second, someone was going to get hurt. Better to insult a person and leave than to kick the crap out of them. My parents weren't too thrilled about me walking out. It was more me creating tension within the family than no job. I ended up helping out doing other odd jobs for my dad. Cleaning the pool, sweeping the grounds and setting up the outdoor furniture. Didn't pay nothin' but made my parents happy. Living there at the hotel was stifling. The apartment was cramped and the people who ran the place were certified assholes. I felt sorry for my father having to work for a cousin who was not only on the verge of being senile, but was a total dick. The trouble with being a multimillionaire is that you get to walk around in short pants with the zipper down, shouting orders at your employees and watching them scurry for cover. If it weren't for Jim and the other cool employees, the place would have been unbearable. I knew that this gig wasn't going to last long and that was fine. The thing is, my parents had given up everything to move here and worked for this prick. There were very few options left for them. Oh yeah . . . and me!

The hotel was located right in the middle of downtown Kona, the coast where the state's annual Billfish Tournament was held. It was a Mecca for fisherman who would try to win the coveted top prize. Tourists flocked here during the summer months to get away from their uninteresting lives. The nightlife was slow in comparison to the more fast-paced Waikiki beach scene. I found it boring. There really wasn't much of anything to do. I had no friends except for Jim and few of the locals. So what do people in my position often do? What else! Drink and get high and party. Anything to escape our pathetic lives. Being free wasn't good enough anymore, I felt as if the world owed me a living. My probation officer never even bothered with me. I checked in once with him before I left the island. He said to stay out of trouble for the next five years or else. And that was that. I was free to pretty much do whatever I wanted. As long as I didn't get arrested. Believe me, I stayed far away from the police. Keeping to the shadows was a snap. With the slow, easy-going lifestyle I was living it was difficult to get into trouble. You had to go out of your way to do that. Life in the free world was great, but I hungered for more. Never satisfied. I should have counted my blessings at the time. I guess I was too busy feeling sorry for myself. Whatever. I needed out of this mundane environment quick . . . the boredom was driving me crazy. So crazy that I started doing LSD on a regular basis just to combat it. There was tons of the stuff going around. I hadn't really done any since high school and I'd forgotten how much I loved it. It turned the shitty days into sunshine and laughter. I once drove my dad's car through an off-road path to some hippy guy's house to buy a few hits. I scraped the bottom of the transmission pan on a rock and then tore it open. The fluid was coming out faster than we could pour it in. It was a bum trip in both the real and the unreal world. Try explaining that to your parent while frying on acid.

Meanwhile, as all of this drama was playing out, Lorna and Ralph were busy developing a 385-acre parcel of land in the country. We'd gone out a few times on the weekends to see their progress. The place was charming. Lush and green, situated next to the roadside with a large open pasture. Ralph had planned subdividing the land into one-, two- and three-acre lots. An exclusive community in the works for only those who could afford it. He was set to make millions on the project. There was no electricity or running water. In fact, there was nothing but barren land. It was located just outside the sleepy town of Naalehu, across from the South Point Road. Tourists often travelled the winding road to the end, where sharp cliffs meet the blue ocean, just to brag that they've been to the southern most part of the USA. The serenity was captivating. It reminded me of my younger days on the dumb shit ranch in Waianae. I could see why my sister loved it so much. Every time we visited, I wanted to stay—I hated going back to Kona.

With no living accommodations, Lorna and Ralph stayed at the nearby Naalehu hotel. It was nothing more than a stopping-off point for tourists who were travelling around the island. No more than six rooms available, but at least it was clean and had hot and cold running water.

Like I said, it wasn't long before the bullshit got old at the hotel. Dad got fed up with his cousin's crap after a year or so and we moved out into the country. Mom and dad lived off their retirement and Social Security and I went to work for Ralph. He made me the ranch foreman for his development project. Although the pay was good, I barely saw any of it. My parents rented an old house just down the road from the property. It was good to be close to my sister again. The whole family was together again. To assist in the project's development, Ralph had enlisted the help of some of the locals. Mainly from a construction company owned by two brothers who didn't mind working under the table. Sam and Jack both worked part-time for the Kahuku ranch—owned and run by the Damien Estate. When they weren't busy stretching barbed wire or maintaining the heavy equipment for the owners, they bulldozed house pads and dug cesspools on the side. They were great big gentle giants, well over 400 pounds each, but their hearts were even bigger. They needed a wheel barrow to carry them. Ellen, Jack's wife, ran the household and kept the books. She was a gracious lady in her fifties with a heart of gold. She fell instantly in love with my parents and did everything to please them. She even arranged to have them permanently housesit a friend's property so they didn't have to pay rent anymore. The place had no running water, electricity or indoor plumbing, but it was up in the hillside, away from everything and everyone. It was heavenly. It was like living on the moon. Everywhere you looked, in all directions, there was nothing but this black, roughly cooled lava. They had accepted us into their family circle and we spent many nights having dinner at their home on the ranch. I enjoyed cooking some of my special dishes for them. A small token of appreciation for their hospitality.

The development project became such a large undertaking that nearly the entire family became a part of it. Both Ellen's sons, Milton and Numb, and her nephews Larry and Bun, worked side by side with me. They were hard working people, strong and loyal. They spent their entire lives in that small part of the island. Pure Hawaiians that often never left the parameters of their comfort zone. The majority of them had never left the island or flown on a plane. They were content to remain in their own world. It reminded me of those isolated tribes discovered by anthropologists in Papua New Guinea. Well, not exactly, but pretty close, considering the madly insane lifestyle that I lived. It was only natural, working in such close proximity, that we'd become good friends. Our work relationship would soon find us inseparable. They eventually exposed me to new heights of adventure, like boar hunting and poaching. The word alone speaks for itself. You could say it was their version of stealing parking meters. Sure as hell kept the boredom away.

The highlight of our land development venture was when Ralph purchased an abandoned Pioneer Federal Saving and Loan building. It was primarily a wooden structure with the same dimensions as a two bedroom house and it sat in the middle of a parking lot in the middle of Naalehu town. The company had gone out of business and the building was just sitting there taking up space. What drew Ralph to it was the amazing Koa wood trim throughout the interior. Koa is a prized hardwood grown locally. The ancient Hawaiians used it for everything—bowls, kitchen utensils and outrigger canoes. Its unusual grain and rich brown color made it highly desirable for furniture and cabinetry. Purchasing the building was one thing, moving it to the land was another. From the parking lot to the property was a narrow two lane highway that, in some areas, climbed at a steep incline. The winding road pathways and roadside tree line made movement even more difficult. Difficult, but not impossible. It would take a professional moving company that specialized in such work. It was not only a huge task, but a dangerous one. Any number of things could go wrong. Cost being an issue, selecting the right contractor to do the move wouldn't be easy. Since the beginning of this venture, money had been a problem. The project was set up on a shoe-string budget with minimum investment that yielded maximum profit. Meeting employee payroll deadlines were bad enough. I would often forgo my pay so that the others could get paid. I was in it for the long haul and intended on cashing in on the final outcome. It was a gamble I was willing to take. One that everyone else was betting on as well. I just followed Lorna and Ralph's lead.

Came the day of the big move, the entire community was out in force to see it. There was a parade atmosphere. People lined the streets to see the crazy haole do the impossible. We hired a company out of Hilo for the job. Caesar and his crew arrived days before and set up shop, preparing for the move. It was an intricate task consisting of semi-trailers, low-boy carriers and hydraulic jacks. Everything was calculated down to the very last detail. The only variable was the weather. The whole move depended on sunshine and dry conditions. Naalehu is a wet climate area with only periodic dry conditions. The month in which we were attempting the move wasn't the greatest. We had already faced a few rainy days which pushed the schedule back and the cost up. For everyday Caesar and his crew sat around it cost an additional $1500. And we really couldn't afford it. Today, all the conditions were right and we set to go. With the house loaded on the trailer and the police escort at the ready, we started out. This would be a once in a lifetime opportunity and, not one to take a backseat, I chose the most dangerous job and the most spectacular. I, along with another worker, would ride the entire distance on the roof, holding up the phone cables as we passed under them. The route was only five or six miles, but it ran through some of the scariest roadways in the country. The view from the top was breathtaking as we made our way along. Although I decided against drinking before climbing over twenty feet into the air, I couldn't resist smoking a doobie. Stoned, but able to function, we negotiated the winding road.

Just when things were going good, we hit a snag. The eaves of the structure overhung into some narrow areas, so we had to chain saw them off. On the move again for only a few minutes, we hit another snag, this time a bigger one. As we reached the local park, we found that part of the roadway was obstructed by a few gigantic trees that lined the length of the park. There was no way we would be able to get through. Unless of course, we cut those trees down. We couldn't turn this whole rig around and couldn't reverse the way we came. These trees had been standing here for over a hundred years. To even attempt to obtain permission to chop them down would require a permit. And no one would grant it.

The operation had come to a complete halt, blocking traffic in both directions. The clock was running and the storm clouds were forming above. It was time to smoke another joint. Ralph feverishly phoned every city official available and was met time after time with the same answer. No. Absolutely No. Ralph, not one to accept no for an answer, and under the threat of arrest and or stiff fines, grabbed a chainsaw and started cutting. Nothing would deter him. The police, caught between the buildup of traffic and an enraged public, wanted out of there fast and stepped back. When all was done, there were two (or was it 3?) dead trees.

And we were off. Now came the fun part. As we drove along the steep, winding incline, the views from the top were fabulous! Probably never seen from this angle by anyone before. We made it in one try and were soon at the entrance to the property. Then the rains came. The place in which the house was to sit was nothing but grass and dirt, which was quickly turning into a muddy marsh. Caesar made his way onto the property and got stuck. He gunned and gunned the motor, but the wheels kept spinning. The rain poured down. We called for reinforcements. With the help of a TD25 Caterpillar bulldozer chained to the trailer, we tried and failed. Then we chained a Caterpillar grader to the dozer, tried and failed. The rain let up for an instant. We then chained Caesar's 4x4 pick-up truck to the grader. And with all four vehicles working together at full bore, in tandem, we finally made it. There was applause all around and cause for celebration. It was quite an experience and one I was proud to have been a part of. Of course, the town was pissed about their trees and Ralph agreed to purchase new ones and pay the fines. Which he never did. Jackass.

With the house settled in the middle of this picture perfect pasture, it was on to the next project. The place would act as a showpiece for the planned development. A lure for potential buyers. After digging the cesspool and hooking up the plumbing, Lorna and Ralph moved in to cut costs. For the time being, they used candles and lanterns. They needed to install two telephone poles at a cost of about a thousand dollars each in order to get the electric connected. A cost that wasn't in the immediate budget. After all, we had trouble paying the workers.

If this deal didn't workout, they'd lose everything. Ralph had a plan up his sleeve that I never saw coming. To celebrate our progress, Ralph decided to take Lorna and me for dinner at a three-star hotel restaurant. The trouble with that plan was that he really didn't have the money. That never stopped him from doing things. When I first met him, he said, "All you need to make a million dollars in this world was a single quarter in your pocket and a payphone." His resourcefulness and eccentric character often made this concept work. On this afternoon, Lorna and I were undecided on what to order. Apparently, our inability to decide had Ralph somewhat annoyed. So he ordered for us—he told the waitress to bring one of everything on the menu. The waitress stared at him in disbelief and said, "Excuse me sir. Did you say the whole menu?" He replied, "Yes, and don't forget the salads and deserts." Lorna and I stared at each other, totally blown away. The guy was nuts. He then motioned the waitress over again and told her to bring him a bottle of Crown Royal. "It was my late mother's favorite," he said. The waitress explained that the liquor laws prevented her from doing so and they began to argue. He convinced her to circumvent the law by pouring the entire contents of the bottle into glasses. She arrived a few moments later with four huge glasses, filled to the brim with the fine liquor. There was no way in hell the three of us could possibly drink even two of those without passing out. There was no dissuading him from the start over his ridiculous request. We just sat back and went with the flow. Then the food started arriving. The other customers stared in awe as tray after tray was brought to the table. There were steaks, chops and fish, pasta, burgers and sandwiches prepared every way imaginable. The table we were seated at was large enough to comfortably seat 8 people. There wasn't any empty space available to place all of the dishes. We just ate bites from each plate, here and there, kept the ones we liked and had the waitress take the rest away to make room for the next. The food kept on coming. I've seen a lot of crazy shit in my life, but this topped them all. After we'd had enough, the deserts started to come. Pies, cakes, ice cream in all flavors, sherbets in a rainbow of colors, shakes, floats, splits, malts and sundaes. They had it all and they brought every bit of it. It was madness. The table was overflowing with goodness. Stuffed to the gills, we began handing plates out to all the kids and other customers. It was a sight to see. How many people in the world even get the chance to experience such a feat? Believe me, not many. Not even the rich go to such lengths. It was absurd, but in a good way. I was so full, I had trouble breathing. When all the mess was cleared, Ralph handed me a great big joint and told me to light it up. I refused. The last thing I needed was to get arrested while on probation. He called me a pussy and lit it himself. The entire room filled with the unmistakable sweet smelling aroma. Every person in the place just looked at us. Their stares burned into me and I wanted to hide under the table. Ralph puffed away, then handed the joint to me. What's a fella to do? I grabbed it and reluctantly puffed away. This was way off the scale of lucid behavior. Out of the corner of my eye, I saw two of the biggest individuals I'd ever seen in my life heading our way. No doubt security. Ralph asked for the joint and he kept on smoking. They walked casually up to him and the larger said, "Excuse me sir, but could you put that out. You can't smoke that in here." Ralph apologized and asked to see the manager. They escorted him away. I sat there with my sister, holding my ass, expecting to be arrested any minute. Lorna looked poised and unconcerned. She saw the worried look on my face and said, "Don't sweat it brah. Ralph got this." She sounded so convincing, but I found it hard to believe her. You blame me? Hell no! Time passed and nearly an hour had lapsed with no sight of Ralph. The waiting was killing me. Thoughts of different outcomes were flooding through my mind. I looked up to see Ralph sauntering towards us. Lorna looked at me, flashed a big smile and said, "Not to worry." He said that everything had been taken care of and that our meal was compliments of the house. The tab easily amounted to over a thousand bucks. I don't have any idea what transpired in the manager's office that day, and I'm still baffled over the whole thing. Ralph sure was a class act.

This quiet little town held a closely guarded secret that I would soon discover. For years, groups of locals had been growing marijuana in large quantities. The place was a haven for organized pot farmers. It had become a family affair, kept within the tightly-knit community. Outsiders were forbidden to interfere or participate in any way. Most of the crop was sold locally but there was a group who shipped product to the mainland. I had no way of knowing that the very people that I worked with and partied with were these farmers. They were referred to as hui, the Hawaiian word for union or partnership. Their marijuana crops were their business. Everything else, including working for us, was their alternative income. These guys didn't just grow a few plants out in the backyard; they grew weed by the tons. It was hard, backbreaking work that took thousands of plants to make a decent crop. These people weren't your average drug dealers. Picture them, instead, as professional gardeners, not unlike orchid or rose farmers. They cross pollinated and experimented with different seeds and strains to achieve the ultimate product. They mix and test soil and fertilizers to provide the perfect bed to plant their hybrid starters. The competition to produce the best product was fierce among rival hui. Most involved were all related, in one way or another. Rivals or not, they were one big happy family. And anyone who got caught up between them was dealt with. They trusted no one. That's what kept their enterprise surviving for so many years. My family was one of the few exceptions to their closed society. It was the love Ellen, Jack and Sam had for my parents that made us different. Lord knows it wasn't Ralph. They despised his presence in their community. Though he brought jobs, he reminded them of the white man's infringement on their native lands.

With funds at an all time low and expenses mounting, Ralph came up with another scam. I don't know if our purpose for being in this town in the first place had anything to do with it or what, I never knew. Out of the clear blue he introduced me to these two hippie dudes. He told me that we were going into the pot cultivation business and that these guys were going to show me how it was done. The guy was full of surprises. I wondered how all this land that was destined for sale was going to be used to grow weed. That's where the insane part of the plan comes to light. You see, adjacent to our property were a few acres of undeveloped land owned by a police captain. Ralph said our patch would be grown there. He said it was the best place and that no one would ever suspect a thing. I don't know if the guy who owned the land was in on it. I never asked. It was a brilliant plan—if it worked. These two hippie dudes were geniuses. Supposedly they were college grads who specialized in botany. They certainly knew their pot. They planned on bringing in the harvest in just ninety days and cashing in. I found that hard to believe but I was no expert. I still had no idea of the scale or immensity of the project. I thought it was just a few hundred plants at most. Boy was I mistaken. It turned out to be more like five thousand. Yup, you heard right . . . five thousand!

You could tell from the start that these guys had their shit together. It was like watching two scientists in a lab display their talent. From the sprouting of the seeds to the transplanting of the sprouts into the ground. They mixed their own soil and tested it with kits to assure the right pH levels. All of this took place under the canopy of a large tree on the property. When the time came to transfer the starters into the ground, it was a huge undertaking. The young plants were over a foot high with leaves as big as my hands. We dug holes a foot deep and a foot wide, filled it with all the special soil—which meant carrying bags of the stuff back and forth—and then we planted four plants in each hole, to insure that at least one of them would grow to maturity and be a female. Only the females of the species are worth anything, the males are discarded due to their lack of potency. It took four of us three days of non-stop work to get the job done. When finally done, we had dug hundreds of holes, carried over a ton of soil by hand and planted over five thousand plants. It was an amazing feat! The patch was set up in the configuration of a hand with sections spread out like fingers. The holes were six feet apart. Now, get your calculator and figure that out. All we had to do now is sit back and watch the fruits of our labor grow. Well, not exactly. Someone had to tend to them, you know, water and weed and keep them healthy. That job was left to yours truly.

Because there was no proper irrigation system set up, all those plants had to be watered by hand. You think planting them was hard? Think about what it's like to make a baby. Conceiving was the fun part. Then there's school, college and all the stuff in between. It took me over five hours a day using two five-gallon plastic containers to water those suckers! It was hard, ass-busting work but I grew to love it. Watching my babies grow big and strong. I never experienced such a closeness associated with growing a plant. They become endeared to you, like children. That year Naalehu had a record drought. Not a drop of rain the entire time those plants were in the ground. It would be a bad year for pot farmers who depended on the rainfall to water their crops, some of which were grown in hard to access places. But not for us. Thanks to my constant care and attendance, our crops flourished. Soon the pollination cycle would begin and removal of the males would happen. It's a period when close attention was needed to insure a good harvest. One mistake could spell disaster for the whole crop, making all our time and money and energy for nothing. I'll save this part of the story for later.

This was surely God's country, no matter how you looked at it. My parents were enjoying their retirement in such a peaceful environment. Even without all the creature comforts of life, they were happy. The only drawback was the isolation. In their late fifties now, concern for their medical needs was an issue. It was miles to the nearest clinic and even further to a hospital. If something serious was to happen, chances are they wouldn't survive it. My dad once had a terrible fall and we rushed him to the clinic for treatment. Lucky, all he had was a few bumps and bruises, nothing broken but it was a wake-up call for all of us. His main concern was for my mother. She was a tough old bird, but after that incident, he worried for her safety. So for their benefit, they decided to move back to Honolulu and civilization. Ellen was heartbroken to see them leave. They all were. They'd all gotten rather attached to the "old folks" as they were referred to. I'd miss them too, but felt good that they were leaving. It was for the best. I stayed behind to bring in the crop and keep an eye on my sister. I never trusted Ralph when it came to her. We once got into a big argument over the way he treated her. I snapped on him and told him if he ever hurt her or laid a hand on her, I'd kill him.

I became closer and closer to the boys and their family. We spent all our waking moments together. I began working for the ranch on a part time basis since things were slow on the land. Work there was a standstill as far as development went. We'd put up lava rock walls and a gate after moving the house to improve the overall appearance. The wall was constructed by an old Hawaiian man in his nineties named Apo. He was an expert craftsman who used no concrete or modern tools to build his works of art. His work was in high demand throughout the island and we were lucky to have him. I learned a lot from that old man who rarely, if ever, teaches anyone other than his own family. The only constant was attending to the plants. It was amazing that up until this point, no one even knew they existed. I slipped away to tend them while the other guys went off to work. Lorna and Ralph spent most of their time away in Honolulu or California on business. I had a feeling that things weren't going well. When I wasn't staying at the ranch with the boys, I lived at the property where my parents did house sitting. My father had fixed the place up nice and had even built a shower room with a water tank that cached rainwater and hooked electricity up by converting a 12 volt battery to play the car radio. We used to spend nights listening to broadcasts like people did before the invention of TV. There was even an old wood burning stove. I loved it!

Harvest time was approaching and our crop was looking great. Some of the plants had started to develop the male sacks that would soon burst open to produce the pollen that fertilized the females. To prevent that, we carefully removed all the males from the patch. There were bags of them. I now saw why those hippies planted more than one plant in each hole! There was a male plant in many of the holes. With the first batch cut out, I planned to fly to Oahu to visit my parents. I made my plans clear to the two white guys and they volunteered to tend the plants. I hated leaving their care to anyone, they had become such a big part of my life. I knew they were in good hands. Or so I thought. The next day, I flew out to Honolulu and the big city life that I'd left behind. My parents were happy to see me again and tried to persuade me to move back. They looked great, comfortable in their old world. I spent my time seeing old friends and family who all thought that I'd fallen off the planet.

The whole time, all I could think about were those stupid plants. They were my children and I'd left them. I called everyday for an update but couldn't reach anyone. After four days, without a word, I cut my trip short and flew back. Something wasn't right. My parents were sad to see me go and for the first time in my life, I felt good about leaving them behind. Living in the sticks is all fine and dandy if you're a spring chicken, but when you're moving up years, the novelty wears off quick.

The knot in my stomach told me that I was heading back to a less than happy reunion with my partners. I hurried to the airport parking lot and broke the sound barrier in my jeep on the way to the property. When I got there the place was deserted. Not a soul in sight. Lorna and Ralph were still away on business and the house was empty. I drove up the trail and bee-lined for the patch. The first thing I saw was a bunch of fertilized females. There were male plants among the crops and their once swollen sacks had opened and distributed their pollen. I walked through the patch and cried. All that hard work for nothing. Ruined. The plants looked dry and neglected, like they hadn't been watered in days. I was enraged! I could've killed those hippies right then and there. I ran to the upper section and was surprised to see that the plants there were immaculate. Being up wind had saved them from fertilization. Maybe all wasn't lost. I began the painstaking task of removing the male plants along with pollinated females. What a waste. It was a shame—in just about a week they would have been ripe for harvest. It took several hours, but I go the job done. When finished, there were hundreds of pounds of green pot stuffed into triple thick black trash bags. The load filled my Jeep Cherokee, front and back. And even though these plants could still be smoked, their potency was diminished. I drove to the house that the hippies were staying in to deliver them their share of the harvest. I held them personally responsible for the blunder. Arriving, I was greeted by the owner's two vicious Dobermans. They were big and mean and off their leashes. I guess they were expecting me. I sounded the horn and screamed through the crack in the rolled up window. No one came. I knew they were there because the owner's truck was parked in the garage. The dogs were in a frenzy, leaping onto my jeep and hungrily circling, like sharks waiting for dinner. All they did was make me angrier. I was too mad with rage to let those dogs stop me from getting hands on those two punks. I screamed a final threat and said, "come out and get your dogs or I'm going to kill them!" Still no one appeared. I reached under the seat and removed the shortened Louisville Slugger that I kept handy for just such an occasion. I got the dogs to the opposite side of the truck, leaped out and as they attacked, I swung. I connected on one at the front shoulder, then on the other's rear hind leg. They yelped in pain and hobbled to the garage. Their bark was worse than their bite after all. The owner's wife finally came out and threatened to call the cops if I didn't leave. It was obvious that the hippie dudes were too afraid to face me, letting a woman do their job, so I unloaded all the bags on the driveway and told her that here was their cut. "And if I ever catch them anywhere near the land, I'll kill them and bury them on it." Something told me I shouldn't have said or done any of it. Sure wasn't going to sit well with Ralph.

With that out of the way, I stopped by the ranch to see the boys. I needed to cool off and a party was in order. We piled into my jeep, loaded in the cooler and went out on the road. "Yeah . . . road trip!" We circled the island and stopped wherever and whenever. Everywhere we went, we were welcomed by the other growers who were anxious to have us sample their product. It was harvest time and pot farmers throughout the state were busy bringing in the crop. Seemed like everywhere we went, the quality just got better and better. At the end of our journey, we stopped at a park where a family gathering was underway. There was food and drink and live music in abundance. It was a fun time for all. The highlight of the evening was when a large circle was formed and everyone lit up their joints. Must have been twenty people in the group. They all began passing the joints around. Not one of them tasted the same. Amazing! Turns out, this innocent looking family outing was an annual gathering of the pot farmers to display their crop for the season. I was the first outsider invited to stand among this secret society. It was an honor and I was warmed by their trust. A week ago, before my trip, Bun and Larry Boy had asked me to drive them to an undisclosed location. When we arrived, we made our way into the brush and came into a clearing. The smell of marijuana was everywhere, but I couldn't see any plants. Bun looked at me and said, "Can you smell that?" I had no idea we were standing in the middle of their hui marijuana patch. The plants were concealed so well that they were undetectable. The both of them looked so serious that it scared me. I thought that I was dead. I got an eerie feeling and my hair stood up, "chicken skin kine." Why would they trust anyone other than family to come here unless they were going to kill me? They saw the look on my face and burst into laughter. Seems bringing me here was their way of showing me how much they trusted and cared about me. That I was accepted as family. Bun pointed to the plants he'd exposed and said, "Pick any one you want." I was stuck for words. "You're joking right?" I went for the thickest, nicest, sweetest plant in the patch. "You got good taste. Burns is going to trip out when he sees it gone." Bernard was the oldest member of their hui and was referred to as Burns. He was the one who had the knowledge and green thumb. It was the greatest honor and show of trust anyone had ever shown me.

Standing in the circle, puffing away, I reached into my pocket and lit up a joint from a plant taken from my crop. It was sweet and potent and I passed it to Bun. He puffed on it and his eyes opened wide. He looked at me bewildered and said, "where did you get this?" It was no surprise to me that these connoisseurs of the pot world, after smoking joint after joint of different varieties, could be fooled. I told him it was mine and that I grew it myself. He smiled and passed it down the line. Each time, it was met with the same puzzled response and seal of approval. There was no better way to have a product tested. By the end of the night, the winner was announced and hailed as having the best weed in the county. His name was Kadink and his weed tasted exactly like a bazooka bubble gum. I kid you not. And it kicked your ass! And with all the different kinds of pot smoked that night, each one dynamite in its own right, the bubble gum weed took the award, hands down.

I woke the next day, still stoned. We persuaded the "king of pot," Kadink, to tag along with us that night. And there he sat across from me rolling joints of that heavenly gum weed. He passed me a joint and said, "good morning." Sure was, now. You just couldn't get enough of a good thing. I dropped everyone off and headed for the land. The property was quiet and vacant. I approached the gate, got out and noticed the shiny new lock attached to the heavy chain. Looked like Ralph was back and I wasn't welcome here. I drove to the same house with the dogs. I found them there. After checking for those dogs, I walked to the front door. My knocks were met with silence. The owner's wife came to the door and I asked to see my sister. At first, she refused to even let me in but I heard Lorna call out to her. She stepped aside and I entered the living room. I could smell the pot the minute I walked in. The place was alive with activity. My sister was busy helping Ralph and the others scale and bag weed into baggies. Not one of them said hello, they just kept on working. I looked into the side bedroom and saw all these plants hanging up, drying. Santa's little helpers have been very busy. There was an awful lot of pot here. Pounds of the shit. I asked my sister what was going on and she launched into a stream of negative responses. Ralph walked up to me and said, "what do you want here?" Then he went off on me. "What gives you the right to treat my friends that way . . . blah, blah, blah." He told me to leave and that he never wanted to see me again.

The two hippie guys feared for their lives and had left town. I knew I shouldn't have done that. There was so much weed here, I wondered it they raided the whole patch. I calculated the amount that was there. I asked my sister if I could have some of the bags and she said "No. Better yet, just leave." Feeling hurt and dejected, I walked out. They hadn't heard the last of me . . . no way, no how.

Tore my heart out to be treated so callously. I always expected that kind of behavior from Ralph, but never from my sister. And after all the things I've done and sacrifices I made for them. Times got so hard, they couldn't even pay me for the hours of grueling work I did. Instead, whatever money came in went to pay other workers. Even that wasn't enough to cover cost. To compensate, they promised me some land on the property. Anywhere I chose when the subdivision was complete. Marked it off and everything. Then, his partner Robert got arrested in the mainland for cocaine distribution and the land deal fell apart. To keep me working and make up for that, they gave me their pet bull terrier, Rocky. And now that I was an outcast, his loyal companionship was all I had left. Animals never let you down. Not like people.

I spent the drive back brooding. What better thing to do in a situation like this . . . party! I rounded up the gang and we headed for the beach. These guys, who only a year ago were strangers, were the only family I had. Reaching out to them now was comforting and I felt less alone in the world. They had no idea what I going through. It wasn't their problem and I needed to sort this whole thing out on my own. Throughout the night, I couldn't stop thinking about the way they treated me. The drunker and stoner I got, the clearer my course of action became. My hurt soon turned into anger and anger into rage. The nerve of them! I had every right to share in the profits—no one worked harder than me! I won't be cast aside in that way by anyone!

That's when it all became crystal clear to me. I'd have my revenge. But for that, I'd need a little help. Why not put my trust in them? It was a long shot, but it was all I had. I looked at Bun and said, "call up Walter and tell him to bring his truck and all the rubbish bags he can get." They were puzzled, but went along. I got Larry Boy to get his dad's Ford F-250 truck with the long bed and all the plastic garbage bags he had. "Don't forget the bolt cutters," I said. I told them to meet me at the gate to the property. It was after midnight when we met. The night was dark and the skies were clear. Perfect for what we were about to do. Up 'til then, I still kept this whole covert operation a secret. No use ruining the big surprise.

I took the bolt cutters and snapped the padlock off the heavy chain. We drove, lights out, along the driveway. We came to a stop at the entrance to the marijuana patch. I grabbed the flashlight, got out of the jeep and said, "smell that?" Being the growers that they were, they each had the nose of a bloodhound. They sniffed at the air, and the sweet smell of fresh green pot filled their nostrils. Their faces lit up. "Follow me," was all I said. I hopped over the rock wall that divided our property line and made my way along the trail. I'd walked these trails a thousand times and knew them like the back of my hand. The closer we got, the stronger the aroma. In the darkness, the distinct, shadowy silhouette of a tree could be seen. I turned the flashlight on and pointed. There, in all its glory stood the first of many eight-foot tall wonders. The white, crystallized formation of THC, the active chemical in pot that gives it its kick, shined like granulated sugar against the beam of light. It was beautiful! Bun, feeling uneasy, asked whose plants these were. Pot farmers had a sense of right and wrong, an unwritten law when it came to entering other fields. These people have been growing pot as their livelihood for years in this town. Now, here I was, a stranger who dropped in and planted an entire crop right under their noses. I felt sorry for them. They'll get over it. I turned and looked at Bun, shined the light under my chin like a Halloween mask and said, "they're mine. Now let's get busy."

When all was said and done, we had filled both pick-up trucks and my jeep with bags. We'd doubled the bags and stuffed them to the hilt with weed. I never thought pot could be so heavy. Each bag weighed at least forty pounds and it took the four of us over four hours of non-stop work to empty the patch. The sun was already starting to rise. The raid had been successful and like they say, "revenge is a dish best served cold." Boy, Lorna and Ralph were going to be surprised. Who cared? They deserved what they had coming.

Ok. The only problem was where the hell do you hide all of this pot? We decided to steal the keys to the gates on the ranch and take the load down to the sea, an area only the ranch workers had access to. It was hours of driving along rough terrain. The sun blazed and in our haste to avoid being caught we had forgotten all about packing water for the trip. We were dying of thirst by the time we arrived but fortunately we had a jug of water I kept for the radiator. There was this old, dilapidated house next to the beach. All the interior walls were broken out, leaving just the outer shell still standing. It was the perfect place to dry the weed. We tied strings throughout and hung every last tree up. There were thousands! It was a big house. Walter and Larry left to get us supplies. They returned later with beer and food, saving our lives. There was nothing else to do but kick back, relax and watch the plants dry.

With the hot sun and cool ocean breeze, conditions were ideal. The air circulated through the house, keeping the temperature just right. After two days, the plants dried to perfection and they took on a golden color. They were gorgeous! There were pounds and pounds of the stuff. The whole lot had to be manicured. Larry Boy and Walter had left Bun and me there two days earlier with the pleasant news that my sister was inquiring about me. Evidently they discovered the rip off. That's all I could think of as I saw Walter's blue truck approaching. I noticed there was a stranger with him, a large Hawaiian man I'd never seen before. He introduced himself and said, "I heard you got some weed for sale?" I sure did. Along with the huge wads of cash he carried, he also brought two ice coolers full of beer, soda and steaks. The guy certainly knew how to do business.

I walked him through the narrow rows of weed as he selected the plants he wanted and then we decided on a price. He pealed the bills from his roll one after another. Five thousand dollars or more later, I had my first happy customer. We packed up the rest and drove to Walter's house to start the difficult, but enjoyable process of manicuring and packaging. Larry Boy was asked to relay a message to me, if by chance he happened to see me. He said my sister was sorry for the way they treated me and that she and Ralph didn't care about the weed, they were just worried about me. Was I OK? I felt guilty as shit, but not guilty enough to give the weed back,

With five or six people working day and night, it took three days to manicure all that pot. Must have been about two or three hundred pounds. Now that's a lot of shit! The weed would be needed to fund our new joint venture of opening a cockfighting arena.

That would present me with a whole new set of challenges that I never saw coming. Alliances would be made, families would be tested and friendships would be broken forever. But that's how life goes for those of us who choose the path of addition and crime.

Chapter 14

Exit, Stage Left

With all this marijuana at my disposal, I now had the financial means to put my plan into effect. Cockfighting, although illegal in Hawaii, continues to thrive. Popular among the Filipino community, it attracts gambling enthusiasts from all walks of life. Well organized, these fights, no different than underground dog fighting, are held in backyards and other secret venues. These so called derbies can be a lucrative enterprise for those willing to take the risk. The idea first came to me one day while exploring the property where my parents were house sitting. I stumbled across a large, naturally formed vertical lava tube that ran to the surface. The pit was about 25 feet deep and 40 feet wide. It reminded me of an arena. Originally, I thought it the perfect place to plant pot. The top of the hole was covered with overhanging tree limbs and vegetation, obscuring the location. It made helicopter surveillance impossible and all it would take was some clearing. You could easily fit a hundred or more people in that pit along with their bird carriers. I kept the spot and the idea locked away in the back of my mind for future use. I suspected that the opportunity would somehow present itself. Just one thing before I progress any further. I'm truly sorry if this plan of mine offends you tree-hugging animal rights fanatics. You're probably foaming at the mouth at this point. Don't get your panties in a twist. Hang in there a little longer; you'll be more than satisfied in the end.

It was a brazen plan and in order for it to be successful it required the assistance of some very powerful and influential people in the underworld. Obtaining permission to operate an organized crime activity had to come straight from the top. From the Godfather of the entire crime syndicate himself. Like any projected future business in the works, you go through channels to get the necessary approval. Lucky for me, the resident enforcer for the man himself was none other than my partner Bun's older brother Archie. He was a soft-spoken, solidly built man who reminded me of a boulder with legs. His physical stature matched his incredible strength. I once saw a drunk woman reverse her Honda Civic into him, pinning him to the side of the bar. The tires were still spinning as he lifted the vehicle up and tossed it aside. All she could muster from the mishap was, "I'm sorry, was that you?" His casual reply of, "I'll live" said a lot about his character. Seeing him perform such a feat so effortlessly made me wonder what he was capable of if he got angry. My father nicknamed him the Hulk. Believe me, the name fit him to a tee. If I hadn't known him personally, I would have been afraid to ever speak to him. It was only because of his intercession on our behalf that we got the green light to go ahead with the plan. Archie was a great person and I was glad to have known him.

In order to insure the safety of our operation, I opted to fly to Oahu with a good portion of the weed, sell it and procure weapons. It was also my intention to fly the whole gang over to celebrate our new venture. A vacation that all of us would remember. Looking back to that fateful trip, I never would have made it if I'd known the outcome. I didn't expect to be off island more than a week at most. Once business was out of the way, followed by a few days of partying with the boys, I'd be anxious to get back. Except for a fresh set of clothes, I packed the two large suitcases to the hilt with baggies of weed. Before setting out for the airport, something told me to stop at my place and cut the tops off of the two marijuana trees I'd planted there for personal stash. They were of the highest quality. Somehow I had a feeling that I wouldn't see them again. Better to take the best part of the tree and leave the rest. No doubt the minute I was gone, someone was going to steal them. I made arrangements for the boys to bring the remainder of the stash with them when they came. I must have packed at least 40 pounds of weed in my bags. That was a fraction of what I left behind. But it was more than enough to achieve my goals. In Honolulu we could get top dollar for my product. With all the weed going around on the Big Island, we'd never get a good price. Besides, I didn't have the luxury of taking too much time. Things had to happen quickly. I said goodbye to Rocky and left him with a trusted friend. I wanted to take him but where I was going, pets weren't allowed. That was the hardest part about this whole trip, leaving him behind. No big deal, I'll be back in a week, so I thought. I was moving at the speed of light when I arrived at the airport, never giving a second thought to checking in all that pot at the counter. Security measures were a joke back then. Smugglers flew back and forth on a daily basis. If anything, they arrived at their destination to find their luggage missing. The cops had nothing to do with it—a greedy and savvy baggage boy with a keen sense of smell. Cost of doing business.

Not until I was safely in the air ordering my first drink did I realize the gravity of the situation. I couldn't believe it. I was actually doing it! I haven't made it yet, but I was unusually calm under the circumstances. I just had the feeling that everything was going to be okay. It was great to touchdown on Oahu again after being away for so long. And even if I was here for only a short stay, I was home at last. Home in the city where the action was wild and the candle burned at both ends. My heart was racing a mile a minute and a surge of excitement rushed through me. Exiting the plane, a brief moment of concern passed over me. It was too late for all that bullshit, dragging feet crap now. My feet were itching and on fire to get busy; I was a horse at the gate. Relax, stay cool, here we go! There they were, among the many bags on the carousel, going around and around. I scanned the area, looking for the fuzz. I took a deep breath, snatched the bags up, braced for the authoritative grab—never came—and jumped into the nearest cab. The taxi delivered me to my parents' house without incident. I gave him a huge tip for his trouble. Unannounced, I rang the intercom and was happy to hear my mom's voice on the other end. Her surprise at my presence was obvious by her tone. I hadn't seen my parents in months and it was comforting to be here. She greeted me at the door with a warm embrace and news of my sister's inquiries. I tried to save the explanations for later but she wasn't having any of it. Naturally, I told her my side of the story with just enough spin to get her on my team. Then I started unpacking all the weed and loaded it into my old chest of drawers. Her eyes went wide and streams of protest were flowing quickly but, like always, she was putty in my hands. Nothing that a few hugs and kisses couldn't brush away. Luckily, my dad was working at his old job as a security supervisor at the Pagoda Hotel, right around the corner. I couldn't wait to see him and have a drink together. I knew he'd flip out when he saw all the pot in his house. I peeled off several c notes from my wad and gave them to my mom. That brought a smile to her face. "I hope you don't mind if I crash here for a week?" She was happy to have me. I grabbed the phone and started calling all my old connections.

They were falling all over themselves to purchase a taste of Aloha.

Reunion with my father was way overdue. He called to check on my mom and I answered the phone. He came right over. I missed him terribly and I squeezed him tightly when he walked in. He looked old and tired but his green eyes were bright and twinkling. There was no fooling the old man. He was wiser than a fox. A silver fox, with his full head of white hair. It was the one distinguishing feature that personified his wisdom. The older my parents got, the better looking they appeared. There's no place like home. My unexpected arrival, complicated by my sister's disturbing phone calls over my indiscretions, only made my parents' concern increase when I suddenly appeared out of the blue. And they knew all too well the lengths I'd go to when backed into a corner. Although they were happy to see me, I could sense the uneasiness in them. Knowing that I was in their immediate proximity exposed them once again to my every movement. That constant in and out jumping bean activity that they frowned upon in the past. Guessing that I was up to no good, yet hoping that I wasn't. All the while praying for my safety. Walking on pins and needles was tolerable at a distance, away from their sight. Out of sight, out of mind. But with the stressful calls from Lorna and me now standing here with suitcases full of pot, it raised their parental feelings of impending doom and panic right through the roof. It pained me to place them in such a compromising position by my selfish needs. Fool yourself all you want, but the silver fox, shimmering with his regal coat, can never be fooled. Wisdom grows with age and his meter was finely tuned to detect bullshit. So rather than exchange unpleasantries back and forth, we took my visit at face value and left it at that. Our human instinct to survive at all costs always leads us, in times of trouble, right back to the nest. Especially if it has always been safe and warm.

It's a dirty rotten shame that predators like myself continue to capitalize and insinuate ourselves into the innocent love of our parents. Demanding everything, every last drop of their love until we suck them dry. And the poor victims continue to oblige and enable. Yet, we have the audacity, the nerve, to say, "after all, that's what parents are for."

Like an old pair of shoes worn again after being put off to one side, I was comfortable running around crazy in my familiar world. I never realized how much I'd missed it. If not for convenience sake, then for the electrifying pulse of the city's heartbeat. The non-stop action flowed at a feverish pace, there was no stopping it. You feel so alive, strong, powerful. If not careful, you can get swallowed up in the mass of confusion. I welcomed it, embraced it, ran to it and I was making money hand over fist. I'd happened on the scene at the perfect time. In just two days I had sold an entire suitcase of weed and made thousands. I kept the weed from my plant at home as my stash. I have to admit, I did a good job for my first try. With half a suitcase of pot left in my drawer, I made arrangements for the boys to fly in with a few more bags of dope. I planned on wining and dining them and showing them the other side of life. No expense would be spared on my part. My new partners deserved nothing but the very best.

The day before the gang arrived, I met with a drug dealer who also dealt in weapons. We were introduced by a mutual acquaintance. Sitting in his living room, just the two of us, I had the strangest feeling, like he couldn't be trusted. He didn't look out of the ordinary, long hair, unkempt, in his late twenties. But in this business, most people look that way and in all honesty, can't be trusted any further than you can throw them. Like I said, comes with the territory. We drank a few beers, smoked a joint of my weed and snorted a few lines of coke. Then we got down to business. He was interested in trading weed for firepower. After sampling the goods, he was sold. He produced two guns from his arsenal for me to look over. One was a Colt .357 Magnum Python revolver with a six inch barrel in blue steel. The other was a Colt .30 caliber carbine, paratrooper style M2 automatic rifle with a 30 round magazine and a folding stock. It was beautiful. Both weapons were like new. The carbine became fully automatic with a selector switch to change the firing mode. We struck a deal then and there for six of each and a box of hand grenades. They were heavy and waffle patterned like the ones used in WWII. Those bitches sure made a big bang. That should cover our operation nicely. I gave him half a pound of weed to seal the deal and promised him the balance when he got the rest of the hardware. I took the guns with me, but left the grenades there for safe keeping. The last thing I needed was a bomb around town. It was party time!

The celebrating started from the moment the guys got off the plane. Bun and Larry went to stay with Bun's older sister in Halawa valley. That made her place party central. From there it was bar hopping and clubbing nightly. We hit the Waikiki strip one night and tried to get into the Jazz Cellar, one of my old haunts. They had a strict dress code and with Larry and Bun bare-foot and wearing tank tops, the doormen weren't agreeable. That is, until I flashed them an ounce of weed as a bribe. The place was jumping with wall-to-wall women. It was a spectacle that these country boys weren't used to. There were tables full of beers, lines of coke and loud rock and roll pumping out. It was a blast! It was good times all around. Welcome to my world! Every night a different spot with the party being carried back to Bun's sister's house. She was all good with that until I showed up one night with a cute Japanese girl on my arm. A special gift for my friends. Boy, did I get my ass chewed for that one. The ironic thing is, she ended up becoming Bun's wife and his screaming sister's sister-in-law. What a small world. Walter arrived a day later with even more weed and the party continued.

We were having so much fun, but it was time to make our exit. I'd paid the guy the balance of the weed and arranged to have all the weapons delivered to the airport and placed on a private plane back to the Big Island. The boys would catch a regular flight and I'd fly back with the guns. Archie had set up a van and a police escort. Yes, a police escort that would accompany me out to the country. Everything was set and in order. Then things got a little crazy. To put it mildly. During my rampage spree of dealings, I'd contacted my cousin John. The same one who got me involved in that home invasion, hostage taking trip that landed me in jail. He was currently mixed up in a sophisticated black marketing scam. His wife Christine worked at a local food distribution center owned by a rich Japanese family. She was secretary to the owner's daughter, who was also in on the scam. She had become hooked on ice, a more refined and potent form of meth that was rapidly spreading throughout the Islands. To pay for her ever increasing habit, she had resorted to stealing mass quantities of food stuffs from her Dad's company. Pallets of canned meats, tuna, rice and other goods just disappeared from the docks. My cousin, who was the dealer that sold the drug to this poor stupid girl, naturally provided the transportation, sale and distribution of the hot goods. This he accomplished by way of a snack shop owned by an older woman who was madly in love with him. It was a smooth operation beneficial to all parties involved.

Well, this lady kept her cash and receipts from all those illegal transactions hidden away at her restaurant in a large wooden box in her office. She avoided banks and accountants so as not to draw attention to her enterprise. Did I mention that she was also addicted to ice? Addicted to meth, addicted to my cousin and being played like a cheap violin. He had the best of both worlds selling his product and getting paid on both ends. Stealing goods from one and selling same to the other. Then dealing dope to the dopes. He was making a killing. In my infinite greed, I'd decided to cash in on a small piece of the action before I left. The snack shop had already been robbed once when a masked man entered the shop, locked the cook and waitress in the walk-in, broke the padlock on the wooden box and walked out with over $10,000 in cold hard cash. They did leave behind all her receipts though. How convenient. Oh, did I mention that the cook was my cousin Marge, my cousin John's younger sister? What a coincidence? The owner never called the cops to report the crime. Couldn't risk a big investigation. The whole thing stunk to high heaven. I later found out the identity of that masked robber—none other than the other cook who worked there, who just happened to work for John, pushing dope on the side. What kind of person would stoop to such lows? Not one to call the kettle black, but damn that was low!

So, as my final act before leaving Honolulu, I planned to rob the 9th Avenue Snack Shop for all its cash. Dennis, the cook who did the first job, would be working alone that day. And as we sat there drinking, getting high, we finalized our plans to take down the place. The owner and John had plans of their own to fly to Disneyland that weekend with their families. That meant there'd be well over $20,000 in the box. A good going away present. Or so I thought. The last night of our trip, we went out drinking and came home late. We'd hit the place early since the cash was already there. I'd then take the loot and catch the plane with all the guns and split town. I woke the next morning on the floor of Bun's sister's living room. I looked around and saw that the house was quiet. I called out to no one in particular and got no response. I got up and as Bun's sister exited the bedroom, I noticed the place was empty. "Where is everybody?" I asked. "Oh, they all left early this morning. They said not to wake you." Chills ran down my spine and I ran to the phone, panicked. I dialed home and my father answered. The first words out of his mouth confirmed all my fears. "You're in big trouble boy . . . where are you? Your cousin is nuts!" I hesitated to even ask, "what happened?" "I know you guys hit the snack shop this morning!" was all he said. My head was spinning. It was like a bad dream. My friends, whom I'd trusted, had gone behind my back. No, not just behind, they'd stabbed me in it. It was a sobering revelation. I somehow convinced my father that I had nothing to do with it, hung up and caught a cab to his apartment. The walls had come tumbling down around me, or rather, right on top of me. The fast life had gotten ahold of the country bumpkins and was about to swallow them whole. I harnessed my anger for now, knowing that I'd soon need every bit of it.

When I arrived at my parents' apartment, my cousin was already there. He had begged my dad for his help. With him taking charge, the shit was going to hit the fan for sure. I'm glad that I wasn't on the other end of this. As I suspected, there was nearly $20,000 in the box when they struck. They even took all the receipts. The shop owner was beside herself and threatened to go to the cops if they weren't returned. Along with the money, of course. We had until the end of the day. As angry as I was at them, I couldn't let that happen. Then I remembered I had a flight to catch. How the hell was I supposed to get all this shit resolved by then? I called to check on the flight to confirm my reservation and ask if my package had arrived. The plane was ready but no package had arrived yet. That was odd. It should have been there by now. Something wasn't right. Why's that a surprise? Considering everything else was going haywire. I told them to place the flight on standby until further notice. The meter was running. I'd have to track them down and quickly. There wasn't a doubt in my mind that Dennis was at the heart of this whole mess. He just couldn't pay attention. The greedy bastard! He'd be the first target on the scope. After a few calls, I found myself speaking to him on the phone. He was standoffish at first denying any involvement. Then I put my father on the phone. Because of John's moaning he became personally involved. It was his mission to recover the goods. That left me no leeway to operate. My dad put the fear of God into Dennis and I could hear him babbling on the phone. I looked at my cousin, sitting across the table and was reminded of when he was a kid. He always got flustered in my father's presence. Whenever he got into serious trouble, my dad would step in and set things straight. He had that exact same guilty, sorrowful "woe is me" look on his face now. I felt sorry for him. Even if it was me who wanted to rip him off. Funny, I was still pissed that those suckers had beaten me to the punch.

We drove to the location where Dennis was hiding out. He had agreed to cooperate but only to my dad. He was afraid that John and I would beat the crap out of him. He was right. I saw my dad stick his snub-nose .38 revolver into his pocket before we walked out the door. When we arrived, Dennis was already standing on the roadside. He looked like a nervous crack addict waiting for a fix. Only this time, he was attempting to purchase redemption. He climbed into the back seat, next to my dad and John turned and smacked him across the face. The crack of the blow echoed loudly. My father pulled the gun from his pocket and said, "I'm only going to ask you one time." Stuck in the middle, fearing reprisals from Bun and the gang, or a bullet in the head, he relented to the more severe. Of course, my dad wouldn't shoot him, but he never knew that. All he saw was the gun pointed at him. He sang like a canary. Showing us the gang's last known hideout. For that, he received a couple more cracks. I'd handle things from here, just in case things got messy.

Even though these guys were my friends, there's no telling what desperate men would do. I told Dennis I'd be seeing him later. His fear could be smelled.

I climbed the steep stairway that led to the house on the hillside. I listened for any familiar voices coming from inside. It was quiet and peeking through the screen door I saw that the house looked deserted. I called out and a male voice answered. He peered at me from a hallway bedroom. His body partially concealed, I recognized the face instantly. Bun's cousin. I'd met him previously during the week. He bid me to come in. "Where's Bun and Larry?" I asked. "Oh, you just missed them." He replied, "come in, they left something for you." The whole thing didn't feel right. I held the gun in my hand behind my back as I entered. He stepped into the hallway and I saw that he was unarmed. "Come, come, I got it right here!" he said. When I was about ten feet away, he ducked into the room and I stepped to the side just as the barrel of the shotgun came up. I grabbed the barrel with my left hand and smacked him hard on the side of his head with the pistol. He yelped in pain and fell to the floor. I checked the shotgun and pointed it at his face. He cried out, pleading for mercy. I wanted to blow his face off! The punk never expected things to turn out this way. Like I said, got to be prepared for anything. He had no idea where the gang had gone but Bun was going to contact him later. I left him a number and told him about the deadline. Then I kicked him a few times for luck and told him where to find me if he wanted to pursue the matter. I left him rolled up on the floor sobbing and walked out with the shotgun in my hand. It might come in handy the next time. The game had changed. Bun had tried to kill me. It was my turn. Payback is a mother!

Meanwhile, I called the gun dealer to check on my weapons. He answered on the first ring and said that the whole deal had gone bust. The Feds were on to him and he had to flee. Just like that! No refund, no nothing. Just a bunch of sorrys and thanks, but no thanks. It wasn't my day. Then it suddenly dawned on me, the guy who sold me the guns was a friend of Bun's cousin. He'd introduced the two of us. I'd been played big time! I was beyond angry. Crazy insane more like it! I wanted to kill somebody in the worst way. There was nothing left for me to do but hunt them down and exact my revenge.

After all that had happened, there was no way I could ever return to the Big Island. The line had been drawn and I found myself the odd man out. What a shame. I had adapted to that country lifestyle once again. I'll surely miss it. Suddenly, I felt lost, pensive as to my unforeseeable future. I had everything worked out down to the last detail. Looked good on paper, but too bad I forgot to factor in the human nature element. I never in my wildest dreams saw this one coming. I was totally blindsided. I had trouble dealing with the betrayal—should have been used to it by now. My life had changed drastically. If it weren't for my parents, I'd literally be out on the streets. I'd left everything behind.

Now, once again, the burden of my irresponsible behavior and visions of grandeur would fall upon my parents. My dad knew the score, but my mother hadn't the slightest idea how screwed up the situation was. As far as she knew, I was leaving today. She'll find out soon enough. I'm sure she'll be happy to have me back. For now, that is. I had a flash about my sister. She was all alone with that madman Ralph. I always worried for her safety. The guy wasn't exactly playing with a full deck. And with her living out in the boonies so far away, there was reason for concern. No doubt he'd take out my ripping his weed off on her. I think back to that day in her kitchen with that knife in my hand. I should have killed that asshole! I only hope that the boys don't hold this shit against her. If anything happened to her, I'd kill all of them. I'd burn their family tree to the ground! I had to insure her safety somehow.

Time was running out and I still hadn't heard from Bun. If worse got to worse, I'd have no choice but to hand them over. I had one last card to play. They'd left me no option—I called Archie. The minute he answered the phone, he took a big chunk out of my ass, "Where the hell are you?" My flight was hours late and the van and police escort were sitting there waiting. It cost him $5000 to arrange the whole thing. I couldn't blame him for being angry. I apologized and broke the bad news to him. Before I left, I had promised him that I'd keep his brother safe. In return for me making good on that promise, he'd forget the debt. He said he'd call that rat, his brother, and have him call. His last words to me were, "please don't let anything happen to my brother." It was a good trade, 20 years to life in prison for $5000. I felt like a rat, telling on him like that. It wasn't in my nature to do that, but he'd left me no other choice. The gloves were off and there were no rules in the game now. He'd dictated the pace, not me. The sad thing is, it cost a hell of a lot more than money. Friendship comes at a considerable price. After what he'd done to me, I should have let him burn! He never knew, even to this very day, how I'd held his life in my hands. I was obligated to see this whole thing through. Last night, when I'd shown up at his sister's house with that sweet little Japanese girl on my arm, my gift for him and the boys, he'd fallen head over heels in love with her. Made me keep the rest of the boys away from her and went in the room with her and never came out. Lucky everyone else had taken their turn. The best for last, I always say. Now here they both were on the run. I hope they are happy and enjoy each other. But wait a minute, he gets the girl and a free pass home. And I lose my life and get a sharp stick in the eye! That's some messed up bullshit! When things were looking thin, I sent my cousin to go buy us some time with his lady friend. Maybe Casanova can extend the deadline. He wasn't too happy when he found out that his Japanese piece on the side had left him high and dry for Bun. I'd managed to totally disrupt his entire life in just a few days. The master of disaster strikes again. He could care less about the girl. All he wanted was to make his cash cow happy. I just wanted out of this nightmare.

Then, like magic, the phone rang. I answered and wasn't too surprised to hear Bun's voice on the other end. Apparently, Dennis had reached him. The prospect of prison had prompted his call. After confronting him over our friendship and betrayal issues, I gave him the ultimatum. Either gives back whatever money was left and the receipts, or keep it all and go to jail. He might make if off the island, but he still had to deal with Archie. Just the mention of his brother's name changed everything. I heard it in his voice—the fear. Then he dropped the bomb. "The money's gone" he said. All that was left was a bag of change. No bills. Impossible. $20,000 . . . gone. He did have all the receipts. We struck a deal. By late afternoon Dennis arrived, with both. He wasn't kidding when he said bag of change. The money was in a Bank of Hawaii canvas bag that weighed in at about 150 pounds. Took two of us to lift it. It totaled roughly $1200 in silver. The receipts were in a pillow case. The case was closed and all parties concerned, happy or sad, could get on with their lives. My father, although furious, was content that I was in the clear. That had always been his only concern throughout this fiasco. He never forgave my cousin for getting me involved with his crap and landing me in jail. Now that I was stuck on the island we'd be seeing a lot of each other. A relationship that would lead to an even more dreadful outcome than the first. But that's for later.

I talked with Bun one last time over the phone before he left the island. We'd never see each other again and parted ways bitterly. I later found out from a nephew that he'd married that Japanese girl and had a bunch of kids. They were living the good life out in the country. I often wondered how things would have turned out if I had also made it back. I miss that peaceful life that I'd left behind and want it again. I'm glad for Bun and his family. They were two people who were searching for something and had found it together. I hope that he gets my message that I forgive him. As for Dennis, we'd meet again in the future, with him swinging from the end of a rope. His wife and her infidelity would prove too much for him and he'd end up taking his own life.

With all the money gone, it was back to working the old 9-5. How do you follow the act I had just been playing? It was difficult to readjust back into the real world again. The world where bills were paid from the hard-earned money you made by breaking your back all day. Living with my parents in their cramped apartment was getting old fast. To avoid claustrophobia, I spent most of the time out. Because of my depression, I went off the deep end. My drug and alcohol abuse reached new heights. I'd somehow managed to get a job as a baker working for some German guy named Eric. But that didn't last. I had the strangest encounter early one morning while taking a smoke break. Leaning against a wall, enjoying my final puffs, I glanced up and looked directly into the eyes of the guy who tried to kill me that Thanksgiving day in Waianae. When our eyes met, there was an instant of recognition on both our parts. Eyes locked in silence, like two predators readying for the attack, we stood there. I had no weapon at the time but knew beyond a doubt that he did. Couldn't have been more than a minute but time stood still and it seemed like hours. Without blinking and without warning, he turned and walked into the building behind him. It took every nerve and muscle fiber in my body to prevent me from dashing over there and killing him. They'll be another time for that I guarantee it. His fear had outmatched my anger. The next morning I crossed the street and asked if he was working. The man said that he quit without notice the day I saw him. I guess my appearance had an even greater effect on the guy than I thought. I never saw him again, but I keep looking. Some day.

Unemployed again, and hanging out with drug dealers to support my habit, life was heading in a downward spiral. What else is new? My mother had gone to work for a security outfit. The owner, Mr. Freeman, was a retired police officer who was on the force with my dad. Because of their friendship, my mom was issued a cushy post at a private building that had the latest security system. For the meantime, I served as her taxi, taking her to and from work. Then, one day, while driving her to the office to pick up her paycheck, we had a chance meeting with a fellow employee. The woman had learned of my unemployment and offered to speak to a friend of hers on my behalf. Who would have thought that her offer to help would find me working at the most unusual and macabre profession? After being idle for awhile, I thought that any job would suit me fine. Boy was I in for a rude awakening.

Chapter 15

Death becomes you

My appointment with Leroy, the owner of Islandwide Mortuary Services was held at the Hosoi Funeral Home. In his early fifties with green eyes and thinning hair, he'd later become more than just an employer to me. His casual demeanor and off-the-cuff humor made any stranger comfortable and relaxed in his presence. Not your average job interview, it was apparent that his questions were directed more at my ability to handle the extreme nature of the work. Leroy ran the only privately owned transportation business for human remains on Oahu. Staring at the brightly painted white station wagon with the dark tinted windows innocently parked in the lot as we spoke, cold chills ran through my entire body. The meat wagons, as they were commonly referred to, stood silently ready to do God's calling. He spoke about the different types of calls, pick-ups, which I'd be expected to perform. Some of which he explained in graphic detail. It was a description straight out of a nightmare. If it was his intent to scare me away, he was doing an awful good job! Just the thought of doing even a third of what he portrayed would be too much. What kind of person gets up everyday and goes to work hauling dead people around? I'd soon find out exactly.

I needed this job and after all my Mom had gone through to arrange this meeting, I'd be damned if I quit without giving it a try. I owed my parents that much after all the disappointment and heartache I subjected them to. My dad got a kick out of it when he found out what the job was. Before he joined the department, he drove an ambulance in Honolulu. He went on to tell gruesome tales of his adventures at car accidents and other gory scenes. "Thanks pop, just what I needed to hear." I was hired on the spot.

I was placed on a trial period and handed over to Robert the operations manager. He'd be responsible for my training. He was a character right out of the Rocky Horror Picture Show. A ghoul of a person with facial features and mannerisms precisely fitting his part as a body snatcher. He reminded me of Igor, the sorry assistant to the mad scientist in old scary movies. He had an uncanny way of speaking in tones and pauses that mirrored that image. At first, I thought he was putting on an act for me. I later realized that it was, in fact, his true character. At the time, I had no way of knowing that I would soon become intimately acquainted with death on an entirely different level. And ultimately, acquiring a rather odd personality myself.

Death, being one of the greatest mysteries in life, can have a profound effect on the average person. All of us know that we will eventually meet the Grim Reaper in our time and way, yet we run around this world ignoring this fact. We choose to put blinders on and live a life of denial. That is, until struck down. Or a friend or loved one dies. Then the realities of our own mortality become all too clear.

People say there's no use dwelling on it because sooner or later we will all get our chance. I myself, who had on many occasions carelessly tossed caution to the winds and risked my life without a second thought, never once bothered to consider what death was really all about. When you're young, you have the luxury of sticking your head in the sand. We hide from death's cold reality. This job will forever change my perspective, awakening me to its harsh truth.

Human beings are cruel and unusual creatures. We all possess the abilities to think logically and reason with ourselves and others in any situation. But when we get hurt, careless, fed-up or angry, we end up bringing our lives to an abrupt end. Some choose the manner in which we depart this world. Our exit can be dramatic and by our own hand with any of a number of implements of death. Guns, knives, cars, cooking or eating utensils, even poison. Maybe a long walk off a short pier. Perhaps a swan dive off a tall building. How about just jumping in front of a bus? Some of us have no choice on the matter and become victims of chance or fate. The wrong place at the wrong time. Five miles too fast at a stop light or intersection. Then there's the sweetest way, simply going to sleep and never waking up. Pleasant dreams. Whatever the means, when your time is up, your time is up.

I never suspected that I could take human life so callously. Though I'd done some bad things in my previous life, I never considered myself a cold-blooded person. That individual will ultimately transform because of the years at Islandwide. No different than doctors who deal with life and death on a daily basis, you have to become detached. Only in this case, there isn't the "life" part in the equation. You don't have to associate yourself with the person himself, the living, breathing entity. There's no soul or mind to contend with. Only the body. The cold, still, lifeless corpse of what was once a person not unlike yourself. Take all of that moral, ethical feeling and stuff it away and all that's left is a shell. Not to offend the squeamish ... a large piece of meat. How does a person reach such despicable depths of apathy? Easy . . . practice! If you do something enough, you get used to it. It may sound cold-hearted but it's true. And no matter how grotesque the work itself, somebody's got to do it.

What some people fail to realize, when a person dies, the body undergoes changes. Basically, the body begins to breakdown. The weather or environment the body is exposed to determines the degree of decomposition. Prolonged exposure to heat can cause more rapid changes than say, a body that was left in the cold. Most people, when they think of death, see that pretty, made-up person lying peacefully in a casket. This vision helps them accept the reality of death as a good thing. They see those who have passed on as forever in a restful sleep.

But that's not the way death is. There is nothing nice or good or peaceful about it. Except in the religious sense, where we who believe look forward to eternity in Heaven. In which case, our bodily remains can be in any state, we are in a better place. Now that I've given you a brief, but less than pretty picture, I can begin to better explain my transformation.

No sooner had I met Igor, he was off on a call at a local hospital while I was left in the charge of a man called Bull. Bull was a large Okinawan who worked part-time. His day job was ambulance driver along with Leroy, who was also his supervisor. He'd been with Leroy for years and was anxious to see if I had the stomach for the job. They laughed and joked about how I'd react to picking up a ripe one. They claimed those would be the worst kinds of cases. And, if by chance, I could handle that, the job was mine. Just listening to them describe—gleefully—the sights and smells made my stomach turn. And as luck would have it, a call came in for just such a case. They laughed and told me this call would make or break me. We jumped into the meat wagon and headed to the scene. When we arrived, there was a crowd of people standing around. Even the news people were there. My heart pounded in my chest and I had trouble breathing. I couldn't get over all those people and the expectant looks on their faces. I felt embarrassed and wanted to hide under the car. I felt that small. The police and crime unit said that a homeless guy had climbed into an old abandoned truck and died. It was a week before anyone discovered him. The rotten odor was awful! I was fifty feet away and I could smell him. It was somehow familiar to me, once you smell that stink ammonia-like aroma, it stays with you forever. I thought about that day, many years ago when we removed those shovels from our car trunk. The ones that were used to exhume that murdered girl who saw too much.

The truck was in the middle of an open field on wooden blocks about three feet off the ground. Bull opened the back door, removed the gurney and handed me a pair of disposable gloves and body bag. He said, "go ahead, show me what you got." We pulled the gurney to the door of the truck cab and he stood there, watching. I climbed up to the cab and opened the door. The smell was so bad that my eyes watered and I nearly heaved my guts out. I looked back at Bull and he wore this huge, shit eating grin on his face. I wanted to punch him square in that face. I'd be damned if I'd give him the satisfaction of watching me barf. "Well . . . what you waiting for?" he said. My madness drove me forward. Should have had a respirator, hazard suit and everything else that was out there. I tried breathing through my mouth, but the taste was worse than the smell. And the maggots! They covered every square inch of what was left of the body. They actually produced a rather distinct clacking noise that was quite audible. I reached in and grabbed ahold of the nearest appendage and yanked. The body slid right out and into the waiting hands of Bull who had, all of sudden, at seeing my performance, changed his facial expression. "Let's see what you got fat boy!" went through my mind. The crowd reacted with a loud "eeeeeu!" We hoisted the poor soul into the wagon and drove off. On the ride back Bull said, "good job . . . you're hired."

I sat silent in my filthy, smelly clothes. I still wanted to punch his face. That day, my life was changed. It was the beginning of my nightmare journey into hell. My emotional turmoil would lead me down the path to insanity.

Now that I'd broken my cherry on the job, Leroy was quick to get me up and running. I rode shotgun with the guys until I learned the routes to the different pick-up points. They consisted of all the hospitals, nursing homes, convalescent centers and retirement homes—I never thought there were so many places, or so many people who died every day. In between those runs, there were house calls—people who died at their homes of natural causes. Islandwide also held the city contract for all the unattended deaths on the island. These were your accidents, murders and suicides. Deaths where the Medical Examiner, Police and Forensic technicians got involved. Those were the real stomach-turning gory calls that nightmares were made of. They took a little getting used to. I'll never forget my first suicide case. Late one night, some poor shmuck took a full gainer off a twenty story building. I trembled so badly that I had trouble walking. I couldn't control myself. It was like standing in freezing weather without a coat. The body had landed on the third floor overhanging structure to the entrance of the building. The police had already left when we arrived. The medical examiner saw the sick look on my face as I stood staring at the pile of guts splattered across the rooftop. "Who's the new guy?" he laughed. After that call, I never shook again. The sight had scared me straight.

Robert did his best to program me into a mold that didn't fit me well. Now Frank, a Filipino/Puerto Rican guy in his middle forties was more my style. He was a rough-around-the-edges alcoholic and he was good at his work. We got along great and I learned a lot from him. He was a no-nonsense guy when it came to a pick-up. He was quick and efficient. The workhorse of the company. If Robert wore the suit and tie, Frank wore the overalls and carried the shovel. He got all the dirty jobs and that's the way he liked it. I often tagged along with him. It wasn't long before I was cut loose on my own. Leroy bought me my very own wagon. I hit the ground at full speed. There was never a lack of customers. I was soon doing as many as seven pick-ups daily. It was nuts! My day began at 8:00am and went until 4:00pm every day, six days a week. After 4:00 we were on call. Being on call 24 hours a day was rough but that was usually when all the fun started. Somehow people seemed to pick the hours from 4:30 pm to 6 am to kill themselves. Drunk drivers, killers, jilted lovers or just plain stupid folk. Well, there are those who have no say in the matter. Whenever that pager went off, someone had gone to meet their maker. Being a spiritual person, I saw it as doing the Lord's work. At first. That is, until the job drove me crazy.

The funny thing about serving God in that capacity is it literally takes over your entire life. You can kiss your social life goodbye. There'd be days when I'd work from 8 am until 8 am the next day, with little or no sleep at all. The job ran me ragged and over time began to take its toll. I felt like a slave to all those dead people. Like I owed my life to them. Like my sole purpose in life was to serve them. Wasn't long before it began to affect me on an emotional and mental level. I'd be out with friends at a nightclub or with family at dinner when my pager went off. It was non-stop, never ending. Relentless! I started drinking even more. Not only that, but I started using speed in the form of black beauties to stay awake. A strong cup of coffee and two blacks and I was good to go, no matter how much sleep I had, or should I say didn't have. One day it all caught up to me when I was flying down the highway with two stiffs in the back and I just nodded off. I came to when I heard a loud bang and felt the jolt. In my momentary unconsciousness, I'd struck a highway divider and nearly climbed completely over it into the next lane. Sobered me up real quick! The damage to my car was minimal, but Leroy wasn't too happy. Naturally I lied and said someone must have backed into me at the hospital. "You better slow down!" was all he said. I was notorious for speeding. The cops never tagged us since we worked for them so I took full advantage. Leroy lectured me about it every time he had to pay the repair bill for the replacement of my brake pads. "You know, that's the third time this year I had to fix your brakes!" He always got mad, but overlooked it in the end because I had gotten so good at my job. I even gave Frank a run for his money. Robert hardly ever talked to me and quit trying to impress me. I blew him away! Bull just shook his head whenever he saw me. He'd created a monster.

It was all fun in the beginning until the novelty wore off. It got to a point that when my pager went off I'd scream out loud. My character began to change. The more I worked, the more callous and indifferent to the bodies I became. I used to have compassion and felt sorry for them. Now, they made me angry and I hated them for what they were doing to me. The City Morgue attendant, Wayne, who also moonlighted on the side at Islandwide, once had to stop me from pummeling a large murder victim. Things got out of control when I went to transport him from the morgue to a funeral home. I was in a hurry, which was the norm, and rushing to transfer his body from the top shelf of the cooler onto my gurney. The drawer was about four feet off the ground, which made it difficult at times to transfer the corpses from the tray to the gurney. There was an electric chain hoist available but it was slow and cumbersome. So we had a technique that we used: with the gurney next to the drawer, we'd lift the feet out of the tray, hang them over on the gurney, then we'd grab the arms and pull and swing, out of the tray and onto the gurney. The body usually

275

landed perfectly. Never failed. Well, this guy was a large male about 6'3" and weighed in at 225 pounds. To top it off, the tray he lay in was full of blood, about an inch of the stuff left over from the autopsy. He also had this huge afro hairdo that was saturated with blood, like a big sponge. I managed to get his legs in the right position, but when I went to lift his arms and upper body out of the tray, his head got stuck. I should have known things were going to go bad right then, but in my haste to get the hell out I got careless. I tugged and pulled with all my might. Suddenly, the guy's head came free and whipped out of the tray in a slingshot manner. The blood that was soaked into his hair flew at me spattering my entire face and white uniform. It even went into my mouth. I went crazy! Something in me just snapped! The body hit the gurney and fell to the floor. That's where Wayne found the both of us. In my rage, I'd blacked out and didn't remember him pulling me off the guy. He told me to go clean up and that he'd load the guy up for me. When I came out of the restroom, he asked if I was alright. I told him no. He said he had to yank me off the guy that I'd been punching and screaming at him. He never told anyone about the incident and neither did I. It was clear that I was losing my marbles.

As time went by, it only got worse. I began to become a bit of a practical joker. One night, when I went to meet Robert for a house call, I parked my car across the street, so he'd think I hadn't arrived yet. He always had a holier than thou attitude, often boasting that nothing could scare or affect him anymore. So on this night, I'd run and hid in the back of his wagon on the gurney. I watched him drive up and scan the parking lot for me. He jumped into the wagon, started it up and was busy filling out the paperwork when I stood up and yelled out, "ooooh." He screamed and launched straight out of his seat and banged his head on the roof. It was hilarious! He never talked shit to me again. I think he even hated me. But that wasn't the half of it. I arrived on an accident scene early one morning, running solo because everyone else was also on the road. It wasn't uncommon for the police or fire department to help with removals. Even the medical examiner was quick to lend a hand. The male victim had been drunk, walking along the roadside, when a teenager traveling at about 70 miles an hour, struck him from behind with his mother's station wagon. The guy flew almost the entire length of a football field. He tumbled along the roadway before coming to rest on the side of the road and down the embankment. There were body parts scattered all across the highway. I had to climb down the dirt embankment to retrieve the body. When I reached him, I saw that whatever was left of this poor guy, needed to be put into a body bag. I first removed all the parts from the road and placed them in a plastic bag. I then got my portable gurney, an aluminum carrier without wheels, the kind fire and rescue uses in difficult recoveries, from the car and walked back to the scene. On the way back, a rookie cop who was busy directing traffic saw I was working alone so he offered to help. And that's when the sick prank popped into my head. No use disappointing the guy, "I'll call you when I'm ready," I called out. The eager beaver had it coming. I placed the portable on the roadside, climbed down and loaded the guy into the body bag. I observed, initially, when I went to check out the scene, that one of the victim's arms was severed almost clean off. It hung on only by a thin piece of flesh. When I had the body ready for removal, I called the unsuspecting rookie over. He came to the edge and I told him to take a hold of the guy's arm that I had kept sticking partially out of the bag. "Hang on tight . . . and when I tell you to pull . . . pull as hard as you can." "Yes sir," he replied. "Ready . . . pull!" He yanked as hard as he could and the arm tore off and he landed on his ass on the side of the road. He screamed and dropped the arm to the ground. Just before he started to throw up, I laughed so hard my side ached. The sergeant looked at me and shook his head. Beneath his laughter, he said, "you been doing this too long." Talk about a sick sense of humor. Like I said, I was losing it. I bet that cop wasn't too quick to volunteer after that.

I really don't think the people who hire us on to do the job took into consideration the psychological effects the livelihood had. And I use the word loosely. Now that I think about it, I believe that I was suffering from some form of post traumatic stress. Military personal returning home from a tour of duty and after witnessing so much death, experience the same symptoms. They suffer in silence and soon their condition worsens. Eventually, it causes them to break into a million pieces. Their emotional state of collapse is apparent to everyone around them. Yet, they themselves continue to exist in a lonely, withdrawn world of guilt, shame and confusion. Death changes a person on a deeper level. Some cope with its pervasive presence with alcohol or chemical indulgence. Others adopt an alternative persona or character. Laughing it off on the outside while crying on the inside, then there are those who resort to all these measures. And maybe you can run from the realities of death for a while, you can even hide from it within yourself, but in the end it catches up to you. Like a wet blanket smothering you. Better still, like having cancer. It's something that you can't get rid of. No matter what you do or how hard you try it never goes away, never leaves you alone.

Although the money I was making wasn't enough, Leroy made up for it by being the best employer I'd ever worked for. He was more like family than a boss and he bent over backwards to help you. He even set me up with his personal banker to obtain an unsecured loan to buy a car. Whenever I was stuck for cash, he'd advance my pay. All of which came in handy when I decided to marry. People marry for so many different reasons, love, money, title, convenience—all of the afore-mentioned. For me, it was a desperate attempt at normalcy. I honestly couldn't say that I was madly in love with Lou, my high school sweetheart with the haunting green eyes. Nor could I say I was even slightly in love. It was more of a mutual need for each other. We were both lost and searching for a better way of life. Why not do it together? Seemed like a good plan if there ever was one. Perhaps a stable lifestyle would give life more meaning. Change me into a human being again. Maybe after awhile, we'd both grow into love with each other. With our financial position in question, we put aside all the traditional fancy fanfare and were married by a judge. No one from her family attended the ceremony. It was a lack-luster quick, wham-bam—thank-you-ma'am. To help us get on our feet, we stayed with my parents. It was a little hard at first, but manageable. Lou eventually got a good job as a personal secretary for a small, but prestigious, real estate company. With her height, alabaster skin and gorgeous green eyes, she was a magnet for customers. The owners fell in love with her and paid her well. We saved most of our money, planning to someday get our own place. I enjoyed married life and adapted to it well. We were far from the ideal couple but we were young, healthy and reasonably happy. The tragedy of it all was that we both had bad habits concerning drugs and alcohol. When we first got married and were barely on our feet, we made an agreement to party and enjoy our life before settling down and actually planning for a family. So we went crazy drinking, drugging and enjoying life. It was one continuous party. And although we were, for the most part, incompatible, our bond as husband and wife grew closer. Then things started to get way out of control and we began to clash and bang heads. We often found ourselves drifting in opposite directions. We attributed it to marital growing pains. Little did we know at the time that it was a means to our end.

There were moments when we couldn't stand each other. Whenever things boiled over, she'd run home to her mother. Eventually, we would reunite, clinging to each other. Through all the ups and downs, we somehow managed to make a life for ourselves. And although my love for Lou had yet to grow, I became rather fond of her. Deep down inside, I still harbored resentment for her past. As she did for me. Those skeletons in our closets do have a way of rattling to life at times. But regardless of all the troubling mishaps, we were surviving. Before marriage, I had sort of a roving eye. I was never faithful to any of my previous partners. Now that I was married, I took my vows seriously. I felt that the sacredness of the act itself should be given every consideration and respected. It wasn't just my religious beliefs that made it easy to adhere to the straight and narrow, with my grueling work schedule, I had time for little else. I was a fool to believe that my newly acquired bride felt the same. Her inability to control her desires proved too much for her and she faltered.

Her infidelity caused me to take a second look at my commitment. Any man who becomes faced with such an issue would doubt. We separated for a while to take a breather. For now, we remained married. It was hard for me to forgive her, for holding our vows so meaningless. I was angry to the point of pure hatred. I'd given up so much and dedicated my entire world to her. It was a slap in the face. I became despondent and sunk deeper into my alcohol and drug anesthesia. I poured myself into my work, piling on insane hours. I took every call I could, anything to stay busy and keep my mind off my failed marriage. I thought about divorce, but wasn't convinced that it was the solution. After some time we reconciled and she came back. This time, we were living on our own. We'd saved enough money to rent a studio apartment in the same building as my parents. That way she could be close to my mom in case she needed anything. It's not that I didn't trust her, I tried not to think about that. I just thought she could use the support. We both could. I hid my true feelings—all the hurt and disappointment about the incident. We were both affected by the problem in different ways. Up until the moment of discovering her betrayal, I'd never put my hands on a woman. In my fit of anger, I hit her. I actually went crazy and choked her nearly to death. I also attempted to throw her out of the window. If it weren't for my parents' intervention, tackling me to the floor, she would have taken the thirteen story plunge. They had no idea at the time what caused the outbreak.

Exchanging hurt for hurt only makes things worse. But if you had to look at it from that perspective, we were even on all accounts. However, beating a woman, especially your wife, is a no-no in every sense of the meaning. I was taught at a very young age to never put your hands on a woman. There's no excuse for that kind of behavior and anyone who does it is a straight-up punk. Her fooling around does, however, bring to mind a crime scene where a man had caught his wife in the act of having sex with his neighbor. The guy was lucky that day as he dove out the bedroom window. The woman wasn't. It's hard to deny what was going on when you're caught red handed. Laying there naked on the bed she shared with her husband, she did her best to convince him that it wasn't what he thought, as he proceeded to hack her to death with the machete he used to cut sugarcane at work. In her futile attempt to block the oncoming blows, he chopped all but a couple of her fingers off. They flew and landed all about the bedroom floor. That blow continued along its arch and landed across the side of her head, splitting it wide open all the way to the brain. Gray matter leaked from the gaping inch-wide wound. He didn't stop there. He went on to chop her in every part of her torso. She was an obese woman with folds of overlapping fat layers hanging from her body. His blows were that of a madman, overcome with anger. The cuts on her stomach and legs were deep and the greasy yellow fat oozed out. The entire room was covered in blood. She had lived for quite a while as he took his anger out on her. There was blood splatter on the walls, ceiling and huge red puddles on the bed and floor. It was the kind of gory scene that horror movie producers dream of. I never thought a body contained so much blood. She had lost all of it that day, bled out. So, punk ass or what, you could say my wife got off easy. I was no less enraged and more than capable of such violence.

The trouble with death is that it owns you. It robs you of everything you hold dear. Your heart, your soul, it even robs you of yourself. If you're not careful, it will take away the people you love and in more ways than one. The horrors of my work only increased. Just when you think you had become immune to its many faces, it shows you a new one. I was fine going about my business picking up the weak, the careless, the pitiful and even the unlucky when a new profile appeared. I was called to the scene of an accident one afternoon and was shocked to see the lifeless body of an eight-year old boy laying on the street. He was covered in a white sheet that blood had already soaked through by the time I got there. A school bus was parked next to him and the driver was seated on the curb with his head in his hands, crying uncontrollably. About twenty feet from the boy lay a clean white bath towel. It stood alone in the middle of the road. To the untrained eye, an innocent object just lying there. But I knew better. The ominous sight called out to me. My heart raced as I approached the covered figure, with his tiny sneakered feet sticking out from under the cover. Lifting the sheet slightly, I could see that something was missing. His face was disfigured and flat. It looked like someone had taken a rubber Halloween mask and put it where his head should have been. How could anyone play such a cruel prank? Then the truth hit me, like a slap upside the head. I looked closer and saw that his brain was missing. I dropped the sheet and stared at the towel on the road. Somewhere in the background, I vaguely hear a voice calling to me. It was the medical examiner telling me it was okay to move the body. He said it so matter-of-factly without any trace of emotion. I wanted to break down and cry. Just sit there on the road and cradle that poor child in my arms and cry like a baby for him. I thought about my nephew, who was the same age as this boy. It took every last bit of my strength to gather up the courage to remove that kid. Children that age are so trusting. They're not yet fully developed and depend on their parents to protect them, to keep them safe. Well, on this particular day this kid's older brother failed miserably in that department. In his aimless, self-centered attempt to converse with his pals, he'd dashed across the street and left his brother running to catch up. In his excitement to reach his brother, he'd forgotten the golden rule when crossing the street. He never saw the school bus as he rushed across its path. When it struck him, his brain flew out of the back of his skull and skidded along the road. And there it sat, in perfect condition, beneath that innocent white towel. It broke my heart when I held it in my hands. With all the death in my life, I never got used to picking up children.

There is a lot of legend, story and myth about the dead. No, bodies don't sit up all of a sudden from the gurney. They do, however, moan and groan when you move them, but only if freshly dead. It's just the body expelling gases that are trapped in the guts. And no, your hair and nails don't continue to grow after you die. And yes, there are a few sick, demented individuals who engage in necrophilia. I had heard rumors of certain people but never actually witnessed anything. I find the practice unimaginable. I don't want to sound cold or unfeeling, but I viewed a dead body as a piece of meat, similar to a piece of steak or hamburger. Raw, cold, lifeless . . . dead! There was no difference as far as I was concerned. And yes, the dead are victims of theft. Things came up missing all the time. I've even seen the gold fillings removed from teeth and collected in peanut butter jars then later sold for cash. Even ten karat gold fetches a good price. Then there were the pacemakers. You couldn't cremate a person with one—the batteries explode like a bomb in the oven. They have to be cut out before you torch them. A brand new one costs thousands, which is why a few hospitals would pay hundreds for a used one. Highly unethical of course, but it happened all the time. Well, it did back then. Walk into the medical department and speak to the right people and the next thing you know, the accounting department was cutting you a check. They would buy all you had. Many people think that their loved ones leave this life with all their jewelry on their wrists and fingers. Don't be fooled. Jewelry can't be burned in the oven either and has to be removed. The funeral director should tell you that, but doesn't happen in all cases. Once a person arrives at the crematorium whatever is left on the body, except for clothing, is removed. So before you say goodbye to a loved one, check it out. To cope with all the stresses of the job, I attended cremations stoned. A repulsive side show for the maniacal, entertainment for the disturbed. Normal people just go the movies. I preferred to drop large amounts of LSD and stand staring through the peep hole of the oven while bodies burned. I'd stand there for hours, sometimes until the body had turned to ashes, mesmerized by the dancing flames. The two old gentlemen who ran the place never protested. They were a bit odd themselves and got a kick out of my weird behavior. To know one is to love one. A crazy that is. We, who live the life of caring for the dead, understand.

I had found my gold mine by cleaning the houses and apartments of those who had died in a decomposed or messy state. Most of these people had no family and were often discovered by the putrid smell. I'd talk to the manager or home owners when I went to remove the remains and we'd make a deal. I usually charged as much as $800 for the cleaning. But the real treasure was what the dead left behind. The owners just wanted their property cleaned, they didn't give a damn about what was in the place. "It's yours if you want . . . just get rid of it!" was the usual order. There was everything—electronics, furniture, pots and pans—you name it, I got it. I had entire roll-off boxes filled with mechanics' tools worth thousands at some sites. Construction tools of every sort. I even found money and guns. The money I kept, but the guns I turned into the medical examiner. I once found $1000 in change and $2000 in money orders. Whatever I didn't, or couldn't keep, because of the smell and contamination, was thrown out. Hauled away to the dump in my van. It was a sweet way to make extra cash. I got 2 or 3 jobs a month when business was good. Other times, I'd get just a single case, then nothing for a couple of months. It was questionable, but honest. I was rendering a service to those who wanted nothing to do with what I dealt with on a daily basis. Where's the harm in profiting from that? I wasn't hurting anyone. I got all the chemicals I needed for the job from the embalmers at the funeral homes, so the overhead was zero. It was 100% profit. Couldn't beat that. The health department may have had a question or two since I wasn't licensed, certified or trained in this kind of biohazard. But who cared, or even knew, about such things back then. Today you have to undergo extensive training and possess expensive equipment to even compete for a job that could pay thousands for a single cleaning. Progress . . . who needs it?

Just when I thought life held no gifts of pleasure, Lou announced that she was pregnant. I was ecstatic! Finally, I was going to be a father. The news had transported me into a totally different state of mind. All I could think about was my baby's arrival. Even though Lou and I were still on shaky ground, I doted on her and tried to put it all behind me. She was a beautiful expectant mother. Her skin took on a porcelain glow, so clean and fresh, and her bright green eyes burned brightly with happiness. I couldn't wait to become a complete family. There was a sign of hope, of better things to come. They say that bringing a child into the world is a wondrous event, one that changes your life forever. I looked forward to it. I counted on it.

On the day of my daughter Keanu's arrival, we rushed to the hospital when Lou went into labor. She had a hard labor that lasted over ten hours. When the time had come, I was there in the delivery room, dressed in the appropriate garb, camera in hand, ready to record the auspicious occasion. Suddenly, the baby's head appeared and everything happened so quickly, as I stood there, shocked and amazed. I felt a warm feeling wash over me. The miracle of life was happening right before my eyes. And I just stood there, frozen, as she arrived. There was a dull ringing in my ears as I heard Lou's voice pierce the veil of fog I was trapped in. She was screaming, "honey, take the picture . . . quick!" The nurse next to me snatched the camera out of my hand and saved the day, snapping away as my beautiful baby girl entered the world at ten pounds, five ounces. Strange, but even though we were expecting a girl, I kept looking for a penis. I wonder if all new fathers do that? She was absolutely perfect in every way. From her fat, wrinkled face to her beautiful blue eyes. With ten fingers and ten gorgeous toes, we were good to go. The minute I held her in my arms, electricity shot through my entire being. It was as if we were physically, mentally and spiritually joined. I was floating on air! I was experiencing a natural high that out-did any drug I'd ever taken. I felt whole.

Bringing Lou and the baby home to our own space proved to be a rewarding and joyous moment and I was still walking on air. I was experiencing feelings I never felt before. When my daughter was born it was by far the happiest day in my life, then and now. But in this cruel world, for people like me, good things never last.

Keanu was a perfect baby. She was my whole world. Like most couples who experience their first newborn, we spoiled her with attention. She slept on the bed between us. They say that such a practice can be dangerous for babies, that parents can roll over the little body and kill them. Not so in our case. I had gotten used to having her tiny figure next to me and we'd surround her with pillows to keep her safe. I'd lay her across my chest and feel her precious breath on my face each night before I slept. In the early morning hours, I'd jump awake at the slightest sound. I would turn and see her big, blue eyes looking back at me, her smiling face happy to have my undivided attention. I'd feed and carry her in my arms, listening to her soft delightful sounds.

I would spread her toys across the carpet and play with her for hours, her mother protesting about our wee hours of the morning romps. Those moments that we spent alone together were the highlight of my days. She was my life. I adored her with all my heart and could never imagine living without her. It didn't matter if I worked the next day or not, if I had enough sleep or not. Those moments I spent alone with my angel were all that mattered.

I worried a lot about my job and the biological waste and hazards that I had contact with at work. The smell of death never washes off no matter how many baths you take. It becomes a part of you. Even if you know you're clean, you always feel dirty. That bothered me constantly. I wouldn't go near my daughter, or even touch her, until I took an extensive shower. I was so afraid that the Grim Reaper's stench and all that he represented would get to her. I was paranoid about it when it came to her. It became apparent to Lou that I was more in love with my daughter than with her. I saw it in her eyes, heard it in her voice, whenever I held or played with Keanu. It was a weapon that she'd come to use against me. A weapon that I was helpless to defend against. Eventually it would become the only power over me she possessed and like a puppet master, she manipulated the strings and made me dance.

There comes a time in a man's life when he has to make a supreme sacrifice. In order to survive and protect his very existence, he has to turn and walk away from all that he holds dear. As difficult a task as it seems, his choice ultimately destroys the lives of many. There was no way, with Lou and I constantly at odds, to prevent our break up. With no common ground strong enough to support our crumbling marriage, our violent battles escalated, resulting in the police having to be called and me over the back fence into the night. Returning the next day to an empty house, without my daughter. I sat crying in the middle of the room and drew in the scent of her. I swore I'd move heaven and earth to get her back as my hatred for my wife burned hotter and brighter.

No longer able to function in a reasonable fashion, I quit my job at Islandwide and became hooked on heroin. With no income, I found myself in the exact same predicament I was in when I defaulted on my custom van loan. Only now I had two cars and an outstanding debt of over $10,000. I couldn't have cared less about any of that, all I wanted was my precious daughter back. If I couldn't have that, then the needle filled with comfort, would do. After three years of wearing the yoke of God around my neck, with the tally at close to three thousand corpses to my name, my brain was fried! So many different factors could be contributing to my fragile state. Dennis hanging from the end of a rope in the middle of a school yard playground? The only time I really associated the job with people—he wasn't just a piece of meat. He was someone I knew. The many faces of the dead hover around me, a constant reminder of a nightmare that passed. Now I can finally sleep. Enjoy the peaceful rest I'd done without for so many years. Seemed like forever. And as I release the belt from my arm, I begin to drift off into la-la land, sweet comfort. Happiness surrounds me and life's worries disappear into the fog. I begin to nod off. Is that a baby's cry in the distance? Only heartache for the wicked?

Chapter 16

Means to an end

Devastated by the separation, I fell into a deep, dark depression. It wasn't the fact that I had a failed marriage on my hands, it was not having my daughter close to me that hurt. I hated Lou for taking her away from me. I never saw at the time that I was as much at fault as she was for the break-up. Too young and immature to accept the responsibility or share the blame, I threw it all on her. I'd experienced hurt from separation before with Elvia, but this was different. I can't say that one hurt more than the other, but if I had to rate them on a scale from one to ten, both were a fifteen. Nothing could fill that emptiness. I drank myself blind and did whatever drug there was to stop the pain. I was lost. I discovered that heroin, although it couldn't erase the hurt completely, was the best remedy to dull the pain.

I found relief in two friendships that would eventually impact my life in very different ways. James was a drug dealer I'd met while in high school. Everybody called him Jimbo and knew him as the guy to see if you needed weed. We met through fellow football players that partied with me. After school, Jimbo and I became best friends and hung out on a regular basis. He had no personal life other than his hustling of drugs.

He fueled my drug addiction for years. We were like brothers, even though his ability to make money from dope and refrain from using, made him somewhat condescending at times. He was a pretty tough guy, about 5'10" and weighed in at around 200 pounds. But even if he could hold his own in a fist fight, he was nowhere near as vicious or cold as I. He knew as well as I did that if it came down to killing, I'd take the front line. Businessmen always have a guy who wears the dirty overalls in the background to do their heavy lifting. All of which would be proven to its ultimate example in our future.

Through Jimbo, I met Derrick. He was a slim and lanky rat-faced individual who was as scandalous as he looked. Derrick was the epitome of the street smart hustler. He'd do anything for a fix. No moral compromise was too low for him. He was the type of guy that, although he was your friend, you could never trust him. His needs and desires always came first. It was like handling a pet snake. They were fun to have and look at from a distance, but if you weren't careful, you'd get bit. Derrick learned most of his street smarts from his dad, Jimmy. Jimmy was one of the last of a dying breed of heroin dealers who distributed their drugs out of a bar on the infamous Hotel Street, the Minatoya Lounge. There was a gambling establishment on the second floor and that's where I went to purchase heroin from Jimmy himself the first time we met. We entered via a long, narrow stairway guarded by a huge scary guy. When we first entered the room, it was in darkness save a naked light bulb hanging from a socket that was shielded by a metal shade. The light shined directly downward, making it impossible to see how big the room was or if there was anyone else there. Derrick introduced us and I handed over the money. Jimmy was a slim Japanese man in his late fifties, well-dressed in aloha attire. Taking the money, he scrutinized me with a questioning look and said, "So, you're the ex-cop's boy?" It shocked me at first to hear him say such a thing, but in his line of work, you had to be careful. All I could say was "yes." "My boy said you're okay . . . I don't usually sell to anyone personally, but I wanted to meet you," was all he said as he eyed me. He handed me the heroin and shook my hand. His grip was strong and sure. "Nice to meet you sir," I said. All at once the lights came on and I was stunned to see that the room was filled with people. They all sat around tables with cards in their hands. There were piles of money on the tables and dealt cards sitting face up. They all stared at me and my skin crawled. Must have had thirty people in that room, seated at those tables. I was blown away! They were so quiet! You'd never know they were there if the light hadn't gone on. Before we exited, Jimmy looked at me with a knowing smile and it was at that precise moment that a permanent understanding of trust passed between us. And so my introduction into the secretive life of heroin addiction was sealed. A life of slavery to a different god—a god that was merciless.

The drug made me sick to my stomach, at first. Soon, your body builds a tolerance for it and the high emerges. The warm, comforting feeling captures you and transports you to a warm and fuzzy place. A place where the cares of the world are forgotten. Heroin is a drug like none other. Far beyond the mental effects, the physical dependency is what forces you to keep on doing it. The high the drug produces is like floating on air. For those of you who have had major surgery, you are well aware of the feeling. Racked with pain, it's that magical medicine that the doctor slams into you with a syringe. Only with heroin, the pain factor isn't present. Only pleasure. Heaven and hell in a needle. Heroin addicts are a different kind of animal. Without their daily dose, they get sick. The physical need for the drug kicks in, the one side effect that can kill you. That is, aside from overdosing. When the jones comes calling, there's no denying it, no ignoring it. It reaches into your guts, grabs them and starts ripping like a giant hand, and it squeezes and twists until you feed it. There's no stopping a heroin addict on the jones from getting that shot. I'd heard stories and even seen friends go through it and now it was my turn to live the experience. You reject it, then you embrace it, then you love it. Soon, it owns you. The devil owns you. That's why they call it "boy."

Without a job, I began running errands with Derrick for his dad. Picking up and delivering heroin to customers and friends. With my own habit through the roof, it was the only way I could get the drug. Every morning, noon and night Jimmy would meet us at Derrick's house and fill the spoon for us. It was payment for our work. He'd drop two or three "papers" (1/20 of a gram) into the spoon, fix himself one then repeat the process for us. That was enough to wipe me out for the morning. It barely got Derrick started, his tolerance for the drug was so high. Heroin affects everyone differently. Whenever I did it, I found myself lying flat out on the floor or sunk into a chair. It was like morning coffee for Derrick and he'd spring to life. He even drove us around town. I'd always have to keep one eye on him the entire time he was behind the wheel. As any moment the drug would get the best of him and he'd nod out at a stop light or whenever. Nothing that a swift backhand to the chest couldn't fix. I hated when he did it while his son was on board. I put a little extra punch in the wake up call on those occasions.

It was ironic that I found myself running around dealing and buying drugs on those very streets that my father and grandfather once walked as policemen years before. I'd often wonder to myself, "How did I ever get into this position?" But the thought lasted only briefly, then vanished. I was way past the point of caring, blinded by my need for a drug that possessed me. Throughout my addiction, I had no way of knowing that the product we were dealing was being provided by a cold-blooded contract killer named Ronnie Ching. The name itself makes the blood run cold in the hearts of some of the most feared men in the Hawaiian underworld. He was an independent hit man who killed strictly for money. Only later, when I'd have the opportunity to meet the man in person, I'd discover that he had a lust for the job. He loved it. I'd previously come into direct contact with his handy work while working at Islandwide. Both were brutal killings in which the men were shot right in the open. One in a nightclub as he sat at the bar, having drinks. Ronnie walked in with an M-16 rifle, took aim from a cigarette machine and shot the victim in the back. Killed instantly. The other was a man who was found shot in a car on Hotel Street. A known gambler, he had over $25,000 in cash on him. He also had two handguns tucked in the waistband of his pants. He never knew what hit him. His two feet were planted on the sidewalk and his torso was slumped on the front seat, door wide open. He even had a pouch of loose diamonds in his pockets. All that wealth and he couldn't buy his way out of dying. When I first shook hands with the guy, it was like death crawled up my arm and into my soul. Believe me, I know death on every imaginable scale and this guy was the grim reaper come to life. Cold as ice. But he had lots and lots of heroin and that's all that mattered. The rest I could deal with. Then I caught a glimpse of the six o'clock news one night, "Police raided the apartment tonight of a suspected contract killer and drug dealer." Right away I recognized the building where Ronnie lived. The raid had uncovered a false wall in the apartment with pounds of heroin, cocaine and a cache of weapons. That was the beginning of the end for Ronnie. And my supply of heroin. The gravy train was over.

Here's where my time line gets a little confusing. I believe, however, that it was around this time that I ran into a former classmate from Lahainaluna days named Ron. We'd stayed in touch over the years, but drifted apart when he went to prison for manslaughter. He was convicted of beating his infant child to death because he wouldn't stop crying. His former wife, Michiyo, was a Japanese national and a lovely person. They used to come visit and bring the baby. It was their first child and they seemed to be a happy couple. I soon found out that Ron had been abusing his wife as well as his new born baby. She stopped by unannounced one afternoon without Ron, sporting a black eye and bruises on her body. She looked deathly afraid and sullen. But that's not what alarmed us. The baby had a large bruise on his face. Michiyo said that she had dropped him while bathing. You could tell that she was hiding something. She was so reluctant to discuss the matter; I had a funny feeling in my gut, but dismissed it. I looked at the bruises on her face and went ballistic. I couldn't believe that Ron could be so stupid. I refused to even consider the notion that ate away at my gut. That he may have hit the baby. Ron soon arrived in our driveway with the look of a madman on his face. He exited his car, swearing and asking for his wife. I was on him in an instant. I grabbed him by the throat, lifted him off his feet and slammed him into the ground. I then began to beat the crap out of him. He pleaded and cried like a bitch and Michiyo and my mom came to his rescue. She begged me to stop. Something inside me said keep going. It just felt so right. I wanted to kill the son of a bitch. If I'd known then what was to come, I wouldn't have stopped. I could see that after all she'd been though, she loved him. They cried and hugged each other, convincingly. I told him that if he ever touched her again, I'd chop his hands off. Later on in the week they showed up again. This time without the baby. He had died days before. They were visibly shaken and stricken with grief. Ron cried in my arms and I tried my best to comfort them. All they had now was each other. I knew it would be hard, but together they could still make a life for themselves. After they left, I had a sinking feeling in the pit of my stomach. I couldn't put a finger on it, but it bothered me. It was a while before I heard any word from either of them. The next news came when he was charged for the baby's death and she had left to go back to Japan. I bit my lip and my heart broke for that poor child and his mother. I should have killed him when I had the chance.

Ron was now working as a loss prevention agent-aka, store detective-for Burns International. Come to think of it, we had run into each other when he was walking the floors at F.W. Woolworth's and I was shopping. The chance meeting, I now believed to be more of an act of fate than a coincidence. I hadn't seen him in years and he took his lunch break so we could catch up. He had an air of arrogance about him that only people who have been in prison possess. The punk-ass baby killing, child molesting, women raping air of phoniness that this kind of lowlife adopts. I wanted to punch his face! In all of his bullshit, the one piece of valuable information he passed on was that they were hiring and they didn't care if you had a police record or not. It was on the job training and with Ron at the top of the ladder, he would more than likely be training me. I told him to set it up. I had nothing else to lose, since Derrick and I had parted ways less than amicably.

One night, while I was passed out from an overdose in the backseat of my car, he decided to commit a burglary. I awoke the next morning parked on a side street down on Hotel Street with hoards of people gathered around my vehicle. The trunk was open and Derrick was busy peddling goods from it. There was all this brand new merchandise—designer sunglasses and one-of-a-kind air-brushed hats. They were selling like hot cakes. Still in the fog, I got out and asked him what the hell was going on. He flashed his hustler smile beneath those gaudy shades and said, "we're rich partner. We hit the mother load . . . ready for a fix?"

There was a stack of bills in his hand. Sensing my uneasiness and confusion, he handed me a pair of shades and a cap, pointed to all the merchandise in the trunk and said, "See?" There were boxes of brand new stuff in there. He then handed me a few papers of heroin and told me he'd be right with me after closing up shop. Didn't have to tell me twice. We sat there, getting high and he divided the money between us. He said there was more stuff where that came from. Boxes more. All we had to do was wait until dark and then go get it. Sounded too good to me. What he failed to mention was that all this shit came out of a van that was parked in a garage at the Pagoda Hotel. The hotel my dad worked at as the security supervisor. Of which I was duly informed when I walked through my parents' front door that afternoon. I was greeted by a parent on the verge of murder. What my accomplice failed to realize was that the private parking structure was littered with security cameras that captured the entire theft on tape. Lucky for us, the owner of the van and goods it held was a personal friend of my dad's. He was setting up business in the tourist shop of the hotel and had left his van there for safe keeping until he could display his merchandise. When the man had gone to his van the next day, he discovered the missing boxes and reported the crime directly to my father. When they reviewed the tapes, my dad recognized my car and Derrick instantly. He could only assume that I was in on it. In an effort to protect me, he made a deal with the owner. Here I was a part of something I knew nothing about, but was just as guilty of. All the guy wanted was his stuff back. Whatever was left. He didn't even want any money from the sales. I wanted to kill Derrick for what he did. I had until nightfall to come up with the goods. Most of the stuff was still in the trunk of the car. I'd given the car to Derrick without my dad's knowledge because his mom had kicked him out of the house; he was currently living out of it. That's where I found him and his girlfriend, sleeping soundly.

I removed the twenty-five pound, six-foot long steel pry bar from the trunk and took a big swing at the windshield. The glass shattered and imploded shards of broken glass into the interior. It showered the slumbering love birds. I continued along the doors and side panels, across the hood and onto the trunk. A rude awakening in every sense of the word. The girl was terrified and screaming at the top of her lungs. "Please . . . I sorry, I sorry. No kill me. Please?" She didn't even know what she was sorry for. Derrick clung to her in a futile effort to protect himself. I broke the window of the backseat out and smashed him in the face with the bar. Blood gushed from his mouth and lips as he screamed apologies for his actions. They yelled hysterically for me to stop as the girl, traumatized, huddled on the floor next to him. She begged for his life as I reached in, snatched him by his long hair and pulled him through the window. He resisted and I slammed his head along the pieces of broken glass that remained. Through my anger, I heard the blood curdling scream of a woman possessed. It snapped me back to reality and I let him go. I pried the trunk open with the bar and retrieved the stolen merchandise.

Again, my father had to come to my aid. No doubt saving me from another stint in prison. The messed up thing about this whole affair was that I was an unwilling participant. If I had been aware of the circumstances, I would have done anything to have prevented it. That made me no less guilty. Rationalization 101.

Ron had gotten me a one-on-one meet with his supervisor, Silos Aqui. He was the head man responsible for all retail and grocery security, which included F.W. Woolworth and Star Markets, a local grocery store. We filled out the necessary paperwork and I was hired on the spot. I had no idea what the hell I was doing, but I'd learn real soon. How difficult could walking around a store, looking for thieves be? It took a crook to catch a crook. The saying would never become more factual than in my case. I learned quick and adapted to the job like a fish to water. It was easy and after training with Ron initially, I met Michael. He was a tall, slim Chinese guy about 6' 3". He came from a rich family and his parents both had their own businesses. The mom was a member of the elite million dollar club where only realtors who sell upwards of a million dollars in homes could belong. His dad had his own photography studio. They both came from money. He lived with his millionaire, land-owning grandmother who constantly reminded him of how his previous bad behavior towards her dead husband would earn him zilch after her death. I liked him from the start and he taught me a lot about the business. We'd spend many hours on the floor as partners and see our way through a few fist fights. He always stood his ground no matter how bad the odds. I admired him for that and trusted him. He in turn, trusted me back. After seeing the viciousness I brought to the game, everyone was soon convinced that I was an up and coming star.

Because of my ability to handle myself, and love for violence, Silos placed me in all the trouble spots. Spots where floor walkers on the average day got beat up or quit because of high threat and probability of violence. I thrived in the environment. I welcomed the challenge and physical confrontation that was associated with the job. I was a natural at the work. My penchant for violence equally matched the people that I hunted on a daily basis. Yes, hunted, because that's exactly what I was doing. I hunted the greatest animal that roamed the planet. Some may say that a charging rhino or elephant is the greatest prize a hunter can bag. I beg to differ. There's nothing like hunting a human. We humans have the ability to think making my prey even more challenging. Even more dangerous. There was nothing like it. Hunters pay millions each year to go on extravagant safaris to hunt and kill a single animal to add to their collection. All for the sport. I got to hunt the most cunning animal there is. And I don't even need a gun.

Before long, I had equaled and in some cases, surpassed all other store detectives before me. With my arrest numbers climbing, along with my total amount of merchandise recovered, I had finally found my place in the law enforcement field. Not exactly the one I thought I was destined for, but close. My father was proud to see me battling for the good guys for once. It never ceased to amaze me what the average thief was capable of. They would fill shopping carts full of stuff and simply walk out the door. Then they would load up the trunks of their cars as casually as can be. When confronted with the reality of jail, they'd reach into their bag of tricks to conjure up an excuse for their larceny. My mother is sick and she needs this or that to get well. I was going to pay for it but forgot. Yeah, you forgot to pay for the whole bag of items you carried out of the store. I've heard every lame excuse there is and then some. Shoplifting is a misdemeanor and many times offenders get a slap on the wrist and do no jail time. That is, unless you steal over $1000 worth of merchandise. Then it becomes a felony. Ever wondered what a shoplifter looked like? Well, all you have to do is take a look in the mirror. Everyone and anyone fits the profile of a shoplifter. You'd be surprised to see just what kind of people steal. Rich people, poor people, black, white, red or yellow. I once arrested an off-duty cop who'd walked out with two shopping carts loaded to the brim with merchandise. One cart alone was filled with liquor. Hundreds of dollars worth. He was a big dude, tall and over 200 pounds. First thing he said when I stopped him was, "I'm a cop!" Just before I jumped up and put a sleeper hold on his ass. Was like wrestling a steer to the ground. But out cold he went. When he woke up, he was hand cuffed behind his back and being dragged, face down through the store. He cried like a baby and begged me to let him go. All he could see was his pension turning to dust. I would have too, but the manager said he came in at least twice a month and did the same things. I chewed him a new ass and called his fellow boys in blue to come get him. Funny, the guys who came to transport him knew him. I clearly saw the distain on their faces as they hauled him away. They kept making excuses for themselves, "Not all cops are like this scumbag!" I guess they felt embarrassed for the Department. Who could blame them? The guy's career was over. I thought about my dad. He would have been pissed. At the guy that is.

Like drug addition, shoplifting holds no prejudice and has no favorites. It can affect anyone. Most people do it on a dare. For kicks. The thrill of getting away with it. Beating the system. Others do it because they simply can't help themselves. Kleptos. They don't even need or want the stuff they take. Crazy people. Some do it because they want an item but don't have enough money to pay for it. Many of these people have never committed a crime in their lives. They just want that item so much—have to have it so badly that they roll the dice. Some first timers get away with it. They experience the thrill, that rush of adrenaline through their veins after having committed the perfect crime. They swear to never do it again. But the high, that rush, haunts them. Nothing in the world has ever made them feel so alive. Just one more time . . . I promise. So they roll the dice again. This time, I'm waiting outside the store for them. Busted—you lose.

When you are the hunter, you hold your prey's life in the palm of your hand. Once I slap those cuffs on your wrist, you belong to me. I'm free to do with you as I please. Arrest you. Set you free. Or even exploit you. Some people would do anything to get those cuffs off. They cry, they plead, they beg. The most desperate, those who need just one more arrest before they go back to jail or get thrown out of the country; those who can't take any more beatings from a parent or spouse, they deal, barter and bribe for their freedom. Gamblers with thousands of dollars in their pockets, young beautiful women with short skirts, prostitutes ready, willing and able to please. In the beginning they made me extremely angry. I'd yell at them and send them down. But with a raging out of control drug habit choking me to death, I began to take a serious look at the gold mine I held in my hands. Forget about all that moralistic bullshit. It was survival of the fittest. The prospect of taking a bribe gnawed at me for awhile until it finally ate through my soul, deciding to do it for the cash only.

The first bribe I ever took was from a Filipino man in his sixties. He'd stolen a bunch of small items amounting to less than ten bucks. When I brought him into the office and searched him, I found over $25,000 on him. I was shocked! I had wondered why he was so reluctant for me to search him. At first, I scolded the man and asked, "why you steal this stuff when you had all this money to pay?" After questioning him, he admitted to winning all the money at a cock-fighting event. Then he said something that flipped the switch on inside my head. "Please, sir, I no can go jail. They send me back Philippines." In his broken English, the words rang loud in my ears. So we talked a little more, "how bad you want to stay in America?" The words came out of my mouth but it sounded like someone else in the room said it. The old man looked at me and smiled. "You like rip me off?" He grumbled in his native tongue and said, "I give you $200, you let me go." I stared at all those beautiful hundred dollar bills fanned out on the desk and said, "$2000." He laughed and told me he'd rather go to jail than give me that much of his tax-free gambling money. Whatevers! I reached for the phone to call the cops. He started to cry and said, "No, no, I pay, I pay." He watched as I counted out the cash, gave the rest to him and stuck my $2000 in my pocket. I photographed him and made him sign a trespass form, basically saying you're not allowed to set foot on this property for one year. Then I cut him loose. It was the easiest money I'd ever made.

From that day on, I began to rethink this whole work for profit thing. I looked around in all directions of the store and thought, "Why stop at blackmail and bribes?" There is so much stuff in this freakin store! Why not just help myself to whatever I wanted? And so it began, my shoplifting career. Remember earlier, I mention the different types of people who shoplift? Well, I left out the ones who do it for a living. The professionals. These people are an entirely different animal altogether. Stealing from stores is their job. They do it every day, it's their livelihood. They even go as far as to acquire clients who special order items from different stores. High-end stores, low-end department stores, grocery, even pharmacies. These boosters prowl the retail merchant world and feed off the teats of the cash cows of society. A professional booster can make hundreds, even thousands in one haul. These are the people you see on the news. They walk into a clothing store, walk up to a rack, grab as much as they can and walk out of the store. Most work in teams. They circle the store like sharks until they spot the right food, then they strike.

Some are lookouts, others are decoys. The decoys help spot the floorwalkers and lure them away from the real thieves. Some teams have a hitter, a smasher or a slammer. These are the guys who drop back and wait for the booster to exit the store. Their job is protection. They roll up on the store dicks from the blindside and clock 'em. I saw many floorwalkers go down hard. Some get knocked out cold by a slammer. But not me, never in a million years. To prevent that from happening, I was always on my toes. Some boosters are the smashers themselves. When you approach them to identify yourself, they turn around and punch you square in the face. So to prevent that, I never followed the rules of arrest. See, there are a few basic elements of a crime that have to occur before your bust can be good. It's universal throughout the retail merchant's security world. First, you have to observe the suspect enter or be standing in that particular aisle he's committing the actual crime. Then, you have to see the suspect remove the item from the shelf, look in all directions to show that their intent is to steal. Then you have to see them conceal the item on his person, either in pockets, down the pants, or in a bag. Some thieves carry empty boxes on them that look like mail parcels. The box usually has a trap door allowing them easy access to conceal the item. Some even invent ingenious suspended rigs with belts or straps between their legs. A woman who had such a device beneath her dress was caught exiting the store with a microwave oven between her legs. Clever huh? Not clever enough. She got caught. But think about all the times she got away with it. Anyway, where was I? Oh yeah, then you have to observe the suspect exit the aisle, walk past the check stand, making no attempt to pay then exit the store. Once three feet out (that's the distance the law requires) he's toast! Last, but not least, you approach the suspect, pull your credentials out and place the suspect under arrest. If all those elements are not present, your case is bust. Observation has to be constant. You must never lose sight of the suspect throughout the entire event—or that's what you write on your report. There you have it. The rules of being a Loss Prevention Agent. Kind of a catchy title huh? The reason why I stress the fact that you should keep an eye on your target is, sometimes the suspect gets cold feet and ditches the item somewhere in the store. Then, when you go outside and place him under arrest, he doesn't have the goods on him. Now you're left standing there with egg on your face and what's known in the business as a "bad stop." Potential lawsuits if you aren't careful; but there's a remedy for everything. We'll discuss that later.

Getting back to my method of prevention from being punched in the face. I do away with the polite element of the arrest. The "excuse me sir, ma'am, but you forgot to pay for that item in your pocket, purse, ass, whatever," while presenting my badge to them like a shield of everlasting glory. I simply grab a hold of the suspect, physically, which is a no-no in the rule book, and slam him up against a wall or into the pavement. They don't ever get the chance to think. Some react with a swing or elbow, but I'm way ahead of them. It happens so fast they don't know what hit them. For those who do attempt to hit me . . . well let's just say they're overpowered. Many agents disagreed with my methods, but I produced results. You can't argue with numbers, they never lie. Oh and those bad stops, I've never had one. All the good agents claim that must be bullshit. They cover it up one way or another. If they didn't, they'd be fired. Yes, I stopped people who had nothing on them. Most just got scared and tossed the item before they exited and I was just too high to see them unload it. They rant and rave and ask for the manager and threaten to sue the pants off me. The thing is, they did try to commit the crime and you know it. So I'd threaten them right back. While their screaming in front of the crowd, I lean in close so that only they can hear what I'm saying, "look punk . . . I know you dropped the shit before you left. So if you want to make a big deal out of this, let's go back into the store . . . I'll grab any item from the shelf and pin it on you and send you down!" That shut them up real quick. The bluff always worked. After all, the intent was there and they knew it. However, there was this one time when I stopped this lady and she didn't have the stuff on her. She opened her bag to show me. I could have sworn up and down that I saw her take it. But it was the way she denied it that made me question what I'd seen. She asked to speak to the manager. I apologized profusely and for some reason, that day when I went to stop her, I was polite. She grumbled and walked away. My heart was pumping and chills ran all over me. Yup, that was a bad stop for sure. It never happened again, no matter how stoned I was.

When I started stealing from the stores I worked at, I stole stupid stuff like cassette tapes, batteries, candy, cologne—stuff for me, not to sell. Although I had stopped shooting heroin, my habit was still substantial. I needed help, an accomplice. I spoke to Jimbo about my plan to rip off the store. When I was working at Islandwide, I had introduced him to a beautiful Samoan girl who was now his steady girlfriend. I asked them to come in together and pick up items that I stashed in the store and carry them out. He was an avid fisherman who was always buying fishing gear. So I started stealing expensive Penn reels from the showcase. I'd wait until the store closed and all the employees were punching out in the lounge. I then made my way to the sporting goods department, removed the items from behind the counter and stashed them in an empty Igloo cooler. The next morning, when the store opened, Jimbo and Rose would come in, walk to the cooler, retrieve the goods and walk out. I traded whatever he took for drugs. But that wasn't enough. I got greedy.

I found out by chance that my old crime partner, Mike, the guy I got busted with on that home invasion trip, had a sweet boosting operation going on. He was making tons of cash stealing construction tools and selling them to a licensed contractor. The guy was rich and bought all that Mike could steal. I set it up for him to come and hit the place on the day I was working. We started off small with electrician tools like insulated needle nose pliers, channel locks and other items. We stole them by the dozens; loaded up large canvas bags. The store had so much inventory, they never missed it. For now. Soon we graduated to stealing power drills, Skill saws and power sanders. Not one, not two, but the entire inventory on the shelf. I made him boost those items on days before I had a two-day off period. He'd come into the store and clear out the shelf right before closing time. No one would notice. The next day, when the other agent worked, they'd see the empty space in the shelf and think that it just happened. We were making a killing! Then the heat got so bad we stopped and the managers were stumped. They'd find all these huge gaps where items used to sit on the shelf. Then I got lucky and caught a guy stealing a couple of power drills and I told the manager that this was the guy stealing all the power tools. Since we had stopped doing it, inventory wasn't disappearing. The guy was the fall guy and I was celebrated as the hero. Worked out fine by me. I got a raise and started working the Star Market grocery chain.

Grocery is a lot different than the retail business. You walk around, smelling food all day, watching couples and little old ladies shop for denture cream. It was slow and boring at first but then I got the hang of it. Soon I was in the groove and my reputation grew. Now, instead of stealing dry goods, I stole food. Nothing but the best—USDA prime steaks, shrimps, lobsters and all kinds of booze. All the good stuff. Most of it I consumed myself or gave to friends. When someone I knew had a party or I had a tailgate, I supplied the food and the booze. It was like having my own personal inventory of merchandise.

The deeper and deeper I fell into the pit of greed and self-satisfaction, the greater the chasm grew between my daughter and me. Although my love for her never diminished, it was my desperate attempt at survival, burying the hurt of loneliness, that drove me onward. I kept in contact with Lou, but our conversations were distant and tart. All I wanted was to hear my daughter's voice over the phone. Her gentle cooing and laughter. Lou never once denied me the joy of hearing her or feeling the love through the wire. It was a bittersweet connection each time it happened. I longed to hold her in my arms again. Perhaps it was too late for that, but I had to give it one more try. My hatred for my wife was far less than my love and burning desire to be with my daughter. Meanwhile, the beast within me ran wild. Unleashed! There was no stopping it. No controlling it. I burned hot with hatred and pain. Trying to quench the flames with soothing, calming waters of drugs and alcohol, but the fire never extinguished. It flickered for a while, then raged once again. Each time it did, it burned a piece of my heart and soul away from me. I begged for relief from this agony.

Then opportunity presented itself. I'd turned to ashes eventually at Burns International and just walked out. As luck would have it, my father had gotten an offer from the owner of Western Intelligence, a security firm out of California. He considered bidding on the security contract for the Safeway stores food chain in the Pacific region. The current local security outfit was below standard and out the door, so the contract was up for grabs. My dad approached me and asked if I could assemble a team of about six guys to start up the workforce. The contract, if awarded, would call for a two-man team to provide plainclothes security coverage for each of their stores. We'd concentrate our efforts on Oahu first and generate numbers (arrests) before expanding. The stores were getting hammered due to the present company's lack of enthusiasm at losing their contract. I contacted Ron and Mike and several of the other guys who I'd worked with at Burns. We held a meeting to discuss the terms of our hire and to plan strategies. We'd all make double the money we made presently. It would be easy for us to swoop in and deliver a blow to stem the flow of Safeway's losses. Together, we were some of the best loss prevention agents in the State of Hawaii. By the time the meeting had adjourned, everyone was in agreement. We all signed our applications, then and there, to work for Western. With the gang on board, we were ready to deliver. With my dad as the operations manager and me as the field agent in charge, we had a formula for success.

Came the day of our inaugural entry into the stores, we all met at a prearranged location. Everyone was jumping with excitement. Out of all the companies that bid for this golden contract, we were the winners. It was an opportunity in the business that all store detectives dream of—a new store, new contract. Now all we had to do was perform and produce. My father looked at me with a glimmer of hope and pride in his eyes and said, "this is it boy . . . this is our chance . . . go get 'um!" And like hungry dogs being let off the chain, we attacked. There were three teams of two men each to provide a blanket of coverage and increase our chances of producing maximum arrests. We chose to cover the stores that got hit the hardest. We'd take the peak hours of traffic and stay there for four hours. Then, each team would change to a different store and cover that store for four more hours. That way we could provide coverage for six stores instead of three. If the action in one store produced high numbers, we'd continue to leave a team there for the duration of the eight-hour shift. The owner and my dad stood close by and monitored our progress. No sooner had we entered our first store, someone got a bust. And the numbers climbed throughout the day. In all, we had some sixteen arrests for the day. An average of two per man or better. Good results for a start up. The owner was happy, Safeway was happy and my father was bursting with pride. We were off to the races. New job, more money, new life, but same old habits.

Chapter 17

Shop 'til you drop

The new job working for Safeway proved to be lucrative in many ways. Not long into the year, the Safeway food chain experienced a union strike. Workers unable to negotiate a contract walked out. That meant our company became responsible for monitoring the strike activity. All picket lines had to be videotaped twenty-four hours a day at different intervals at select locations. Because the company paid us for mileage, the amounts totaled into the thousands. My travel allowance for a two week work period amounted to even more than my regular pay. I was bringing in over $4000 a month. That's in the early 1980's. With all that cash coming in, I tried one last time to bring my daughter and wife home. I'd gotten an apartment and convinced Lou to come back to me. I still had a habit, but I managed to control it to just using pot and drinking in moderation. Nothing but beer. It was a wonderful feeling to hold my daughter in my arms again and to come home from a hard day's work to her warming smile. Lou and I were trying to put the past behind us and start our life over. We'd stopped all the intense partying, but the desire still smoldered, like burning coals between us. Our lives revolved around Keanu. She was

310

the glue that held us together. However fragile the bond was, it was because of her that our family existed at all. It felt good to be a family again, no matter what currents flowed underneath. I was surprised to find that we had picked up exactly where we left off. Just your average newly married couple with their first baby.

I went to work walking floors during the day and Lou stayed home playing housewife. I came home at a reasonable hour and didn't have to worry about that stupid pager going off in the early hours of the morning. I had the entire evening to devote to my family. The American dream in the making, living it, loving it.

I tried my best to make things work but in the end, I guess my best wasn't good enough. Those skeletons rattled much too loudly for either of us to ignore. I knew initially, when Lou and I had gotten together again, that she had been having a gay relationship. Throughout our marriage it appeared that her feelings for this other woman couldn't be denied. It had also become apparent that she was seeing another man. It was with him I had dropped her off at one of the times we had separated. I was suspicious when she said it was a cousin's house. The final time we parted ways for good, I came home to find the apartment empty and every stitch of clothing I owned, along with my high school diploma and cherished baby pictures of my youth, cut to pieces in a pile on the floor. I knew then that it was over for good. There I sat, in the middle of the room with my head hung low, alone and cried for my loss. I cried for my baby girl. It would be over a year before I'd hold her in my arms again. By then Lou would give birth to a second child. A girl she named Kano'eau. I would not be present for her birth or even see her until much later.

I poured myself into my work. Jimbo had gotten married along the way to that gorgeous Samoan girl, Rose. Although best of friends, I was not invited to the wedding. We had become estranged because of Lou's inability to keep a secret that was entrusted to her by Rose. They were getting drunk together one night when Rose let slip that her younger brother, who was about five years old, was in fact her son. She had gotten pregnant from a doctor on the mainland when she was a teenager. She kept the baby and her mother adopted the boy and Rose got on with her life and her loose lifestyle. It would be both our lustful desires that would ultimately cause the destruction of our friendship permanently. Well, Lou couldn't keep the secret and blabbed it to me one night at the dinner table. The good friend that I was, thought I was expected to tell Jimbo. I told him not to marry the bitch or she'd ruin his life.

When a man, who hasn't had much experience with women, falls head over heels in lust and love, well, there's just no reasoning with him. She had convinced the chump that she was a virgin; he strapped the blinders on and charged ahead. She could have been Medusa herself and he wouldn't have listened. Needless to say, he took her side and lived to regret it.

Meanwhile, I had started a relationship with a 21-year-old Korean-German fox named Cindy. She was a stunner! 5'4", 120 pounds, 36-24-36—absolutely perfectly built woman. And she was still a baby. Yes, I was robbing the cradle. You'd rob it too if you saw this girl. We'd met one sunny afternoon when Lou brought her home to go swimming in our pool. Seeing her in that bikini drove me wild! I couldn't take my eyes off her. She too saw that look of desire in my eyes and blushed. I got more than a few elbows in my ribs that day. I fell madly in lust with this girl the moment I laid greedy eyes on her. I had to have her—but being all married and stuff, I resisted temptation. She was hired as Lou's personal secretary at work. We soon became good friends and even had dinner together with her boyfriend. I liked the guy and we hit it off from the start. But I liked Cindy even more. We ran into each other again at a nightclub after Lou and I had separated. She was now a hostess at a Korean bar that her friend owned. She made tons of cash sitting on men's laps and pretending that she cared about them. I hated it! But it paid the bills and she spent all her money on me. She was my sugar momma.

The contract with Western Intelligence was going strong and I tried to keep myself together enough to show up for work. My drug and alcohol habits soon had other forms of indulgence to accompany them. Mike had introduced me to the Korean bar scene around the time Cindy and I got together. It was a fabulous lifestyle reserved for lonely men with money to burn. Then there was the strip club scene. You know those bars where men watch beautiful women rub themselves on brass poles, and on you. And take their clothes off. Both became another addiction I added to my collection. It was a very expensive habit. It wasn't uncommon to drop $600 a night in these places. And if a certain girl caught your eye, well, what can I say? There's no price for desire. I usually enticed them with cocaine and jewelry that I got from tweakers—desperate drug users that would sell their mother for a fix. My life was beginning to spin into a new realm of insanity. My hunger for the fast action lifestyle which was once fed by violence, was now fueled by sex. I soon had a favorite girl in every hostess bar and strip club. I'd shower them with gifts of drugs, stolen jewelry and cash. I'd work all day, then hit the clubs and bars every night. There wasn't enough money in my paycheck to support my habit, so I sought alternative measures.

Being two of the top loss prevention agents, Mike and I knew the business inside and out. We soon came up with a plan to help pay for our nightly escapades. We'd just steal merchandise from other stores and sell it to the bars for cash. This wasn't no ordinary run of the mill theft. These were well organized, professional shoplifting boosts. Felonies to be exact. Stealing on a grand scale. Just like the big boys and the best of the best we hunt down do. And then some. It was no coincidence that we targeted our former employer, the Star Market food chain. We knew every aisle and all the blind spots. We joined forces with another ex-agent, who was currently unemployed. The three of us loaded two huge coolers with ice, placed one in the backseat and the other in the trunk. Starting early in the morning we worked our way along the chain of stores. Our goal was to take nothing but the steaks, seafood and booze. Needed lots of ice to keep the goodies cold until sale, it could be a long day.

The method we used was simple. We would each enter a store with these large canvas bags, folded and tucked into the front of our pants. Then we'd grab a shopping cart and split up in different directions. We'd search for the floor walker and our third man, who knew them all, would keep him busy while Mike and I loaded up the carts with items. Before I loaded up, I prepared a drop point where we'd load the goods into the bags. I liked to use the detergent aisle. I'd pick a spot on the bottom shelf, where they kept all those big boxes of laundry soap. I would clear out all the rear boxes and leave the facing boxes in place, concealing the large gap in the shelf. It was the perfect camouflage. Undetectable to the casual observer, it would store the already filled bags. Once we filled the carts with specific items, we'd drive to the drop point and I'd load up the bags and stash them behind the fronting soap boxes. When all three bags were filled, Mike would signal the third man to come make his pick-up. The store Dick had no idea what was going on. We then met at the aisle and we would load up with huge black bags and the three of us would simply walk up to a closed check stand, unhook the chain, and walk right out the door. Most checkers just stared at us in amazement. Bewildered as to what could possibly be in those gigantic bags slung around those gentlemen. I called it caravanning, comparing it to ancient camel merchants, whose animals came filled to capacity. One store after another we repeated the trick. Often the car was off-loaded at a house to make room for the next load. By the end of the day, we'd amassed shit-loads of stuff. Twenty to thirty twin-packs of fresh frozen lobster tails, twenty-packs of shrimp, fifty pounds of Prime cuts of meat. And then the most precious cargo of all—the liquor. Totaling thousands of dollars in merchandise. A felony.

When night fell, we'd clean up and make the rounds from bar to bar and club to club, peddling our goods. Some places never bought the food, only booze. Others took whatever we had, all we had. Sometimes we made one stop and the owner took the whole lot. We'd get around forty cents on the dollar. Some nights, we cleared over $2000 plus free drinks and goodies of all kinds. It was a sweet deal. Not a bad day's work. We tried our luck at least once or twice in a month. Then things got hairy.

With things going great with the Safeway contract, the owner of Western Intelligence rewarded my dad by sponsoring him for his private investigator's license. It was a big honor and they would become partners in the business. Obtaining a P.I.'s license was difficult in Hawaii because you had to have connections in the law enforcement community and the reputation to go with it. My father possessed both. The hardest part was paying for the bond, which cost thousands of dollars. Most civilians who start up a private investigation business and can't afford the bond use another security company's license to operate. Such was the situation in our case, my dad named the company L & L Investigation, taking the first two initials from both our names. It was to become the beginning of our legacy together. One of our first assignments was to shadow a rich business executive's wife. She vacationed here in the islands with a girl friend each year. He suspected that she was having an affair with an ex-lover who met up with her in Kauai. My mom and I flew to Kauai as a team, with her backing me up. We observed the subject's every move for a week. At a club, I had drinks with her and her friend at the bar and even danced with them. Every night, they retired to their apartment alone. We got over $5000 for that one job, plus expenses. It was fun working with my mom. She was also hired as a shopping agent for Safeway. Her job was to pose as an impatient customer. She'd rush through a check stand with a carton of cigarettes and the exact amount in cash in her hand. She'd plop the cash down and exit the store before the cashier had a chance to react. The cashier, busy ringing up another customer's items, would have to finish before ringing up mom's purchase. The proper procedure would be to place the money for the cigarettes on the top of the register, then when she had time, close the register and ring in the purchase. Cashiers aren't allowed to carry any money on their person at any time during their shift. They are also not allowed to carry more than ten or twenty dollars in their purses at work. After my mom exited the store, we'd observe the cashier's every move with binoculars. If the cashier stuck the money any place other than the register, she was busted. Crooks often just shove the cash into their aprons. I once caught a veteran cashier, making $27 an hour and with the company for over 25 years. All that hard work down the drain. All for a lousy ten bucks and some change.

At our P.I. business, we were starting to get jobs in the private sector. A missing person here, stolen vehicle there. Rent-a-car companies paid us $400 just to locate one of their missing vehicles. Most were left abandoned on the side of the road and ended up sitting in an impound yard. One phone call from my father to a source in the police impound section was all it took to find it. We didn't even have to leave the house.

But with the hectic schedule and constant pressure from the Safeway gig, there just wasn't enough time to split between the two careers. So we had to concentrate and devote our time to the job that produced the more steady income. It was a shame to see our company dissolve. It had a lot of potential and with my dad as the boss, we couldn't miss. There was none more qualified. When thinking back, we should have hung on to it. At least until we could have afforded to pay for the bond ourselves. I saw the disappointment in my father's eyes the day he told me of his decision.

Not long after that, I got fired from Safeway for kicking a regular customer's son out of the store. He was an asshole! A spoiled, rich kid who went around the store grabbing items off the shelf and sticking them in his pockets to get my attention. When he saw me watching, he'd toss the items back onto the shelves and duck around the corner. I was far less amused at the game. I finally approached him and warned him to stop. He laughed in my face and said, "I saw you watching me . . . you can't catch me." I lost control, grabbed him in a hammer lock and threw him out of the store. I should have filed an incident report and trespassed the s.o.b. Not that it would have made a difference. Seemed like the new district officer didn't care much for my physical methods of apprehension. My arrest numbers and recovery amounts couldn't be matched, but that didn't count for anything the day I was summoned to the main branch office. Silly me, I went there with the impression that I was getting a pat on the back. When I walked into the conference room, I saw my father sitting in the middle of the other big whips. They all looked way too serious. The room was so quiet, you could have heard a pin drop. I sat down and the district manager started asking me about the incidents with that spoiled brat. My blood froze and I was surprised. Even with my plausible explanation, he said, "I'm sorry, but we here at Safeway

can't tolerate such behavior from our agents . . . you're fired!"
His words pierced me like a dagger. I looked at my dad and he
just stared back at me.

No one else said a word. "So that's it . . . after all I've done for
this company?" I thought about that back door employee theft
ring my dad and I had broken up. I hid in the bushes for two
days and nearly got shot by a cop. I had surprised him when I
leapt out of the bushes in the darkness. We were all waiting for
the pick-up man to recover the stolen goods. We were lauded
for the achievement. And what about all the professional
cigarette thieves I put out of business? Boosters who stole cases
and cases of cigarettes from stores that amounted to tens of
thousands of dollars. Many of whom permanently retired from
the business because of me. "That's it . . . you're fired!" was all
he said. I stormed out of the room. I felt betrayed and alone. I
never blamed my dad. He was only doing his job as operations
manager. I knew deep down that it broke his heart to see me
get the boot that way. I'm glad it was me getting fired instead
of him.

I buried my sorrows in the usual fashion—binge drinking
and drugs. After a while, the boys persuaded me to go back to
work for Burns International and my old boss Silos welcomed
me back. There were no hard feelings about stealing away his
best agents to Safeway. I saw the puzzled looks on the cashiers'
faces of those same Star Markets that I used to boost from
with those big bags. Now I dragged thieves through the stores.
Although I could see it in their eyes, no one had the guts to say
anything. I just smiled and they smiled back.

Walking floors can be boring. Walking in circles for eight
hours makes you crazy. The only relief from the boredom is an
arrest. At Star we worked alone without back-up, so you could
spend all your time writing an arrest report for a small crime,
while chances are a bigger fish is getting away. I only locked up

the cheap stuff when I was desperate for numbers. It was the big stuff that made you a legend. The professional thieves that stole large amounts counted most. They all knew me by now and they knew that they ran the risk, of not only getting caught, but getting hurt in the process. Every store, whether retail or grocery, had a hot sheet of criminals to watch out for. Sort of a ten most wanted list of big timers. Those are the ones that I became obsessed with. Made it my mission in life to arrest one and when I did catch them, they went down hard. I'd look them in their bleeding faces, with their dislocated fingers and arms and say, "the next time I catch you stealing in my store, you'll spend some hospital time!" They believed me. The ignorant ones I had to convince. It got to a point when they saw me on the floor, they split. Some even waved or saluted before leaving. The brave ones walked up to me and said, "I'm here with my family shopping . . . . promise. I ain't going to steal."

After a few months of walking in circles, I quit and moved in with Cindy. She had a big, two-bedroom condo that her sugar daddy paid for. He was a rich rental car company owner who lived on a different island. Too old to give a damn and too rich to use her other than for his own pleasures, he cared less about our relationship. She flaunted it in front of him whenever he flew in. She'd invite me along for a wild night of partying at his expense. While he was busy paying for the champagne, she and I would be in the parking lot getting high on coke and necking. It was hard to keep a straight face when we went back. At one point, she had three, over-the-hill millionaires paying for her charms. When we fell in lust, she cut two of them loose. She didn't really need their money any longer since she worked for her girlfriend, the owner of the hottest hostess club in town. On a good night, she could make over $2000 and even a slow night netted $500. She kept her own hours and only worked three or four nights a week. Her only problems were drugs and booze.

She drank nothing but hard liquor, vodka and cognac—her favorites. It was easy for her to drink a bottle a night at work. She was a good drunk and an excellent lover. I was denied nothing. She paid for all my drugs and alcohol and even gave me a car to cruise around in. All she really wanted from me was to be at her beck and call. Oh yeah, and not to go drinking with the boys in strip clubs. It made her jealous and angry. She knew full well what went ón in those places and wasn't having it with me. Can't say I blamed her. What she wanted never concerned me in the least. She held a special resentment for Mike since he was the one who introduced me to the club scene. He knew all the good places and the sweetest girls. To curb my hunger, Cindy often invited us to her club for drinks. Didn't cost us a dime. She'd come by and drop cash on the table all night long until we left. The table was always filled to capacity with the finest food—fit for a king. It made her happy and I indulged her. Mike and I always showed up when we were broke. When we had money we'd hit the other places. Whenever Mike and I were out together, Cindy was nervous. Nervous because we did dangerous things and could never be found. I used to have to sneak out while she was slumped in a drunken stupor. I'd creep out of bed and call Jimbo to come pick me up. But not before removing a few bills from her clutch. The thing was always so stuffed with cash that it sprung open like a jack-in-the-box when I opened it. Money just popped out. She never missed it. I should feel like a rat for stealing from her after all she did for me. But considering the bullshit I had to endure because of her choice of occupation—I didn't enjoy sharing my girlfriend with strange men. I hated it! But, the sex was so good that I forced myself to put up with it. While all those rich suckers were busy chasing her tail around, I was getting paid to have it. When you look at it from that perspective, who am I to complain? The boys always teased me that I was whipped. I admit it, I was. It was a reciprocating relationship. She was happy with me being her bitch. Being a sex slave to a nympho ain't easy.

There's something about being a kept lover that is unsatisfying. I don't mean to gripe about being spoiled by a younger woman, but it leaves your manhood locked away between her legs. I felt useless and my life had no purpose. It was incomplete. So when Ron called to tell me that F.W. Woolworths was going in-house with their new security and was looking for a few good men, I jumped at it. Because of my work experience, I was a guaranteed hire. They never cared or bothered to ask about my previous arrest history. All they cared about was numbers. Cindy thought it was a great idea. Now she wouldn't have to worry about me during the daylight hours while she slept. My immediate supervisor was Diane, a gorgeous, buxom Portuguese woman in her early thirties. With her perfect features, milky-white skin and piercing green eyes, she was a stunner! And she had the personality to compliment the package. But make no mistake about her resolve when it came to handling her business. The woman was tough as nails. I fell instantly in love with her. But more as a sister than anything else. She was not disappointed by my performance from the start. I brought an air of confidence to the team that Ron couldn't provide. His arrogant character and narcissistic bravado was as transparent as Scotch tape. And just as weak.

I recall an incident when we both were partnered at Safeway. One night, a local gang of four guys walked out of the store with cases of beer under their arms. I had no idea what happened. All I saw was Ron running out of the door. I was right behind him. He had no idea that I was there. He confronted the four in the middle of the road, fronting the store. When he went to place them under arrest, the smallest of the group dropped his beer and attacked him. He punched Ron in the face, knocking him to the pavement. Then he went for me. I let loose with a barrage of punches and decked him. He went down next to Ron and didn't get up. Ron jumped up and ran for the store. I could see the scared look in his eyes. Then, two of the other guys dropped their beers and approached me menacingly. Hands up and fists clenched, I proceeded to kick the crap out of them. Knocking one to the ground after breaking his nose and then the other after landing a solid blow to his chin. By then, the first guy had gotten up and ran for his life, leaving all that beer behind. The last two guys also turned tail and ran. The fourth guy just stood there, with his jaw hanging, clutching the case of beer like a life preserver. I screamed, "What? You too . . . let's go punk!" He let out a scream, dropped the beer and ran for the fence. I chased him down, caught his ass and slammed him to the pavement. After all that shit, I'll be damned if I don't send somebody's ass to jail! The cashiers, some of whom had exited the store and witnessed the event, cheered. They jeered at the suspect saying, "good for you!" Apparently, these thugs had been coming into that particular store for years and helping themselves to free beer. Everyone was too afraid to confront them. Even the managers just turned a blind eye. I handed the prisoner to Ron, just as the cops arrived. The look on his face was worth a year's pay. One of the cashiers recognized the suspect and said he lived just on the other side of that wooden fence. The same one the other three leaped over to make their getaway. The patrolman jumped over the fence and I went after him. When we reached the other side, there was a party going on with lots of people milling around. The cop began yelling orders and the music went silent. We searched the house and found the other three suspects in different clothes, trying to disguise themselves and blend into the crowd. They couldn't hide their swollen faces though. I never forgot that frightened look on Ron's face as he ran for cover. Now here we were again. This time, he was my boss. It didn't bother me in the least. He knew the score. So would everyone else in the business. It was here in the largest shopping mall in the state, the Ala Moana Shopping Center, that I would make my legendary mark on the loss prevention business.

F.W. Woolworths was a new store in a different location from the old, beat-up, run-down site. It was next to the Sears store with an open access near customer service that ran directly into their store. At that time, Sears had the most modern and sophisticated security camera system in the state. The 52 camera, closed circuit T.V. screens system covered the entire three levels of the store. Security Chief Bernie Ching was a former Honolulu police sergeant who knew my dad. He'd sometimes invite me over to help train his new agents in the finer art of floor-walking. Many of the new generation loss prevention agents are taught to use the camera as their primary source of observation. And although I must admit that a surveillance system is useful, it's not fool-proof. On any given day, it can be beat and I was a master at doing just that. It's one thing to sit on your ass all day and play with knobs and switches, but it can't compare to the actual hands-on floor-walking method. Yes, there are many agents who are virtuosos of the security monitor, but you still have to arrest the guy in person. Some just depend too much on the camera. They lose that personal element that makes the thrill of the business worthwhile. That's where I came in. Whenever a hot shot group of newbies would arrive, especially a camera enthusiast, Bernie gave me a call.

Such was the case on this beautiful summer day. A cocky, attractive blonde sat at the controls. She was much too confident for her own good. The challenge was simple—I bet her lunch for my whole crew, if I could steal the store blind without her catching me on camera. She looked at me with that smug smile spread across her face and said, "Deal!" Bernie shook his head, looked at her and said, "I hope you brought your wallet."

I left the office with the other three agents in tow and instructed them to follow my lead. When we reached the floor, I walked them through the exercise. I kept them close to me so they could hear what I said as we walked about the aisles. To the casual observer, we appeared to be just a bunch of guys browsing through the store, killing time. There's no doubt that the pretty blond girl was zoomed in on our every move. Each section of the store I walked, I assigned them strategic points of observation that I wanted them to move to when I said "go." I verbally relayed my orders so as not to alert the, by now, impatient blonde of my intentions. All she saw was the four of us walking in circles. The camera couldn't hear the words I was speaking. I pointed out the blind spots where it was impossible for the camera to see, sharp corners with high shelves that impeded the camera's view. When I had the plan set, I walked past a specific area where she could get a good look at the four of us, then I said, "go." With that, we all split up and went our separate ways. Everyone headed to the prearranged hide-out spots. There, they had an unobstructed view of me committing the crime. How do you like them apples . . . sassy white girl! She couldn't observe all of us at the same time and had to settle on one of us as a target. Most likely the honor would be mine. The trouble with that idea is, the spot I chose to divide up was located next to an aisle that was a blind spot for the camera. She'd only have a split-second before I vanished. I counted on the diversion of our four-way split to break her focus. She'd panic and by the time she regained her composure, I would be gone. I ducked out of sight of the camera, slipped around a corner, grabbed two large plastic shopping bags from a nearby stand and proceeded to the denim aisle. There, I removed stacks of Levis and stuffed them into the bags. Then I turned the corner and weaved in between clothing racks, avoiding the cameras, and made my way to a rack of Polo shirts. I started loading them into the already full bags. Throughout the entire time, the prospective agents casually looked on in amazement. I called out to them from my spot whenever I concealed the items. That way, although staged, they'd have a feel of seeing the actual crime take place. Watching them pretend as if they were looking at clothes on the racks made me chuckle. I knew by now that the bitch was going crazy. Panning the cameral back and forth watching the three decoys, all the while swearing to herself as she feverishly searched for me. At this point she'd probably be in a panic, Bernie leaning over her shoulder smiling. When the bags were stuffed full to capacity, I signaled to my crew to make their exit from the store. They all proceeded to leave the store via different locations. By then, I had already left the store and was waiting for them outside on the sidewalk with the stolen merchandise. We made our way back to the security office undetected. I walked through the doors and found her over the console, still searching in vain. I dumped the two bags of stolen property onto the floor behind her and said, "Mushroom steak, extra rice, extra salad from Masu's Kitchen." She turned and the surprise on her face said it all. She was so busy looking for me she didn't even hear us come in. She turned bright red, shook her head and said, "you're good . . . you got to show me how you did it." I pointed to the other three agents and said, "ask them." Bernie laughed and said to her, "told you so." I shook her hand, told her better luck next time and said, "don't forget the drinks," and walked out. I did it all while on my break. I sat down in Diane's office and she hung up the phone and said, "show-off!" That was Bernie on the other end of the line praising my performance.

Being good at something is never enough for an addict. The only thing that we are ever really good at is getting high and concealing it from both the people around us and ourselves. We claim to be above the rest of the affected drug population because we are able to hold a job. We call ourselves functioning alcoholics and drug addicts. But that's just a myth. A word invented to help further enable and fool us. I can't say when my addiction to using cocaine intravenously actually started, I can say how and why. Cindy had been a lover of crack cocaine. She and her fellow bar maids would often get together after closing time and smoke their brains out. In my effort to please her, I began smoking the shit too. I hated it from the get go. It made me paranoid and no matter how much you did or had there was never enough. But a drug addict's a drug addict and we manage to make do with whatever is out there. I've shot cocaine up before in the form of speedballs when I was hooked on heroin. Speedballs are a mixture of heroin and cocaine. When injected, the user experiences an intense rush as adrenaline surges through the body. It's like opening the floodgates in a dam. Tie yourself to the front of a dragster or the nose of the space shuttle during take-off would be the only way to duplicate the sensation. Then, when the effects of the coke wear off, the heroin kicks in. Imagine being so tired that you just nod off, but multiply the drag by a thousand times. The whole rush from that shuttle ride, but this time you're rushing in the opposite direction. Like sleep is grabbing a hold of your eyelids and pulling you through the floor. I loved it and it became my favorite high. It was an expensive and dangerous addiction to be caught up in. When Derrick and I parted ways, I left the needle and my love for that method of getting high behind. Somehow the taste of cocaine and the rotten method of smoking it in rock form pushed me back into shooting up again.

The strange thing is, throughout the entire time I shot up heroin, I never injected myself. I had always depended on Derrick or other addicts to administer the fix. Then, one afternoon, while sitting by myself in a store parking lot with an ounce of Peruvian Flake cocaine, I decided to fix myself a shot. The first time was easier than I thought it would be. Releasing the sling from my arm, I felt the familiar rush flow through my veins like hot running water. The taste of cocaine soon entered my mouth, filling my taste buds and tongue. I hit the latch from the bucket seat of my Toyota SR5, stretched out and enjoyed the ride and listened as the roar of the freight trains rolling at top speed deafened my ears. And that was the beginning of a love affair with the drug that punks you out. You can never get enough of it or get rid of it. Even sex or beautiful women, whatever you're into, you don't need it like you do heroin. You want it, desire it all the time. That's why they call it "girl," the "devil's mate", the "man-boy."

I started using on a daily basis. Every waking moment was devoted to it. To support my ever increasing habit, I began buying it by the ounces, breaking it down into quarter grams, then selling it on the streets for $30 a pop. When I wasn't walking the floors at work, I was peddling cocaine to anyone and everyone who had the cash. I started selling right out of the store. Selling to employees and using the place as my personal pick up and drop off point. During work hours, my customers would walk through and I'd meet them in a prearranged section of the store and make the exchange. In between walking in circles and arresting people, I could be found tucked away in one of the two employee restroom stalls, fixing and ringing my brains out. One afternoon, still flying on coke, a professional booster came in and started stealing the store blind. The effects of my last shot were still clanging in my ears when I spotted him. I shook my head in an effort to clear my vision, but it did me no good. I thought about just letting him go, but the amount this greedy bastard was helping himself to was just too much to ignore. I sat back and let him load up. He slung the bag and headed for the Sears store entrance near customer service.

I caught up to him as he was making his way out the Sears exit. I grabbed him and slammed him up against a pillar. Since he had already left Woolworths, technically he'd left the property and I could legally arrest him. I got him to his knees and retrieved the bag with the merchandise. Just as I was about to handcuff him, he leaped up and broke flat out for the exit door. It shocked me how fast he was. Before I could regain my senses, the guy was already out the door. I should've been happy with just the recovery, but I wanted this guy bad! I gave the bag to a Sears employee, told him to take it to customer service and gave chase. When I got into the parking lot, the guy was already across the street, over a hundred yards away, running at full throttle. He turned back, flashed me a smile and turned on the afterburners. Under ordinary circumstances, I no doubt could have run him down. But wacked out as I was, there was no way. Still, I had to try. I chased him and got within twenty yards—so close I could almost reach out and touch him. Just when I was about to nab him, I felt a searing pain in my chest that knocked the breath out of me. It brought me to my knees. The guy, sensing that my engine had run dry, leaped over a fence and disappeared. I'll never forget the look of relief on his face as he reached the top, turned and smiled at me. He knew that he'd gotten away. He was the only suspect that had ever gotten away from me. We'd run nearly a mile by that point. As I huffed and puffed, it felt like my heart was ready to explode. Scared the shit out of me! I knelt there on the sidewalk for what seemed an eternity. I made a promise that if I lived, I'd give up shooting coke for good. But that was just a lie. When the pain had subsided, I walked the distance back to the store, ever so slowly. The afternoon would again find me locked in the bathroom stall, ringing my bells.

My cocaine addiction had become so out of control, that I could no longer hide it from my father. He'd walked into my room one day and found me sitting with a huge pile of coke on a table in front of me. With all the bullshit going on in my life with Cindy and Lou, I'd taken to staying off and on at my parents' place. It was my hideaway. A haven where no problems could find me. He asked me, "how much shit is that?" "Thousands," I answered. He glanced up to see a dart board I had filled with dozens of used syringes. He shook his head and told me, "you shooting that shit!" The disgust and hurt poured from him like thick syrup. I was so far gone that I just sat there and said, "I'm sorry dad . . . close the door when you leave." The worst was when my mother caught me in the act of injecting myself in her kitchen. I'd thought her asleep and in my greedy haste to fix and feel the rush, I'd ignored my own rules of only using in my room. She startled me when she screamed out, "What are you doing?" I turned to see her staring aghast with her hand to her mouth and tears streaming down her cheeks. The needle was still in my arm and I hadn't yet slammed the plunger home. Even with the sight of my hurt mother's face burned into my soul, I injected the contents of the syringe. I looked down at the rig, then up to where she once stood. She was already gone. I heard the slam of her bedroom door. I went to the door and tried to console her, but she refused to open the door or talk to me. All I could hear was the racking sobs of her despair. I turned and left. It was then that I made up my mind to quit shooting cocaine for good. When I returned that afternoon, my father was waiting for me in the living room. He had a drink in his hand and from the looks of the cigarette laden ashtray by his side, it wasn't his first. I asked him, "where's mom?" He looked at me with the coldest stare I'd ever seen, a look that gave me chills and said, "she caught the plane to Arizona to stay with her sister. You stupid kid! Get all your shit and get out of here and don't come back."

Chapter 18

Voodoo dust

I made myself scarce from my parents' place and dropped off the planet. Jimbo and I had gotten together again, after the warning about Rose rang true. He called one morning out of the blue crying and despondent. Said he was sorry and that he needed to see me. He talked about killing. I phoned Diane and took a sick day. After the way he'd treated me he didn't deserve my friendship, let alone my undivided attention. He showed up at my door with a half-gallon of Vodka already half gone and all of his dope. "Let's get wasted!" was all he said. It appeared he'd caught his lovely wife in a compromising position. On her knees in the back of a limo pleasuring four strange men. I hate to say I told you so, but what the hell. I couldn't just turn my back on the guy. He was my friend. We drank and smoked some weed, then he said that he wanted to kill her. After hours of non-stop partying, he passed out on my floor. I stared at the troubled figure, snoring softly, for now at peace with the demons that haunted him. I thought about the beautiful baby girl that both he and Rose had brought into this world. When he awoke, I told him to go back to his family. For now, I had defused a bad situation. And while I seriously doubted that he had it in him to actually follow through with murder, you never know what a troubled individual was capable of, given the situation. Hurt is a powerful motivator and the anger that stems from it has destroyed many.

The not so happy couple showed up without warning one afternoon, minus the baby. From their biting exchange of rude remarks, the relationship was headed for the rocks. Seemed like their reason for being here was to have someone referee their ongoing battle. The words she said cut him deep. His anger rose as his face turned beet red and the tears flowed from his eyes. I finally separated the two, taking Jimbo into my bedroom. She sat there on the living room floor pleading her case to my parents. She had enough of his drug addiction and late night carousing. She suspected for some time now that he'd been having an affair. Payback for her cheating. He sat there crying and downing a bottle of vodka. He talked about how he should have listened to my warning and apologized for how he treated me. In his drunken ranting, he talked about killing her. It made me angry! In fact, the both of them were driving me crazy with their bullshit. Through his raving, I heard her tell my parents, "I should have married your son." Jimbo looked at me and became quiet for a second. "Bitch, I'm going to kill her!" The look in his eyes spoke of Rose's and my history. When she and I had first met, she had become smitten with me when I beat up her ex-boyfriend for slapping her in front of me. After that incident, she'd left the abusive relationship and started flirting with me. Being married to Lou at the time, I denied her advances. I shifted her attention to Jimbo's direction. All I wanted was to do a friend a favor. You know, get him laid. I told him from the beginning that she was just for fun and not to get serious. I never expected the jerk to fall for the bitch. Ever since the day we met, she'd been hinting how much she'd love to get me in bed and I avoided an opportunity to be alone with her. This whole scene kept playing over and over in my mind as the two of them went on and on about each other's faults. It finally got to me in a way that no one, not even myself, expected. I grabbed Jimbo by his shirt with two hands clenched, pushed my face into his and screamed, "You want her dead? That's what you really want?" I then reached under my mattress and removed the Smith & Wesson .357 Magnum pistol. I had enough of this crap. I dragged Jimbo into the living room, walked up to Rose, grabbed her by the hair, stuck the gun to her head and yelled, "This is what you want . . . you want this goddamn bitch dead?" Everyone in the room froze. My dad told me to put the gun down. My mother leapt back in shock. She begged me to lower the gun. I screamed at Jimbo for an answer. Rose, feeling the gun barrel to her head, said, "You see, the punk doesn't even have the balls to do it himself!" I nearly blew her head off there and then. Jimbo screamed, "NO, no, please . . . don't shoot!" I came to my senses then and released my grip on her hair. Lowering the weapon, I looked down to see Rose as calm and cool as a poisonous snake looking back at me. I saw the look of excitement in her eyes. The bitch had gotten off on my performance. I had no way of knowing at the time, just how much. They reached for each other and locked in an embrace. All the while, she looked at me over his shoulder with a knowing smile and a twinkle in her eyes. I kicked them out and told them to get their act together.

My cocaine addiction, by now, had reached extremely dangerous levels. I was shooting nearly half an ounce of coke a day. As my hunger for the drug increased, I sought whatever means possible to maintain it. I started spending every night on the streets, dealing to support my habit. Jimbo had hooked up with a Japanese dude who worked in Waikiki as a front desk clerk at a four-star hotel. The guy supposedly held ties to the infamous Japanese underworld gang known as Yakuza. The guy had the best Peruvian Flake cocaine in town. Not since the days of Ralph and Lorna had I seen such quality. The stuff was dynamite. Jimbo was totally against me shooting drugs but had no choice but to deal with it. See, this guy also dealt the drug crystal meth, or ice. This was the drug of the future that was sweeping through the state and would soon reach epidemic proportions. Well, Jimbo had become addicted to meth and was in the process of establishing a relationship with this Japanese guy. The catch was, this guy had all this cocaine he needed to get rid of before he could start dealing the ice. That's where I came in. With my enormous habit and coke selling network in place, it was no problem for me to help unload all of the product.

I remember the first time I met this guy. He was a tiny, nondescript looking fellow about 5'4" and less than 145 pounds soaking wet. He wore nerdy-looking glasses, those black-rimmed ones. He could easily pass for a tourist. We shook hands and he removed this huge manila envelope from the front of his pants. It contained about a half-a-pound of cocaine. "I need to sell all of this by tonight," was all he said. He opened the envelope and dumped some out on the table. The room filled with that familiar hospital smell of ether and alcohol that assaults your nostrils when you enter. I started to gag. A reflex action that all coke addicts experience. I said the only way I could be 100% sure that the stuff was good was to shoot it. Jimbo protested at first, but relented. I rushed to the bathroom, locked the door and proceeded to fix a syringe. The powerful scent wafted around me, filling the small room with its potent mixture. I heaved and shook as I removed the clear wavy liquid from the ball of cotton in the silver spoon. Finding the vein, I poked the needle slightly into it, drew back on the plunger, saw the telltale sign of blood and slammed the contents home. The rush was immediate and intense. The taste surged into my mouth and over my tongue. My ears felt hot as if on fire and they began to ring. I sat back on the toilet and enjoyed the ride. In the far away distance, I thought I heard a voice calling my name. It was Jimbo pounding on the door yelling. I had slipped into a world of ecstasy. I gave the product the Good Housekeeping seal of approval and was ready to do business.

I sat there, making phone calls and taking orders, while Jimbo weighed out our clients' orders on a triple beam scale. By the end of the night the entire contents of the envelope had been sold. Minus the portion I took home with me. From that moment on, that little Japanese dude was my cocaine connection and Jimbo's crystal meth line. It would be a cold world that neither one of us could control. But for the moment I was satisfied that the cocaine kept on flowing. The price soon went from $1200 an ounce to just $500. I had more coke than I needed. Check this math out. I bought an ounce for $500, that's 8 eightballs to sell on the street for $420 each, which gets me $3360. After my share, my profit is $2860. Try getting your head around those figures. I even stretched the profit margin by shaving just 2 tenths of a gram here and there, and drove my bottom line up to $3600. I could easily sell all the coke down on Hotel street in a single night. Times that by a Friday and Saturday and you are making over $6000 a weekend. There's no other business in the world that could produce those numbers. Like I said, I had more coke than I could use. That didn't stop me from trying.

Ever since I walked out of my parents' house, I had been on a mission. A mission that consumed every bit of my mind, body and spirit. A mission that would eventually lead me down the path to annihilation. I had little contact with my parents other than the usual phone call or visit to check on their well being. That's a joke! "Well being." How the hell do you think they're doing moron?! As long as I was hooked on drugs, they'd never have a moment of peace. I loved my parents with all my heart but was just too weak to exercise that love. To use it in my favor to help get me out of this living hell. I was so far gone, caught up in the drug lifestyle that I had become blind, distant, cold and unfeeling. My own selfish needs, wants and desires took precedence over everything and everyone else. I had lost myself. Lost my identity as a human being. In the brief moments of clarity between highs, I knew. Those thoughts of normalcy vanished much too quickly for me to react. To question and reason with myself. So I continued on the runaway train of destruction. Jimbo, in an effort to help me, had confided in my father. They were both desperate to see me kick the habit. And although he himself had become a slave to ice, he recognized my situation as tragic. Since he was basically the one supplying me with the coke along with his friend, he could stop the supply any time he chose. After months of watching me wrestle with my addiction, he decided to put me out of my misery.

I had no idea what he had planned for me. All I knew was that it was swift and drove the point home quickly. It was a rude awakening that would take me by surprise. Whenever I got done selling my drugs, I'd stop at Jimbo's house in the early morning hours, while he was asleep or out tweaking and stuff my money under his door. The next day, after he'd gotten the coke, we would meet up and go our separate ways. However, on this day, I waited all day for him to call. I called and searched frantically for him, but he was nowhere to be found. I had no way of knowing that he was deliberately avoiding me. By nightfall, he still hadn't contacted me and my supply was nearly gone. I had no time to deal with this shit, because it was my turn to work graveyard shift standing guard at Woolworth's sidewalk sale. All the other stores in the mall hired private firms but Diane thought it a good idea for us to get the overtime pay. She was always looking out for us.

Sometime after midnight, Jimbo's van pulled into the parking lot. I was relieved that finally I'd get my drugs. I raced to the van in anticipation of having my next fix. I'd run out of coke hours ago and was way passed the jittery stage. I sat in the seat next to him and asked what took him so long. I said, "where the hell is my dope?" He told me to grab a beer from the cooler as he lit a joint. The way I felt, the last thing I needed was a beer. He passed me the joint and told me if I didn't pop a beer he wouldn't give me my coke. Sipping on the ice cold beer, beside myself with irritation over his slow motion, I asked again about my drugs. He handed me back my cash and said, "Here . . . there's no more coke." I went crazy! "What, you kept me waiting all this time just to tell me the guy didn't have my shit?" He said the guy had plenty of cocaine, but I wasn't getting any more of it. "Your line is cut," he said. "No more, finished, over, done." Then he started telling me about how he'd been talking to my dad and that the both of them decided it was time for an intervention. His hollow words echoed in my panicked brain which refused to hear or comprehend what he was saying. I started to sweat and beg him to stop messing around and give me the shit. It was a bad joke, that wasn't even the least bit funny. He stood his ground and told me to get used to it. I wanted to dash to my car and head to the nearest dealer. I told him to stay and watch the store until I got back. I knew a guy who sold cocaine no more than ten minutes away. I'd be back in half an hour. No one would even know I left. He said that if I got out, he would drive away. I was desperate and jumping out of my skin. He said to calm down and drink another beer. I wanted to strangle him! We got into a heated argument and he said if I didn't cool off, he was leaving. I was stuck between a rock and a hard place. It was hours until my shift was over. By then, I'd be crawling up the walls. He said he had a solution to my problem but that I had to calm down before he told me. At that point I would have agreed to anything. I was an addict, going through extreme withdrawal. It was not only a cruel thing to do on his part, but dangerous as well. Kids, don't try this at home. Even a trained specialist, knowledgeable in the field of treating addicts, would be alarmed at Jimbo's method. I forced myself to calm down, hoping to find relief from this agony. Then, he produced this tiny, zip-lock pack and showed it to me. He held it up so that the streetlights of the parking lot illuminated its contents and said, "Here's the answer to your problem." I stared at the clear rock forms at the bottom of the bag. At first glance, they appeared to be rock salt, the kind used for food preparation or preserving. I shook the little plastic bag and laughed, "You nuts. What the hell is this shit?" I was so angry that I could have killed him right then and there! He went on to explain about the drug crystal methamphetamine. Ice was the beginning of the end for me. From that night forward, I would become enslaved to the greatest demon of all. A demon that would become more than just a god to me. It would become the very breath I took. Every thought my mind would think. The food and drink that the human in me needed to survive. It would, in the end, change me into that very demon itself.

I left the store that day wondering why the crystal I had smoked in that strange-looking pipe, shaped like a bowl with a tiny hole at the top, left me invigorated and alive. How it made me forget all about my hunger or craving for a syringe full of cocaine. I had become instantly, literally, overnight, cured of my previous addiction. And now, without my knowing, addicted to ice. When I entered the store to punch-out, after leaving the confines of Jimbo's van, I couldn't help but notice how brilliant everything in the store appeared. The colors were brighter than ever before and leaped out at me from the displays. I became so focused on my surroundings I could practically read the labels from every item I passed. Not only could I hear, but I also comprehended every conversation that went on around me. It was amazing! I had worked all night, smoked more than just a few joints and consumed nearly a case of beer, and felt as fresh as if waking from a good night's sleep. I was wide awake and ready to go. The sensation was nowhere near the sudden instant rush that comes from shooting up coke or heroin. It was more of a creepy, spacey high that was just there. With all of my newly discovered powers, I felt like superman. As though I could walk through walls. I never picked up a needle but once after that night. I did, hated it, and never shot coke again. Coke was now considered rubbish to me and you couldn't give it away to me for free. My new love was ice. And when I say love, I mean like how you love your wife or your children. But more.

Soon I was using crystal meth on a regular basis. The drug was less expensive than cocaine and a little bit went a long way. I had become so addicted to the drug that I spent my entire paycheck on it. I moved back with my parents after Cindy and I parted ways due to my inability to deal with her overpowering desire to work in the bars. That way I could spend all of my money on meth. After years of hard core addiction to every kind of drug from pot to prescription pills to cocaine and heroin, I never once dreamed there was a drug out there as fantastic as ice. I mean, where have you been all my life? There wasn't enough money in my paycheck to pay for my habit so I resorted to drastic measures. I started stealing large amounts of merchandise from the store—clothes, electronics, whatever could be traded or sold. Although ice had been around for years on the mainland, used mainly by biker gangs who manufactured the drug, it was relatively new to Hawaii. The newer and more potent form of the drug was fast becoming more popular among Islanders. Not only by the younger generation, but by the adult crowd as well. During WWII, the Japanese military was rumored to have given the drug to their workers to improve their production of war machines and munitions. Adolf Hitler was said to have used the drug intravenously which could account for his eventual madness. No one really knew, or cared about for that matter, the dangerous side effects of the drug back in my day. Everyone was more concerned about marijuana and cocaine. They should have paid more attention. We all should have.

Crystal meth is a devious, all-consuming drug. It captures your mind and imprisons your body. The physical effects of the drug are more apparent than the psychological effects. The user loses all appetite and his physical appearance changes rapidly. Extreme weight loss and sunken facial features turns the user into a walking skeleton. When they look into the mirror, the image projected back at them is one of a super being, totally together and in charge. That's nothing more than the drug's sadistic psychological aspect playing tricks on the mind. With the lack of sleep and improper nourishment, the mind undergoes a series of changes. You start to hear voices, you become paranoid to the point where you're convinced that people are watching you or are after you. Your skin crawls and you think bugs are moving about beneath the surface of your skin. Some users acquire a nervous disorder and start to pick at themselves, trying to remove whatever imaginary creatures attack them. This results in small open sores that cover the person from head to toe. They never do rid themselves of those bugs that haunt them. Those individuals with stronger wills succumb to the power of the drug in different ways. The violent become more violent. The weak become weaker. The creeping sneaky demon eventually takes over its host like an alien bacteria and sucks the life out of them. Like throwing a wet sponge onto a hot grill, you fry and dry and turn to dust. That's why I called it voodoo dust. You become a zombie answering the call as it drives you closer to death. Then you turn to dust and, "poof," you're gone.

The drug turned me into a madman. I traded one ugly, fiendish mask for another. A more colossal, hideously, monstrous mask than I ever wore before. When I used cocaine or heroin, I found no need to arm myself. As my paranoia set in, the need to carry a gun was a must. I needed the weapons to protect myself from the demons that sought to destroy me. Although some of those demons were nothing more than my vivid imagination, many were real-life people who themselves had become victims to the crystal's voodoo spell. They were mad, crazy addicts that would do anything for the drug. Hyped up and moving at the speed of light, these crazies never slept. They wandered the city streets 24/7 in search of their next bowl-full of ice. It was like living in a different world, with all the people on the planet, except for us users, just standing still. You weaved and maneuvered in and around them without their having an inkling as to your existence. It was not uncommon for me to go days or even weeks at a time without sleep. I'd go to work during the daylight hours at Woolworths, walk the floors for eight hours, then stay out all night travelling from place to place, dealing meth. Days turned into nights and nights into days and before I knew it, two weeks had passed. I was so sleep deprived at some points that if I stayed still for even a brief second and didn't take a hit from my pipe, I'd nod out. But only for twenty minutes. I'd wake to find the pipe clutched in one hand and the lighter in the other. I felt as if I'd had a full night's sleep, took a hit, and was ready to go. I cranked on that glass dick like a soldier preparing for battle, because that's exactly what I saw my life on ice as—going to war. The pace was grueling and a lesser man would have shriveled up and died. Many did. Turned to dust and blown away. But I was stronger than most, in both mind and body. And my heart, that pumped my desire and resolve, was a machine that ran on nuclear power. A nuclear reactor that ran hot and at full speed even when I slept. The drug that fueled the source of power was needed by the grams-full. But what price was I willing to pay to feed my insatiable appetite? The answer to that question is easy and quite obvious. I would pay any and all to keep the fires burning.

My addiction to ice drove me deeper into the world of darkness. Jimbo had once been my main supplier but could no longer keep up with my hunger. I had begun an alliance with several family members including my cousin John and his brother-in-law, Mike. The same guy I was first arrested with on that home invasion years before. I never stopped to think how like minds thought alike. Especially drug addicts. Yesterday it was coke, weed, pills and heroin, today it was ice. Never stopped to think that the results of rekindling our relationship would lead to anything other than a tragic outcome. Who cared! All I wanted was to get high. Didn't matter how or who I had to go through to get it.

To support my habit, I staged organized shoplifting sprees at the store. I had also begun seeing an older Filipino girl who worked in the make-up department. She was older than me and had two children from a previous marriage. They both stayed with their father. Kathleen was gorgeous with long, black hair that fell below her knees, and lovely brown eyes. The special feature that drew me to her were the big dimples on both cheeks. I'm a sucker for dimples. I kept all of my drug habits and extra-curricular activities a secret as I didn't want to scare her away and ruin our relationship. More than one time, she vehemently voiced her protest on the use of drugs. She herself had once been addicted to crack cocaine. We eventually moved in together with my parents after she had gotten kicked out of her friend's house. I admit my motives for helping her at first were selfish and devilish. I couldn't just leave her stranded on the streets. My parents weren't too thrilled about the arrangement, but it was only temporary until we got our own place. Yes, there I go again, taking advantage of my loving parents. Call me an asshole, call me whatever name comes to mind, but hey, you know what kind of person you're reading about by now, so save the comments for later. You'll need them.

With Jimbo and Rose helping, I managed to boost whatever I could get my hands on that was worth anything. I'd spend hours walking around the store removing certain items of interest from the shelves and stuffing them into huge plastic Woolworth bags. When the bags were full, I hid them under clothing racks where the employees or customers couldn't see them. The employees were easy to deceive. They trusted me implicitly and thought of me as their protector. Writing about it now I feel like a rat for misleading them and breaking that trust. Especially Diane. She was such a honey and I loved her. (I'm sorry for being the person you always suspected me to be, but always hoped I wasn't. You were right in doing what you did that day in your office.) Getting back on track. With the bags packed and ready for pick-up, I'd call Jimbo and him and Rose would stroll in all casual-like, grab the goods and walk right out. I never bothered to cut off the security tags because I was so busy I just left them. When I saw Jimbo approaching the alarms, I grabbed an item with a tag on it and walked ahead of him. When the alarms triggered, and they were loud, I handed the item to the clerk in customer service and apologized for setting them off. By the time they reset the alarm, Jimbo was long gone. Was genius, if I may say so myself.

But, like all devious plans, it didn't last long. It had become obvious to Diane and her boss, a sweet German lady, that my activities were questionable. I was getting too many phone calls during work hours and leaving the store early, asking the night managers to close up for me. When you're high on ice, you're always the last to notice that you're screwing up. Oh, but you never screw up, the whole world is wrong and you are right! Because of my behavior, I was called into her office for a conference. The two women had become more concerned for my welfare than anything else. Diane sat pensive as she asked if I was all right and if there was anything wrong in my life. Anything that she could help with? They asked if I needed a few days off to gather myself. Me being high as a kite, I took a defensive position and began throwing figures at them. Were my arrest stats down? Was my recovery of stolen merchandise off? The whole guilt trip.

My smug over-confidence and exaggerated sense of self-worth had led me to believe that I was not expendable. Months earlier, I had captured a notorious felon that had murdered three people in Washington State. He had made his way to Hawaii and was attempting to fly out of the country when I arrested him in the mall for taking a bunch of stupid items. When I went to apprehend him, he made a sudden reach for something in his pocket. He never got the chance as I slammed him to the ground, over-powering him. When I searched him, I found a .357 Magnum over and under in the pocket he was reaching for. My own unique style of violently taking a suspect into custody had no doubt saved my life that day. The guy looked so young and innocent, you would never suspect he was a killer. The local paper wrote it up mentioning an F.W. Woolworth's security agent as being instrumental in the man's arrest. What, no name? They could have at least used my name. No matter, I became the rave of the retail merchant's community and the talk of the mall. Diane was elated! Even the big boss was so proud, he'd personally congratulated me on the bust. My lightning fast reflexes that day had been due to my drug use. I was lucky to have had some sleep or the bad guy would have won and I'd be dead. If I thought such heroic acts had earned me a get-out-of-getting-fired free card, I was sadly mistaken.

I was too stupid and too far gone to realize when people were really concerned about me. Really cared about me. I was so caught up in this world of fantasy and illusion that I couldn't recognize a true friend any more. They tried but failed and warned me to straighten up my act. I promised them I would and left.

I should have seen the signs then and there. I needed to change, to stop using and pay attention to the program. What do you think? Did you expect me to suddenly see the light and snap back to reality? Hell no! In fact, things went from bad to worse. And in a hurry. First, Kathy got drunk one night and smashed a beer bottle in my face. She always had trouble holding her liquor. When we started seeing each other, I told her to never try and make me jealous, you wouldn't like when I got angry. Just like the Hulk used to say. But women like to test their man. To see what kind of a man lies beneath the calm exterior. After a few episodes of letting the beast out in public, for her own drunken amusement, you'd think the bitch would have learned her lesson. I said she was gorgeous, not smart. My reaction to getting hit with a beer bottle was simple, I beat the shit out of her. The cops were called and that was the end of us. Then I left the store early one night to go make a drug deal. I forgot all about the lecture I'd gotten a few weeks back. The next day I was called into Diane's office. She told me to close the door behind me. She looked serious and as she sat down at her desk in front of me, she broke into tears. They streamed uncontrollably and I wanted to reach out and hold her. "Didn't I warn you not to leave the store early . . . didn't I tell you not to do it?" I apologized and she said it was too late for sorrys. I asked her if I was fired and she just nodded. I told her not to cry and she, being the person she was, handed me two envelopes. One held a month's pay in cash. The other held a check for the same amount. I looked at all this money, then up at her tear-filled eyes, "I can't take this," was all I said. I didn't want her to get into any trouble over me. "I want you to have it . . . I okayed it with the boss. So take it." I grabbed both envelopes, stuck them in my pocket and said, "you know I love you . . . if you ever need me, if anyone ever hurts you, call me." I turned and walked away. I never saw or heard from her again. Now there was nothing to stop me from losing myself in the demon realm.

My life had now become dedicated to the pursuit of smoking myself into oblivion. I had gotten so obsessed with ice that I spent every waking moment chasing it down. No longer able to pay for the amount I used in the usual fashion, I began using my talent as a cold-blooded thug as a commodity. I became a gun for hire to all the dope dealers and drug houses that needed their money collected. In return for services rendered, I was paid a percentage of whatever I collected on the debt. Usually a quarter of the total amount owed. If I had to use my gun in the collection, the price went up to half of the take. With the amount of people out there running around crazy on ice, there was more than enough business for a guy in the bogeyman trade. I took Lincoln Continental town cars away, cabin cruisers, jewelry, even people, whom I kidnapped and held until the debt was paid. I once snuck into a guy's house while he was asleep next to his girlfriend. I stuck the barrel of my pistol at his head while covering his mouth and whispered in his ear, "make one sound and I'll kill your girlfriend." I walked him to a waiting truck and drove him to the guy he owed the money to. When we arrived, the entire living room was covered in blue plastic tarps to avoid getting any blood on the rug and furniture. We tied him to a chair in the middle of the room and I proceeded to beat the crap out of him. He called his dad who was, at first, unwilling to pay the debt for his drug addicted son.

If he didn't I told him to say goodbye and held the phone to the beaten man's lips. The next day, bright and early, we met at the bank and we made the exchange. I thought that was the end of it. Just another flawless collection plan gone right. Boy was I ever in for an unpleasant surprise. Seems that this guy's father was a well-known big time gambler with ties to the local crime syndicate. He tracked me down and put a contract on my head. The killers followed me around and nearly fulfilled the hit. If it weren't for a chance meeting with a police patrol car that pulled out in my direction at the precise lucky moment, the woman that I was out on a date with would have been killed along with me. Fortunately for me, my ex-boss Leroy had friends in the underworld and informed me of the hit. He called me two days later and asked me to meet him at his work place. When I arrived, he told me all about the night I was passing by that gym where I dropped my date off. I was totally taken aback. It puzzled me how he knew about it. Then he explained about the contract and the father. He knew it all! It gave me goose bumps as he described the event and what could have been my final day on earth. I suddenly became enraged. I wanted to kill those bastards! How dare they try and kill me for some other stupid jackass' mistakes! Leroy calmed me down and assured me that these guys weren't to be taken lightly and that if I did anything stupid, they'd kill my whole family. That took the air right out of me. He said to lay low for a few days and not to leave my house to go anywhere. Not even to the store. I followed his instruction to the letter. Four days later, he called and told me the contract was lifted, but to stay away from the area where I kidnapped the guy. All this trouble over a measly three grand. It scared me for an instant, but not enough to prevent me from doing what I was doing.

Throughout my entire time in the ice world, I was constantly looking for the man. That one person who had the mother lode of crystal meth. The main supplier who had pounds and pounds of the stuff, an unlimited supply. It was an elusive search that took me far beyond the reaches of sanity and reality. My search took me to places I never knew existed and I met people I never suspected walked the planet. The harder I searched, the more elusive the imaginary figure became. But he was not a myth. He existed and many times I got close to finding him. I would find him! Hopefully, before I myself am turned into dust. Just when I began to think that all was lost, I got a phone call from my cousin John. He said he needed my help and to meet him at a certain address. When I reached the house it looked quiet and abandoned. I knocked on the door and a man's voice spoke, "go around to the back." You'd never know anyone was there the place was so shut up. When I entered I saw my cousin seated at a dining table along with two other men. One was a large, fat man with a dark complexion. The other was a thin, lanky man with bushy hair. They each had a glass pipe in their hands. John introduced me to the men and we shook hands all around. Then the fat guy, named Stan, handed me the pipe. He said that he heard about me from my cousin and that he needed my help collecting his money. He showed me a list that tallied into the tens of thousands of dollars. I was astonished! And like a hungry animal set to attack, I looked across the table to my cousin, who flashed a knowing smile, cocked his head, raised an eyebrow and said, "Just what you wanted huh cuz?" I finally found the man and he was asking me to work for him. It was a dream come true in the world of crystal meth. For a crazed addict that is. Our relationship would further lead me down the rabbit hole into the strange dark world of the damned.

They say one of the worst possible things you can do is to lend money to family. Or to have a family member working for you. The kind thought is there, but it's just bad business. I concur! In this case, Stan had a brother-in-law who owed him money, around $2000 for an ounce of ice he fronted to him. Fronted meaning given to the person up front with nothing down in lieu of future payment. In a timely manner of course—ASAP! It wasn't the highest amount on the list, but it was more the principle of the debt. He had broken the rule and his brother-in-law had taken full advantage of his blunder by playing the family card. In the drug business, there's no such thing as family. Only customers. That's why I never sell to family. I just give it to them. It avoids all the mix-ups that tend to happen. That way, I don't have to get nasty when they don't pay me. Stan had tried everything short of sending a collector over and stomping on the deadbeat to get his money. I guess he saw this collection as sort of a test. You know, see if I could really do the job.

I borrowed a huge Smith & Wesson .44 Magnum revolver with a long-ass 10" barrel from John and said I'd be back in a jiffy. Stan said, "Whatever you do, don't kill the guy!" "I'll try not to, but I can't promise you anything," I replied. When I arrived at the house, I recognized it in an instant. This was the place where Tim, my ex-boss Leroy's son and I came one time to get high with two stiffs in the back of the wagon. All the people in the house couldn't believe that there were two dead bodies in the back of the car and rushed out to have a look. The owner, who I met that day, was the guy who owed Stan the money. What a small world. I drove past and parked down the street. I noticed that there was a bunch of guys, maybe six or eight, hanging out in the garage. They all looked high and from the way they were dressed were packing guns. I stuck the gun down the front of my shorts, the barrel nearly protruding out the bottom of the seam and walked slowly towards the crowd. With my casual attire, tank top, shorts and flip-flops, no one would suspect that I carried a cannon on me. That would give me an advantage if any of those guys decided to get stupid. While they were busy posturing up and ruffling their feathers. I'd be able to fast draw and kill a few of them, then duck out of sight before they knew what hit them. I reached the group and their relaxed demeanor suddenly stiffened. I asked the tough closest to me, most likely to get killed first, if Darryl was home. "Darryl not home. Go away!" he barked. "How about you guys, you seen Darryl?" I asked the others. They closed in and the same guy said, "Darryl not here I said, so split!" At that point my anger had peaked and it appeared that things were about to get ugly. Those stupid Filipinos with their greasy hair, dark shades and idiotic accents had no idea how close to death they were at that moment. They looked too laid back to consider the threat that stood before them. Not one of them even made a move to reach for their weapon. They thought their strength in numbers was menacing enough to scare me away. They had another think coming. I screamed out, "Darryl, Darryl!" The gang was shocked to see that their plan to scare the big guy in the shorts away didn't work. The first guy with the big mouth took a step toward me and swore something in his native language, an expletive that Kathy had taught me. I was about to pull my gun and start shooting when the screen door swung open and out walked Darryl. He moved toward us and everyone turned and looked. As he walked passed, I called his name again. He was only a foot away as he turned to me, "Yeah" was all he said. "I want to talk to you about Stan," I told him. He got spooked and almost fled but he saw my hand on the butt of the gun and froze. Then I said, "remember me? Timmy's friend, we came here and got high with you and had the bodies in the wagon?" He smiled and called off his dogs. We shook hands and he jumped into my car and drove to a nearby market. We sat in the parking lot and discussed the matter of his debt. Apparently Stan had been trying to extort the kid for a little extra payment because of his failure to pay on time. The original debt was $2300 for the ounce and he'd already given Stan $1000. That left a balance of just $1300 but because he was late a couple weeks, Stan upped it to $2000. Darryl got angry over the extra and decided not to pay him a dime. It was all a misunderstanding between two pig-headed family members that dealt drugs. What a hassle. That's why I never deal with family. I told him that I needed a payment right here and now before I left or I'd have to get mean. The look of shock came over his face and he stared into my eyes. He reached into his pockets and removed a stack of bills. All he had was three hundred in cash and a gram of ice. I took both and told him to meet me here in three days with the rest. He agreed.

When I got back to the house, about an hour later, the three men were in the same position, at the table smoking their pipes. I sat down next to Stan and he glanced at me with a skeptical look, "What happen . . . things didn't go right?" The doubt was etched on his face. "On the contrary," I replied and emptied my pockets onto the table. Stan's jaw dropped wide open. "You mean he paid you?" John laughed and said to Stan," I told you my cousin was the real deal." I explained the payment plan and told Stan that if he wanted me to work for him, he had to play straight with me and do it my way or no deal. He shook my hand in amazement and agreed. Four days later, I met Darryl in the same parking lot and collected the balance. I had made a believer out of Stan.

The ice world could be considered a close knit, I wouldn't say family because everyone who existed in it wouldn't hesitate to stab the next person in the back to take what they had, network of dog-eat-dog lowlifes. Every addict that used the drug more or less knew everyone else who either dealt or used the stuff. The only difference was between the casual users and the full-on, hard-core abusers, people like me, who made it a business of getting high. The greater the usage and quantity of the drug trading hands, the higher the probability of violence. You could never tell when that crazy person running around with little or no sleep would snap. Even the most docile of humans could become a raving lunatic at the drop of a hat. All that mattered was the drug. I was often surprised at the lengths people went to obtain the drug. They lied, they cheated, they stole, even killed to get it. There were no rules or organized order in this game. Your best friend could become your worst enemy overnight. Morality and kinship tossed aside like a discarded piece of rubbish. I would soon become all too familiar with this crazed phenomenon among my fellow users. When the reality of true humanity touches home in a world where the id in each of us is worn on the exterior of all who fall victim to voodoo dust . . .

Chapter 19

In this bowl, the world is cold

Trust is something that is reserved for the normal, hard-working populace that can appreciate the word and know exactly what it entails. The mere mention of the word conjures up images of relationships both old and new on which all friendships, marriages and families are based upon. But in the world of crystal meth, the word trust is a misconception. Even when mentioned it can never be taken at face value. The word simply doesn't exist. Only the empty echo when spoken from the mouths of scandalous individuals. Hollow and meaningless. A word used to deceive the naïve. It possesses no more value than the dirt beneath your shoes. For those of us who were stupid enough to believe the people in this distorted world who preached the concept of the word, our very lives would be tested.

Working for Stan opened up an entirely new profile for me in the world of ice. You could say it broadened my horizons. It was a higher plane of drug dealing. I met people who from all accounts, were in a different bracket of handling the drug. Not the usual nickel and dime penny pushers, but the people who called the shots. One of these people was Rex. Apparently, I was doing such a good job for Stan that his supplier wanted to have a face to face meeting with me. All this time I thought I was working for the "man" himself when in reality I was working for his "boy." The night I met Rex, we hit it off from the start. He wasn't anything like the person I expected. They called him by the name "Old Man" yet here was this young Filipino boy in his late twenties. He was a gun nut like myself and had quite a collection of illegal firearms. When we first arrived, I was awed by the amount of ice that was spread about the coffee table. John had to elbow me in the ribs to wipe the hungry look off my face. I never saw so much crystal in a single place before. But as the conversation turned to weaponry, I found myself totally wrapped up in Rex's gun collection. He was amazed at my prowess and knowledge of the weapons he presented for my viewing, how I was looking over and examining each one with authority and loving appreciation, opening and closing the bolts and removing the magazines like a professional. It must have been the twinkle in my eye that sealed the deal. Before the night was over, he asked me to come work for him. The hatred and glare of jealousy in Stan's eyes was obvious and even John noticed it. To make matters worse, before I left he presented me with two gifts. One was a .30 caliber Colt carbine and the other was a Remington 12 gauge pump shotgun. If looks could kill, I would have been a dead man in Stan's eyes. To prevent things from getting any worse, I told Rex that I'd let him know about the offer. It was a quiet ride home as Stan stewed in his own juices. I'd find out soon enough just how pissed off Stan really was.

From then on, every effort to contact Rex was sabotaged by Stan. This I would later confirm to be true following an incident that would cause me to sever my relationship with Stan. It started when Rex had asked Stan to contact me about a drug dealer heist. Rex's competitor was bringing in a huge load and would be distributing the crystal from an airport Holiday

Inn. It would be a basic home invasion take-over robbery. We'd use a girl posing as a party-goer to gain access through the front door. Along with John and myself, Stan had asked a friend of his, an ex-navy man to come along on the hit. The guy brought to the game a Mac 10 automatic machine pistol that held a .45 cal round. It was the perfect weapon to use in a closed room environment. The gun spurted out over 600 rounds a minute and could easily kill a lot of people in a hurry if need be. The moment I laid eyes on this guy I had a bad feeling. He gave me the creeps!

The night of the robbery, we met at a room that was rented under an assumed name in the same hotel. In the midst of the planning, Rex walked in and came straight up to me and embraced me. Then he said, "Where you been . . . I been trying to reach you?!" I turned to look at Stan and he looked away. He made me promise to come meet him at his new home after this was over. When Rex had left, I overheard Stan and his friend Alex quietly discussing what sounded like a plan of their own. From the looks of things, the two were planning to be the only ones walking out of that hotel room alive after the hit. I called my cousin over and told him that, whatever he did, don't enter that door. Alex had conveniently chosen to follow up at the rear with Stan while John and I breeched the door first. I felt more than a little uncomfortable entering a strange room with a creepy guy carrying a "Miami chopper" following close behind me. I told Stan that the only way I'd enter the room first was if I had the machine pistol. Alex refused to give up his gun. Debating turned to arguing. I was so angry! I just wanted to kill Alex and Stan right there. Forget about all that ice and money that was to be had. After awhile we agreed that Alex would come with me and Stan would go with John. We'd each take different approaches to the room and meet up when the girl started knocking. I had no intention of going through with this robbery, especially with these two shady characters. I told John to take Stan on a wild goose chase and wait until he heard shots, then run to the car. I said I'd be there waiting.

We split up and Alex followed me into a stairwell where we'd wait until the girl arrived at the door. Alex had no way of knowing that I was about to kill him. As long as the robbery hadn't taken place, Stan and his plan to murder John and me was on hold. I was shaking with rage as I stood behind Alex on the steps. His gun in hand and head peering out the door, I pointed the .38 special towards his head and was all set to fire when the door on the level above swung open and a couple entered the stairwell. I lowered the gun. If I had shot at that moment, the couple would have walked right into it. We entered the hall just as the couple went by. It was a close call. I was pissed! This punk needed killing! When we exited the hall, I saw Stan, John and the girl standing next to the car. The relief was evident on my cousin's face. Stan was livid and started arguing with Alex. I had managed to lead Alex to a different building of the hotel across from the one we were going to hit. We jumped into the car and left. In all the excitement, Alex had forgotten where he left his machine gun. Which I found and now held in my hand, pointed in his direction. He panicked and searched everywhere, protesting to Stan as he drove. "Looking for this?" I said. Alex looked down in the dark and saw the muzzle pointed at his gut. He turned white as the reality of the situation hit home. "Thought I lost it" he replied. He asked me for it and we sat staring at each other for a long second. John's voice broke the spell, "cuz, cuz, everything's cool . . . be cool." I took the magazine out, ejected the round from the port and handed Alex his weapon. "Should be more careful where you leave your gun . . . someone could get hurt," I told him. I rode home the entire distance with that .38 pointed at him from my coat pocket. I wish I had emptied that clip into his ass. I parted ways with Stan and my cousin after that night to seek greener pastures. Well, safer ones anyway. I told you trust wasn't worth squat.

Venturing out on my own, I had become pretty adept at the game. With all the new connections I made it was easy for me to set up my own operation. It wasn't what I'd describe as a big time set up, it was more of a one man band kinda thing. I really didn't need anyone's help to establish myself. I'd had enough help from Stan to last a lifetime. Although he turned out to be a rather loathsome person to work for, I have to admit he taught me everything there was to know about crystal meth, from smoking it to dealing. The one thing I possessed that he did not was the ability to do my own dirty work. I didn't have to hire someone to collect my money or, if it got to that, kill someone. I was the total package. Purchaser, sales person, bookkeeper, collector and enforcer, all rolled into one.

There's no one better to trust than yourself. The thing with that last statement is, with this drug, you couldn't even do that. Being under the influence of crystal meth is like having ADHD. When the mind altering chemical kicks in, you have difficulty focusing. Your body is moving a mile a minute as it keeps changing channels like a TV. It takes a feat of strength to maintain a clear train of thought. Once you lose focus, the channel changes and you're off in another direction, doing who knows what. That's why many meth addicts have projects that sit around the house in various stages of incompletion. Their minds can tune in for only brief moments of concentration, but then they drift off. I've seen stereo sets, TV's, washers and dryers, even cars, in pieces at some addict's house, waiting to be reassembled. The sad thing is, none of these people ever possessed the knowledge in the first place to repair any of that stuff. It was just the drug convincing them that they could. You begin to see visions of grandeur and act upon it. It made me believe that I was invincible. That I was the smartest, most bad-ass drug dealer around. And that's what made me dangerous. I focused 100% of my mind on that thought and never lost it, no matter how messed up I was on the drug.

I soon branched out to all sections of the island. I had safe houses in five different locations. These were houses where families lived and at least one of the couple had a steady job. The other stayed at home watched the kids or sent them to school and sold drugs for me. I'd show up once a week, stay for a day or two, deal drugs, then move on to the next house. When business was good, I'd hang out a little longer to maximize my profit. I dealt mostly in small quantities because I was still busy looking for the "man." The closest I'd gotten was Rex and that nearly got me dead. But until the next good prospect came along I had a habit to feed, one that had grown into an enormous appetite. Somewhere along this pipeline I met Fred. He was a country boy who I'd been introduced to by a friend. We began hanging out and doing deals on and off together. He was a good businessman, at first, who really knew the game. But then the ice got the best of him and he ended up getting gunned down by a drug dealer he'd ripped off. I knew it from the moment I first met the guy, he'd get into trouble. I tried to warn him the day he showed up at my house with a machine gun in his knapsack. He refused to listen. Up until the day his girlfriend called to tell me that he had been shot nine times. When I arrived at the hospital, they were wheeling him into surgery. I was suspicious from the beginning because of his injuries. All the bullets had hit in the lower portion of his body, mainly on one side in the leg area. The leg would have to be amputated, but he'd survive the shooting. I was mad as hell and itching to take revenge on the people who had done this. When you decide to go gunning for someone, it's best that you get the story straight. That way, only the right people end up getting killed. After talking to his girlfriend, who had witnessed the shooting, I found out that Fred had been wearing a bullet proof vest—the reason for the wounds only to his lower body. She said Fred had gone to the guy's house he owed money to and was ambushed. The whole thing didn't make sense at first. Then I got the full version. Fred was partners with this guy who fronted him the ice, which he started to abuse and could no longer pay for. The guy, who was a killer himself, got disgusted and told Fred to forget about the bill and to keep the machine gun he had lent to him because he was going to need it. Fred decided to take matters into his own hands, strapped up and tried to sneak into this guy's house. He walked right into an ambush. The shooters just opened fire on him from the darkened interior of the house. He'd lied to me about what happened, he could have started a war. I walked away from that one.

Eventually, a friend who lived and dealt drugs at one of those safe houses introduced me to a female drug dealer who was down on her luck. Like many of the independent dealers operating on their own, without the benefit of protection, she fell victim to pirates who robbed her of all her stash and cash. The difference between this particular individual and the rest was, not only her ability to make money, but she also had a harem of young girls working for her. We met in a hotel room where she asked me to sell her an ounce of crystal meth. Because of her situation, all she had was half of the purchase price. She said if I trusted (that word again) her for the balance, she'd get me the rest by that evening. Since Joe swore to her solidarity, I gave her the drugs. I don't know what it was that convinced me to give her the chance. I didn't even know this lady. It sure wasn't the sincerity in her promise to pay me. The dirty dog that I am, I saw myself in a room full of these hot girls, partying! To get to that was worth the risk of half an ounce of dope.

That's exactly where I found myself that evening after she called me to come pick up the balance of my money. In a nest of young and tender babes. When I entered the room, I thought I'd died and gone to heaven. The girl who answered the door was herself a stunner. She escorted me in and my eyes were greeted by six or seven females, scantily dressed in short shorts and tube tops, lying around in suggestive poses. From the looks of them, they all appeared to be in their late teens or early twenties. They all chimed in an excited welcome and told me that Aunty Jerry was waiting in the next room. One of the girls asked if I was Jerry's new boyfriend. Another of the girls approached me before I reached the bedroom and said, "hi . . . so you're the guy with all the dope. Are you going to kick back and smoke with us?" She looked so young and innocent, I was at a loss for words. When I entered the bedroom, I noticed the stack of bills on the nightstand next to the bed. Jerry had a pipe in her hand and was busy puffing from it. She turned and said, "thanks for coming. I got your money. How do you like my girls?" All I could answer was, "what do you mean, your girls?" She explained that these girls all worked for her selling drugs and that was all. No funny stuff. She considered them her family and was very protective of them. Whatever scam or setup this lady with the short red hair had going, I wanted in on it. Yes, forgive the perv in me for pecking out or don't forgive the perv in me . . . whatevers. I thought her angle enticing. Strictly from a business point of view, these girls were honey to the flies. Every dealer in town would die to do business with someone who paraded around a stable of beauties before their eyes. It was an ingenious idea. Scary and dangerous for the parties involved but with the right muscle behind it, such a gig could take off. I just couldn't bring myself to believe that these young girls could handle themselves in this game. Hell, I couldn't imagine them smoking the drug. I was soon put at ease as Jerry assured me they were all of legal age and that they smoked like carburetors. Somehow, my skepticism got the best of me and I opted to put her information to the test. I suggested that since our business had concluded, lets get down to partying. Jerry laughed and we both adjourned to the living room. The girls smiled with delight as I made myself comfortable on the sofa. Then the sea of females closed around me and I was in heaven for sure. They each introduced themselves in their own seductive manner as I broke out the batu. Batu is a Filipino word for rock, the description and most commonly used word for ice in Hawaii. Everyone called it that. I was mesmerized by these girls who nearly smoked me dry. They were charming and I had a great time. But time was money and I certainly wasn't making any here. Before leaving, I gave my number to a few of them. I put them on the back burner to simmer. That play would come in handy one day.

Throughout my frantic world, my need for companionship was lacking. When the pace slowed, I longed for a normal man and woman relationship. Not the meaningless physical union I sought because of my incompleteness. Because of my lifestyle, it would be next to impossible to find a mate that was willing to accept me for what I had become. Who'd ever consider being with a monster? To my surprise, the answer to the puzzle arrived in a phone call. One of the girls I'd met that night in the hotel room phoned and asked if I wanted to get together. Her name was Celestine and who would have thought that our friendship would one day end so tragically? An innocent, vivacious Filipino girl in her twenties with brown eyes and hair, 5'3" of perfection. Of all the eye candy in the hotel room that night, she had caught my attention over the others. My attraction to this girl was more than sexual. I didn't desire her in that sense. She reminded me of a wounded animal. A newly born fledgling that had fallen from the nest. I felt compelled to protect her. The night we met, it was obvious that the other girls saw her as anything but their equal. They teased and abused her jokingly, as if she was the court jester. Although they all grew up together in a low income housing project and attended the same schools, their unconscious degrading attitude towards her seemed unintended. After sitting with them awhile in that small room, while the devil possessed us, it became apparent to me that their years of abuse were the result of Celestine's slight handicap. Not visibly noticeable but evident in her character and mannerisms. She was adorable and I loved her from the start. Like a parent would a child born with a physical deformity. We were both alike, she and me. Two broken spirits who were lost—searching for a way out of the crooked maze that life had stuck us in.

We'd met up again along with a couple of the other girls. They were all hopelessly addicted to ice and could hold their own in a smoke-a-thon. They painted me a colorful picture of their lives under the expert tutelage of their mentor Aunty Jerry. She treated them well and looked out for them as best she could. But after the incident where she was robbed, the girls had become shaken and reluctant to go on working for her for fear of their welfare. I saw this as an opportunity to lure them into working for me. In a limited capacity to start. A trial basis, if you will. They were all for it, but felt bad about leaving Jerry high and dry. In this business, with its pernicious consequences, you have to lower the odds of getting hurt or killed in your favor. These poor innocent girls had no idea what they were getting themselves into. Neither did I. Even the factor of life and death in this game was all fun and games to me, just as it was for these girls. Only in my game, we played by a different set of rules, we played for keeps. Only time would tell if they had the right stuff. Ladies, it was time to step your game up!

I agreed to eventually supply them with Batu and take care of all the protection and enforcement. They were safe as they could be under the circumstances. On our very next meeting, I was introduced to the matriarch of the clan. Her name was Sarah. She was twenty and busy working at a KFC the first two times we gathered. Sarah was a tough, speak your mind girl who shot straight from the hip. A voluptuous hapa haole (Caucasian/Asian mix) beauty with a happy-go-lucky personality to match her bubbly charismatic presence. She was almost the mirror image of myself, only in the female version. I was taken with her from the moment we met. I focused all my attention on her the entire night. But it was more the mishaps that happened over the course of the evening that made my mind up about her. First, I popped a beer in her face that drenched her, just as I was displaying my charm. Then, as we left the hotel to move the party to my house, I dropped a six pack of beer on her foot. And last, as we all piled into my car, I slammed her hand in the door. Each accident was met with a clever response on her part. "Thanks bra, I already had my shower." Or "If you don't like me, I'll leave, you don't have to kill me with the beer!" then, "Man, if you don't want me here you don't have to chop my fingers off!" I wanted her more than anything then.

From that night on we became a couple and she, along with her friends, were swept into my nightmare. I depended on her to keep the girls in line. Celestine wasn't too happy at first. She had always held out hope that I'd take to her in that fashion. She told me as much when she saw Sarah and me sleeping together. She was slow at some things, but way too smart in other areas. Regardless of her still being my favorite, I desired Sarah on a more intimate level. Although there was a difference in our ages, I was thirty at the time, we were meant to be together. The two women learned to share me, each in their own way. I was lover to one, protector to the other. We hung out together and spent almost all our waking moments as a family. Sarah and I treated her as a sheltered child. While Sarah went to work, Celestine drove me around as I took care of business. She was an excellent driver and I trusted her, as far as that was concerned, with my life. Collectively, with the help of the girls, I had established a rather efficient drug dealing operation. It was far from a multimillion dollar organization, but it was smooth and made money.

The girls were like candy to a baby. After all, isn't that what grown men really are? Big babies. Whenever I needed to make a drug deal go my way, I'd use them as bait to capture the customers' attention. After flaunting them around in front of their hungry eyes they were ready, willing and able to give me anything I wanted. All they had was lust on their minds. The girls all knew their roles and played them well. You could enjoy the goods but look, don't touch. Unless, of course, the girl was interested. Let's get one thing straight. My relationship with these girls was strictly a professional one. People would see my motives as being that of a dirty old man enjoying a perverted arrangement. That was in no way the case here. I cared about these girls. They were my friends. I looked out for them, made them safe. It was they who chose the lifestyle, I didn't choose it for them. I know it sounds sick and a warped way of seeing things, but these girls wanted this. Lived for it! Whether I was there with them or not, they'd be doing the same thing. They had a nickname for females who used their bodies as payment for crystal meth in the business—batunas. It was a hateful slur reserved for only the worst kind of woman who had no heart. These girls, who appeared to fit the description, were far from it. They possessed hearts of gold and truly cared for people. Even if the pipe did get the best of each and everyone of us, these girls were too pure of heart to let the drug consume them in that manner. It was a good life for everyone involved. But, as always, death sat on its dark horse, waiting in the shadows.

The end for me would come soon. In between my own drug trips, Jimbo and I would connect and do business together. I came a long way in the crystal meth business, but always attributed my humble beginning to Jimbo's intervention. He should have left well enough alone and let me shoot my life away on cocaine. At least, back then, I wasn't really hurting anyone, physically that is, except me. The moral bullshit will always be the same, no matter which way you tilt the picture. I'm wrong, it's wrong, etc. He being a certified ice monster himself seemed to have his act together. Always made money, paid his bills on time, took exceptionally good care of his family and controlled his consumption of the drug. From the days in high school when we first met all those years ago, he'd remained the consummate drug dealer. He never wavered. But crystal has a way of changing a person. When the reality of the illusion begins to sink in and tiny cracks begin to develop in the hardened exterior, you're the last person to notice that you're breaking. The telltale signs become evident to everyone around you, but not yourself. The veil of denial encircles you within a fog of blindness. You continue to function at full speed ahead, unaware of the crumbling world around you. Jimbo never saw the signs. Never paid attention to the caution signs warning him to take heed.

The drug soon consumed him. Gobbled him up! He spent more time on the road. Away from his family, hungrily drowning himself in the fountain of greedy pleasure. The voodoo dust had found its latest victim. He was a strong one. Stronger than most, but the crystal that burned within the glass bowl, the Demon, was much stronger. No human can resist its calling. Its alluring whispers, like a cold winter frost, ascending, turning a heart and soul into something as cold as ice. He began seeing another woman, more like a girl in her early twenties. I had been the one responsible for their meeting. She was the girlfriend of a friend of mine, named Joe. They were both madly in love and it broke his heart when he found out about her infidelity. I went to see him in the hospital after he tried to kill himself over the betrayal. It was there that he told me it was Jimbo who had taken her away. I was shocked. I had no idea at the time that he was being unfaithful to Rose. I wondered if my past and recent relationships with Cindy and Sarah, both in the same age group, or having our young friends working for me had anything to do with it. Perhaps it was payback for Rose's bad behavior or it could have been just plain lust. Either way, it stank. I couldn't believe it until I saw them together one afternoon. I don't know why, but I was pissed at him. Must have been the fact that Joe had tried to kill himself over it. When it's over, it's over. No excuses necessary.

About a month later, Rose called and asked me to come over. When I arrived she said she'd had enough of his shit and she was leaving him. She was taking the baby and moving back to the mainland. I tried to convince her to reconsider, but her mind was made up. She asked if I'd help move her stuff to her mother's house. I asked her if Jimbo knew and she said no. I told her I didn't want to get involved. I gave her the whole best friend speech. She pleaded with me and the sucker in me gave in. I showed up the next day to find the baby gone and her standing in the midst of disarray. I felt uncomfortable and said as much. I just wanted out of there. She looked so distraught and alone I couldn't just leave her there. I felt like a rat, sneaking behind Jimbo's back, conspiring with his wife. It was a no-no. She said her plane left the next day and to hurry before he finished work. Okay, I'll pack her shit up then drop her off and that would be the end of it. Jimbo would be crazy mad if he found out I helped her. But hey, after what he'd done, he deserved it.

My anger for what he'd done to Joe pushed me on. I told her to leave me out of I; say she caught a cab. I knew from the start this whole thing was a bad idea. It was the cool way in which she spoke. Sweet and suggestive. I remember how she used the baby as an excuse to lure me into coming the day before. I had completely forgotten just how persuasive this bitch could be. But aren't all women when they use that irresistible charm of theirs? Men are weak!

The quicker I got this covert operation done with, the better. When we arrived at her Mom's and unloaded her junk, she asked me to drive her to a friend's house. Why not, in for a quarter, in for a dollar. She ran in and returned less than ten minutes later with a big grin on her face. She looked at me with those dark eyes of hers and said, "Let's go to your house and smoke!" Things were about to get complicated. "What about the baby" I said. "Don't worry, she's fine." Sap. It was more the drugs than anything else. I was just too stupid to decline the offer. When we got to my place, my mom said that Jimbo had called. Great! Just what I needed. We headed to my bedroom for a perfectly innocent time of smoking. I never, for the life of me, expected what happened. Only one thing weakens a man more than drugs. Sex! It was that day that I broke every rule in the books. It was the beginning of our torrid, whirlwind affair. All the mystery was revealed as our desires exploded when we explored each others lust. There was no question about it, we were in deep shit. In the middle of our lovemaking, she confessed that she'd always wanted this. Deep down inside, so did I. I never imagined it to be like this. I had no right to destroy my best friend's life under any circumstances. Blame it on the meth? Now that's a lame excuse. Justify it any way you like, you messed up big time!

Like two newlyweds, we hid ourselves away from everyone. Lost in our forbidden passion, we never left the bedroom. The phone continued to ring off the hook, met with excuses that I was nowhere to be found. I'd hidden my car in an underground parking stall to avoid detection. This whole damn thing was all wrong. But my unbridled sexual desires made it seem right. I'd have to surface sometime. I thought about lying to Jimbo the night he called with his heart on his sleeve, telling me that Rose had left him. It was agonizing to hear his hurt, but not enough to make me turn back. I had failed as a person. Sarah kept calling and I kept dodging her. How long could I keep this up? My ecstasy was the answer to that question. As long as it took!

The whole game caught up to me one day when I went to pick Sarah up from work. I'd left Rose home alone and told her not to answer the phone under any circumstances. Jimbo had been calling daily to get a hold of me. He'd been pounding the pavement, looking for his wife. Rose's mom told him she had no idea where Rose was. Things had gotten way out of hand. I tried to break it off with Rose, but couldn't. When I returned from picking up Sarah, I noticed Jimbo's van parked on the street in front of my parents' condo. I looked through the seven-foot high wooden lattice fence that enclosed our patio and saw Jimbo pacing back and forth. He was screaming obscenities at me. He was also carrying a 12 gauge pump shotgun. Sarah freaked and wanted to call the cops. I told her to go get my dad, who was working security at the hotel across the street. The sun burned brightly in the sky above and its beautiful blue color was a stark contrast to the ugly drama that was about to play out. The stupid bitch had answered the phone! I walked to the apartment, opened the door and entered the hallway. I was greeted by an angry husband with a .357 magnum pointed at my head. "What's my wife doing in your house without her panties on?" The distance between us was about fifteen feet. Much too far for me to rush in and attempt to disarm him.

Seeing that gun pointed at me made me angry. I told him to put the gun down. He refused. Tears were streaming down his face and the weapon was unsteady in his grip. Any moment now I expected to be shot. I tried to reason with him, but he was way past reasoning, he wanted blood. Mine. Men who have been around weapons all their lives, like myself, never pull a gun on someone unless they were prepared to use it. Then it was just bang. "Never point a gun at someone unless you intend to kill them," is all I said. He never had it in him before, but this time it was different. No telling what he would do in his present state of mind. I tried to get closer, but he yelled at me to stop. From the living room Rose launched into a shouting match over his behavior. He turned to focus his attention on her and I stepped closer. She stood up and suddenly reached up and grabbed a handful of his hair. That was the distraction I was hoping for. I leaped on top of him and closed my hands around the gun. We wrestled to the floor. Somehow I managed to choke him and unload the pistol. He started to turn blue and his lips went purple—I almost choked him to death. I stared into his frightened eyes and felt his body go limp. I relaxed my hold on him and he started gasping for breath. He started sobbing. He asked me "why?" I told him I'd let him up if he calmed down. At first he agreed and we both rose to our feet. Then, in a blink, he snapped and ran towards the kitchen. I heard him rummaging through the drawers. I turned to retrieve the gun I'd given to Rose during the struggle. It wasn't there. She'd given it to Sarah who'd showed up in the middle of the fight. She hid it along with the shotgun in the bedroom. I turned to see Jimbo exiting the kitchen with a huge butcher knife in his hand. I sprinted for the front door. I ran into the parking lot and hid around a corner. By that time, my father had appeared and was confronted by Jimbo who had left the apartment. He had abandoned the knife and was loudly voicing his discontent. My father tried to calm him, but in his rage he refused to listen. All I heard him say was that he'd be back before he stormed off. I saw him jump into his van and speed off down the road. I came around the corner and my father said he was calling the police.

Even on a good day, it was more than likely to take the cops about fifteen minutes to get here. Jimbo lived only a mile or two away. And from the way he was driving, it would take him no time at all to get to his house, rearm himself and return with guns blazing. I walked past my dad and headed for the apartment. He reached for me and said, "wait for the cops." I told him that there wasn't time for that. "What you going do?" he said. "I can't let him get here and start shooting up the place . . . I got to stop him." It was my intention to arm myself, track him down, and kill him if need be. As far as I was concerned, he'd had his chance. Now it was mine. I asked Sarah where she hid the guns and she took me right to them. I locked and loaded both weapons and told her I'd drop her at her mom's house down the street before I went hunting for Jimbo. No sooner had I gotten the car started than Sarah screamed, "babe, there he is!" I turned to see Jimbo's van racing around the corner, tires screaming. He pulled behind me, blocking my exit. Sarah ran for cover through the hotel lobby. I reached for the shotgun that was in its case, but had trouble getting to it. I knew that Jimbo had a variety of weapons, including high powered rifles and shotguns at his disposal. The shotgun would be the perfect weapon to use at this distance. All I'd have to do was point and pull the trigger. I couldn't miss. Maybe the sight of the gun aimed at him would scare him back to reality. If it didn't, I was prepared to shoot. I settled for the colt .357. It was in my hand in one smooth motion. I covered it with a red bandana to keep it hidden.

I swung out of my seat and faced the left side of his van. I held the gun low in an unassuming position, next to my leg. He swore at me and yelled that he had something for me. It's then that I saw the snub-nosed pistol in his hand. He was screaming at me and said, "This what you want?" as he showed the gun to me. Never strong arm the strong arm! Remember, "shoot first and ask questions later son," was all I heard, my dad's familiar voice echoed in my head. And as calmly as I'd learned as a child, I raised the gun, took aim, and fired. The sound of gunfire was deafening within the confines of the high rise buildings and streets. I fired five shots in total. The bullets found their mark and I saw Jimbo's gun hand fall. He cried out in pain as each round entered his body. I saved one bullet in the cylinder for good measure. A resounding silence and peaceful calmness overcame me before the shooting and after. In all the years of carrying a gun, though I had gotten very close, I had never had to use one. Somehow I had always managed to avoid it. Lots of people I'd known needed killing, but Jimbo wasn't one of them. As I approached the van, an eerie stillness surrounded me. There was no yelling or traffic sounds or people's voices. Curious on-lookers, who had been treated to a wild west show in their urban environment, were silent. I slid the van's side door open to see the collapsed body of my once best friend sprawled out on the carpeted floor. He was conscious and bleeding. Even fired through the passenger side door, the trusty Magnum had done its job. He looked up at me and in a low, haunted voice cried, "why you shoot me?" He sounded so child-like. Gone was the angry crystal meth addict. I yelled for one of the bystanders to call an ambulance.

I recovered the revolver that lay beside him and saw that it was my dad's old service weapon. How he had obtained it was lost to me. I placed both weapons on the back seat floor of my car, retrieved the gun case that held the shotgun and walked to my parents' apartment.

The police finally arrived, after all the excitement was over and done with, just as I predicted and took me into custody. I was charged with first-degree attempted murder, felony possession of a firearm and ammunition. If convicted of the charges I would spend the rest of my life in prison. There was no chance for parole in this case. It would be the same outcome whether Jimbo survived or not. When the police handcuffed me and escorted me to the blue and white, my father was there to encourage me. I hugged him and said, "I really messed up this time Pops." "At least you're alive," he replied. It was heart-wrenching to see the sad look in his eyes. One that I'd seen so many times before.

I was booked in at the very same receiving desk where I'd once lived and passed through years before. There was a glimmer of hope in those days, when the light at the end of the tunnel shined brightly with the promise of freedom. As the empty sound of metal on metal slammed behind me, the reality of what had happened hit home in an instant. The adrenaline drained from my body and a sudden heaviness washed over me. I had actually shot a man! Surprisingly it enough, it barely bothered me one way or the other. I'd done precisely what I was trained to do—survive. Albeit for all the wrong reasons, I had performed perfectly. There was nothing else to say about it. It was time to face the music. Reward for my stupidity. Only God above could help me now. Or so I thought. The detectives of the case grilled me about the particulars of my involvement and I gave them my statement. They said that according to witness statements, Jimbo had been the aggressor. I could possibly be looking at a self-defense case. If they could verify my statement. There was a glimmer of light after all. All I had to do was prove that I was telling the truth. That shouldn't be so hard? How the hell was I supposed to do that locked up?

The next day, the turnkey came to tell me that I had a visitor. I was overjoyed thinking that my parents had gained access. Visitors weren't usually allowed to see prisoners under investigation. I've seen all kinds of stuff happen over the years concerning rules and regulations. Especially when it came to my dad. I was led into an interrogation room where a serious looking gentleman in his fifties sat alone at a table. Here we go again I thought at first glance. Another round on the barbecue! I sat down across from the man, who stared intently at me though his black rimmed spectacles. "My name is Michael and I'm a polygraph expert. Your dad called and asked me to help you." It caught me totally off-guard. In the dark recessed of my confinement, once again my father had reached out to save me. The light at the end of that tunnel was brighter still.

He explained to me that he was going to conduct an examination on me to check the veracity of the statement I gave to the police. He said he and my dad knew each other back in the day when he was in the department. The man spoke nothing but praise of my dad. His being here was a favor for a friend. After a stern warning, we entered the examination room. I was a bundle of nerves and he could sense my apprehension. While hooking me up to the machine, he spoke to me in calm, relaxing tones. "All you have to do is tell the truth. The machine will do the rest," he said. For the first time in my life I had nothing to hide. When the polygraph test ended, he commented that the results looked promising but not to get my hopes up. We shook hands and I thanked the man who held my life in his hands. It was an impossibility that was unimaginable. But I clutched tightly to the last vestige of hope I had left.

Late the next evening, I heard footsteps coming down the hall. It was the detective handling my case. I rose to face him. Must be pretty bad news if he came here in person to deliver it. "You're out of here. We're releasing you on your own recognizance pending further investigation. Tell your dad I said hi . . . and don't get into any trouble," he said. Then turned and walked away. It was unbelievable. It was miraculous! I walked through the doors and past that all-to-familiar buzz of the last barrier into freedom. The night, particularly beautiful, displayed stars high above, cool trade winds washed against my face as I made the short walk down the road home. It was a walk I never expected to make again. I do believe in miracles.

My parents were overjoyed with my return. We hugged and held each other for what seemed hours. My mother's tears of happiness streaming as I wiped them from her face. I embraced my father tightly and the tears flowed freely from all of us. It was a familiar scene, played once again. I whispered chokingly, "thanks Pops . . . I never thought I was going to make it out of this one." "You almost didn't," he replied. "Now behave yourself and cut out all the bullshit!"

To my surprise, I saw Rose there as well. She came out from the bedroom and flew into my arms. Her embrace was warm and her kiss sensual and welcoming. I clung to her. I asked about Jimbo. He was still alive, but critical. The doctors said if he made it through the next few days, he would live. All five bullets had struck him in the torso. I remember having a perfect head shot when I first sighted the weapon, his head framed directly in the middle of the passenger side window. I had adjusted my aim lower to the door at the last moment. I attributed my change of heart to our friendship, however damaged or destroyed. I was happy he was alive. I asked Rose if she had been to see him. Under the circumstances, it would have been a difficult decision for her to make. After all, she was the reason for Jimbo lying in that hospital bed. Well, I couldn't put all the blame on her. I'd have to accept half of the responsibility. Maybe all of it. I could never see my involvement in the situation as being my fault. But as the years passed and I sit here writing about it, the picture is all too clear. It was my weakness and inability to control myself that put Jimbo in that hospital bed that day. It was my fault and I'm truly sorry for all the hurt and pain I caused him, his family and everyone else. I turned out to be a terrible friend.

After such a sobering experience, and barely avoiding spending the rest of my life in prison, you'd think that a fool would learn his lesson. You couldn't be further from the truth. People like me never learn a lesson. It's in our blood to mess up. Hardwired into our DNA to continue the onslaught of destruction. To make our loved ones and family suffer. To make them pay for our greedy, selfish pleasures over and over again. Stupid people don't learn! They can't change! They can only continue to do what they were destined to do, destroy lives. To step one foot closer to the grave. We never cared about anyone else but ourselves in the first place, why start now? Portrait of the crystal meth addict.

Chapter 20

Final solution

Like a mad dog, I had the taste of blood in my mouth. I had nearly killed a man by shooting him. Oh, but it was a grand, sensational, spectacular event. Covered in every newspaper and T.V. station in the state. I had become an infamous outlaw in the public eye, my picture plastered in every form of media. Like the wanted posters in the wild, wild west, I was considered armed and dangerous. Unconstrained while on my own recognizance, the state continued to build its case against me. I had a free pass to roam the streets with impunity. So long as I didn't break the law—or more like didn't get caught—I could do pretty much whatever I pleased. In the underworld of crime that was the key to the city. I had become a celebrity to my peers. They now knew that I was the real deal. People who messed with me in the drug game ran the risk of getting shot. It was one thing to pretend and maneuver your way around, posing as the real thing. Chances are, unless you come face to face with a person like me, you'd be able to bluff your way through. Even scare a few of the other fakers into believing that you were authentic. Convince yourself all you want. But with me, you knew exactly what you were dealing with. You were dealing with death. Death from the end of the barrel of a smoking gun.

Those who weren't ready to put their lives on the line to do business with me, avoided me like the plague. Ran for cover just at the sight of me. Those brave and honest enough to deal with me felt safe and were rewarded. Transactions went smoothly and they prospered. Suddenly I was in demand with dealers and drug houses who had outstanding debts owed to them. Forget that! I was out to take care of number one. With the clock ticking on the state's timetable, I couldn't afford to waste time working for others. Besides, I didn't need anyone else. It was still my intention to hook up with the all elusive "man." The one person who could take me to the promised land of riches. I would be both his most prized asset and worst enemy. Depended on how you looked at it.

Wherever I went, the heat increased ten-fold. Big-time dealers are discrete. They handled their business on the down-low, below the police radar. The last thing they wanted was someone on fire drawing attention to their drug operation. I know what it feels like to be on the bottom of the ladder—always reaching for the next rung while the guy ahead of you kicked back. All the while hoping you would slip and fall. These were my people in the business. When they played by the rules and toed the line, I bent over backwards and looked out for them. The rest of the maniacs out there were food! The necessary source of fuel that fed the machine's insatiable appetite. Lives were gobbled up in my path. My habit was past the point of paying for the crystal meth I gorged upon with mere money. The price tag had become much higher. No amount of cash, gold or even diamonds could quench my desire for the drug. Figuratively speaking, it required living, breathing individuals. Not only the blood that ran through their veins or the heart that pumped it, I swallowed the person whole! Consuming body and soul. Sometimes, even that wasn't enough to pacify the beast. He wanted more. I disposed of entire families completely. I watched as their lives were destroyed one after another. Their delicate structures turned to dust by the demon's greedy lust.

I sucked and drained away life from the ultimate supply the world had to offer. How could such a vicious animal exist? The answer is easy—we walk among you. The unknowing, the innocent, the normal, the hard-working, law-abiding populace. And as taken from the bible when Jesus, our Lord and Savior asked, the tortured man and demon, "What is thy name?" "Legion!" he answered. The devil in human form. The personification of evil. There is no escaping us. We will have what you have. We will take what is yours. We will take everything. And everything will turn to dust.

The girls who once hung out in my little circle of confidants became scarce. Except for Celestine and Sarah. Throughout the whole ordeal, they were there for me. We still partied with the rest, even did business occasionally, but things had changed. I guess the reality of the violence hit home. I briefly continued my affair with Rose following Jimbo's recovery. I had to let go—our relationship was jinxed from the start. It ended when Jimbo got released from the hospital. He called me and asked to see her. She was afraid to see him at first. Who could blame her? After all the crap of the last few months, she went back to him.

That week, Sarah and I decided to live together. She was a fantastic girl and I cared about her dearly. I wouldn't say it was head over heels love, but it definitely was love of a sort. I was glad to have that crazy portion of my life behind me. The cops hadn't come to get me yet and so far the prosecutor's office hadn't issued a warrant. Things were pretty much up in the air. They had a year or two before they could bring me to trial on the charges or they'd have to drop them. The technicalities involved and the contradictory evidence of the shooting kept dragging things out. Jimbo had in effect broken into my parents' apartment and assaulted his wife and me. He held us at gunpoint with a stolen firearm. Not to mention the .12 gauge Mossburg pump-action shotgun, which itself was part of a cache of missing firearms stolen from the sheriff's department arsenal. Then there was the damage he caused with that butcher knife. He chopped the heck out of my dresser, stereo and other stuff. And finally, leaving and returning to the scene carrying yet another weapon. In this case, a retired detective's .38 snub nose revolver and threatened us all over again before being shot himself. And that's how I was able to get myself OR'd. But being a felon in possession of a firearm, even to protect myself, was against the law. I might escape the attempted first-degree murder charge, but not the gun charge.

Sooner or later, I was headed back to prison. The charge carried a maximum sentence of five years. I'd probably be out in less than two. That's where things stood as of now in my life. The reason why I had become a man on a mission. Relentless. There was no time to waste.

I stayed close to home and rarely went on the road. Sarah's dad got lucky and scored some Hawaiian homestead property way out in Waianae. It was a chance of a lifetime. With a limited amount of ceded lands available in the state, getting selected was like winning the lottery. The waiting list was a least ten years long and his name had come up. I had the opportunity to live once again in the community where I'd spent my childhood. It had no less of a fierce reputation as it did in the sixties. Sure, gone was the old regime of underworld figures and killers, but that made the place even more dangerous. Here to stay was a new breed of bad guys. Replacements—younger, pistol-packing, crystal meth smoking, unpredictable criminals. It all came down to the drug they used. They stayed hidden in the shadows and came out under the cover of darkness to feed.

Like zombies, they never slept. And as the days passed, days of restless wandering, they transformed into the cold-blooded demon they fought to conceal. In whatever manner, on the outside, the quiet town of my youth remained the same. I never realized how much I missed it.

Having another residence to escape to was a gift from above. It was my city of refuge away from the maddening pace of downtown Honolulu. Since my arrest for the shooting, I felt as if a huge sword hung over my head, poised directly above me, waiting. When the police sorted out all the details of that day, the sharp point would fall. I made it a habit of moving around from place to place, staying at those safe houses or with friends and clients. It was a game of hopscotch designed to confuse the cops. I changed places every couple of days, never staying in one place twice if I could help it. I was on the run. Everywhere I went, people recognized me. It started to take a toll on business. Only the most loyal and brave of the brave wanted anything to do with me. To generate cash flow, I started forging checks and cashing them at retail stores and markets. My cousin John had gotten his hands on a defunct construction company's paycheck ledger. The company had been attached by the feds for tax evasion. In the process of liquidation, some of his friends had burglarized the office for the computers and other equipment. They came upon the book of printed checks with the company logo on them but the tweakers never knew the goldmine they had. John had no use for them so he gave them to me. I was now in the white-collar crime business. Classic case of forgery and fraud.

I rustled up a group of five or so meth addicts with fake ID, typed their names on the checks in different amounts and they cashed them at the markets. I let them shop for grocery items they needed to cover the ten percent service charge. Then I paid them a hundred bucks cash and sent them on their way.

I found it quite amusing walking into a store with nothing more than useless pieces of paper and exiting with thousands of dollars in cash, food stuffs and liquor. It was a great windfall that kept the crystal machine operating. I cared less about the charges I was accumulating. Just add them on. I'd hit the food chains on Friday nights when the banks were closed. That way they couldn't verify the checks and they wouldn't be discovered until Tuesday at the earliest. Then they'd be reported and investigated. By the time the alarm was sounded, we were into the next week. The scam would be over for them. On to the next. When the weekend came, the people were lined-up waiting for the chance to go shopping. I netted nearly thirty thousand a month. Not counting the food and booze tab. I threw lavish parties in rented hotel rooms for my friends and workers. It was like having my own teller machine. I was all set to take my scam on the road when I learned of a good friend's passing.

His name was Shorty and the name was in no way close to describing this one of a kind individual. He was a fun-loving, hard-core party animal who just as soon shoot you between the eyes as offer you a beer. People in the business feared him. He had been working with Stan and John before I arrived on the scene. We met by chance at a drug dealer's home. He'd recently gotten out of prison and was running wild and loose through the city. He'd taken to me when he found out I was in partnership with his cousin Fred. The same Fred that was destined to get nearly shot to death. Since that meeting, we became friends. Shorty never took shit from anyone. And when he found out that a certain wannabe gangsta was strong-arming his old lady's massage parlor for cash, he went nuts. He shot up a few residences and kidnapped a few people and held them hostage before the cops finally caught up to him at a friend's apartment. They surrounded the block and he barricaded himself inside with hostages. He wasn't going to be taken alive.

He was there looking for the guy to kill him when the "friend" dropped a dime on him. The cops had already been combing the city for him. After a lengthy standoff, the police tear-gassed the apartment, rushed in and killed him. The day I attended his funeral was the only time I came out of hiding. I knew the cops would be there in mass, taking pictures, so I disguised myself and showed up early. I didn't stay more than a few minutes. There were undercover cops everywhere. I snuck in, paid my respects to his dad (who smiled when he recognized me), said goodbye to my friend and left. Just standing there at his casket with all those cops breathing down my neck made the hair there stand up.

The last time we'd crossed paths was when we both were on the run. He'd shown up at a dealer's house where I was doing a drug deal. I heard a voice calling to me while on a pay phone. I turned to see Shorty sneaking among the parked cars in the lot. He was carrying two large plastic shopping bags filled with guns. He was taking them to that same apartment where the cops would later catch up to him. I was there buying the drugs for a Japanese guy who had a cast that ran the entire length of his right leg. He worked for my cousin John's wife, Chris. On that day, he mistakenly chose to use the company car to do the deal. We began to party and lost all track of time and before we knew it, night had fallen and the booze was gone. Shorty had offered to buy more if we drove him to the store. It was almost 11 pm. We had ten minutes to get there. The three of us jumped into the company station wagon and sped off to the market. It was already too late when we reached there, but Shorty said he would take care of it. I watched from the sidewalk as he entered the front entrance dressed in his signature trench coat, shirtless, with short pants pulled high above the waist and ankle length work boots. He had the body of a Greek statue, chiseled from the years of intense workouts behind prison walls.

I saw Shorty walking around the store and enter the liquor department. The area had been cordoned off with rope, signifying that the deadline to purchase had passed. He ducked beneath the rope, hunkered down, removed two suitcases of beer from the display and left the area. From the window, I saw the store manager heading in his direction. Shorty began to scoot in and out of aisles, avoiding the angry manager's pursuit. I saw one of the checkers on the phone while looking about the store for Shorty's whereabouts. No doubt she was on the phone to the police. I stood at the pay phone holding the dead receiver in my hand, pretending a call. In all the confusion I'd lost track of Shorty. Just then, his head popped up and he smiled at me through the glass. I signaled to him that the manager was two aisles over and that the cops had been called. He disappeared again and as he did so, a police cruiser entered the parking lot. He drove slowly towards us and the Japanese guy with the cast yelled to me. The car kept its slow pace but never stopped. He continued out the other end of the lot and left. Just then, Shorty came sprinting out of the store with the two cases of beer. He handed me the beer, pushed our frightened driver into the passenger seat and said, "I'll drive!" The guy was crazy. We burned rubber out of the lot as the angry manager reached the sidewalk. He screamed and shook his fist at us, but his words were muffled by the squealing tires. "I told you I had it handled." Shorty laughed.

We drove in and out of abandoned streets as the sounds of sirens and speeding patrol cars raced to capture us. Shorty tossed me a pistol and said that if they got any closer, to open fire on them. "Are you kidding me," I thought to myself. What had started as an innocent cruise to the store had turned into an all-points-bulletin manhunt. We eventually pulled into an empty garage and sat in the dark. We drank beer and smoked on our pipes as the cops went around and around in circles.

It was quite a show. Shorty went to the door and knocked. A pretty young girl answered and he struck up a conversation. After about 2 hours we left. On the way home I said, "lucky you knew those people where we hid out." "What people . . . I never knew those people" he said. I was floored. That was the kind of guy Shorty was.

We arrived safely back at the apartment around 3 am with the driver begging to leave. After a stern retort from Shorty, he shut up. When the sun rose the next day, Shorty asked if he could catch a ride with the guy. The guy pleaded with me but was persuaded in the end. I stayed there partying with my new friend the drug dealer and soon four days had gone by. Shorty showed up again. I'd forgotten all about him or the liquor run. When he opened the door to the room I was in, I glanced into the living and saw a white cast come into view. It was the Japanese guy sitting on a chair. When he saw me, he leaped out of the chair and hobbled over. He looked unkempt and scared to death. He cried and begged me to speak to Shorty. Apparently, when they left that night, he ended up being held hostage. The guy was beside himself and panicked, "please, please let me go. You can keep the car. I just want to go home!" I started to bust out laughing. I can only imagine what this poor guy had been through at the hands of this madman. Shorty had gone on a rampage in the space of those four days, shooting up houses and threatening people at gun point. The guy had witnessed it all. I was surprised that he wasn't dead. The cops were on a state-wide manhunt for him. He'd just as soon shoot this guy where he stood. Didn't matter one way or the other. Regardless of what the guy witnessed, Shorty was already headed to prison for the rest of his life. I convinced him to let the guy go knowing that he wouldn't say anything. I gave him bus fare to get home. He'd probably have nightmares for days.

I saw my friend only two more times alive. He appeared in the darkness early one morning at this same apartment. We partied together and he gave me a bunch of dope and a Remington .20 gauge semi-automatic shotgun before he left. Our last meeting was in a parking lot next to the apartment complex. He showed up as I was getting ready to kill the drug dealer I was staying with. It saved the guys life. I often think about Shorty and the kind of man he was. He was the real deal. Live by the gun, die by the gun. Rest in peace my friend.

Eventually I ran across that Samoan gorilla named Leo. The same guy Shorty set out to kill that day. He'd pulled a double barrel shotgun on a street dealer kid who worked for me. The kid was busy slinging papers for me when Leo drove up, stuck the gun in his face and ripped him off for all of my drugs. When I went to collect my cash, his partner told me what had happened. The poor kid was so frightened that he went underground. I finally caught up to him hiding out at his mother's house. Being Samoan himself, he knew Leo wouldn't disrespect his mom by showing up there. He was also worried that I'd beat him for losing my dope. I cared less about the loss of my drugs. It was the second time I had heard about this tough guy who thought he was bulletproof. He had to be taught a lesson. I asked the two boys to show me where this punk could be found. The thing that pissed me off the most about this mess was the fact that this kid, being Samoan, had a struggling family. He was selling dope to help pay the bills. Now this grown man comes along and scares him half to death. I'd dealt with bullies all my life—hated them. But this guy was off the scale.

We passed a side street and they pointed him out. The idiot was busy working on his car with his shirt off in front of his house. I dropped the boys off and told them I'd be right back. I locked and loaded the Colt .30 caliber carbine with a 30 round magazine and drove up his street. I stopped and parked my van on the roadside next to his car, blocking the lane. I kept the motor running. At the sight of my arrival, he looked up from his task with a questioning look. I said, "you Leo?" He walked to the passenger side of my van and said, "yea, who the hell wants to know?" Then he leaned in the window and froze as he saw the gun pointed directly at his face. I said, "you the punk-ass mother that stuck a shotgun in the kids face and stole my dope?" The blood drained from his face. I introduced myself and he said if I knew who he was. I said I didn't give a shit and that I came for my drugs. If not, I asked if he was prepared to die. He stood there helpless, wishing no doubt that he could reach the gun he probably kept on the front seat of his car. I saw it in his eyes. The indecision, the fear. "Don't try it . . . you'll never make it." I said, making his mind up for him. He said my name out loud and asked if I was John's cousin. Turns out he was friends with my cousin and had heard about me. He apologized, "I'm sorry . . . I didn't know the kid worked for you and that it was your dope." I asked him again if he had my drugs. He said he didn't but reached into his pocket for a wad of cash. He counted off $400 and handed it to me. I grabbed it from him and asked for the rest—he'd taken over $700 worth of drugs. He produced a packet of cocaine from the other pocket. It was about four grams. "This is all I have left . . . if you want, I'll get the rest later?" I hated cocaine and didn't want anything to do with it. But payment is payment. Throughout this conversation I thought about Shorty and what this scumbag had done to his old lady. That was personal, this was business. I took his coke and he apologized again. I told him that if he had hard feelings and wanted to pursue the matter, feel free to come up town and we'd settle it. He declined. I drove off. He later pursued me in a different aspect. As a friend. We did some business together, but only briefly. With friends like that, who needed enemies? Guys like Leo never last long in this business. Sooner or later, their shoulders become too big for their own good. There's always someone out there tougher than you are. If you keep putting yourself to the test you're bound to run into someone that's scarier than you. Which was the case with Leo. He was found shot to death in his own vehicle. The person who committed the murder also set the car ablaze. He was pretty much roasted when the cops found him. Saved a lot of people grief. The guy needed killing in the worst way. Now my friend Shorty can rest in peace knowing that he got his. It would be years down the road that I'd shake hands and look into the eyes of Leo's killer. Strangely, the guy's boyish good looks and polite demeanor were contrary to the popular belief of what you expect a cold-blooded killer to be. Never judge a book by its cover.

The more money I made, the more I spent. The more went up in smoke at the bottom of the glass bowl. There never seemed to be enough. I spent less and less time sleeping. I went as long as a week without even closing my eyes. I once stayed up for 28 days with nothing more than ten-minute catnaps. I took lots of showers, drank plenty of beer and ate even when I wasn't hungry. At times I hardly ate a thing—just drinking and smoking ice. I hired other people to drive me around so I could concentrate on smoking and doing the next deal. Celestine had gotten leery and became distant. I found Kenny sleeping behind the sofa of a friend's house. He was homeless and down on his luck. He turned out to be the best driver and most loyal friend a person could have. Solid as a rock. That night, I threw him the keys to my SR5 and asked him to pull it out front and wait for me. We'd become inseparable and he became my preferred wheel man. I drove him to a deserted area one night and while we cruised along the pitch-black deserted highway I pulled my gun and fired it out the window. He slowed the car a little, but never panicked. I could see the fear in his eyes. I told him if he continued driving for me he had to get used to gun fire. I also said to him never, ever, stop the car. When and if he heard it, step on the gas and get us out of there—fast! Kenny was down for the challenge. His loyalty would soon be put to the test.

It was a year since my arrest for Jimbo's shooting and the cops still hadn't showed. It was looking as if they'd drop the case entirely. Then I got a call from a detective who worked in the Morals section. He was a friend of a friend who also knew my dad. He said my name came up in his division concerning some bad checks and they were considering bringing fraud and forgery charges against me. That is, unless I would cooperate. They wanted to know about my network of drug associates. The world of crystal meth had become such a serious problem in the islands that they were willing to do practically anything to get a handle on it. One of the girls who helped me run the check scam had gotten arrested passing a bad check on a Navy base. She was handed over to HPD and she'd given me up. My friend was the head investigator on the case and would gladly flush it down the drain if I went to work for him as an informant.

I was insulted that he would even consider me for that role. Maybe he saw this as my chance to get back on the good guys' side. Now that I think about it, that is what he hoped for. It was a get-out-of-jail-free card I should have taken. The trouble with that was the price—too high. I may have acted like a rat in some cases, but to be a real life, squeaking rat was out of the question. "You got me mixed up with somebody else friend," I told him. Then he played the guilty father card. "What about your dad . . . don't you want to make him proud?" I hit the roof on that one! "Don't even go there," I shot back. As a last resort he threatened, "If you don't cooperate I'm coming for you!" he said. "This conversation is over . . . come and get me!" I replied and hung up. The noose around my neck was closing. Time had run out.

Everywhere I went I made people nervous. They wanted nothing to do with me. Not even to smoke the precious batu I always kept with me. They'd rather do without than run the risk of getting involved. I moved around more frequently now. I never stayed in one place for long and I was searching for new hideouts daily. I couldn't trust anyone. People wouldn't think twice about ratting me out to the cops. They'd be safer with me gone. I hardly ever went home to my parents place and when I did, to pick up a change of clothes or to say hi, I snuck in at night and never stayed for more than a few minutes. One time, I had no choice but to go there during the daylight hours. I needed to get a bunch of numbers I kept hidden in a drawer. My dad, who was on lunch break, showed up unexpectedly. It was good to see him. I hadn't seen him or my mother in weeks. She'd gone on another vacation and wasn't there. While in the middle of catching up, the doorbell rang. I stopped him before he answered it, telling him that it might be the cops. I hid in my room with a sawed-off shotgun in my hands. I hadn't slept for days and was tweaked out of my mind. I heard him answer the men through the closed door. Sure enough, it was two detectives asking to see me. I heard my father stall them without opening the door. He said he was on a lunch break and hadn't seen me in days. They insisted that he open the door and let them search. He brushed them off and walked to my room. When he entered, he saw me gripping the gun and was stunned! He said the cops wanted to see me. "Whatever you do, don't let them in the apartment." He tried to convince me to give myself up. Hell no, that wasn't happening. "Get rid of them," I told him. He could see the madness in my eyes and hear it in the tone of my voice. I had no way of knowing what I was prepared to do at that point, but I sure wasn't going to give up.

I heard the front door open and I braced for whatever came next. I heard the cops trying to smooth talk my dad into letting them in. He stood his ground and said I wasn't there. They started getting angry and saying shit like, "oh so that's how it's going to be?" One of them even said, "I thought you were one of us . . . the good guys. We know he's in the house." They tried pushing past my father, who blocked their entrance. They couldn't enter without a warrant unless my dad let them. They were trying their hardest to get by and were already in the hall. I was so pissed off at that point that if those two assholes came down the hallway I would have blasted them. Then I heard my dad yell at them, "get out of my house. I told you my son is not here. You want to look around, get a warrant." The door slammed on their threats. The relief washed over me like a breaking wave. I sat on the floor as my heart crashed in my chest. I released my grip on the gun. My father came in and saw me sitting helpless on the floor. "You better get out of here before they come back," he said. I hated placing him in such an awkward position. I felt exhausted. I stood up, hugged him close and the words he spoke to the cops as they left resounded in my ears. "I don't care if you guys are the good guys and I was a cop . . . that's my son you are talking about. Now get out!" "I'm sorry for everything pop . . . everything," I said as I checked that the coast was clear. As I headed for the door he told me, "don't get killed boy." I looked back to see the worried look in his eyes and replied, "I'll try not to pops," and left.

After months of being on the road, the constant shell game began to take its toll on me. I longed to just stay in one place and relax. That wasn't an option at this time. I had made my bed of nails, now I had to sleep on it. Regardless of how things appeared, in reality, they weren't as bad as they seemed. What did the police really have? A couple of five-year beefs that they would probably run concurrently. That wasn't much. It was the thought of going back to prison that got to me. Five years? Five minutes was too much. Now that's if I don't get stuck with that first-degree attempted murder charge. The way I saw it, I'd just keep on trucking until they caught me. Hopefully, I'd be smart enough at that time not to throw down on them. When you're running crazy on crystal meth, no telling what might happen. For the present, I was having too much fun to lie down. My main objective was to hook up with the "man," make a ton of cash and store it all away for the winter. The winter being a lengthy prison term.

Somewhere along the road, I ran into the chick who got caught passing those bad checks and gave me up to the cops. She was once a good money maker in the game. They all are in the beginning. Once you get busted though, you become somewhat gun shy. The hunger for the ice never goes away, only the extreme methods in which you obtain it. She apologized for getting busted and rolling over on me. I forgave her. Wasn't her fault for being an addict. I mean, it was, but us addicts had to stick together. She was no different than me and after all, she was my friend. Hell, I'd been going to jail with or without her help. We partied into the night and she had one last surprise to lay on me. She told me the cop who was after me wanted to speak to me. After our last conversation, I didn't think it was a good idea. She insisted, saying that he thought about cutting me some slack in the cases he had hanging over my head. Why not, what could it hurt? I was already drowning. Maybe he could throw me a lifeline?

I called him the next day and he said he was willing to cut me a break and slow down the investigation on me "if" and here it comes, I would help him with a problem he had. He needed a favor for a favor. All he was interested in was locating someone. Seemed fair enough. The person he wanted wasn't even going to be arrested. He wasn't wanted. He did, however, possess certain information on an on-going case. Just so happened, I knew the person and where he could be found. I wasn't about to turn rat now. I told him to ask the girl who snitched on me. She already wore that jacket. Evidently he got what he wanted. The heat was off and I was free to roam. I went to my parents place for a rest. Sarah and I then went back to the country with her dad. We spent the time out in Waianae painting and fixing up the place. Mike, my ex-crime partner, had given me an active purchase order from his old job as a townhouse manager. I made good use of it racking up a $3000 bill for paint, brushes and other building materials for the house. I simply drove my van to the warehouse, selected all the materials loaded up the van, gave the manager that number and rode off into the sunset. Piece of cake.

It felt good to have the cops off my back. I had no qualms about the reality of the temporary respite I was given. When they were ready they'd come knocking again. Hopefully by then my nest egg would be filled. I tried to keep my business transactions strictly between close friends and familiar acquaintances. The girls went their separate ways, but kept in touch. We got together now and then to party and hang out. Sarah had quit her job because she wanted to spend more time with me. And the drugs. We lived from day to day in a haze of meth. Money was sparse, but we always had ice. Neither one of us could go a day without it. The more I smoked it at this stage, the more paranoid I became. I started to hear echoing voices and see shadows wherever I looked. The constant abuse was slowly taking effect on me. One afternoon, while the girls were gathered together in my room, smoking, I lost control. For no reason at all, I fired a bullet from my .25 caliber automatic into a bag of laundry in the closet. Scared the shit out of everyone. I had suspected one of them of sharing information with my competitors. I later found out that one of them was sleeping with the enemy.

It's not nice to accuse people of divulging privileged information to your rivals. I became suspicious when certain individuals started showing up at safe houses where I did business. They'd try to intercept the drug deal I had set-up. If it weren't for my prompt arrival, they'd have gotten away with it too. The first couple of times, I wrote it off as coincidence. Crazier things had happened in this game. But, as it became more frequent and the level of the players involved became scarier, I was convinced. Then a worker of mine who'd accidently showed up at a rival gang's party out of the blue said, "guess who I saw at Howard's last night?" In my wildest dreams I'd never suspect the name he mentioned. "Who?' I asked. "Celestine," he replied. "She showed up on the arm of Pat," he added. I was totally blown away! Now the whole picture fell into place. Patrick had once been one of the biggest ice dealers in Hawaii. After falling from grace because of his addiction and divorce, he was on the rise again, making a comeback. I knew then that it wasn't just my paranoia getting the best of me. Now there's nothing wrong with trying to get yours by whatever means possible. But playing for the other team was strictly against the rules. People got killed in this game for that. My heart broke with disappointment then. I'd been nothing but good to her. Looked out for her, gave her the shirt off my back. "Loved her!" Made me angry as hell.

I sent everyone looking for her. She showed up that day with the guiltiest look on her face. I sat her down and asked her what she was doing. She was so innocent. I couldn't blame her for any of it. Whether she was guilty or not. She told me she'd met Patrick at a hotel party. He was nice to her. Treated her good and bought her nice things. He gave her drugs. "What did you give him?" I lashed out. She cowered in her chair and answered, "nothing." "You mean you never did sleep with him?" I shouted. Patrick was in his late fifties, fat and as slick as a snake. Guys like that had only one thing on their minds. They went around recruiting young girls and exchanging sex for drugs. I hated them! Sarah slapped her hard on the head and she started to cry. I told her if she continued to see Patrick she wasn't welcome in our house. Don't even come around us, I said. She apologized and promised not to go near him. I forgot all about her betrayal. She really had no idea what she had done, "simple minds lead simple lives." All she wanted to do was smoke. How could I fault her for that? I had been partly to blame for spoiling her. We all hugged and I forgave her. But the demon makes you say things. Things people want to hear. You promise anything to anyone. As long as it gets you to the next bowl full of ice. I believed her only because I wanted to.

In this game, you never look a gift horse in the mouth. I had her watched. Just to make sure. She came and hung out more often. Everything was like before. Then she started making excuses and disappeared for days at a time. I knew what she was doing, where she was and who she was with. I refused to believe it. She had promised! Then the phone call came that confirmed my suspicions. She and Pat had been spotted together. She'd lied to me. I was outraged! The next time she showed up at my place, I played coy with her at first. I could smell the fear on her. Like a frightened animal. In the middle of conversation, she blurted out about being at a hotel room party with Pat. She realized in an instant what she'd done. She gasped, putting her hand to her mouth. As if the simple motion could erase the mistake. The lie! I yelled at her, "what the hell did I tell you?" Then I kicked her out and told her never to come back. I couldn't understand why her deception had affected me so much. I found my emotion confusing. The only other times I had experienced such a reaction was when my relationships with Elvia and Lou ended. Only now it was different. I felt as though I was being lied to by family. I rationalized and compared it to a daughter telling you she was pregnant at 13. The hurt, disappointment, and anger were profound. I thought about my family. My two growing daughters and how Lou had tried to get me to stay with them one night. "For the girl's sake," she said. "Don't you want to see your girls?" she begged. I somehow knew that it was just an evil ploy on her part to torture me. To use them against me. I knew that when morning came, she'd be taking them away again. I couldn't deal with the thought of losing them all over again. It would break me for sure. They stayed the night at my parents' place and it made me happy to see the joy on their faces to have their grandchildren with them. It was one of the hardest things I ever had to do. Saying goodbye to them as they clung to me and cried their eyes out. Celestine stirred those hurtful memories in me. I had to let her go.

Weeks went by and it was business as usual. I was still out on O.R. and free. I had adapted a low-profile mode of operation. With no conscious intent of doing so, I crawled deeper into my addiction. It was a pathetic, meaningless existence. Waking each day, doing dirty, low-down things to get my next fix. It had been weeks since we'd heard from Celestine. I'd lost track of her. Then, out of the nowhere, she called. Her voice sounded far away and sad. She apologized for what she'd done and asked to come over. Her sincerity had struck a cord in me. I invited her over. Sarah and I had begun hanging out with two of the girls who had been dating big time drug dealers. They all knew each other and like vicious cats were jealous of the next. Michelle was the more daring and rowdy of the two. Haole Girl was the more relaxed and business minded. Being a single mom, although hooked on meth, made her more responsible. Together they provided us enough cheap deals and freebies to keep us in drugs. They both frowned upon Celestine's behavior and choice of friends. You know, giving up the goodies to get high. It was like the pot calling the kettle black. When you change and start running with the school, a tuna is a tuna. The three of us sat around smoking and catching up on the latest news. It was good to see Celestine again. I had missed her and forgot all about being mad at her. It seemed like old times again. The way it was when we first met. She said that I'd been right about Patrick—he only cared about her body and all he could get out of it. She finally realized it when he'd tried to pass her off to a friend. Discarded baggage. Hand me downs to the next user. I felt sorry for her. To top it off, her father had thrown her out of the house. She had nowhere to go. We took her in.

For awhile, we were peas in a pod. Family. However dysfunctional. I hardly ever went out on the road to do business. When I did, Sarah and Celestine came along. I could always rely on Sarah. She was a tough customer and didn't scare easily. She used to tote my gun, the .357 Magnum, around in her bag just in case the cops got the drop on us and searched me. Ever since Jimbo's shooting the cops had taken away all of my fire power. I had resorted to borrowing weapons whenever I needed one. What's a gangster without a gun? Just another face in the crowd. With my notoriety it was difficult to find anyone willing to sell me a gun. I finally purchased a Browning .25 caliber automatic thanks to Haole Girl. It wasn't much of a weapon with its small caliber bullet, but it was better than nothing. It was still a gun and it could still kill you. Like I mentioned before, it's not the gun but the man behind it. I bought it for $200 cash and a half a gram of ice. Expensive by any standards. It came without the magazine. Being an old weapon it was a bitch to find. At least I was armed. The gun would prove to be more of an obstacle and deadlier piece of hardware than I anticipated. It would eventually be the end of me.

I used the tiny gun to reassure myself. I'd always loved the feel of a cold piece of steel against my naked flesh. Made me feel safe. I wished it were bigger and I would have liked it to contain more than one bullet at a time. The way it stood, I'd have one shot and one shot only to get me out of a jam. That was bad odds anyway you looked at it. I sent Kenny out to buy a box of ammunition. Copper jacketed for maximum effect. He looked for a magazine but the only way to get one for that model was to special order it. We kept looking for it and for other weapons. Kenny had found a girlfriend and spent most of his time pleasing her. While working for me he managed to save enough money to buy a car. What he was short I gave to him. His life was turning for the better. So Celestine became my driver again. She had begun to tow the line again. I started to trust her more and more. Up until now, she'd earned it. Why can't beautiful things just stay beautiful?

Late one night, after partying with Haole Girl, Sarah and Celestine, I told her to drive me to Darryl's house. Since Stan, we'd stayed in touch and did business together now and then. He owed me money, so I went there to collect. I'd been up for days without sleep and wanted to collect all the money I had out there before I crashed. On the way, I'd taken two rainbows, a strong barbiturate, to counter the meth. I started to feel the effects as we pulled up to the house. I was nearly out on my feet by the time we left. They had to practically carry me to the car. Before I passed out, I placed my gun, drugs and money in a Crown Royal bag and stuffed it beneath the driver's seat. I thought no one had seen me do it. I woke the next afternoon hung over and dazed. My first reaction was to look for my bag. I needed a pick me up to help clear the cobwebs. It took me a moment to remember where I'd left it. I always leave it next to my bed on the floor for easy access. I searched the room but couldn't find it. I yelled for Sarah. When she entered the room, I asked her, "where's my bag?" She went to her bag and retrieved it. Then I remembered sticking it under the car seat. She had a worried look on her face. She then explained that she'd found it in Celestine's bag. She had no idea where it was until she saw it there. I opened it and saw that everything, including the gun was still there. I got so mad at Celestine for touching it. She knew better. I screamed for her to get her ass in here. She came in and sat beside me on the bed. The look on her face was enough to convince me of her guilt. She looked like a frightened rabbit caught out of her burrow. "What you doing with this in your bag?" I questioned as I held it up to her face. "I found it in the car . . . I was only holding on to it." She replied. "Why didn't you give it to me last night?" Sarah chimed in. "I forgot," she said. "Yeah right!" Sarah snapped. "What did I tell you about touching my stuff? Especially this?!" I scolded. Showing her the gun in my hand. "I'm sorry", she responded, barely audible. "What did I say?" I shouted. "Not to touch your things, your gun," she said. "Don't ever do that again. The next time I'll hurt you!" No telling what she would have done with it if Sarah hadn't spotted it in her bag that morning. She'd be long gone! She never had the chance to leave the house with her bag of goodies. It was obvious that she meant to take it. Stupid girl. It bothered me that she'd even consider doing it. And in my own house. As angry as I was I forgave her for it. There was no excuse to steal from me. I tried reasoning within my own mind that maybe she had forgotten and would have given it back when she awoke that day. I had to give her the benefit of the doubt. This time, whichever way you saw it, the whole thing hurt my feelings and made me wonder. So she made a mistake. A mistake she'd never repeat. Why would she? No one's that ignorant. I let it slide and put it away in the back of my mind for now. Why dwell on something so trivial? I had more important things to worry about then some broad's sticky fingers.

Chapter 21

Just reward

Crystal meth inhibits the way a normal person thinks and reacts under everyday conditions. Interface this with an abnormal person's slight character flaw or mental disability and the result is a stupid person. A person who lacks the ability to distinguish between right and wrong, friend or foe. Everybody basically becomes one and the same in their eyes. Good, evil, right, wrong, yours and mine. It's all good. What's the difference? The hell with everyone else. As long as I get mine, who gives a damn? Who cares who suffers? It's all about me. I've seen this exact same story before. In the hearts and minds of many in this shitty drug business. When it gets down to the nitty-gritty, we all fall victim to our own greedy wants and desires. I can picture a complete stranger living up to my cynicism and expectations of disappointment. But a friend who you love and care about? I can't picture that in my mind. In a perfect world there's no excuse for it. Can't condone it. Won't stand for it! Fair warning was issued to all parties involved from the onset. This wasn't no game in the practical sense. You weren't out playing in the sand box with your kiddy friends. The drug world was stone cold serious business. Male or female, if you messed up, you can expect to be treated the same. No double standards allowed. The least you can hope for in your dirty, low-down state, is a bit of favoritism. Even that can be pulled out from beneath you if you're not careful. Constant abuse gets a person nowhere in this racket. That's why it's best you determine between the wolves and the sheep quickly. Then choose a side and stay in your place. It's the crossing over that can get you hurt.

Fits of rage are a common factor for meth users. Lack of sleep and proper nutrition changes a person physically and mentally. Over prolonged periods of constant abuse, the addict can literally go insane. See things that aren't there, hear things that weren't said, believe things that aren't real. You become encapsulated in a world of make-believe and lies. The imagination is stretched far beyond the limits of reality. Latent complexes that were once buried, emerge. Amplified. You convince yourself that all is well and that you're functioning in a normal, sane capacity. People who love and care for you try to talk to you. Warn you about your crazy behavior. They try, but can't reach you. Only the people around you who are themselves possessed, appeal to you. Worth listening to. The blind leading the blind. Destined for doom.

A couple of weeks following the incident with Celestine, we'd been partying hard for days. Traveling from place to place, visiting friends and doing business. We ended up at my parents' place. I hadn't slept for days and started crashing. I had just gotten connected with a new source who was providing me with, not only ice, but barbiturates as well. With the number of days I went without sleep, I found it difficult to lie down and fall asleep. I started using downers to help me. I would lay there in bed for hours as my body twitched. It was no different on this particular night. I left Sarah, Celestine, Kenny and Arthur, another friend who worked for me, to their partying and went to bed. The next afternoon, I woke rested but anxious to get busy making money. I wanted to get out on the road as soon as possible. Before sleeping, I'd given the gang enough dope to last the night. I placed my Crown Royal bag, containing a quarter ounce of meth, 200 rainbows, half an ounce of weed, $400 in cash and my .25 caliber under the bed, next to me. The first thing I did was reach for my bag. It was gone. I searched everywhere with no luck. Did I forget? I distinctly remember giving them all drugs from it before entering the bedroom. I heard voices in the living room and I yelled for Sarah. When she entered the room, she had my bag in her hand. "What you doing with that?" I snapped. 'Honey, don't get angry. I didn't take anything." She said. I snatched the bag from her grip and emptied the contents onto the bed. The gun was there but the weed was gone. So was $200 and some of the other drugs. I went ballistic!

Sarah had been trying to explain what had happened, but my anger made me deaf to her words. The only sound I recognized from her stuttering was Celestine's name. Apparently sometime during the night, she'd crept into my room and had stolen it. She then said her goodbyes and left. No one would have known it was missing except the stupid girl showed up at a hotel party across the street carrying it. Most of the people there were either friends or worked for me. She had gone on a party trip with my dope. Handing it out and turning on the entire crowd. Everyone there was surprised to see that she had so much and was being very liberal with it. It was way out of character for her. Just so happens that the chick who got arrested for that check cashing scam was there and saw her reaching into the bag to fill her pipe. She recognized the pouch instantly and grabbed it away. I couldn't believe how dumb the girl was. It was the ultimate betrayal in my book.

I was beside myself with anger, pounding on the bed with rage. Sarah said that Kenny and Arthur were holding her hostage at the hotel. I reached for the phone and dialed the room. Ken answered on the first ring and I asked him where she was. He gave the phone to her and when I heard her voice, I said in a cold tone, "what did I tell you about touching my shit?!" She started to apologize when I swore at her and told her to put Arthur on the phone. "Bring that bitch to me right now!" I said. When I hung up the phone my anger had become so heightened by the sound of her voice that I began to shake. I filled my pipe to overflowing and began smoking. There was no pot to calm my madness and I didn't want to take a barbiturate. I wanted to fuel the anger I felt. Then I did the stupidest thing that would lead to the biggest mistake of my life. Remember when I said I'd never pick a needle up again and shoot drugs into my veins? Well, there was one last time. I don't really know what compelled me to reach for that gram of cocaine. I'd forgotten all about it until now. I found it right where I'd left it months ago along with a fresh syringe. I had meant to give it to Sarah. I dumped half the bag into a spoon, tied off my arm and injected. The rush was immediate. The roar of those freight trains and ringing my ears. I tasted the familiar flavor of cocaine as it entered my mouth along my tongue. The buzz was overpowering and it left me rattled. Totally hyped out. I fought the intensity of the rush.

The phone rang, signaling their arrival. Trapped in the thrall of my cocaine haze, I had momentarily lost track of time and events. As the rush subsided, I suddenly remembered who, what, when, where, and how. Kenny entered the room with Celestine, Arthur and Sarah behind him. Seconds before they entered, I'd grabbed my gun and chambered a round. I held the gun in my hand, concealed behind my back. It was my intention to scare her with it. I never thought about actually using the weapon. Maybe the sight of the gun would make her a believer. She sat next to me on the bed and I could sense her fear. She was sullen, nervous. I pulled the gun around and placed it on my thigh. Her eyes went wide with fright as I said, "how many times do I have to tell you not to touch my shit? I gave you everything, take care of you and that's what I get in return." Everyone in the room was frozen. Then Celestine started stuttering excuses as I poked her in the ribs with the gun. She slid towards the end of the bed in an effort to escape as she pushed the gun away. I pulled it away and as she rose to walk away, I pointed the gun in the direction of the ceiling, towards her head. Then I heard the shot. I didn't even realize that I'd pulled the trigger. The sound filled the small room and yet was no louder than a firecracker. Celestine stopped in her tracks, sat back down on the bed and looked at me. She appeared normal, composed and still. Then she told me her head hurt. When I first heard the weapon discharge, I looked up at the ceiling to find the hole. There was none. Her eyes rolled back and she collapsed on the floor. I was shocked! Kenny and Arthur freaked out and made for the door. Sarah stood there, with her hand to her mouth. "Babe, babe, you shot her!" She kept repeating it over and over. "Shut up," I yelled. I then pointed the gun at Kenny and Arthur and said, "Where you guys going?" "Nowhere, don't shoot." I reached down and cradled Celestine's head in my hands. I felt the bullet hole in the back of her skull. She was complaining about her headache. The rush of the coke had all but vanished and the paranoia of the meth kicked in. I couldn't think straight. I panicked! My instincts for survival went into action. Like the sick monster that I had become, my will to survive and escape was greater than saving a friend's life. By now, Celestine had slipped into a coma. If I had done the right thing and called 911, she might be alive today.

Instead, I chose to cover my tracks. Cover up the crime that I'd committed. Looking down at the motionless girl at my feet, my mind raced for answers. I couldn't believe what had happened. I never meant to hurt her. Never meant for this to happen. It was an accident. The safety on the gun was faulty and had failed. Who would believe that? Believe a convicted armed robber and attempted murderer? I stood there convincing myself, weighing the pros and cons of my future. For those of you who continue to read from this point on, feel free to hate and despise me.

The paranoia and amp of the cocaine, combined with the ice, sling-shot me into a different realm of conscious awareness. I felt the walls closing in on me. My fight or flight instincts warred with each other, suspending me in a state of indecision. I could hear Kenny and Arthur running scared through the apartment, trying to get out. With the deadbolt firmly in place and the bars on the windows and doors, that was impossibility. Sarah had run out of the room and was standing dazed in the hall. In a state of shock, she mumbled incoherently, too softly for me to hear. I'd reached for a towel and placed it behind Celestine's head to stem the flow of blood. Surprisingly, there was very little. I threatened Ken and Arthur with the gun after the shooting. Telling them they'd end up just like her if they told anyone. Standing there, alone in the room, looking down at the still figure that had once been my friend, thoughts of a life in prison flashed through my cloudy mind. It was a hideous thought that instantly jerked me back to reality. I would do everything in my power to prevent that. I sprang into action.

I ran out into the living room and confronted Ken and Arthur. Once I made up my mind to conceal the crime there was no turning back. No one but the people in this apartment knew what had occurred. Killing everyone here was an option but not the smartest thing under the circumstances. One body would be difficult enough to dispose of. Four was unthinkable. Could I run the risk of exposure by "trusting" (ah, again my favorite word of choice) these people? If the killing ground had been in a more remote location there's no doubt that the body count would have increased. But here in my parents' apartment, it was out of the question. There's something about witnessing a murder that changes a person. It scares them into a place that transports them back to the womb. That safe, warm sanctuary where troubles don't exist. A place where your mother waits to comfort and protect you. People caught in such a position who aren't used to savagery, switch to flight mode. All bets are off and escape becomes their only option. They flee the scene and seek protection for themselves. Running from the evil that pursues them. They forget all about the victims left behind. Self preservation is a strong motivator. It brings out the worst in people. Scared people only have one thing on their minds, "living!" Now I'd finally get the chance of seeing what these chosen individuals who I lived, laughed and cried with, were really made of.

Up until this very moment, I'd never considered myself a bad person. Sure, I did drugs and took advantage of good people and hurt the ones I loved, but it was unintentional. My weakness for drugs and inability to stand on my own as a man governed my behavior. I never set out to purposely hurt anybody. Certainly never meant to kill anyone. All the training and preparation in my previous life wasn't a prelude to murder. Every violent episode encountered beforehand was purely incidental, regardless of my involvement. In an instant I had taken everything to a whole other level. I had become a killer! It wasn't the actual act of killing that bothered me. It was the person I had killed. She was an innocent. A sweet troubled girl who had put her trust in me. Believed in me! She never in a million years deserved what I'd done to her. I was torn between the guilt I felt at my mistake and my primordial instinct for survival. My predictable selfishness and failure as a human being would be the deciding factor in my decision to cover up the crime.

Initially, when I entered the living room, I tried to get Kenny and Arthur to help dispose of the body. They were visibly shaken and begged me to let them go. They cried and pleaded, saying that they just couldn't do it. So much for that idea. I had no choice, aside from killing them both, but to let them go. They promised to remain silent. To keep my deadly secret. I threatened to kill them if they didn't. For some reason lost to me I believed them. I unlocked the door's deadbolt and the two men ran out into the freedom of daylight. I was gambling that their witnessing the murder itself and my fierce reputation would deter them from calling the police. With them gone, I was faced with the cold hard reality. You read about it in the newspapers or watch it on the six o'clock news but you were just a spectator. Your distance from the actual crime of murder made it no more real than Santa Claus or the Easter Bunny. Now here I was living in the moment.

Entering the bedroom I looked down at the lifeless body. She appeared to be in a state of peace, her face emotionless and calm. My emotions ran the entire spectrum as I fought to take control of myself. I've done this a thousand times before. Lived the story over and over again through countless crime scenes. Struggling, I snapped back to the present and yelled for Sarah. She had been sitting on the bed in the living room hugging her knees to her chest. She appeared at the door and I sent her to get a large black garbage bag from the kitchen. "Is she dead?" she asked. "Get the bag!" I shot back. In a state of shock, it must have been unimaginable the pain she felt staring at her childhood friend laying dead on the floor. She returned with the bag and I closed the door. After years of removing human remains in all kinds of situations and under various conditions, it's a talent that you never forget. It comes as natural as riding a bike. I covered her head with the plastic bag to prevent any blood from spilling out. I grabbed a plain white sheet from the drawer and wrapped her body in it. There was only a single drop of blood left on the carpet beneath her head. With the easy part done, there was only the hardest part left to do. Committing the crime of murder is easy. Anyone is capable of doing it. It's getting rid of the evidence that's difficult. Never had to worry about that at the mortuary. All the bodies had a designated location. This was different. I couldn't just throw her over my shoulder in broad daylight, toss her into the trunk then drive off. I'd have to wait until the cover of darkness. I couldn't just leave her here to be discovered. I began to stress out. The only option left to me was to hide her in the closet. I removed all the bags of clothes and junk I had in there, placed her on the floor at the bottom, and piled everything back on her. My mother was away on vacation and my dad was busy at work. He'd be home soon but he never came into my room. With my mom away no one would ever know. I just needed some time. I had no idea what I was going to do with the body at this point. I was still trying to process what had happened.

Kenny and Arthur called that afternoon to check on the situation. I reassured them that all was well. They came over later with food and beer. My dad was home and we spent the early evening drinking and talking. He was tired and retired to his room after dinner. It felt strange hiding a murder that happened in his home from him. I could never get him involved with any of this. Everyone acted as casual as possible and didn't let on. However, they all had a different look about them. It was the face of fear. To people in the know, it was unmistakable. The police haven't showed up yet, so the boys must have been true to their word. Michelle and a few of the gang called and asked to come over. They wanted to party and needed a location. Under different circumstances I would have rented a hotel room but there was no way I was letting that body out of my sight until I got rid of it. I had to be ready for the first opportunity that came along. That was all I could think about. The party was by no way a means to help draw a ray of sunshine onto the event. It was more a way of keeping account of everyone. Acting natural. Who'd a thought that it would turn out to be my downfall. Serves me right for being so shallow.

During the night, Michelle had asked me for some barbiturates. Sarah forbade her to take any because she often got silly and loose when on them. She begged and I gave in. Before long, she was stumbling and hanging on every available male. Including me. Sarah got pissed and put her to bed in my room. The party lasted until the early morning hours. By the time all the guests had gone the sun was coming up. Sarah and I were in the middle of cleaning when I went to use the bathroom. As I passed my bedroom down the hall, I noticed that Michelle was awake. She was sitting at the edge of the bed, clutching her handbag. The look on her face said it all. I knew that she had somehow discovered Celestine's body. I walked in and knelt in front of her. "Who's that in the closet?" she said in a quiet voice. Her shocked expression and pale white color gave me chills. "There's nothing in the closet . . . what you talking about?" I said, trying to sound convincing. She insisted that she'd seen someone in the closet. She had woken and couldn't remember where she'd hidden her purse. While searching the room, she'd come across the body. She babbled and rambled on about finally finding it and how she recognized the tattoo on Celestine's ankle. "Why is Keala in the closet?" she asked, starting to cry. The capital K and B letters of her nickname, visibly tattooed on her ankle, were known to everyone. I hugged her then and tried to console her. Like Sarah, they had been raised together and played together as kids. I explained to her what had happened and why. She sensed by the calm, soothing tone of my voice that she'd never be leaving that room again. She looked into my eyes, hers filled with sadness and said, "Please don't hurt me. I won't tell anyone." I slowly reached into my pocket and felt the butt of the gun. She had left me no other option. I told her how sorry I was and as she held on tightly and cried into my shoulder, I raised the gun and placed it to her head. Just as I began to pull the trigger, I heard a loud, "No honey!" I turned to see Sarah standing in the doorway. Her urgent protest startling me. Michelle had looked up to see the gun to her heard. Sarah ran to me and threw her arms around us. She cried and begged for her friend's life. They both hung on to each other trembling. Another second later and Michelle would have been dead. I was far beyond reasonable thought. Desperate. Now there were four people who knew about the murder. I couldn't possibly cover up the crime with so many people in the know. Killing another person at this point would make no difference. Oh so I thought. Michelle would ultimately turn out to be the weakest link in the chain.

The three of us sat there for what seemed like ages. Them crying and me full of indecision. The girls finally convinced me and I let Michelle go. She was a hard-core drug addict who had a boyfriend who was a gangster. She'd seen pretty much all there was to see in the game and learned to shut her mouth. She'd be the last person, among the four who had knowledge of the crime, I'd expect to talk. Perhaps if Celestine had been some stranger, I could have guaranteed her silence. Somehow, seeing the death of a childhood friend occur and being forced to shut up about it carries little weight to sway an individual's decision. I knew one way or another I'd live to regret my actions on all accounts. I was however, glad I didn't kill Michelle that day. Two wrongs never make a right. The grave injustice I'd already done to that poor innocent girl was terrible enough. It was stupid of me to even ask how things had gotten so messed up. That question kept playing over and over in my mind as the hours passed. I still hadn't devised a plan to dispose of Celestine's body. I knew that I just couldn't leave her there in the back of my closet. Sooner than later she would start to smell. It had been over 24 hours since the murder and by the next day, decomposition would be in the early stages. I thought about burying her in my mother's garden by the patio, but I couldn't bring myself to do it. I felt guilty enough about killing her in my parents' apartment and the act itself. I wasn't about to leave her anywhere near the area. My only option was to transport her to another location under cover of darkness. But where? I had no idea. All I knew is that I better come up with a plan real soon.

I found it difficult to sit around with my dad and carry on a conversation. The guilt of involving him in all of this was eating away at me. Up 'til now, he had no idea what had happened. I wasn't about to put any of this on him. Meanwhile, the clock was ticking. It was into the next 24 hours and I could start to detect a slight odor coming from the closet area. You couldn't smell it unless you stood directly in the front of it. Soon the smell would spread into the entire room. By then my dad would be sure to notice it. I couldn't let that happen. I wouldn't want to say "as luck would have it" because years after the event, it sounded so callous but the following night the opportunity presented itself. Haole Girl dropped by with a friend who wanted to sell a pair of house stereo speakers after midnight. Stolen goods he wanted to trade for drugs or money. They were of the highest quality and less than half the market price. The boxes they came in were about four feet high and two feet wide. That's when the idea hit me. They were perfect to help conceal the body. That morning, after they left, I removed the body from the closet, wrapped it in plastic bags and another sheet to prevent leakage and carried the box to the dumpster out front. I covered the box with debris and bags of garbage to conceal it.

You couldn't distinguish the smell of decomposing flesh from the garbage. I stood there staring at the green metal dumpster that contained my friend. Although relieved that she was out of my parents' apartment, there was a profound sense of loss and an overwhelming feeling of guilt that washed throughout me. Meaningless and useless, I whispered, "I'm sorry," and returned to the apartment.

The box sat there for another day before I heard the sound of the front-end loader dumping its contents. The deed was finally done and the not so perfect crime was on the way to becoming a part of history. I hadn't gotten away with it yet and being a God fearing man, I knew that I'd never get away with it. Even if I did conceal the actual murder from the eyes of the law, you can't hide from God! I had broken the most important commandment in the bible. Unforgivable in the eyes of the church. My feelings of being a good person in my heart were done. I was now for certain not only a bad guy, but a bad person.

For weeks, I existed in a state of limbo. Never knowing when or if the police would come for me. So far no one had said a thing. It appeared as though I had gotten away with it. Arthur and Kenny called now and then to reassure me that they were staying solid. Michelle, however, had started to display strange and unusual behavior. She was no longer the outgoing, carefree spirit that she once was. She spent her days locked away in her bedroom in fear. Smoking large quantities of crystal meth only increased her paranoia. She became convinced that I was out to murder her. The phone would ring at odd hours of the night with Michelle on the other end insisting that she saw my car circling her block.

We never left the house. I became concerned that she would break. I knew then that it had been a mistake to let her go. Sarah and I tried to get her to come over and party, but she refused. I had no intention in the beginning of harming her. But as the weeks passed and her paranoia worsened I knew that I'd have to get rid of her. I tried to lure her close so I could get to her but she was too cautious. The one time she ventured out to come visit, she showed up with two other people and wouldn't budge out of the vehicle. I made several attempts to catch her alone even with the assistance of other people, but she was too afraid and smart to fall for the trap. She must have sensed that her death was imminent because unbeknownst to me, she had written a letter, which she kept in her bottom drawer, addressed to her mom. The letter pretty much summed up what she had witnessed. It was her insurance policy if she was killed. Bringing her killer to justice from the grave. Her letter would become the one thing to bring the entire house of cards tumbling down.

Her mom, a crystal meth user herself, worked as a dispatcher for the Honolulu Police Department. She had seen her daughter go from an active, party going animal to a recluse in a matter of weeks. Michelle's sudden change in character had peaked her mom's concern and curiosity, prompting her to scrutinize her every move. She tried talking with her, hoping she'd reveal the source of such a drastic change. But Michelle shrugged her off. She stood solid. The thought of her ending up like her friend must have kept her quiet. I can only imagine how difficult it was for her to wrestle with the demons that haunted her. Her mother came upon the letter one day while Michelle was out. She was no doubt searching for clues to her daughter's troubling behavior. After she'd read the letter, she contacted a detective friend of hers who started an investigation into the murder of Celestine. I often wonder if things would have turned out differently if Michelle hadn't written that letter. Could she have held out long enough to forget about the murder of her childhood friend? Highly unlikely. Sooner or later, she would have cracked. That letter had saved a lot of lives. Hers, mine and the many other innocent victims that would have been preyed upon by the monster who wrote these words. Justice was served in the end and I was at peace with my God and myself for the time being. Nature has a way of balancing the scales in the course of its life cycle. Good overcomes evil and survival of the fittest takes a back seat.

Epilogue

The knock broke the silence and could be heard with authority throughout the apartment. Outside, on this glorious Sunday afternoon, the police stood ready. They had blocked off the roads and surrounded the building. Dramatic as it seemed, they weren't taking any chances. After all, they'd come here to take a suspected murderer into custody. Mom and Dad had gone over to Grandma Marjorie's and Grandpa Joe's for drinks. Sarah and I had stayed behind and considered heading out to the country to stay with her dad. I missed the country so much and the place called Waianae. The place where I once lived and grew into a man. There was nowhere left to hide. No place to run to. I looked into Sarah's scared eyes and detected the sadness in her heart. I hugged her close and told her I loved her and that everything would be alright. I called my grandparents' house and spoke to my father. "Better come quick before the cops take me away." was all I said. They arrived in minutes, just after I'd opened the door to surrender. No gun battles, no going out in a blaze of glory. I've done enough damage. We embraced each other tight for the last time with me as a free man. The tears started to flow from all of us. I looked into the eyes of my father and saw a shadow of peace come over him. He can finally relax, knowing for certain, that I would be okay. No more wondering, guessing, worrying for my safety. The animal that he'd created can now be locked away. His love for the monster that visited him through his nightmares can rest. My mother's broken heart for the loss of her only son shattered all hope for dreams of recovery. She couldn't understand why her precious son was being taken away. Forever young, the baby in her arms at birth could do no wrong in both their eyes.

Charged with murder in the second degree, various gun charges, terroristic threatening and both fraud and forgery charges, I was booked and remanded into the custody of the Department of Public Safety. Bail was set in the amount of $975,000. Pre-trial status lasted for four long years waiving my right for a speedy trial. In the end, I was found guilty of all charges and was sentenced to a life-term with the possibility of parole. After thirty years that is. Michelle, Arthur and Sarah were there to give testimony against me. Although Celestine's body was never recovered and there was no physical evidence, I was convicted solely on eyewitness testimony.

Throughout the trial, my mother sat stoic and listened as her son the monster was revealed. She never believed a word they said. She had hidden herself away in place of denial. Whenever possible my dad was there to support her and me. But he knew the outcome from the start. He'd seen it many times before. The familiar words he often said rang true in the back of my mind, "you always got to learn things the hard way!" That's me. My heart broke for them as I looked over. They had suffered so much for love.

The judge was an angry man with the nickname, "the hangman." Even though all was lost, my father had somehow managed to protect me. With all the charges against me, the judge was seeking an extended term of imprisonment. Possibly a trigger lock with a mandatory sentence of seventy years plus. Maybe the career criminal act which could as much as double my sentence. To convict me of that, he'd have to prove that all the charges against me, including the murder, were connected. That the forgery and fraud charges were acquired by me in an effort to fund my drug activity. With the threatening charges and murder occurring when I tried to cover up those drug activities. Remember that attempted murder charge I had hanging over me when I shot Jimbo? Well, the prosecutor dropped that charge but charged me with the felony in possession of a firearm charge. Along with the present firearm charge for Celestine's murder, he could tie the whole criminal history together and throw the book at me. Or so he thought.

Before the start of the trial, Judge Takao had decided to take a vacation. You know, come back nice and fresh, ready to fry my ass. While he was gone, mysteriously, those other charges, the fraud, forgery and gun charge for Jimbo's case got transferred to Judge Leland Spencer's court where I pleaded guilty on all counts. Judge Spencer had been a good personal friend of my father who campaigned for him when he ran for City Prosecutor. He didn't win the election, but went on to become a judge instead. Now, I don't suggest there was any impropriety on Judge Spencer's part but Judge Takao sure hit the roof when he found out that some of the ammunition he would need to put me away forever was gone. Thanks dad! He further hit the roof when the prosecutor, Lance Goto, told him during my sentencing that I didn't fit the criteria for either trigger lock or the career criminal act. There'd be no extended term forthcoming. He wouldn't need it.

Here I sit today in a medium security prison somewhere in the middle of Arizona. Paying my debt to society. Twenty-one years have since passed and I've experienced the death of both my beloved parents. They're at peace now, watching over me from heaven. Because of my situation, I was unable to attend either funeral. I knew it in my heart the last time I hugged them both at our last contact visit in Hawaii, prior to being moved to the mainland, that I'd never see them again. I find hope and peace knowing that someday we will all be together once again. Lorna and I are all that remain. She lives in Wyoming with her husband Mike. We keep in constant contact and I'm expecting her visit one day soon. I haven't seen her in over fifteen years. But when we talk, it's as if it were yesterday. We're both getting on in years and have learned not to fight like cats and dogs as we used to. I love her dearly and would move heaven and earth to put a smile on her face. It is my hope to see her before one of us leaves this world.

In my life, I have come to know man in every aspect of his pitiful existence. From his strengths to his weaknesses. But what causes the nature of the beast to emerge? Excessive unconditional love provided by paranoid parents who had every right to feel so? Maybe a repressed memory which held a deep dark secret of being molested by close family friends at a tender age? Perhaps it was the witnessing of a father's many violent outbursts? No on can say for certain. As we delve into the mysteries of the human mind, I invite you to render a verdict as to how each and every one of us becomes a product of our environment. How our elementary stages of life and the people responsible for our nurturing coincides with the actual imprinting of our thought patterns and character. How their inadequacies and insecurities, shattered hopes and dreams, become projected onto us and establishes the basic building blocks of the person we eventually become. Empirical evidence has shown that the manner in which each individual develops into adulthood is attributed to that person's surrounding and intellectual input provided by their caregivers at various stages in their life cycle. Who knows the complexities of the human psyche? The vulnerability of the human spirit is as unique to each person as the their fingerprints. We all possess ghosts that haunt us and govern our motives.

Experts would argue the point and attach labels to the many phobias, scenarios and environmental factors that are involved in the production of a normal human being. They can even go on and on to argue and hypothesize about what produces a cracked, broken and damaged product of society. What it all boils down to is our own personal individuality as a people on this small revolving blue marble. The ups and downs, the cries and laughter, the loves and hates, the caring and the sharing. There's really no one to blame. Except everyone and no one. We are what we are and become who we become because that's the way life goes. The weak perish and the strong survive? But sometimes the tables get turned and the weakest somehow overcome and become the strong. They fight their way to the top and survive. That's human nature. Our will to survive and persevere is awesome. We find it in our hearts to live to fight another day. Place all the labels you want on it. Attach whatever professional, legal or clinical mumbo jumbo term to it. When all is said and done, the key to the whole mystery is you. It may take years, even decades to arrive at the solution, but the answer's still the same. So stop playing the blame game—the what if game, the holier than thou game, the mine is bigger, mine is better game, and get off the pity pot and get a life! Your life! Whatever it is, make the best of it. Forgive yourself and those around you. God is watching you . . . don't disappoint him!